WOMEN of DEVOTION

❧

A Daily Devotional Guide
for Spirit-filled Women

WOMEN of DEVOTION

A Daily Devotional Guide for Spirit-filled Women

International Department of Ladies Ministries

Pathway
P·R·E·S·S

1080 Montgomery Avenue
Cleveland, TN 37311

ISBN: 0-87148-959-7

Library of Congress Catalog Card Number: 91-062657

Copyright © 1991
PATHWAY PRESS
Cleveland, Tennessee 37311
All Rights Reserved

Printed in the United States of America

Foreword

Each day is a new adventure, an exploration into the wonders of God's created universe. Even in the midst of *routine* that can lull us to sleep or when involved with the *ordinary* that can haze our spiritual vision, God often sends just enough shock waves to make us conscious of Him. And if you are like me, you probably have discovered more than once that it is best to begin these daily sojourns with prayer and a spiritual devotion.

Surely C. Austin Miles must have been thinking along these same lines when he composed *In the Garden*. Over and over his words have touched our hearts:

> I come to the garden alone,
> While the dew is still on the roses;
> And the voice I hear, falling on my ear,
> The Son of God discloses.
> And He walks with me, and He talks with me.
> And He tells me I am His own;
> And the joy we share as we tarry there,
> None other has ever known.

Whether your lifestyle, work load or daily responsibilities permit an early-morning devotion or a late-night sit-down with the Lord—or, for that matter, even if you must cram your devotion right into the middle of a busy day, during break at work or when the babies are napping—the personal and poignant experiences found on the pages of *Women of Devotion* will launch you into new realms of spiritual truth. Keep the book near you. Read it daily.

This Ladies Ministries project is special for yet another reason. We women of the church have accomplished it together, as a team and as sisters in Christ. Ladies from all over the world, who serve in numerous and varied ministry roles, have contributed intimate portions of their lives to the making of this book.

Each day you will identify with the pain, the struggles and the disappointment of others and will get a feel for how horrifyingly bleak life would be without Jesus. You will also discover the triumph, the joy and the victory of those women who, just like you, are discovering that through faith we are always "more than conquerors" (Romans 8:37).

This is one publication you don't have to begin reading at the front. Start with the date you receive it. If you purchase the book on November 15, start with that day's devotion and follow through.

As we each focus on a central theme, thought or prayer for each day, our reading will bring us together with the Lord and nearer to each other.

Can't you just imagine phoning a friend or receiving a call and sharing the blessing you have just gleaned from your daily quiet time with the Lord?

My prayer is that *Women of Devotion* will minister to you now and for many years to come.

Iris Vest
International President
Department of Ladies Ministries

List of Contributors

Valerie Abbott
Anita L. Allen
Patricia A. Allen
Ligia R. Ambriz
Wilma Amison
Sharon Anderson
Anne Arledge
Oleda Atkinson
Judith Ayers
Cheryl Ann Bailey
Beulah (Bea) M. Baker
Mary Sue Baker
Wanda R. Baker
Annette Ballard
Debra Ballard
Geraldine Ballard
Lala B. Bare
Jean Barnett
Mamie Alice Barwick
Sharon K. Bass
Edith Bean
Virginia Beaty
Lou Beaver
Pamela Binda
Marge Bingham
Sandy Bishop
Dorothy J. Black
Ulna B. Black
Ina Boling
Dora Bonilla
Ruth R. Bordeaux
Linda F. Bostic
Debra Rivers Boutwell
Aurelia Brewer
Edith Brock
Pat Brock
Ethel Ray Brummett
Debbie Burdashaw
Beatrice Burroughs
Erlene J. Burton
Robin Caddell
Lynn R. Caffrey
Jimmi N. Campbell
Katherine Lee Cantrell
Evelyn M. Carroll
Wilma Carter
Anita Chamberlain
Trudy L. Chapman
Deborah W. Childers
Dione A. Clagg
Deborah Schierbaum Claudio
Florence Clawson
Therese M. Coen
Gloria Colbaugh

Earlene Coleman
Brenda Combs
Teresa Conlon
Jeanette Cook
Kathy Countryman
Lynne Couzens
Mary N. Coward
Mildred Cox
Elaine Craig
Ruth Starnes Craven
Brenda W. Crisp
Phyllis Crissey
Jean Hampton Crumbley
Jennifer W. Cummings
Patrice Curtiss
Edith Daniel
Louise Daniels
Willie Lee Darter
Marilyn Daugherty
Pat Daugherty
Glenda Davis
Peggy Decanter
Sharon DeFino
Yvette S. DeHaney
Patricia Dempsey
Naomi R. Donaldson
Alicia A. Dotson
R. Louise Douglas
Nancy Downing
Dorothy J. Driggers
Sandy Duncan
Tannis Duncan
Evaline Echols
Sharon Echols
Virginia Eure
Diane Falco
Marlette Finger
Donna McCarn Fisher
Mary Fisher
Linda Joy Fox
Ellen B. French
Charlotte Frye
Barbara Fulbright
Becky Fulton
Margaret Gaines
Shana Garner
Lois J. Garrison
Charlene Gay
Emeline Gayle
Sarah Glover
Lexie Golden
Lorna V. Gosnell
Atha Grassano
Mary E. Graves

Charlene Gray
Sonia Griffey
Laura Griffith
Wanda Griffith
Brenda Gunter
Denise Hacker
Jewell W. Hammons
Ruth Hampton
Naomi Hancock
Rita J. Harper
Dorlene Harris
Kim Hathaway
Terry Hathaway
Linda Hayes
Barbara Henderson
Geri Henson
Rachel Corley Higgins
Dorothy Hilton
Betty J. Hockensmith
Mary Hocker
Carolyn M. Hodges
Darla Hodges
Linda M. Holdman
Eveylene Holt
Joy Hostetler
Loretta C. Huffman
Anita Hughes
Margaret Hughes
Sonjia Lee Hunt
Charlotte Hurst
Debbie Irwin
Judith S. Isaacs
Kathy Isaacs
Pauline James
Sandra Jeffords
Rebecca J. Jenkins
Aurelia Johns
Norma Johnson
Billie I. Jones
Joan Jones
Liz G. Jordan
Alma Kelley
Susan C. Kelley
Lee Kincaid
Deborah King
Margaret W. Lackey
Zelma LaFevor
Deana Landers
Hazel P. Landreth
Sharon L. Landreth
Debbie Lanier
Katherine Lankford
Bobbie Lauster
Susan LeBuhn

Elaine Lee
Myrtie Lee
Sherry B. Lee
Gladys Lemons
Linda Lemons
Marie Leonhardt
Wanda LeRoy
Lori Libby
Linda Lippolt
Beth D. Lirio
Judy Lowdermilk
Michele Lugo
Donna Luna
Alice Lynd
Pat McBride
Ruth J. McCane
Karleen McCarn
Marge M. McClain
Enetha McClung
Kay McEachin
Brenda A. McGarity
Joyce R. McGlamery
Joann McIntire
Holly K. McIntosh
Sheila McLaughlan
Carolyn Martin
Wanda Martin
Dorothy E. Matthews
Freeda May
Joan May
Shirley Meadows
Martha D. Mecum
Betty Mickovich
Joyce Miles
Patricia Miller
Sandra Miller
Donna Moore
Marsha J. Moore
Marianita Moreno
Judy Morgan
Shirley Moss
Karen Carroll Mundy
Nancy A. Neal
Nancy M. O'Bannon
Wendy Obenauer
Roxanne Pasanen
M. Joyce Pennington
Sue Perritte
Sharon L. Perry
Nancy Peterson
Flo Petry

Brenda Pettyjohn
Johnna Phillips
Carolyn L. Poitier
Wanda R. Porter
Judy L. Poteet
Sharon Powell
Frankie Powers
Anna L. Pratt
Gail L. Price
Betty J. Proctor
Lynda Pruitt
Lois Carol Pushkar
Rachel Quinley
Patty D. Rains
Monte L. Ratchford
Andrea C. Reid
Xernona P. Reid
Vilot Reynolds
Betty Rice
Wanda Landreth Rice
Tina M. Rightnour
Ann Roberts
Evelyn Scogin Robertson
Paulita M. Rodriguez
Bertha Rogers
Saundra Jennings Rose
Evelyn Roset
Marilyn Rushing
Ginger Sanders
Kathy Sanders
Peggy Scarborough
Delta Schrade
Shirley Scott
Eleanor S. Sheeks
Kitty Shelton
Brenda Short
Dorothy H. Sibley
Elizabeth S. Sikes
Melody A. Skoog
Mae Smith
Mary A. Smith
Oneta Smith
Peggy J. Smith
Val Sovdi
Marion M. Spellman
Patty Stallings
Samara Stanfield
Joyce Stephens
Monica Stewart
Vicki Stewart
Patti Stigman

Jean C. Stines
Lilly Gay Stockton
Mary Ruth Stone
Miranda Stuthridge
Phyllis M. Sustar
Joan Swank
Siema Bailey Swartzel
Mildred Taylor
Alice Thomas
Gladys Thomas
Nellie Thompson
Jane Thornton
Margaret K. Tioaquen
Ellen Treadway
Julie Trusty
Irene G. Tunsil
Wanda Turner
Lillian Turnipseed
Charlotte Tygart
Beverly Usherwood
Jeanette A. Vance
Joy A. Vanoy
Jennifer Vassell
Jewell Vaught
Iris Vest
Lucille Walker
Shirley Strawn Walters
Marilyn E. Ward
C. Annette Watson
Judy Y. Watson
Kathy D. Watson
Rhoda Watson
Barbara A. Weaver
Clarice Weaver
Wedis Webber
Rachel E. Weir
Belinda West
Kathryn S. White
Pat Whitehouse
Blenda Wicker
Carolyn Wiggins
Rachel Corley Wiggins
Roberta Wilhelme
Shirley Wilson
Joyce Bouschard Wingo
Esther Witcher
Martha S. Wong
Versell Wood
Jan Wright

8

Introduction

Women of Devotion is the book many women have requested—a devotional guide, written by Spirit-filled women for Spirit-filled women. I am pleased that the Department of Ladies Ministries has conceptualized, initiated and produced this valuable ministry resource.

Women of Devotion is dedicated to the valiant, courageous women servants of yesterday who have generously and unreservedly devoted themselves to Christ, His church and His kingdom's mission. This book is dedicated as well to the conscientious, inquiring women servants of today who have grasped the torch of His purpose with a firm determination to meet the challenges of this generation.

Each day as you consistently glean strength and encouragement from the pages of this devotional guide, pray for the mothers, homemakers, teachers and professionals—the many gifted women—who have contributed to this endeavor. Pray as well for all those who will be uniting their hearts in thought with you as we read and meditate upon the Word together. Ask the Father to strengthen our hearts so we can become faithful and godly women.

Many have contributed to the success of this publication: Iris Vest, international president of the Ladies Ministries of the Church of God, who enthusiastically endorsed this project; the Advisory Council and Board of Directors, who encouraged and supported the concept; the staff of the Department of Ladies Ministries, who graciously and willingly assisted with the many processes of preparation for publication; Wanda Griffith, who assisted me in the compilation and initial editorial work; members of the Book Committee at Pathway Press, who agreed to share ownership of the project; Nancy Neal, book editor, who embraced the concept from the beginning with an unusual spiritual commitment; members of the Pathway Communications Group and the Editorial Department, who followed through with the creative process.

Women of Devotion is foremost a tribute to our heavenly Father; His precious Son, Jesus; and the abiding Holy Spirit, who brings us into daily communion and fellowship with God. We, the women of the Church of God, offer this devotional guide to you as an acknowledgment of our total commitment to and dependence upon God as our only source of help, health, strength and sustenance. To God be the glory!

Sherry B. Lee, Director
Department of Ladies Ministries

REMEMBER TODAY. We can be assured that when our feet carry the good news of Christ and bring the message of peace, even the details of our lives like our feet will be under the keeping power of God.

Karen Carroll Mundy
Cleveland, TN
Related Scripture
Nahum 1:15
January 1
Isaiah 52:7

How lovely on the mountains are the feet of him who brings good news,
who announces peace and brings good news of happiness (Isaiah 52:7, NASB).

FEET THAT BRING GOOD NEWS

The blessedness of the men and women who carry the gospel is alluded to in numerous scriptures. Often this blessedness is described by referring to the feet of those who bring peace and good news. Nahum wrote, "Behold, on the mountains the feet of him who brings good news, who announces peace!" (Nahum 1:15, *NASB*).

In scriptural passages the usage of feet indicates a willingness to go, to accept the call of Christ. History gives us numerous examples of distortions in the purpose of feet. For example, the feet of upper-class women in ancient China were too abused to fulfill any function. Parents would bind the feet of their infant girls with heavy cords, preventing their normal growth. In crippling their daughters and making them unfit for service, Chinese families displayed to the world that they were privileged class, a cost exacted in terms of pain and suffering.

Many Christian women are also crippled and bound. Our crippling may not be as apparent as was that of our sisters in China, but we are unfit for service. Our culture encourages women to be ornamental rather than substantial. Our privilege is indicated by well-groomed feet that dwell in safe places. Limited by the cultural conceptions of female service, women invest the fleeting minutes and hours of their lives in safe but spurious activities.

Christians are not called to be safe; we are called to act, to go where there is a need for good news. And today there is a desperate need for good news. But our feet are constrained by the narrowness of our vision. If women would heed the call of Christ, their feet could carry them to the impoverished nations of the world or to the impoverished children of our own society or even to the darkened wards of dying AIDS patients. Indeed, the call of Christ could require us to teach, preach, lead, follow or pray unceasingly.

When we accept the call to go, the Lord will keep us, even down to our feet. Thus, Nehemiah described how the Lord kept the children of Israel for 40 years in the wilderness and "their clothes did not wear out, nor did their feet swell" (Nehemiah 9:21, *NASB*). As our feet carry us to new territories of ministry, the Lord will not allow our feet to stumble or slip, even in treacherous places (Psalms 56:13; 66:9). He will set our feet upon the rock (Psalm 40:2), and the Lord himself will guide our feet in the way of peace (Luke 1:79).

REMEMBER TODAY: We can be assured that when our feet carry the good news of Christ and bring the message of peace, even the details of our lives, like our feet, will be under the keeping power of God.

Sandra Jeffords
Doraville, GA

Related Scripture
Romans 12:1, 2

January 2
2 Corinthians 5:17

Therefore, if anyone is in Christ, he is a new creation; old things have passed away;
behold, all things have become new (2 Corinthians 5:17, NKJV).

NEW ... ANEW ... RENEWED

I'd say we all like new things—new clothes, new cars, new houses, new carpet, new beginnings, a new year, new interests, a new life.

When a new year begins, we make New Year's resolutions. Most often we don't follow through, however, because we aren't totally committed to them.

Newborns really express the meaning of new. Seeing God-given life for the first time and realizing a child is the express image of God is indescribable. A little one is full of life in every respect—moving, breathing, eating, sleeping and crying. He is helpless, totally dependent for love and nourishment. He needs unconditional love and the God-ordained family for caring, nurturing and loving.

Christ loves us unconditionally and gave us new birth—physically and spiritually. The newness He gives means we can be new in every sense of the word. We can start over, make an about-face, be completely changed and love the unlovable. This is the meaning of unconditional love.

What a rewarding experience to see sinners—child molesters, pimps, rapists, drug dealers, homosexuals or murderers—completely transformed and made anew. *New* is defined as "clean, pure, unused, fresh—something just made, just created or developed." It is not old and familiar, not usual or common, but made anew.

How can it be that something so defiled is made *anew*? "Therefore, if anyone is in Christ, he is a new creation; old things have passed away; behold, all things have become new."

REMEMBER TODAY: We are to stay spiritually renewed—clean, pure and fresh—totally committed to Christ.

Eleanor S. Sheeks | Related Scriptures | January 3
Cleveland, TN | Psalm 1; Galatians 6:9; Ephesians 6:13 | Revelation 2:10

*"Be faithful until death, and I will give you the
crown of life".* (Revelation 2:10, NKJV).

GOD'S DEFINITION OF SUCCESS

A perennial on the Most Admired Women's list is a very plain aging woman who spends most of her time in the squalid streets of Calcutta, India, rescuing from alleys and gutters those who are dying. Beggars with just days to live are brought to her shelter, cleaned up and loved. Mother Teresa believes a loving God created every man and woman in His image and that there is in every person an innate need and right to be treated with love and respect. Her commitment to this belief has led her to a life of prayer and incredible personal sacrifice and physical endurance.

"How do you stand it?" someone asked her. "Don't you know that with all you are doing you are not touching 1 percent of the suffering in Calcutta?"

"I was not called to be successful; I was called to be faithful" was Mother Teresa's profound response.

We are success-driven. We fear failure. Each of us has a personalized definition of success. Whatever that definition is, it propels us. It translates into goals, occupation, lifestyle. We tend to become too occupied with "success" and too concerned with how others perceive our "success" or lack of it.

But Mother Teresa is right! God defines success in terms of faithfulness. He does not evaluate me on the basis of numbers, dollars, position, title, recognition, address, press ink or any of the usual components of "success." He measures the depth of my commitment to the ministry He has given me. He measures the length of my faithfulness to those things He has revealed to be right and good for me.

Psalm 1 says the successful person is like a tree planted by a river—committed to the place it stands, firmly rooted, consistently drawing from the water of life, faithfully producing fruit.

REMEMBER TODAY: God's primary call is to faithfulness. The ultimate success comes as the result of being faithful "until."

Patty Stallings
Rapid City, SD

Related Scriptures
Philippians 1:2; 1 Timothy 1:2; Ephesians 2:5-9;
Titus 3:7; John 1:17; Romans 5:17; 2 Corinthians 12:9;
Hebrews 12:15; 4:14; James 4:6; 2 Peter 3:18

January 4
Hebrews 13:25

Grace be with you all (Hebrews 13:25, *NIV*).

THE FRIEND WE HAVE IN GRACE

I first met Grace as a child. She stood beside me when I chose to stand up for what was right, and Grace knelt beside me when I needed to ask God for forgiveness for wrongdoing. Grace has counseled me, whispered encouragement to me and hung around when other friends didn't. When I went into emergency surgery, my husband and family were not allowed in the operating room, but somehow in all the commotion, Grace slipped through the door, held my hand and assured me that God was watching over me. Grace has been around when times were good, when times were bad, and even on the ordinary days when I haven't given much thought to Grace at all.

You probably know Grace also, because this friend is the same Grace that Paul mentioned in every book he wrote: "Grace . . . to you from God our Father and the Lord Jesus Christ" (Philippians 1:2, *NIV*).

Grace usually walks hand in hand with the companions of Mercy and Peace (1 Timothy 1:2). Grace is the facilitator for salvation (Ephesians 2:5-9) and justification (Titus 3:7). The source is Jesus (John 1:17). God has given an abundant provision of grace (Romans 5:17), and He promises that His grace is sufficient (2 Corinthians 12:9).

With such a tremendous friend offered, is it possible that some actually miss out on or even defy God's grace? Hebrews 12:15 tells us that a root of bitterness does just that. An unforgiving heart can be so covered with weeds of bitterness entwining every relationship that grace can no longer affect that heart. When grace goes, peace and mercy follow. In their place is a critical, legalistic, uncompassionate spirit that affects everyone else.

I need grace to help me in my relationship with God. I need grace to oil the relationships with my family, friends, coworkers—even the cashier at the grocery store. I cannot afford to frustrate God's gift of grace in any way. Can you? If you need to find grace, God would like to introduce you to a place called the throne of grace (Hebrews 4:14-16). He gives grace freely to the humble (James 4:6). That is an offer you can't afford to refuse.

REMEMBER TODAY: "Grow in grace, and in the knowledge of our Lord and Saviour Jesus Christ" (2 Peter 3:18).

Anne Arledge
Lahaina, HI

Related Scriptures
Deuteronomy 30:6; Galatians 5:25;
Ephesians 3:19

January 5
Deuteronomy 6:5

"And you shall love the Lord your God with all your heart and with all your soul and with all your might" (Deuteronomy 6:5, NASB).

MUNDANE TASKS

When did you last ask, "God, how can I really know You more?" Perhaps you've had this similar thought or prayer: "Lord, I want to love You with my whole heart. Show me how to serve You more."

I believe Christian women especially desire to love Him completely—with heart, soul and might. After searching through Christian books on the subject, I had yet to realize the practical yet profound answer I ultimately came to know. My husband and I had signed up as counselors in a crusade meeting in our area. On the last evening the music minister called me aside. I heard him begin, "Our crusade team was having breakfast at the local pancake house this morning when we saw your family. I watched you feed your son spoonful by spoonful, and I couldn't help but notice your expressions the whole time."

I was taken aback, hardly hearing what he was saying for thinking how messy the scene must have appeared! Our child is handicapped and must be fed like a baby. I was totally unprepared for being observed so closely. I expected his conversation to be on soulwinning or on the happenings of the crusade. Instead, he addressed something so basic, yet so practical and spiritual.

Even the simplest, most mundane tasks can portray the reality of our walking in the Spirit. These are opportune times for revealing through our actions that we are loving the Lord with our heart, soul and might, and are entering fully into a love relationship with Jesus.

REMEMBER TODAY: We have been provided the love of Christ through the power of the Holy Spirit.

Oleda Atkinson	Related Scriptures	January 6
Birmingham, AL	Psalm 30:4, 5; Revelation 21:2-4	Psalm 126:6

He who continually goes forth weeping, bearing seed for sowing, shall doubtless come again with rejoicing, bringing his sheaves with him (Psalm 126:6, NKJV).

TEARS, TRUST, TRIUMPH

A most surprising spiritual message occurred while I was visiting the cemetery where my mother is buried. As usual, my dad was painstakingly removing the weather-worn floral arrangement from the headstone. Lovingly, he scraped away the debris and old arrangement to place a beautiful silk pastel arrangement on the headstone.

All at once I saw something in the tattered flowers that intrigued me. Stooping lower, I discovered a perfectly symmetrical, miniature bird's nest with three tiny eggs. My first impression was that someone had placed an artificial nest in the flower. Suddenly, I noticed a small bird frantically flying nearby. Tenderly we moved the nest and its precious contents to a new place in the new flowers, hoping we had not disturbed anything. In a flash the small mother bird made a dive into the flowers to make sure her treasure was safe.

What usually was an uneventful visit turned into one of excitement and hope because of the beginning of new life in a depressing environment. It was special that the mother bird had chosen my mother's flowers for a home for her babies. What a tribute to a lady who always saw so much of God in nature!

Traveling back home, we wondered what would happen to our little "adopted family." A phone call came in a few days from a relative who also has parents buried there. "You won't believe what happened in your flowers. Three tiny birds have hatched!"

What a beautiful and loving Savior to direct a small bird to just the spot where heavy and sad hearts could be lifted and reminded of the promise of new life! Hope for the hopeless, light for darkness, health for sickness and eternal jubilation will be the order of the day. He cares about the smallest details of our life and the greatest pains we feel.

My mother's grave symbolizes tears, but we have the confidence of God's promise for those who die in Christ. It seemed that God allowed the little bird to reiterate the fact that there is triumph over tears for those who trust Him. Life goes on for the believer!

REMEMBER TODAY: Tears are common, trust is confidence, and triumph is celebration.

Margaret Gaines
Jerusalem, Israel

Related Scriptures
Proverbs 23:4, 5; Matthew 6:19-21;
Philippians 4:11; Hebrews 13:5; James 5:3

January 7
1 Timothy 6:6

*But godliness with contentment
is great gain (1 Timothy 6:6).*

TRAPPED BY MY TRAPPINGS

"I think I have missed the point in life. My trappings are my trap, and contentment has always eluded me."

This is what a good friend told me recently. She went on to explain how her determination not to be a poor, mediocre nobody compelled her to harness every power of spirit, soul and body in order to be and stay beautiful, to have a big elaborate house, and to maintain godliness in it all.

"If it were only I whom I compelled, it would be different," she added. "But I manipulated, even dominated, my husband by my feminine ruse and charms to mobilize his help to reach my goals. But now he has died of a heart attack, and I am left with the shell of my illusions and discontent."

She explained how her husband would have been satisfied with a small but lovely frame house and a pretty lawn bordered with flowers. He had even tried to convince her at first that they would be happier with simple pleasures and less pressures.

"But I despised his simplicity and, at times, secretly felt disgust and impatience with his 'lack of ambition.' "

How fortunate this friend is, even in her misfortune, to be able to analyze her situation and to understand. That is the important first step in finding contentment.

REMEMBER TODAY: If God is not the authority on the nature and value of material possessions, there is no other.

Edith Bean	**Related Scriptures**	**January 8**
Brownfield, TX	Psalm 37:5; John 16:23, 24	Matthew 6:8

Your Father knoweth what things ye have
need of, before ye ask him (Matthew 6:8).

HELP ME FIND A JOB

Our finances were so low that I was going to have to return to work. How I dreaded all involved in the process of filling out applications and knocking on business doors to find a suitable job. "Lord," I prayed, "help me find a job soon."

Since I had worked at a credit bureau in another town and enjoyed my job, I decided to call the local credit bureau to see if there were any openings. According to protocol, I knew I should make contacts in person rather than call, but the urge was so strong that I called. The man in charge said the office was only a two-person operation. He suggested another place where I might inquire. This was Friday afternoon. I knew that on Monday I would have to start making contacts.

Saturday came, and my telephone rang. "Are you the lady who called yesterday looking for a job with the credit bureau?" the man asked.

"Yes," I replied.

"Well, the girl who works here came in Friday afternoon, turned in her keys and left. I would like for you to come down and apply."

I started to work on Tuesday and was eventually offered full management of the bureau.

So many times we try to solve all of our problems, while Christ stands ready to help if we ask. We are instructed in 1 Peter 5:7 to cast all our cares upon Him because He cares for us.

REMEMBER TODAY: God's Word reminds us that we don't have because we don't ask. Although He knows our needs before we ask, He still wants us to ask so we may receive and so our joy may be full.

Dorothy E. Matthews   **Related Scriptures**   **January 9**
Kotzebue, AK   Psalm 44:5; Luke 10:19;   Romans 8:37
John 16:33; 1 John 5:4

Nay, in all these things we are more than conquerors
through him that loved us (Romans 8:37).

MORE THAN CONQUERORS

The memory of the words still echo in our minds from time to time. Many in the Eskimo villages above the Arctic Circle were saying, "You people are crazy; it cannot be done. It is impossible. Alcohol, beer joints, liquor stores, night clubs and dance halls have been a part of our community for over 20 years. We have tried several times to vote liquor out, but we've always failed."

We replied in faith that it would be different this time because of prayer and fasting. God would make the difference.

Finally—after much persecution, threatening phone calls, public ridicule on the radio, four slashed tires and the kidnapping of our daughter—voting day arrived.

We will never forget that day. The polls were in the middle of town. Husbands, wives, sons and daughters gathered, marching with signs of encouragement for the community. The temperature was about 18 degrees, with the chill factor around 40 degrees below zero. People tried to run over us with snow machines and vehicles. But through it all, we believed God.

Finally, the voting ended. We all gathered in a circle in the middle of town, raised our hearts, hands and voices to God, and thanked Him for His protection and the answer He was going to give.

When the votes were counted, God had given His people the victory. We were made more than conquerors through Jesus Christ our Lord. The dance halls are now silent, the liquor stores are closed, and the beer joints are shut down.

REMEMBER TODAY: We can do all things through Jesus Christ. Through Him you can triumph and be more than a conqueror.

Shirley Scott **Related Scriptures** January 10
Sylvania, OH Proverbs 31:11-31; Proverbs 12:4 Proverbs 31:10

A capable, intelligent, and virtuous woman—who is he who can find her? She is far more precious than jewels and her value is far above rubies or pearls (Proverbs 31:10, *Amp.*).

THE BALANCED LIFE

"Mom, I can't find my red sweater. Did you remember to pick it up at the cleaners?" my daughter asked.

"Honey, don't forget to drop the car off at the dealer," my husband reminded me.

Suddenly, the phone rang. Someone from the school was informing me of an appointment in 15 minutes.

How in the world can I get it all done, God?

When looking at all the roles I must play—wife, mother, homemaker, career woman—my life seems hectic and out of balance. All too often the rapid pace of today's living leaves me physically exhausted and spiritually anemic. Then I hear Solomon describing how it ought to be: "The virtuous woman of Proverbs 31 is a commendable wife and mother who lives for her home and family, is consistently industrious, self-disciplined and orderly, a sharp business woman with good taste, has the grace of hospitality, and is still spiritually minded."

Hope rises in me as I meditate on these words. In times past this was not my favorite portion of Scripture. Now I understand this woman's success.

A virtuous woman is consistent, balanced and organized. She is not weak but has a mind of her own. She is not alone, and in her hands are riches, substance and wealth.

In verses 15 and 30 we find the key to her accomplishments: "She rises while it is yet night and gets [spiritual] food for her household. . . . A woman who reverently and worshipfully fears the Lord, she shall be praised!" (*Amp.*)

REMEMBER TODAY: A balanced life is possible only when it is centered in the Lord Jesus Christ.

Edith Daniel
Cedar Rapids, IA

Related Scriptures
Isaiah 65:10; 2 Chronicles 20:1-30

January 11
Hosea 2:14, 15

"I will lead her into the desert and speak tenderly to her. There I will give her back her vineyards, and will make the Valley of Achor a door of hope. There she will sing . . ." (Hosea 2:14, 15, NIV).

ACHOR—A DOOR OF HOPE

Achor means "trouble." Sometimes we find ourselves in the valley because of our disobedience. At other times we get there because God is leading us and wants to teach us a special lesson. Whatever the reason, God wants to change the Valley of Achor into a "door of hope" for us. Our need becomes God's opportunity. It becomes His opportunity to show us His love and "speak tenderly" to us. It becomes His opportunity to restore to us the "vineyard" we may have lost in our busyness.

Achor can become a door of hope or a place of despair and discouragement, depending on our response. We can respond to our circumstances with grumbling or with singing (praise). Whenever the Israelites faced a problem on their journey through the wilderness, they usually responded with complaints and grumbling. But the Lord wants us to respond like King Jehoshaphat did when he was faced with a large army coming against him: " 'O our God . . . we do not know what to do, but our eyes are upon you' " (2 Chronicles 20:12, NIV).

The Lord instructed him, "Don't be afraid or discouraged, the battle is Mine. Face the enemy; I am with you." Jehoshaphat encouraged the people, " 'Have faith in the Lord your God and you will be upheld' " (2 Chronicles 20:20, NIV). And the people went away saying, " 'Give thanks to the Lord, for His love endures forever' " (v. 21, NIV).

Will I face a Valley of Achor today? Maybe. How will I respond to my circumstances? The Lord's instructions are the same as they were to Jehoshaphat. As we look to Him with trust, our trouble becomes His opportunity to reveal Himself to us in a greater way—to move mountains, remove obstacles, or bring healing and restoration.

REMEMBER TODAY: My need becomes God's opportunity, but I must choose to trust Him.

Jeanette Cook **Related Scripture** **January 12**
Kingsport, TN Jeremiah 9:23, 24 Proverbs 3:5, 6

Trust in the Lord with all thine heart; and lean not unto
thine own understanding. In all thy ways acknowledge
him, and he shall direct thy paths (Proverbs 3:5, 6).

EVEN WHEN YOU DON'T UNDERSTAND

"She cannot live! Her lungs are gone. She will probably die from heart failure, and it could happen at any moment." These are the words my husband and I heard from a lung specialist about our 16-year-old daughter, Tracey, who had been rushed to the hospital. Tracey had cystic fibrosis. Her brother, Bill, a handsome, Spirit-filled Christian, had passed away at age 16.

A few days before this, I had been studying Proverbs 3:5, 6 in preparation for a Wednesday-night class. God had really opened up this passage to me. I had always considered our understanding as limited before an all-wise God, and so it often is. But I came to realize that even though we do have the capacity to understand many things clearly and correctly, we do not trust in that understanding but in God who has the power to change any circumstance.

I had stood in this same place in my son's hospital room, hearing these same words, and I knew what was happening. Even as the doctors spoke, God, through the words I had studied, was speaking to my spirit. He said, "Trust Me. Don't lean on what you know; lean on what I can do." I clearly understood that from all physical evidence, Tracey was dying. But God said, "Lean not unto thine own understanding."

"We don't know what has happened," said the doctors. One doctor who was a Spirit-filled pediatrician and longtime friend visited Tracey, not only as her doctor but also for the laying on of hands in prayer for her healing. Tracey was healed. She experienced some of the most rewarding and dream-filled days of her life after this. Many lives were changed after seeing this miracle. You see, I thought I was preparing for a Wednesday class, but God was preparing me to see Him work as He directed Tracey's paths.

REMEMBER TODAY: Whether you clearly understand the situation you're facing or not, it doesn't matter. Trust in God!

Cheryl Ann Bailey **Related Scriptures** **January 13**
Vacaville, CA Isaiah 62:11; Luke 12:7 Ecclesiastes 11:1

*Cast thy bread upon the waters: for thou shalt
find it after many days* (Ecclesiastes 11:1).

MOTHER AND CHILD REUNION

"Oh, David, you just don't know how much Pastor and I appreciate your help. Thank you for patching the hole in the ceiling this Saturday evening, especially since the general overseer will be here with us in the morning service," I expressed sincerely. Immediately my mind recounted the story of David's recent conversion.

Randall had accepted our first pastorate in Fortuna, California. We were expecting our second child; our first had died. I was experiencing a lot of stress. One senior lady, a Church of God exhorter with extraordinary grace and spirit, ministered to us. Her name was Margaret Bolt. She taught me so much.

Now, 17 years later, we are pastoring a thriving church in Vacaville, California. We have seen a great revival among the youth. Subcultures of all kinds—including satanists—have been born again. I accompany our youth group out on the streets witnessing to troubled kids every Friday night.

One night, three years ago, the Holy Spirit prompted me to ask the name of one young man whom I'd never seen. Reluctantly, he said, "David Bolt."

Under the unction of the Holy Spirit I blurted out, "David, I know your grandma, and she is at home right now on her knees praying for you."

His eyes grew as big as saucers. Then I thought in my mind, *Sister Bolt might not even still be alive. Are you crazy, Cheri?* I hadn't heard from or seen her in years. *He might be from a different Bolt family,* I thought.

Suddenly I laid my hand on his blond head and began to pray. He threw his cigarette away and began to pray. Sister Bolt is his grandmother, and I later discovered that she was praying for him that very night. The next Sunday morning David, along with his mom and dad, was in Sunday school and church.

I am sure this situation occurs all the time. If we allow the Holy Spirit to guide us, lives can be changed. The Bolts are now faithful members and a great blessing to our church.

REMEMBER TODAY: Keep praying, Grandmas. God listens.

Rita J. Harper
Brunswick, GA

Related Scriptures
Psalms 25:1-6; 121:1, 2

January 14
Hebrews 12:1, 2

*Let us run with patience the race that is set
before us, looking unto Jesus the author and
finisher of our faith* (Hebrews 12:1, 2).

TURN YOUR EYES UPON JESUS

It was one of the most wonderful prayer conferences I had ever attended. It was more than challenging, more than inspiring—it was life-changing. My life would never be the same again.

Upon returning home, I received some of the most devastating, heartbreaking news of my life. Bill and I had faced many hurtful experiences with church members, family and friends. Now he and I must face this situation alone. There was no one with whom we could share this burden, no one to talk with about the hurt.

As I turned to Jesus, He brought to my mind and heart the words of the old song "Turn Your Eyes Upon Jesus." As I began to sing and meditate on this chorus, God gave the strength.

The Scripture tells us to "run with patience the race that is set before us, looking unto Jesus the author and finisher of our faith." The race is an obstacle course where the Enemy continually throws stumbling blocks in the way.

Your obstacle may be a child in trouble (involved in drugs, smoking, drinking, sex; keeping wrong company; a runaway), a husband in midlife crisis, or an aged parent or relative needing care. When you look full in His wonderful face, you will realize that no matter what the obstacle, with Him nothing is impossible to overcome. This is but a fleeting moment when viewed in the light of eternity. No matter how difficult the circumstance, He will give you the wisdom, strength and healing for every situation.

REMEMBER TODAY: Even hurts will grow strangely dim when you look full in His glorious face.

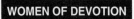
Roberta Wilhelme
W. Burlington, IA

Related Scripture
Isaiah 54:10

And the peace of God, which passeth all
understanding, shall keep your hearts and
minds through Christ Jesus (Philippians 4:7).

HIS PEACE REMAINS

In 1980 my husband died suddenly of a heart attack in the driveway of the parsonage. That same night I was also admitted to the hospital with a heart attack. In the days that followed, the Lord spoke such peace to my heart that I was able to attend and briefly minister at my husband's funeral. During this time of loss, I was aware of the presence of Christ and His constant peace.

In January 1990 I faced quadruple-bypass heart surgery. The doctors and nurses gave little hope for my survival during the surgery. Never had I felt such a need for the peace of God. I asked specifically for a scripture to sustain me during this time of need. Immediately, Isaiah 54:10 came to my mind: "For the mountains shall depart, and the hills be removed; but my kindness shall not depart from thee, neither shall the covenant of my peace be removed, saith the Lord that hath mercy on thee."

Not only did the Lord bring me successfully through the surgery, but He provided a Christian surgeon, opened doors for me to minister during my hospital stay and kept me from pain during my time of recovery.

His peace remains unchanged today. When we are in need, He overshadows us with His peace. There are times when we don't understand the things we must endure, but His promise remains true.

REMEMBER TODAY: No matter how high the mountain or how low the valley, His peace remains.

Jennifer W. Cummings
Vero Beach, FL

Related Scripture
Isaiah 40:11

January 16
Psalm 23:1

*Because the Lord is my Shepherd, I
have everything I need!* (Psalm 23:1, *TLB*).

NEVER ALONE

We'll be together always, I thought. Having four brothers and sisters, I thought surely I would never be alone, unprotected and insecure. I had an older brother and sister and a younger brother and sister; I was the middle child.

As the years passed, things changed. My older brother and sister left and began living a new life away from home. The secure, protected feeling I once had was gone. Yes, I still had Mom, Dad, and my younger brother and sister, but things seemed different. I now felt alone, empty and stripped of family ties. Before they left, I was the bridge between the older and the younger sisters and brothers. I thought it would last. I thought we would be together always and nothing would change that. I was wrong.

A few months later my father preached a sermon, taking his text from Psalm 23:1: "Because the Lord is my Shepherd, I have everything I need!" *(TLB)*. I accepted the truth of that sermon, and the Shepherd has filled every need in my life, built a fortress of protection around me, infused me with true security and brought a new dimension of the family in my life. All this time, I've had everything! I've never been without, empty, unprotected or even alone. Yes, I finally realized that . . . because the Lord is my Shepherd, I have everything I need.

REMEMBER TODAY: The Lord has everything we need—and more!

Wanda Griffith
Cleveland, TN

Related Scriptures
2 Peter 1:3, 4; 2 John 6

January 17
James 2:17

Faith by itself, if it is not accompanied
by action, is dead (James 2:17, NIV).

TURN THE HANDLE

"Change is stressful; change is risky; change is scary; change is challenging; change is a part of Christian growth." If these were part of a multiple-choice quiz, the answer would be "All of the above."

Although change produces stress, fear and challenge, when God is in control, we also experience growth. Times of adjustment, reprogramming and sometimes confusion accompany this growth process. It is then that we have to remember that He provides the door; all we do is act in faith and turn the handle.

I had been working at Lee College since I was a teenager. My job was more than keeping accurate student records; it was my life—my ministry. Through the years I had opportunity on several occasions to travel with STEP teams and student groups. More and more I felt the Lord leading me into writing and sharing my testimony of His faithfulness to me. When the time was right and a new position for this type of ministry opened, I was afraid to turn the handle. It was difficult to leave my "comfort zone" and be stretched into broader and more diverse fields of ministry.

Once I was willing to turn loose of the familiar, He was faithful to lead me one step at a time. No one could discourage me or persuade me to change my mind. I am presently serving as administrative assistant to the director of Pathway Communications.

He provided the door, but I had to turn the handle. I now face this challenge with confidence, knowing "He guards the lives of his faithful ones" (Psalm 97:10, *NIV*).

REMEMBER TODAY: God wants you to turn the handle when He provides the door.

Pamela Binda
Mississauga, Ontario

Related Scriptures
1 Kings 19:11, 12; Mark 6:31

January 18
Psalm 46:10

Be still, and know that I am God (Psalm 46:10).

SILENCE

It was an impressive two minutes—no counter service, no cash registers, no movement along the aisles. What was once a busy thoroughfare was suddenly brought to a screeching halt.

Being a part of this frozen theater scene, I listened to the words which echoed loudly over the P.A. system: "Would our customers now join our staff for two minutes of silence to honor those who gave their lives for this country." I shared the pride and respect for this patriotic expression.

Those fleeting moments of solitude reminded me so vividly of Psalm 46:10: "Be still, and know that I am God." Almost without thinking, I was also honoring the One who died, not just for me or my country but for the entire world. Perhaps the writer of this great psalm was saying there would also be a day when the whole world will stand still to recognize Jesus as Lord. What a tremendous privilege we have as Christians to do so now!

What started out to be another anxious day filled with daily demands was now punctuated with a tremendous peace and quietness penetrating the inner levels of my soul. This quality of silence in our fast-paced society is golden!

REMEMBER TODAY: It is in the times of solitude that we can recognize the voice of God.

Terry Hathaway
Wahpeton, ND

Related Scriptures
James 1:26; 3:1-11; Proverbs 10; 19; 25:11

January 19
Proverbs 20:19

A gossip betrays a confidence; so avoid a man
who talks too much (Proverbs 20:19, *NIV*).

WATCH YOUR WORDS

Working as an in-service director in a nursing home, I have an obligation to discuss confidentiality with my employees.

I remind them, "Be careful what you say, where you say it and to whom you say it."

Recently a friend shared her new resolution with me: "I have stopped attending a Bible study I've been involved in for the past three years."

"Why?" I asked.

"The burden was just too heavy. There were just too many details of other people's lives being shared."

As a Christian, confidentiality is an important issue. What do we say about people? Do we speak well of others? Do we use prayer time to share intimate details of others' lives? Prayer time can be a special time of sharing, but if we are sharing another's needs, we should keep the request simple or "unspoken."

Where do we hold our conversations? In a potluck line, during a ladies meeting, at Bible study, at the dinner table? When sharing intimate details of another's life, consider whose ears might be tuned in.

We must always be careful not only what we say but also where we say it and to whom we say it. Proverbs 10:19 states, "When words are many, sin is not absent, but he who holds his tongue is wise" (*NIV*).

REMEMBER TODAY: "A word fitly spoken is like apples of gold in settings of silver" (Proverbs 25:11, *NIV*).

Johnna Phillips
Hamilton, OH

Related Scriptures
Proverbs 10:12; 11:13; 15:23, 28; 16:28;
17:9; 20:19; 26:20; Romans 13:10;
Galatians 5:13-15; Colossians 4:6; James 3:1-12

January 20
Ephesians 4:29

*Do not let any unwholesome talk come out of your mouths, but
only what is helpful for building others up according to their
needs, that it may benefit those who listen* (Ephesians 4:29, *NIV*).

WHAT DID YOU SAY?

"Sticks and stones may break my bones, but words can never hurt me," the little girl yelled as she walked away crying, proving her statement to be false.

Words have tremendous weight. Words can confuse, embarrass and hurt. Words are often tragically destructive. "How long will ye vex my soul, and break me in pieces with words?" (Job 19:2). We must constantly be aware that our words carry impact. That's why God holds us accountable for our words (Matthew 12:36, 37).

"The tongue also is a fire, a world of evil among the parts of the body. It corrupts the whole person, sets the whole course of his life on fire, and is itself set on fire by hell" (James 3:6, *NIV*). Fire is one of the few forces that does irreparable damage. Fiery words often destroy relationships that, even when restored, are never the same again. We should wear signs that say "Caution: Life is a combustible commodity—douse your tongue!"

On the other hand, words have the power to heal, encourage, help and teach. We are to "encourage one another and build each other up" (1 Thessalonians 5:11, *NIV*). My mom always told me that if I didn't have something good to say about someone not to say anything at all. In other words, "Build up, or shut up!"

Matthew 12:34 tells us, "'Out of the overflow of the heart the mouth speaks'" (*NIV*). All talk is really "heart talk." Our words simply reveal what is happening inside us. When I was a little girl and said things I shouldn't say, my mom would threaten to wash my mouth out with soap. But I really needed more than a mouthwash; I needed a heart wash.

How do we tame our tongues? By allowing God's love to be manifested in our lives. "Love is patient, love is kind. It does not envy, it does not boast, it is not proud. It is not rude, it is not self-seeking, it is not easily angered, it keeps no record of wrongs. Love does not delight in evil but rejoices with the truth. It always protects, always trusts, always hopes, always perseveres. Love never fails" (1 Corinthians 13:4-8, *NIV*).

REMEMBER TODAY: Begin each day praying Psalm 141:3: "Set a guard over my mouth, O Lord; keep watch over the door of my lips" (*NIV*).

Ruth J. McCane	**Related Scriptures**	**January 21**
Chattanooga, TN	Deuteronomy 16:17; Luke 6:38;	Acts 3:6
	Romans 8:32; 2 Corinthians 9:6, 7	

. . . But such as I have give I thee (Acts 3:6).

A PIECE OF YOUR MIND, PLEASE

While visiting in Baltimore, Maryland, my sister-in-law and I attended a series of child evangelism workshops to learn how to prepare visuals for children's ministries. We learned how to create clever, attractive, affordable visual aids by using things around the house. This knowledge I shared with teachers of children in many struggling churches with limited budgets where my husband served as state overseer. Many years later I still drew from this resource to instruct teachers in how to utilize this skill when using the church's Sunday school curriculum.

"Do you mind sharing a copy of those patterns you used in your workshop in Dallas?" asked a friend of mine whose husband was in youth work.

"I would be glad to," I responded. "What you need is in my mind. I'm not an artist, but when I get home I'll attempt to make a sketch of each for you. Hopefully my elementary art work will provide the guidelines and patterns needed to make your own."

It seemed ages since that workshop. The market was flooded with professional visual aids for teaching children. Yet, budgets were still limited and the need still existed to share this knowledge. I kept file samples to share when needed—that is, until our home burned. It appeared all was lost.

Not so!

I remembered the anointed words in my hymnal: "Give as 'twas given to you in your need, love as the Master loved you . . . Make me a blessing . . . today" (George S. Schuler and Ira B. Wilson).* The Holy Book at my side promised me, "Give, and it shall be given unto you" (Luke 6:38). What I learned in Baltimore, I gave away to others to be taught and shared. His promises are true. After a simple phone call, the patterns I had sent my friend were returned to me by mail. God reminded me, "What you saved, you lost. What you used, you had. What you gave, you have."

* "Make Me a Blessing." Copyright 1924 by George S. Schuler. Renewed 1952, Rodeheaver Company (a division of Word, Inc.). Used by permission.

REMEMBER TODAY: You may know a better way, so share your skill. As you share that which God has given you, you will be richer.

Jean Hampton Crumley	Related Scriptures	January 22
Sharpsburg, GA	Psalms 9:1, 2; 22:3; 34:1	Psalm 40:3

And he hath put a new song in my mouth, even praise unto our God;
many shall see it, and fear, and shall trust in the Lord (Psalm 40:3).

A NEW SONG—EVEN PRAISE

As a church musician I search for new songs to learn for worship in groups, solos and praise choruses. Many authors, publishers and performers contribute a wealth of material from which to choose.

With all this music available, I am still drawn to the words of the psalmist David: "He hath put a new song in my mouth, even praise unto our God." When the heart has been transformed by the saving power of Jesus, the mouth echoes with this new song—even praise. From the mother's lullaby to the majestic strains of the great classics, from the familiar old hymns of the church to the more contemporary praise choruses and songs, the praise keeps resounding.

Among the benefits of praise are these:

1. Praise lifts the spirit.
2. Praise builds faith.
3. Praise glorifies God.
4. Praise is contagious—it has a positive influence on others.
5. Praise defeats Satan, the enemy of the soul.

Let us continue the praise as we spontaneously respond to the love of the heavenly Father. He desires close fellowship with His children. He inhabits the praises of His people, according to Psalm 22:3. This new song is never outdated; it is always fresh and exhilarating. It soothes body, mind and soul as it flows from within like an overwhelming stream.

Allow the Holy Spirit to fill your heart with praise; then fill your home and your world with the song of salvation and hope. Your family, friends and the world around you will be blessed.

REMEMBER TODAY: "His praise shall continually be in my mouth" (Psalm 34:1). Enjoy God's presence now!

C. Annette Watson	**Related Scriptures**	**January 23**
Ocala, FL	Proverbs 22:6; Matthew 18:2-5;	Psalm 127:3
	2 Timothy 1:3-5	

Behold, children are a heritage
from the Lord (Psalm 127:3, *NKJV*).

HAVE YOU HUGGED YOUR CHILD TODAY?

I was sitting at my desk at home when a motion outside the window attracted my attention. It was a beautiful, blond-haired boy about 5 or 6 years old. He was new to our neighborhood, and I watched with delight his antics in the early morning dew. He was running. Those short legs were pumping as hard as they could, as if to gain flying momentum!

Quietly meditating, I wondered, "Has anyone, with a loving hand, cupped that little chin and planted a kiss of undying love on his soft, smooth cheek? Has anyone cradled that precious little body next to his/her heart, looked into those innocent, smiling eyes and said, 'I love you! You're so-o-o-o precious to me'? Has anyone told him,

> 'Jesus loves . . . [you]! this I know,
> For the Bible tells me so;
> Little ones to Him belong;
> They are weak but He is strong'?"
> —Anna B. Warner

The psalmist proclaimed, "Children are a heritage from the Lord." How wonderful that godly heritage is. Their ways, their talk, their lack of sophistication, their innocence, their unfolding, and even their very frailties are of perpetual interest, relief and delight. No pleasure in life should ever equal the joy you have in the children who bear your image and who in miniature reflect you.

Webster defines hugging as "pressing tightly, especially in the arms; holding fast; cherishing; staying close to." Ask yourself these timely questions: Have I held my child close to me, wrapped in loving arms? Have I cherished my child? Have I made a special effort to stay close to my child? Have I hugged, really hugged, my child lately?

REMEMBER TODAY: A child is like a flower—the more tender care you give, the more beautiful it will bloom.

Patti Stigman	**Related Scriptures**	**January 24**
Burnsville, MN	Mark 9:35; Luke 22:26; Philippians 2:3	Matthew 25:40

*Inasmuch as ye have done it unto one of the least of these
my brethren, ye have done it unto me* (Matthew 25:40).

LIVING OUT THE GOSPEL

The day we arrived was extremely hot and humid. The camper I had been assigned to for the week told me of her bathroom needs. I had no previous training and was completely unprepared for what I was facing. Not only had it been years since I had changed a dirty diaper, I had *never* changed one on an adult.

Linda had spina bifida and lay on a cart, unable to do anything for herself. We had been introduced only moments before, and now I had to change her soiled diapers. I had been told she used a bedpan, but as the week progressed, I found out such was never the case. My immediate thought was of my family at home, eating their juicy steaks and enjoying a relaxing day around our lovely swimming pool.

Suddenly I was angry with myself for committing to serve as a counselor at a camp for the physically and mentally impaired. This was going to be a difficult week, and I was off to a dreadful start.

In that moment, however, the still, small voice of my Savior whispered, "I am the One lying on this cart. Whatever you do for one of the least of these, you have done for Me." His love filled my heart as I saw Linda through His eyes. I became His hands and His feet for this precious woman. I shall never forget that week, nor do I want to lose its memories. It was, indeed, one of the most blessed weeks of my life.

I was quickly reminded of a prayer I had prayed months before: "Lord, help me to die to myself, that You might live more fully in me." He chiseled away many of my rough edges that week, and I experienced His presence in a new and wonderful way.

REMEMBER TODAY: God can only use us when we make ourselves available to Him. He is made strong in our weaknesses.

Gloria Colbaugh
Wichita, KS

Related Scripture
Matthew 6:7, 8

January 25
Romans 8:32

He that spared not his own Son, but delivered him up for us all,
how shall he not with him also freely give us all things? (Romans 8:32).

HOW MUCH CAN I GIVE?

As my husband and 8-year-old daughter were on their way to church, Johnna took money from her purse, showed it to her dad and asked if she could give that much in the offering. Of course her dad said she could.

A few minutes later Johanna took several more coins from her purse, added them to the first ones and asked her dad if she could give that much. And as before, his answer was "Yes, you may give that much."

As they drove near the church, Johanna turned her purse upside down, allowing all the coins to fall into her lap, and asked her dad if she could give it all in the offering. My husband's answer was "Yes, you may give that much, but God doesn't expect you to give all you have."

When they reached the church, my husband was proud of Johanna for her willingness to give all she had. Then he realized that Johanna knew she could freely give all she had because she could get more from her father.

What a marvelous comparison to our heavenly Father! No matter how much we give to Him, He is always ready to replace anything we have given to Him and His cause.

How much can I give? I can give my all. Romans 8:32 says, "He who did not spare His own Son, but delivered Him up for us all, how shall He not with Him also freely give us all things?" (*NKJV*).

Dear Lord, thank You for Your Word promising that You know my need even before I ask. Help me to understand that You love me and desire good things for me. I can never give You too much. Amen.

REMEMBER TODAY: He has freely given His best for me; how much can I give Him?

Earlene Coleman
Wichita, KS

Related Scriptures
Psalm 91:9-11; Isaiah 26:3

January 26
1 John 4:18

*"There is no fear in love; but perfect love casteth out
fear: because fear hath torment"* (1 John 4:18).

A CHAIN OF FEAR

As 1 a.m. approached, the screen door was silently opened. The man, seeing by the light of the front porch, stepped around the sleeping children on the floor. I was startled awake when he leaned against my bed. Realizing this was a stranger, I began to scream. A chain of fear held me in its grip.

I had drifted into a light sleep, waiting for my husband to come home from his second-shift job. The night was hot and sultry, so the doors and windows were open. This was 40 years ago when air conditioning was something to dream about. Also there was not as much crime, because people watched out for each other.

That night, as the neighbors were awakened by my screaming, the man left just as silently as he came. Pulling his car out of the driveway without lights, I watched him as fear engulfed me. Fear became my constant companion. My pastor quoted some scriptures to help me, and I began to lean on 1 John 4:18. I realized I would have to go to my heavenly Father in prayer.

As a young Christian, I knew there was nothing I could do but rely on my blessed Lord and His promises. I began praying for the perfect love I needed, and God in His mercy answered my prayers. He removed the chain of fear and replaced it with love.

For the past several years I've lived alone, and the torment of fear has not returned. If a thought of something fearful tries to enter my mind, I remind the Lord of His promises in Psalm 91:9-11, and the amazing security of God surrounds me.

REMEMBER TODAY: If we meet the condition of Isaiah 26:3, "Thou wilt keep him in perfect peace, whose mind is stayed on thee: because he trusteth in thee," God has already provided the promise.

Sandy Bishop
Yakima, WA

Related Scriptures
Psalm 46:1; Proverbs 18:10;
Hebrews 13:5

January 27
Psalm 27:5

For in the time of trouble he shall hide me in
his pavilion: in the secret of his tabernacle shall he
hide me; he shall set me up upon a rock (Psalm 27:5).

THE SECRET PLACE

Sleepy and groggy, I reached for the telephone at 5:45 a.m., January 27. A desperate voice from another area of the country pleaded, "Pray for me! I just can't walk out my door and face life today. I can't go to work; my mind will not focus clearly. Please pray for me!"

Perhaps you too have been at this point. I have. For days emotional pain had gripped me and stripped me of the ability to concentrate clearly. Life seemed like a blur. The words or sentences on my Bible pages appeared as one dark line. Desperately I fought to cling to the one thing in life that I knew was sure . . . solid . . . secure. Yes, I knew the Word. I knew that "God is . . . [my] refuge and strength, a very present help in trouble" (Psalm 46:1). I knew "the name of the Lord is a strong tower: the righteous runneth into it [Him], and is safe" (Proverbs 18:10).

That early January morning all I could think to pray was "Lord, hide him in your pavilion. Hold him secure in your everlasting arms. As his world is crumbling around him, let him know Your love in a way he has never known You before."

Following the telephone call, I crawled out of bed, prepared my cup of coffee and picked up my Bible. How do I remember it was January 27? I read a chapter in Psalms every morning coinciding with the day of the month. I read other divisions of the Psalms in a systematic way which makes it possible to read through the Book of Psalms each month. I read Psalm 27 that morning. Verse 5 says, "In the time of trouble he shall hide me in His pavilion." What a promise with which to face the day—any day!

REMEMBER TODAY: When feeling alone, overwhelmed or unappreciated, remember there is a place of refuge and renewal—His everlasting arms.

Atha Grassano
Farmingdale, NY

Related Scriptures
Isaiah 40:31; Exodus 14:13

January 28
Psalm 91:15

He shall call upon me, and I will answer him: I will be with him in trouble; I will deliver him, and honour him (Psalm 91:15).

SAVED . . . IN THE NICK OF TIME

Driving to the hospital at 6 in the morning, I was talking with my heavenly Father. I did not quite understand why my husband had not received a healing touch. "Father," I said, "he has prayed for many people who have been healed, and now he is scheduled for surgery this morning."

Thomas had been suffering for over four weeks with extreme pain. The internist had sent him to a urologist. Extensive tests revealed nothing, yet all symptoms pointed to kidney stones. Finally, his kidneys stopped functioning; the pain was excruciating. I rushed my husband to the emergency room. Again they did tests, and this time the solution would not pass through his kidneys. Exploratory surgery was scheduled along with additional tests. Of course, I was most anxious.

When I arrived at the hospital, Thomas was ready for surgery. I noticed a small red spot on his lower right side. I asked to speak with the doctor. The nurse came with the pre-op shot, the stretcher was at the door, but I was insistent upon seeing the doctor before surgery. By the time he came to the room, the "small red spot" had become a large mushroomed area. The doctor threw up his hands and said, "Surgery is off."

Quickly he ran to the desk, phoned to cancel the surgery and returned to my husband's room. "Do you realize what you have been spared? If we had done surgery, it could have been fatal. You have shingles and have had them for four weeks. They have been on the inside. We have never seen anything like this."

I know Jesus came just in the nick of time! All day people came to investigate what had happened. The surgical nurse said, "I see you're Italian. Why are you not of the traditional Italian religion? Why are you Church of God? What made you change religion?" With a thick tongue and dry mouth (from the pre-op shot), Thomas testified of our family's conversion. Praise God for answering our prayers at a critical moment!

REMEMBER TODAY: God saves today and answers prayer . . . sometimes just in the nick of time.

Xernona P. Reid
Cocoa, FL

Related Scriptures
Romans 8:37; 2 Corinthians 2:14; 4:8, 9

January 29
Psalm 61:2

From the ends of the earth I call to you, I call as my heart grows faint; lead me to the rock that is higher than I (Psalm 61:2, NIV).

JESUS THE UPLIFTER

We are living in critical times. In these days of uncertainty even the Christian is not exempt from times of perplexity and distress. We need to consistently focus our full attention on the sustaining power of the Word of God.

When the Enemy has come in like a flood, God himself will raise up a standard against him (Isaiah 59:19). What a mighty God we serve! We take heed that we do not allow our hearts to become weighed down with the cares of this life (Luke 21:34).

It is uplifting to know that no weapon formed against us shall prosper (Isaiah 54:17) and that God will provide us with the needed courage and strength to endure. Yes, in this world we will have tribulation, but we are to be of good cheer. We can overcome! (see John 16:33). With assurance we must prepare our hearts and minds with the words of the apostle Paul: "We are troubled on every side, yet not distressed; we are perplexed, but not in despair; persecuted, but not forsaken; cast down, but not destroyed" (2 Corinthians 4:8, 9).

By allowing the Spirit of God to take full control of the situation, we can truly know the lifter of all lifters. God is still on the throne, and He will never forsake His own. It's good to know that when my heart is overwhelmed, He will "lead me to the rock that is higher than I."

REMEMBER TODAY: Only God can lift us above the shadows and plant our feet on higher ground.

Beulah M. (Bea) Baker	**Related Scriptures**	**January 30**
Princeton, WV	Genesis 28:10-16; Luke 2:13, 14	1 Peter 5:7

Casting all your care upon him;
for he careth for you (1 Peter 5:7).

GOD'S TENDER LOVING CARE

Our heavenly Father truly cares for His children with tender loving care!

Our daughter became quite ill and required surgery. I immediately made plans to be with her and take care of my grandchildren, then 18 months and 5 years old. They lived several hundred miles away, so it was necessary for me to fly.

One night while preparing for bed, I was cleaning my contact lenses and lost one of them. My glasses were old and would not stay on my face. This made it difficult for me to work and take care of the grandchildren. After searching everywhere again and again, I began to grow weary.

That night as I prayed before retiring for the night, I asked God to help me find my contact lens. After prayer, I did not feel worried. I went to sleep.

That night God showed me in a dream where the lens was. In my dream there was a baseboard near a window. The next morning I felt along the baseboard, and there was the lens—all dried up like a leaf! After a few minutes of soaking in solution, it was as good as new. Praise the Lord! (Incidentally, the baseboard was behind a chest where I always kept the case for my contact lenses.) This little incident of God's concern was for me a miracle from God.

REMEMBER TODAY: God is always near us, watching over His children with tender loving care.

Pat Daugherty
Charlotte, NC

Related Scriptures
Psalms 61:4; 68:13; Matthew 23:37

January 31
Psalm 91:4

He shall cover thee with his feathers (Psalm 91:4).

TRUSTING GOD FOR PROTECTION

Wild and tame ducks made their home on the beautiful lake on the South Georgia campground. Their "home away from home" was the top of my car, carport and patio. One morning while sweeping away the feathers, I noticed something sparkling in the rising sun. Picking up the iridescent green feather, I realized a mallard had left his calling card. I thought, *This is too pretty to sweep into the wind—but what use do I have for it?*

Centuries ago it would have made a nice pen, duster or down pillow if I had more to put with it. If Yankee-Doodle could do it, so would I. I'd stick this feather in my husband's hat! Gently pushing it into the hatband of his black Stetson, I wondered what use the Lord would have for feathers. He clothed the fowls of the air, from sparrows to eagles, with them. Suddenly I saw what the psalmist meant as he penned Psalm 91:4. God uses feathers to cover me!

Feathers are soft and light but easily carried off with the wind. I would have suggested to God a more substantial covering—perhaps a bomb shelter! When my wounded spirit is smarting with pain and the burden seems more than I can bear, how I thank Him for choosing a light covering for me! Is He teaching me to trust Him?

How do I know a fragile feather covering is adequate for me? The feathers are under the same law as the wind. Is it any harder for Him to speak to the feathers than to the wind? He can say, "Peace, be still," and both must obey. How grieved our Lord was when Israel refused to come under the protection of His feathers. I can't see or feel them, but the warmth that surrounds me assures me His feathers are attached to the strong wings (arms) of my Lord!

REMEMBER TODAY: When the storms of life threaten our security, remember He is covering us with His feathers!

NOTES

Donna McCarn Fisher	Related Scriptures	February 1
Cleveland, TN	Psalms 8:2; Matthew 11:25	John 14:27

Peace I leave with you, my peace I give unto you: not as the world giveth,
give I unto you. Let not your heart be troubled, neither let it be afraid (John 14:27).

OUT OF THE MOUTHS OF BABES

My husband was gone on a college-recruitment trip, and all was quiet on the home front. Supper was finished and the kitchen cleaned, so my two children and I settled into the den for a peaceful evening at home. Amanda, my 1-year-old, was digging into the unknown depths of the toy box, looking for buried treasures. Her 4-year-old brother, Grant, was seemingly engrossed in his play world of Tinkertoys and turtles.

Since the children were content to play on their own, I decided to relax by watching television. But to my distress, there was only more coverage of the military crisis our country was in. It was quite apparent that things were escalating to dangerous levels and war was imminent. For the first time, I found myself actually getting beyond the fearful stage to feeling all-out scared.

With Cameron gone, there wasn't an adult at home to talk with about my feelings. I surely didn't want to arouse fear in my children. So, quietly I trembled and prayed. I really just wanted to have a good cry.

"Mom," my son called.

"Yes, Grant," I halfheartedly replied.

And in the voice with the excitement only a child can truly reflect, he said, "Ya know what? Jesus has power! He can just stretch out His arms and go *pow*! Jesus can do anything!"

"You're right!" I said through flowing tears.

In a moment when I was weak, it took the mouth and mind of a 4-year-old to minister to me. Never did I dream that God would use my child's interest in power to speak peace to my troubled heart.

REMEMBER TODAY: God does have power. He can even speak peace to our troubled hearts from the most unexpected sources.

Sherry B. Lee
Cleveland, TN

Related Scriptures
Psalm 34:4-7; 17-19

February 2
James 3:2

For we all stumble in many ways (James 3:2, *NASB*).

STUMBLING ONE, TAKE HEART

I lost my footing! Tumbling headlong over the edge, I plunged into the darkness, hurt and misery of failure. Failure—again.

My flesh ached as the sharp edges of present circumstances intermittently jabbed me, interrupting my fall. Scenes of yesterday's triumphant journeys flashed before my eyes as I slid past all of them toward defeat. Cries—desperate cries—formed inside me, but my lips were silent sufferers. Heartbreak and disappointment stirred my eyes to fiery tears, my mind to the precipice of pain and my will to involuntary submission. Propelled along by the force of failure feelings, I fell long, far and hard. Landing in a solitary corner of fear and regret, I lay sobbing, feeling hopeless.

The Scriptures never support an unreal or glazed approach to life and its personalized traumas. The apostle Paul openly confessed his emotional, physical and spiritual struggles. His honesty in the midst of pain, even depression, ministers comfort in times of affliction. David's cries from the pit of despair strike cords of harmony in every soul who has hurt because of his own sin or sins committed against him. He said, "I sought the Lord, and He answered me, and delivered me from all my fears. . . . This poor [afflicted] man cried and the Lord heard him, and saved him out of all his troubles" (Psalm 34:4, 6, *NASB*).

The New Testament instructs true believers to bear one another's burdens—yes, even the burdens of "strong" Christians who hurt. We are to pick up stumbling ones, reminding ourselves all the time of our own areas of failure. We must minister encouragement and love among ourselves, strengthening each individual member for the sake of the whole.

Feelings of depression, fear of failure, emotional hurt, mental battles, scarred memories—all these Jesus came to heal. As many times as I need healing, Jesus can handle it.

Returning to that original lonely corner of personal struggle, I take comfort in this short sentence found in James 3:2: "For we all stumble in many ways."

REMEMBER TODAY: Stumbling one, take heart. We all have been there.

Valerie Abbott
Yakima, WA

Related Scripture
Psalm 37:24

February 3
Isaiah 40:31

*They that wait upon the Lord shall renew their strength; they
shall mount up with wings as eagles; they shall run, and not
be weary; and they shall walk, and not faint* (Isaiah 40:31).

WAITING ON THE LORD

My 2-year-old has finally adjusted to his new Sunday school class in our large church. Consequently, when we get out of the car in the parking lot, he will make a beeline for the building where his class is held.

"Hold my hand!" I scold him as we trot along, dodging cars from every direction. He wiggles his fingers until they're free again and proceeds to jog a little faster. Grabbing him, I become hysterical, "Hold Mommy's hand!"

Just as I clutch hold of his tiny fingers, he takes a nosedive onto the pavement. Pulling the weight of his small frame, I am able to barely prevent his face, knees and hands from taking a bruising. Realizing Mom has saved him from a major catastrophe, he slows down and nestles his hand safely in my grasp.

As we continue our cautious journey to the church, God whispers His message to my heart. Many times in my walk and work for Him, I go too quickly or head in the wrong direction. He wants so desperately to hold my hand and save me from taking a nosedive! But often I'm so determined to make it on my own that I fail to wait on Him. Regardless of the dangers that may surround me, I charge toward my goal, eluding His protective touch that would assure my victory!

What lessons He can teach us from our own little ones!

REMEMBER TODAY: Hold tightly to God's hand through the "parking lots" of life!

Becky Fulton
Syracuse, NY

Related Scripture
1 John 3:16-18

*Greater love hath no man than this, that a man
lay down his life for his friends* (John 15:13).

CHRIST'S DYING LOVE

Years ago I heard a man preach on how love should be shown and not just spoken. He shared that while on a missionary trip he was preaching on God's love when a man from the congregation stepped to the platform and walked up to him. His face was half eaten away with cancer, one ear was gone, and his arm and leg were crippled from the disease. He said, "You say you love me?"

The minister replied, "Yes!"

The sick man then said, "I don't need your money, for I'm going to die soon. I don't need your material goods, for I have no home. My wife is dead, and my children are also sick and dying; but you say you love me, so, please, love me."

The preacher asked the Lord to help him show love to this man who desperately needed it. Without thinking twice, the preacher walked over and cradled this sick, dying man in his arms. He went beyond spoken love; he showed his love.

Christ said He loved us. Then He went one step further and showed a love this world has never seen before or since. He loved us enough to die for us.

REMEMBER TODAY: He died so we could live.

Glenda Davis
Somerset, PA

Related Scripture
Philippians 1:21

February 5
Galatians 2:20

I died on the cross with Christ. And my present life is not that of the old "I," but the living Christ within me (Galatians 2:20, Ph.).

GROWTH THROUGH CHANGE

Why do things packed in a box never fit back exactly the same after they have been removed? I guess it is the same reason things are never the same when you return to visit a childhood dwelling. Change produces a different shape to our lives.

I remember returning to my high school reunion many moons ago and seeing my old classmates. Some had changed so drastically that I didn't recognize them.

So it is with the change that God brings into our lives. "Lord," I pray, "take those inner conflicts in me and make them unrecognizable. Whether it be fear, worry or anxiety—make the necessary changes."

A religious leader said concerning Nelson Mandela, who had just been released from 27 years of imprisonment for his political views in South Africa, "When Mandela entered prison, he had wandered away from his Methodist background. While in prison he renewed his faith, and through prayer he gained hope." Through suffering and spiritual change, Mandela's life took on a new shape and meaning.

If you could take all the inner conflicts and character flaws in your life and pack them away in a box in the attic, when you unpacked the box, hopefully they would no longer fit in your life. Why? Because your life has taken on a new shape through growth and new meaning through the Cross.

REMEMBER TODAY: Change produces different shapes in our lives. Let's allow these changes to reflect spiritual growth and strength of character.

Charlotte Frye
Aurora, IL

Related Scriptures
Psalms 19:14; 139

February 6
Psalm 139:14

Thank you for making me so wonderfully complex! It is amazing to think about. Your workmanship is marvelous—and how well I know it (Psalm 139:14, *TLB*).

UNIQUELY CREATED

The argument was between classmates in junior high school. I don't remember what the disagreement was about, but I shall never forget how our best friends reacted to the situation.

Bertha's friend stood beside her, bold and strong, to win or lose, the perfect loyal companion. My friend, my best friend, said to me as we were confronting the opposition, "Don't expect me to take sides." I stood alone.

Within a couple of days the argument was forgotten, but deep in my heart I felt I had failed or my best friend would have stood by me.

One Sunday afternoon, years later, all those feelings surfaced again. A lady whom I admired expressed to me how my personality had affected her. My heart crumbled as she described a person I never wanted to be. I remember crying all afternoon.

All my life I have looked up to my mother. She possesses a temperament of meekness and inner beauty that every Christian woman desires. I feel like an ugly duckling because I'm loud, talkative, persistent and sometimes overbearing.

God fearfully and wonderfully made me. In order to serve effectively, I must maintain my relationship with Christ, allowing His Word to become a dominant force in my life. He has helped me improve the quality of my life by my acknowledgment that I was created with a uniqueness as clean and fresh as the morning dew.

REMEMBER TODAY: You have a rare combination of talent and ability to work for God. Seize this moment.

Margaret W. Lackey   **Related Scripture**   February 7
Mt. Holly, NC   Hebrews 7:25   Romans 8:34

*Who is he that comdemneth? It is Christ that died, yea rather,
that is risen again, who is even at the right hand of God,
who also maketh intercession for us* (Romans 8:34).

JESUS, TALK TO GOD FOR ME

Bernice, our dear family friend from Texas, was at her lowest ebb. Her husband, Jim, had been in prison for three years for a crime we all believed he did not commit. Extremely ill with emphysema, the once-vibrant man, now broken, was dying in the prison hospital. Pleas for an early parole had been denied twice.

Prison officials had told Bernice that his release had been set for July 1991. Her letter spoke her heart so painfully clear: "But he won't live 'til July. We had so many happy years together, why does it have to end this way?"

We had prayed so long. Day after day in my prayers, I had said, "God, please let Papa Jim go home. Don't let him die there." When I received the letter on February 7, my heart sank. Somehow the words I had repeated so many times sounded empty as I knelt again beside my bed to pray once again for them.

"Jesus," I cried out through my tears, "You said You would go back to the Father to plead our cases. You said You would be our intercessor. You didn't say we had to beg for anything; You said for us to ask. But I've asked for so long, I don't know what to say. Jesus, will you intercede to the Father for Jim?"

And I left the matter with Him.

Four days later, another letter came in the mail. I tore it open as quickly as I could. The smiley-face sticker on the envelope said "good news." Hurriedly I read, "Dearest Margaret, Jim is coming home. About 11 p.m. on February 7, I received a call that his release had been moved to February 12."

Tears of joy rolled down my face when I realized what I had just read: 11 p.m. on February 7 was only moments after Jesus had interceded to the Father for Jim.

Have you come to that place where you feel like the heavens are brass and your prayers are not penetrating the darkness? Jesus is your intercessor. He can reach God for you!

REMEMBER TODAY: Jesus is interceding for you.

Trudy L. Chapman
Chattanooga, TN

Related Scriptures
Psalm 29:11; Isaiah 26:3;
Jeremiah 29:11; Philippians 4:6

February 8
Psalm 23:1, 2

The Lord is my shepherd; I shall want nothing. He
makes me lie down in green pastures (Psalm 23:1, 2, *NEB*).

HE MAKES US LIE DOWN

How many times have I quoted this familiar scripture when I didn't truly know the meaning of peace and contentment? More times than I like to admit.

Being the perfectionist that I am, I always think I can make things turn out right. All I have to do is reorganize things again . . . and again . . . and again. What this often does is rob me of the experience of true contentment. Fears develop and anxieties grow.

On February 8, 1985, my husband and I were faced with a fear we had never experienced. Our son was diagnosed with a muscular disease that could possibly leave him crippled or lead to an early death.

These were days of great fear and, like frightened sheep, we were not at rest. Worry and anxiety were the thieves of our peace. We could not "lie down" on our own. Only the Good Shepherd could "make us lie down." It was only through our trust in His goodness, power and wisdom that we found perfect peace in this situation.

Phillip Keller in his book *A Shepherd Looks at Psalm 23* points out that four conditions must be met before a sheep will lie down: (1) The sheep must be free from fear; (2) the sheep must be free from the friction of and aggravation with other sheep; (3) the sheep must be free from insects; (4) the sheep must be well fed.

I have found that by choosing to let Christ be my Good Shepherd, I can be free from fear, free from meaningless conflicts, free from agitation over little things that "bug" me every day and free from spiritual hunger.

In 1985 I found His peace and, yes, ultimately His healing for our son. The Lord brought calmness, serenity and peace in place of our fears.

REMEMBER TODAY: In our very hour of struggle, Jesus brings perfect peace and contentment and makes us "lie down."

Michele Lugo	**Related Scriptures**	**February 9**
San Antonio, TX	Luke 22:41-43; Romans 12:2	Luke 23:23

*And they were instant with loud voices, requiring that he might be crucified.
And the voices of them and of the chief priests prevailed* (Luke 23:23).

THEIR WILL OR THY WILL?

For years I thought everything that had happened to me was decided by others. My mother had decided to treat me in a certain way, as had my father, family, friends. I blamed the world for the rude, self-centered, cynical and scared individual I had become. The voices surrounding my life were molding me, and I had no control.

Coming to Christ brought me face-to-face with the reality of the Lord, whose essence, personality and behavior were not influenced by anyone else. While the crowd shouted loudly, the silence of the Lamb of God spoke louder.

God had spoken many years before, and His voice, not the loud crowd, prevailed. When I think about it, I realize that Jesus' behavior was not molded by Herod, Pilate, the priests or by the shouting crowd. Before this incident with Pilate, there had been a Mount of Olives where our Lord had submitted His will to the will of God.

Today my life has a different perspective. Before I become confused, threatened or molded by the loud crowd, I look to the Master and retreat to the Mount of Olives with Him. There I prepare myself to accept and submit my life to His will, His requirements and His voice.

An encounter with Him at the Mount of Olives makes the voices of a shouting crowd easier. I do not have to be molded by the world; I do not have to give in to what the crowd wants or decides. Even when it is difficult for me to understand, His divine will is what will be done.

REMEMBER TODAY: In a loud and confusing world, God offers us life in Him through His Son Jesus.

Betty Rice
Cleveland, TN

Related Scripture
Psalm 46

February 10
Psalm 46:1

*God is our refuge and strength, a very
present help in trouble* (Psalm 46:1).

GOD'S STRENGTH, NOT OURS

The truth that God supplies all our needs stands as a fitting motto for every believer in Jesus Christ. Even in severe trials we can find comfort and support in the assurance that God's strength is more than adequate for every situation in our lives.

On February 10, 1990, I stood over the grave of my oldest sister, Maybelline. Momentarily my mind was filled with questions and even doubts. You see, just two years earlier I had buried my precious mother. But standing there amid the beautiful flowers, I received a glorious message of hope: "We shall see those we have loved again." We will embrace again those vanished forms who have been changed to immortality and will forever be with those we loved and lost. It is only till He comes.

As Christians we experience storms and trials in life that overwhelm us. We come to the end of our own strength. But we must remember the source of strength. When we lean on God and trust the promises of His Word, we can survive every crisis. It's His strength, not ours, that is sufficient.

REMEMBER TODAY: When you have nothing left but God, you find that God is enough.

Therese M. Coen
Elkins, WV

Related Scriptures
Romans 14:17; 15:13

February 11
Psalm 16:11

*You have made known to me the paths of life; you will fill
me with joy in your presence* (Psalm 16:11, *NIV*).

LIVING IN JOY

Many women seem to have misinterpreted what it means to serve Jesus. I remember one in particular who let her housework go, left her family for hours at a time, neglected her husband—all in the name of Jesus and her "ministry." But mostly I remember her lack of joy in service. She always appeared to have conflicts in her life.

As I study the life of Jesus, our example, I notice He enjoyed life. Though He experienced much heartache, I believe He enjoyed life to its fullest. He could relate to strong fishermen, yet the children ran to Him and women felt comfortable in His presence. This does not sound like a hard, sad person who was unable to interact with people. Far too many feel that in order to have Christ's love, we have to stop enjoying life. This is not true. When we receive God's love, we can then experience joy in all areas of our life.

Life is made up of family, friends, fellowship, prayer time, devotion time, rest and recreation. What the woman did not understand is this: It is true that we should give Christ first place in our life, but this commitment will not conflict with the natural responsibilities of home and family. Time must be allotted to each area of responsibility, and we should feel joyful, not guilty, about giving time to each.

REMEMBER TODAY: God has promised joy when we give Him all of our ministries.

Lois Carol Pushkar	**Related Scriptures**	**February 12**
Belle Vernon, PA	Psalm 24:7; 2 Corinthians 3:18	John 4:23

But the hour cometh, and now is, when the true
worshippers shall worship the Father in spirit and in truth:
for the Father seeketh such to worship him (John 4:23).

TRUE WORSHIPERS

Someone has said, "You are the company you keep." Those who spend enough time with the Lord will become like Him! Some married couples have been together so long that they begin to talk, walk and even look alike! Our heavenly Father is seeking that quality of a relationship with us, His children.

Thinking back over the years of walking with the Lord, I can recall wondering why it was so important that I worship God. From my early childhood I have always loved to sing and make melody in my heart. Now that I have learned that God is seeking for that song of worship in me, I find joy and fulfillment as I direct my praise to the King of Glory. When we worship with uplifted countenance, we reflect the Lord's glory. Little by little we are changed into His likeness.

Being a true worshiper changes us. That is why our worship is so important to the Lord. Scripture records how at the birth of Jesus the very learned Magi curiously sought Him out. Their search led them to the perfect Truth. Their superstition led them to the Light of the World. God truly knows how to reach each of us at our point of need. The Magi did not return to Herod after they came face-to-face with the Christ child, but they returned a different way. Worship had truly changed them.

When we have an attitude of worship that is acceptable to God, He brings us to a place of communion with Him. This veil of flesh is gone, and we are lost in His love to adore and worship Him. We are then adorned with a priestly garment—a garment of beauty and fragrance. As women we have various roles in life, but the greatest is to become a true worshiper of God, to minister to the King of Glory.

REMEMBER TODAY: Opening the gate of a pure heart toward God will give entrance to the King of Glory.

Carolyn Martin
Portage, IN

Related Scriptures
Psalm 31:7; 1 Thessalonians 5:11, 14;
Hebrews 4:15, 16; 1 Corinthians 13

February 13
2 Corinthians 1:3, 4

Blessed be God, even the Father of our Lord Jesus Christ, the Father of mercies, and the God of all comfort; who comforteth us in all our tribulation, that we may be able to comfort them which are in any trouble, by the comfort wherewith we ourselves are comforted of God (2 Corinthians 1:3, 4).

HIS LOVE EXTENDED

As librarian of a Christian school, I had become well acquainted with most of the students. As the first-grade class checked out their books, I heard Charna say, "Nobody likes me, Mrs. Martin. Will you be my friend?" My heart overflowed with compassion, and I wanted somehow to assure her she wasn't alone.

When Charna laid the books of her choice on my desk, I looked at her. She smiled that little smile which seemed to say, "I've got you, Mrs. Martin." The titles of her books were *Nobody Likes Me* and *Will You Be My Friend?*

After she left, the Lord reminded me of some truths on compassion. First, we are able to feel more compassion when we have personally experienced what another is encountering.

Second, we can only show compassion as we have received it from God, who comforts us in all our trouble. Through receiving God's comfort, a faith is built within us that assures us He will always be there. Third, as yielded vessels of God, He desires that we allow His comfort to flow through us to others. He uses our arms of flesh to give hugs, smiling lips to encourage, caring words from an obedient tongue, and sometimes a single tear to loudly proclaim, "I am with you!"

The world is filled with hurting people who need the Lord. The apostle Paul said it best when introducing the love chapter: "And yet I show you a more excellent way [love]" (1 Corinthians 12:31, *NKJV*). Let love prevail, and *you* be that love reaching out in compassion.

REMEMBER TODAY: You are God's love extended to a world in desperate need.

Mary N. Coward	**Related Scriptures**	**February 14**
Greenwood, SC	Luke 6:38; Romans 5:8;	1 Corinthians 13:8
	1 Peter 4:8; 9; 1 Corinthians 13:1-8	

Charity never faileth (1 Corinthians 13:8).

LOVE NEVER FAILS

"My husband doesn't tell me he loves me anymore," cried a Christian woman. Her heart was troubled and frightened. "What can I do?" she wept. Continuing, she said, "I want to see him saved."

My mind quickly said a prayer, "Lord, give me the words to say to this newborn in Christ. She desires to hear the vital words that every wife needs to hear, and she wants her companion saved."

As always, the Holy Spirit gave the answer. The words poured forth: "Go home and put love to work by keeping a clean, warm home. When he arrives from work, greet him with a hug and kiss. Look and smell nice and prepare his favorite meals."

Then I asked her, "What was it that you loved about your husband when you first married him? Was it his beautiful eyes, his smile that made a big dimple in his cheek, his hair? Whatever it was you liked, express your love for those qualities again. It works!"

Protesting, she said, "But it is so hard when he doesn't seem to love me!" The Holy Spirit brought to my mind how Christ loved us when we were yet sinners and unlovable.

With a gentle reminder of these truths, she yielded to the Spirit and put love to work, giving of herself for a week unbegrudgingly. The following week she had a glowing report. Did love work? Her husband told her four times that week, "I love you!"

In weeks to come she came to hear those beautiful words over and over. Months later her husband was saved, sanctified, filled with the Spirit and is now working in the church.

REMEMBER TODAY: Love never fails. Put it to work and observe the beautiful fruit it produces.

Wilma Amison
Cleveland, TN

Related Scriptures
Psalm 103:1-4; Mark 8:22-25

February 15
Exodus 15:26

I am the Lord that healeth thee (Exodus 15:26).

GOD'S HEALING POWER

We called her Sister Cleo. Although some 35 years our senior, she wanted to be called by her first name—to be one of us—and indeed she was! We added the "Sister" to her name out of respect. Our oldest was only a baby then, and we were stationed thousands of miles from home, across an ocean. She and her husband, Brother Andy, became like another set of parents to us, their home providing a welcomed warmth, their friendship providing acceptance, love and spiritual guidance.

Years earlier, before she and Brother Andy met, she had experienced a painful divorce. Grieving over her loss, she became so severely depressed she lost her will to live. Being a diabetic, perhaps she could have accomplished her desire without a great deal of effort. As she sat at home one day, she realized she could not see. Her diabetic condition had resulted in blindness. When her three children became aware of their mother's plight, they became desperate. Crowding close to her, they waved their hands in front of her face and asked, "Can you see me, Mother?" On receiving a negative reply, they pressed their faces close to hers and fairly shrieked, "Can you see me now?"

Hearing the panic in their young voices and realizing their need for her, she quickly regained her desire to live and asked God to heal her. And in His graciousness, He answered her prayer—gradually, she said. Her eyesight was restored; she grew stronger; then she was well. She began to add previously forbidden food back into her diet. And when she finally was able to spread her bread with jelly with no ill effects, she knew her healing was complete.

She is with the Lord now, but this touching experience she related so many years ago continues to be a reminder to me of God's healing power and of His concern for His children.

REMEMBER TODAY: God's healing power continues to be available even now.

Rhoda Watson   **Related Scripture**   **February 16**
Glendale, AZ   Matthew 11:28   Hebrews 4:16

Let us therefore come boldly unto the throne of grace, that we may obtain mercy, and find grace to help in time of need (Hebrews 4:16).

NEVER TOO BUSY FOR YOU

Whether by plan or by lack of a plan, busy lives have forced most of us into living by a list of priorities. The memo tagged "urgent" gets typed first. At home, the shopping, cooking and surface cleaning are done; the closet has to wait. In the yard, that patch of weeds must go; we will smell the roses tomorrow.

At times in our relationship with the Lord, we tend to humanize Him by seeing Him with a list of priorities. As we live in a world of much suffering and need, we naturally put ourselves at the bottom of this list, thinking, *Why bother the Lord with this? I should be able to handle this myself.*

Have you ever thought that at the busiest, most important time of His life, Jesus focused on the desperate needs of one heartbroken and sinful soul? While He was on the cross dying for the sins of the world, the agonizing cry of a repentant sinner touched His compassionate soul—"Lord, remember me when thou comest into thy kingdom" (Luke 23:42). At that moment, as far as the thief on the cross was concerned, the blasphemous crowd, the Roman soldiers, the mocking passers-by ceased to exist! He was alone with Christ and had His full attention. As is always the case, Jesus' response to him was overwhelming: "To day shalt thou be with me in paradise" (v. 43).

Whatever you need today, you do not have to stand in line.

Your name will not be put on a waiting list. You will not be put on hold. You have an invitation to come boldly to the throne of grace for that one-on-one encounter with the Lord.

REMEMBER TODAY: Jesus calls us His friends. As friends we can confide in Him anything at any time. He'll be there!

Anita Chamberlain
Tampa, FL

Related Scriptures
1 Samuel 15; Matthew 26:39, 42;
Hebrews 5:7-10

February 17
1 Samuel 15:22

*Behold, to obey is better than sacrifice, and to
hearken than the fat of rams* (1 Samuel 15:22).

OBEDIENCE

Obedience to God is often a difficult lesson to learn. Because of obstacles we face, such as fear of failure and low self-esteem, we fail to realize that God has given us the tools needed to accomplish His will. Just as He said to Moses, " 'What is that in your hand?'" (Exodus 4:2, *NKJV*), so we must realize that all power is His and that He has not called us to do more than what *He* can accomplish.

I have found that if I persist in going my own way, in my own power, terrible consequences may follow. However, if I inquire of the Lord and go in His power, God works *for* me, *in* me and *in spite of* me.

When God called my husband and me into the ministry, we were already in our 30s. My husband had a successful health-care practice and was a faithful church worker. As I kicked against pricks, the days of not surrendering to His will became tough days indeed. I did not want to give in! My strong will was like hard ground that had to be broken before it could be useful. And broken I became. But what relief when I prayed the words of Jesus, "Nevertheless not my will, but thine, be done" (Luke 22:42). The Holy Scriptures tell us that the giving of our sacrifices is proper. But hearing His voice and obeying Him is better and more pleasing. Our sacrifices—whether they are in praise and worship or through the giving of our time, energies and finances—are not overlooked by God. They are necessary. But our obedience reflects our relationship with Him.

❦

REMEMBER TODAY: Hearing His voice and yielding to His will produces abundant life.

Debbie Lanier
Winston-Salem, NC

Related Scripture
Matthew 10:42

February 18
Matthew 6:33

Seek ye first the kingdom of God (Matthew 6:33).

THE KINGDOM AND THE KITCHEN!

I enjoy listening to ministers share the exciting good news. I am also challenged by good books encouraging me to do all I can to further the cause of Christ. But I must confess, the kingdom of God is not always a glamorous pursuit for me. Much of my day is filled with dirty diapers, dirty dishes and rushing about meeting the growing needs of my baby. I sense my awesome responsibilities as a minister's wife.

However, I am discovering something quite exciting in my quest! Kingdom work is doing those things I wish everyone could see, but they don't. And Kingdom work is also doing those things I wish no one could see, but they do. I am learning that living for the King and seeking to acknowledge His reign in every dimension of my life is all that He desires of me. My only obligation is obedience.

I may never travel to foreign lands sharing the gospel, but when I accept the lordship of Christ in my home and share Him with my family and friends, I know I am fulfilling His will for my life! And yes, changing dirty diapers and cleaning dirty dishes can be Kingdom work. After all, it isn't the nature of the task but my willingness to obey that places me on the frontlines of service.

REMEMBER TODAY: Success is not measured by what you can hold in your hands but by whose hand you are holding!

Blenda Wicker
Somerset, PA

Related Scriptures
1 Samuel 2:8, 9; 2 Samuel 22:32-37;
Psalms 56:10-13; 116:5-9

February 19
Jude 24

*To him who is able to keep you
from falling . . .* (Jude 24, *NIV*).

THE LIFE NET

My daughter, granddaughter and I decided we'd spend the day shopping. Like any other grandchild, little Amelia decided she needed a new toy. The toy she chose was a small figurine of Alice in Wonderland.

After much walking, Amelia looked up and said, "Gooma, will you hold me?" As I held her, she fell sound asleep with Alice in hand, or so I thought. I suddenly noticed Alice had been dropped from the little hand. Amelia's mommy went back and searched, but there was no Alice. There was not another like her in the store. Amelia would probably awaken to find Alice lost and be most unhappy.

As I got into the car and leaned against the seat, something stuck my back. On the shirt I was wearing was a hood, and Alice had fallen into the hood. The hood had served as a catching net for the figurine.

When Amelia awoke, she asked for Alice, and as I handed the small figurine to her, she smiled happily.

This incident caused me to think of the many ways our heavenly Father cares for us. He doesn't want us lost or unhappy. He's prepared many nets to catch us, just when we think all is gone and we're hopelessly falling toward the bottom.

As the life net is to a victim trapped in a fourth-floor fire with no alternative but to jump, as the life net is to the one on the flying trapeze who loses his grip, as the life net is to the one walking the high wire who loses his footing, so is the life net of love prepared for us by our heavenly Father.

REMEMBER TODAY: He cares and will keep us from falling and being destroyed.

Shirley Meadows   **Related Scriptures**   February 20
Hampton, VA   Galatians 6:2; Colossians 3:12   1 John 3:18

My little children, let us not love in word, neither in tongue; but in deed and in truth (1 John 3:18).

PRIORITIES

The yellow legal pad was the first thing I saw when I entered my kitchen that morning. The evening before, I had made a list of my commitments for the day and the obligations I had to fulfill. Just a glance at the list reminded me of the realities of the day.

Quite frankly, I was rather proud to see the schedule I had arranged. I remember thinking to myself that absolutely nothing can interrupt this day. Then the phone rang. *Nothing unusual, this is the parsonage,* I reasoned. *Probably looking for my husband.* He had just left for the office. *I'll give them the phone number and be on my way with my day.*

But when I heard the voice on the other end of the line, I knew that although they did indeed need the pastor, they also needed me—right away. I could not give them a phone number or pass them on to someone else. The message I received that morning stopped my day. My carefully written list became unimportant at that point. An elderly couple had just received news they had been dreading to hear. The body taken from the James River a few days before had been positively identified. It was their missing son. What words could describe how they were feeling? There were none. What words of comfort could I offer them? I began praying, "God, give me the words You would have them hear. Somehow let me, by Your Spirit, minister to them until the pastor can get there."

My well-laid plans, my carefully organized day that nothing could interrupt, were changed very quickly.

REMEMBER TODAY: Lord, help us not to be so preoccupied with our own lives that we feel it is an interruption to offer encouragement to others.

Dorothy J. Black
Cleveland, TN

Related Scriptures
1 John 5:15; Matthew 7:7-11; Luke 18:1-8

February 21
1 John 5:14

*Now this is the confidence that we have in
Him, that if we ask anything according
to His will, He hears us* (1 John 5:14, NKJV).

LEARNING THAT GOD ANSWERS PRAYER

Some faith-building experiences we have in our youth are so unforgettable that they linger with us all through life. When I was a child, my father was the pastor of a small, rural church in North Dakota, but he worked for a railroad company to earn our living. When I was 17, my father became gravely ill and had to give up his job on the railroad and enter the hospital for major surgery.

My mother, brothers, sister and I were worried that my father would not live. So we prayed earnestly that God would give him healing and recovery, and the Lord answered our prayers. My father recovered from that illness and lived another two years, in which he was able to minister and work, before dying quietly and suddenly one day while kneeling by his bed in prayer.

Until this day I am certain God gave my father and us those two extra years in response to our prayers. And memories of that time of crisis in the life of our family still encourage me to seek God's help in times of need.

❧

REMEMBER TODAY: God has given you special opportunities to trust Him and learn of His faithfulness.

Brenda Short
Chattanooga, TN

Related Scriptures
Philippians 1:14; 1 John 4:18

February 22
2 Timothy 1:7

*For God hath not given us the spirit of fear; but of power,
and of love, and of a sound mind* (2 Timothy 1:7).

FACE YOUR FEAR

When you think of the word *fear*, you probably think of alarm or dread. The word may bring to mind a feeling of terror or a painful experience of the past.

The Word of God plainly tells us that fear is not of God. One of the most often repeated commands of Jesus was "Fear not." Yet many people live in fear. Fear holds people in bondage. It cripples lives. To overcome, you must face your fear.

There was a time in my life when I was very fearful. I was especially terrified of speaking to groups of people. When I got up to speak, my heart would race, my hands would shake, and my throat would get so dry I could hardly speak. I knew God had called me to speak and teach. I wanted to obey, but I felt so afraid. I was focusing on my fear rather than on the call of God upon my life. The more attentive I was to the fear, the bigger it became. It's important to realize that what you concentrate on will be magnified.

As I prayed and searched the Scriptures, I realized God really loved me and didn't want me to live in fear. His Word tells me that He has given me power and love and a sound mind. In Proverbs 28:1 I read, "The wicked flee when no man pursueth: but the righteous are bold as a lion." The word *bold* means "fearless and courageous." I began to say over and over, "I am as bold as a lion." Hearing those words caused faith to grow in my heart. I began to feel less afraid. As I focused on the Word of God, my fear did not have priority in my life. Proverbs 3:26 became my motto: "For the Lord shall be thy confidence, and shall keep thy foot from being taken." God's Word gave me confidence to face fear and trust Him.

REMEMBER TODAY: Fear not. God is our confidence and strength.

Saundra Jennings Rose
Norcross, GA

Related Scriptures
Isaiah 55; 1 Timothy 6:6-8;
Philippians 4:10-13

February 23
Isaiah 55:13

"Instead of the thorn shall come up the cypress tree, and instead of the brier shall come up the myrtle tree" (Isaiah 55:13, *NKJV*).

BRIERS AND THORNS

One morning after moving to our new home, I was having devotions and sharing with the Lord just how difficult this adjustment period as a minister's family had been for all of us. My prayer went something like this: "Lord, I trust Your sovereignty . . . but Minot, North Dakota? Lord, surely You made a mistake this time!"

The Holy Spirit seemed to direct me to Isaiah 55:12, 13: " 'The mountains and the hills shall break forth into singing before you, and all the trees of the field shall clap their hands. Instead of the thorn shall come up the cypress tree, and instead of the brier shall come up the myrtle tree' " (*NKJV*).

I was excited to find out exactly what God was saying to me that morning. Hurriedly I went to the encyclopedia and found some interesting facts about cypress and myrtle trees. Both are evergreens and stay alive, green and growing regardless of their surrounding circumstances. The cypress tree is a tall tree which adapts readily to various climates and situations.

The myrtle is an attractive evergreen with shining blue-green leaves and fragrant white flowers. Even the bark and berries are fragrant, and manufacturers use them in making perfume. Both evergreens are often used as ornamental greens in a garden setting.

My heavenly Father gave the assurance that day that the briers and thorns of discontentment in my life could be exchanged for beautiful ornamental evergreens that would give forth the lovely fragrance of the Rose of Sharon. I did not have to depend on any particular place or circumstance to remain alive, glowing and growing!

By the way, the Dakotas proved to be one of the most challenging and enjoyable experiences of my life.

REMEMBER TODAY: Contentment and a joyful spirit are independent of circumstances and are based on a vibrant relationship with Jesus Christ!

Violet Reynolds	Related Scriptures	February 24
Falmouth, ME	Exodus 4:10, 12; Jeremiah 1:6;	Proverbs 20:24
	Psalm 37:23; Proverbs 3:5, 6; 16:1	

*Since the Lord is directing our steps, why try to understand
everything that happens along the way?* (Proverbs 20:24, *TLB*).

GOD'S GUIDANCE

My husband had often said he would like to visit the New England states sometime, but to live there was quite a different story. I had no desire to leave my Southern heritage to live and work in the extreme North, leaving my family and friends in the South.

The mother of six children and a pastor's wife, I had always been involved in church work and activities; but when I thought about being the Ladies Ministries president of Northern New England, I was overwhelmed.

Perhaps I felt somewhat like Moses did when he was called to speak on God's behalf. He hedged, saying, " 'Please, Lord, I have never been eloquent . . . I am slow of speech and slow of tongue' " (Exodus 4:10, *NASB*).

Jeremiah also objected when God called him. "'Alas, Lord God! Behold, I do not know how to speak'" (Jeremiah 1:6, *NASB*). Although neither Moses nor Jeremiah considered themselves talented speakers, God still called them to this task.

I can relate to the opening of Nancy Alford's book *Who, Me Give a Speech?* "You approach the podium, noisily your tongue peels itself from the roof of your mouth. You wonder where the saliva went until it pops out on your forehead and cascades down the side of your face. . . . "

I do believe that "the steps of good men [women] are directed by the Lord" (Psalm 37:23, *TLB*). I trusted the Lord to be with me, to teach and guide me in everything I undertook for Him. "Trust the Lord completely; don't ever trust yourself. In everything you do, put God first, and he will direct you and crown your efforts with success" (Proverbs 3:5, 6, *TLB*).

REMEMBER TODAY: "We can make our plans, but the final outcome is in God's hands" (Proverbs 16:1, *TLB*).

Wanda Griffith
Cleveland, TN

Related Scriptures
Nahum 1:7; Habakkuk 2:4

February 25
James 5:14

Is any sick among you? let him call for the elders of the church; and let them pray over him, anointing him with oil in the name of the Lord: and the prayer of faith shall save the sick, and the Lord shall raise him up (James 5:14).

LIVING BY FAITH

My mother often sang a song from the old red-back hymnal titled "Living by Faith."

One of my earliest lessons of the reality of living by faith happened when I was a child. Daddy was pastoring in Roanoke, Alabama, a small community where there had been great opposition to establishing a Church of God. Daddy accepted the challenge to build a church and parsonage. While he was working on the parsonage, we lived in two rooms of an old frame house, with another family living in the remainder of the house.

This particular winter was unusually cold and snowy for Alabama. Because our living conditions were so bad, Daddy continued working even in the cold weather, trying to finish the parsonage. Because of this unaccustomed exposure to such severe weather, he became very ill. Even though he did not visit a doctor, the high fever and raspy breathing indicated that he had pneumonia.

When the unexpected snows came, church services were canceled and no tithes or offerings were received. What would we do? How would we eat? And what was going to happen to Daddy?

We practiced what Daddy had preached—we called for the elders of the church to pray for him, anointing him with oil; and he was instantly, divinely healed. No period of recuperation was necessary. He immediately resumed work, and in just a few months we moved into the new parsonage.

REMEMBER TODAY: His Word is truth. You can live by faith today.

Nancy Downing
Manchester, NH

Related Scripture
Psalm 71

February 26
Psalm 71:1

In thee, O Lord, do I put my trust: let me never be put to confusion (Psalm 71:1).

THE BAFFLE BOWL

Have you ever been confused? I knew you'd say yes. Join the group! At one time or another we have all experienced feelings of confusion and dismay. Life is an irregular course of ups, downs, ins, outs, curves, mountaintops, valleys, dead-end streets, busy thoroughfares and quiet country roads. Questions attend our journey: Where should we be? When should we be there? What should we be doing? What is God's plan?

Elijah knew about confusion. He ran to escape the death threats of Jezebel. Finally he sat down under a juniper tree and wished he could die.

Confusion reminds me of the squirrels in our front yard. They are always trying to get in our bird feeder. The squirrel baffle we erected to deter them didn't work. Somehow they figured out a way to circumvent this contraption and accomplish their mission. Then my husband had a better idea. He turned the baffle upside down, forming a bowl instead of a hood. These funny little critters now sit in the "baffle bowl," totally confused. As a result, they sit and start to chew around the outer edge of the baffle.

Life quite often becomes a "baffle bowl." Circumstances and situations threaten to consume us. Instead of the proverbial "bowl of cherries" that some tout life to be, we find ourselves suffering from the "baffle bowl" syndrome. The more we focus on our situations and start to chew around the edges of our circumstances, the more confused we become.

It is then that we must refocus our thoughts and understanding and rest in the Lord Jesus Christ. To know that He is with us, that He loves us and cares for us, and that what appears to be a "baffle bowl" is really His mighty hand guiding and directing our lives makes life manageable.

Best of all, He is not baffled at all! He knows every curve, every hill, every bump and every turn of the way, and He has "made straight the way of the Lord" (see John 1:23). Rest in Him and in His Word. Let Him restore you, giving you peace and direction one more time.

REMEMBER TODAY: He cares for you.

Edith Brock Cleveland, TN	**Related Scripture** Psalm 91:1	**February 27** Psalm 121:4

Behold, he that keepeth Israel shall neither slumber nor sleep (Psalm 121:4).

THE LORD OUR KEEPER

What comforting words to a widowed mother who had left her home unprotected, expecting her son to return to take care of it during the night!

I was at work when the call came, close to midnight. My son Steve called to say he had decided to stay over with his brother, Ron, who was in college. The desire to enjoy campus activities at Lee College had overpowered Steve's promise to be home before I left for work.

"Oh, Steve," I exclaimed, "I've left the house unlocked and the lights all on! What will I do?"

Immediately I became anxious about what could happen. My imagination left me stranded with only negative options. As I turned from the phone to resume work, a voice spoke to my spirit: "He that keepeth Israel shall neither slumber nor sleep."

Imagine! Instant peace enveloped me. I needed no explanation. My few earthly possessions were safe—safe! I have since tried to explain this peace to others, but I still find it indescribable. Even in this brief devotion I continue to search for words to convey what I felt. But this peace defies description; it must be experienced.

The pilgrims making their way to Jerusalem for one of the annual feasts were on a long, tiresome journey. Their journey sometimes led them through the parched desert region. Along the way they had to stop and set up camp. At night sentries were strategically positioned to protect their camp against sudden attacks from robber bands. These robbers knew well the traveling seasons of the pilgrims and through thievery enriched their own camps.

But in this psalm are reflections of one pilgrim's thankfulness to his Keeper for His ever-present protection. Perhaps on this particular night he saw beside the sentry another guardian. But this was not a human guard. As he continued to gaze, he recognized this form as his Almighty Keeper—Israel's Keeper, who neither slumbers nor sleeps!

REMEMBER TODAY: To abide under the shadow of the Almighty is to always know who your Keeper is.

Lillian Turnipseed	**Related Scriptures**	**February 28**
Parchman, MS	1 Corinthians 13:13;	1 John 3:18
	John 13:34, 35; 1 John 4:7	

Little children, let us stop just saying we love people; let us really love them, and show it by our actions (1 John 3:18, *TLB*).

LOVE IN ACTION

My husband was out of town, and I was 25 miles from home. It seemed as if everything that *could* go wrong *did*.

I was hearing the dreaded words, "You seem to be having a major problem with your car." After the Lord led me to a mechanic, I was finally ready to go shopping four and a half hours later. While shopping, I encountered a white friend with whom I briefly shared my ordeal concerning the car. She said, "You know if you ever need us, all you have to do is call."

When I had completed my shopping, I rejoiced to finally be on my way home. I got in the car, turned the key in the ignition and nothing happened. Fortunately, I was able to contact the same mechanic. This time it was a different problem. Again he repaired the car. I offered to pay him for his services, but he simply said, "You don't owe me anything; I just wanted to make sure you got home OK." I thanked God that I had met this kind stranger.

Upon arriving home, my daughter shared our experience with one of our Baptist friends. About two hours later, there was a knock on the door. This friend had dropped by because she felt that I could use the company.

As we talked, the Lord quickened in my spirit this thought: Love knows no color, creed or denomination. God only asks that as we have freely received, we should freely give (love, kindness, finances, and so on).

REMEMBER TODAY: Sometimes we can be God's hand extended with just a simple act of love or kindness.

Belinda West
Newburg, MO

Related Scriptures
Habakkuk 3:17-19; 2 Corinthians 5:7

February 29
Habakkuk 3:19

The Lord God is my strength, and he will make my feet like hinds' feet, and he will make me to walk upon mine high places (Habakkuk 3:19).

WE CONQUER BY CONTINUING

The prophet Habakkuk found himself in very difficult times. Many times we find ourselves in similar circumstances. Like Habakkuk, we determine the outcome by our response to God. A story is told about a little snail. On a cold, bitter winter's day, the snail inched his way up a barren apple tree. As he crept upward, he woke a sleeping worm. The worm said, "There is no use in going any further; there is nothing up there."

The snail just continued to inch his way upward. Several times the worm yelled, "I say, there is no reason to go on; there is nothing up there." Finally, the snail looked down at the worm and replied, "There will be by the time I get there."

We can have confidence even when we cannot see the answer. Our responsibility is to trust God and realize He sees the big picture.

In Habakkuk 3:17-19 a desperate time is described, but a worthy response is given: I have made my choice to rejoice because "the Lord God is my strength."

REMEMBER TODAY: Faith is the ability to grasp nothing and hold on until it becomes something.

NOTES

Jean C. Stines
Eden, NC

Related Scriptures
Psalms 37:23-25; 46:1; 91:15;
Romans 8:28; Hebrews 4:16

March 1
Philippians 4:19

*But my God shall supply all your need according to
his riches in glory by Christ Jesus* (Philippians 4:19).

NEEDS SUPPLIED

The job was all I desired—an honest employer, a prestigious title and excellent reviews. But suddenly my comfortable little world fell apart. A change in management made me uncomfortable and bewildered. Each new day became more difficult as I realized I would have to seek other employment. I didn't understand what God was trying to do in my life.

My husband's limited income from pastoring a small church and the expense of having a son in college made me even more anxious. As other doors of opportunity were shut in my face, I must admit I asked the Lord, "Why?"

Then my son heard of a job opening at the college he was attending. When I walked on campus, a calmness settled over me. I felt I belonged here. The interview ended, and the door swung wide. God had made a way! In addition, many extra benefits were attached to the job, including free tuition for my son. The Lord answered my question with blessings. Isn't that just like Him?

Now, having left this all behind and moving to another pastorate, I am again facing obstacles. But my Lord is able to take care of the matter. After all, His Word offers me these comforting words: "But my God shall supply all your need according to his riches in glory by Christ Jesus." It is a walk by faith, not sight. He consoles me in Psalm 91:15, "He shall call upon me, and I will answer him: I will be with him in trouble; I will deliver him, and honour him."

REMEMBER TODAY: God does care about those who serve Him and will supply their needs. Wait patiently on Him.

Judith Ayers
Greenwood, SC

Related Scriptures
Psalm 119:103; Isaiah 40:31; 55:1-3;
1 Peter 2:2

March 2
Psalm 34:8

O taste and see that the Lord is good (Psalm 34:8).

DRIVE-THRU QUEEN

Ronald McDonald and the golden arches have become familiar sights to millions in America. I drive through so often that one of my friends nicknamed me the "drive-thru queen." Our hurried lives leave us little time for daily turkey-and-stuffing meals. Burgers, fries and a quick milkshake will do the trick.

On one of my little trips to "hamburger heaven," I took a quick look around the place. It dawned on me that these drive-thru restaurants are designed for only one purpose—to get the customer in and out as quickly as possible.

The drive-thru queen waits in line, speaks hurriedly into a box, gets her high-calorie, low-nutrition, tasteless "quick" food and drives away. She misses out on the warm atmosphere, lingering conversation and offer of refills.

All too often our spiritual food is taken with somewhat the same haste. We rush in, take a verse from the promise box, say a quick prayer and tell God we'll do better next time, when we're not in such a hurry. There's no warm atmosphere, no lingering conversation with our Lord and certainly no chance for a refill. How can growth occur from such an unhealthy meal?

Do you spend your life as a spiritual drive-thru queen? Why not be transformed into a "lady-in-waiting"? "They that wait upon the Lord shall renew their strength; they shall mount up with wings as eagles; they shall run, and not be weary; and they shall walk, and not faint" (Isaiah 40:31).

As you wait upon the Lord, you will experience the warm atmosphere of His presence and enjoy a lingering conversation with Him as He refills you with His Spirit. Your spiritual meals will then become strengthening, and you will say as David said in Psalm 119:103, "How sweet are thy words unto my taste! yea, sweeter than honey to my mouth!"

REMEMBER TODAY: A sweet relationship with the Lord requires spending time in His presence.

Joyce Stephens
Chattanooga, TN

Related Scriptures
Matthew 6:32, 33; Proverbs 3:1-6;
Joshua 1:8

March 3
Matthew 6:6

*But you, when you pray, go into your room, and when you have shut
your door, pray to your Father who is in the secret place; and your Father
who sees in secret will reward you openly* (Matthew 6:6, NKJV).

GOD STILL ANSWERS PRAYER

Our nephew, Chris, was in Saudi Arabia serving with the Marine Reserves during the Persian Gulf crisis. Because he is an only child, so far away from home and in imminent danger, we were frightened and worried. He was in our thoughts, our conversation and our prayers daily.

Jeanna, our 11-year-old daughter, sent word to him not to worry, that he was going to come home safely. Chris called her from Saudi Arabia to thank her for her message and prayers. I was amazed as I listened to my daughter share with her 20-year-old Marine cousin about the times God had answered her prayers. Jeanna explained that she had prayed for him and knew God would bring him home safe and sound. She assured him that God answers prayer.

Now I understand why Jesus told us to become like little children. A child takes Jesus at His word. Children believe He will do what He says He will do. Jeanna did not have any doubts. She knew Chris would come home safely. Her faith was a source of comfort to Chris and the entire family during this difficult time.

Praying with faith moves God. He does not respond to mere verbal calisthenics. However, when a true believer (regardless of age) asks Him for help, He always answers.

The Lord knows every detail of today's circumstances in advance. He has the desire and the power to deliver His people from oppression. He only wants us to seek Him in full faith so that He can reward us openly!

REMEMBER TODAY: When you pray, believe that God hears and answers and is helping you through your battles of life.

Sharon Anderson
Rochester Hills, MI

Related Scripture
Matthew 6:33

March 4
Psalm 37:4, 5

*Delight yourself also in the Lord, and He shall give you the desires
of your heart. Commit your way to the Lord. Trust also in
Him, and He shall bring it to pass* (Psalm 37:4, 5, *NKJV*).

THE DESIRES OF YOUR HEART

When we start on our Christian journey, we find ourselves praying for many spiritual and material desires. Some, God gives us right away; others are never answered or come in unexpected ways. The key is in Psalm 37:5: "Commit your way to the Lord." He knows what is best for us. If it is our desire to work for Him, He will make a place for us in Kingdom service.

Sometimes our desires may not match His will, but if we delight in the Lord, the desires of our heart will be met. After pastoring churches in South Carolina for 13 years, my husband was asked to accept an appointment as state youth and Christian education director. This was a new challenge and learning experience for my family. We moved to Arkansas for two years, then to Michigan for two and a half years. We had many good times and met many wonderful people, but all the time I had a burning desire to return to pastoring.

I missed my Sunday school class, being a part of the music program, and special bonding with people on a daily basis. Many times during our youth work I would pray, "Lord, give us another church." Churches became available, but it just didn't work out for us to pastor them. So I would cry and ask, "Why, God?"

If we wait, He will give us the desires of our heart. On February 10, 1991, we were appointed pastor of the Walton Boulevard Church of God in Pontiac, Michigan. You can guess what scripture came to my mind as I walked through the doors of my church.

REMEMBER TODAY: If you are still praying about a desire of your heart, hold on. God hears and will answer in His time.

Evelyn M. Carroll
Cleveland, TN

Related Scriptures
Matthew 6:31; 24:44

March 5
Romans 12:2

Be not conformed to this world: but be ye transformed by the renewing of your mind, that ye may prove what is that good, and acceptable, and perfect, will of God (Romans 12:2).

READY TO GO

Christi, our 2-year-old granddaughter, lifted her hand and placed it into her grandfather's hand and said, "Paw Paw, I weady go!"

Our son, Christi's father, had just graduated from medical school. They were staying with us for a short time until they could purchase a house and move to the city where he would be doing his internship and residency in surgery.

Early one Sunday morning my husband and I were ready to leave for church where he was to preach that day, when we saw Christi coming down the stairs. She had awakened before her parents and was coming downstairs to find us. When she realized we were leaving, she was "ready to go." It didn't matter that she was wearing pajamas, was barefoot, had not combed her tousled curls and had not eaten breakfast. The only thing she was concerned with was seeing her Paw Paw leaving. She knew she wanted to go with him.

My heart is grieved when I think of the millions of people who are not concerned with being ready to meet God. Their concern is for what they will wear, how they will fix their hair, what they will eat or what others think about them. Jesus tells us in Matthew 6:31, "Therefore take no thought, saying, What shall we eat? or, What shall we drink? or, Wherewithal shall we be clothed?"

Paul admonishes us not to let the world squeeze us into its mold but to allow God to remold our minds that we may find and follow God's will. "Therefore be ye ready: for in such an hour as ye think not the Son of man cometh" (Matthew 24:44).

REMEMBER TODAY: Through Jesus Christ it is possible to maintain Christian integrity so that when He calls to us, we can put our hand into His hand and say, "I'm ready to go."

Tannis Duncan   **Related Scripture**   **March 6**
Sevierville, TN   Psalm 37:5   Proverbs 3:5, 6

Trust in the Lord with all your heart, and lean not on your own understanding; in all your ways acknowledge Him, and He shall direct your paths (Proverbs 3:5, 6, *NKJV*).

CHILDLIKE TRUST

"Our hearing is this week. We go before the judge and we may get to go back home," 13-year-old Linda spoke with eyes filled with hope. Before coming to the Home for Children, severe depression had its grip on Linda, so much so that she had even tried to take her own life. Now, after several months of healing and nurture at the Home, there was the strong possibility that she might be reunited with her mother.

"Is that what you want?" I asked.

"Oh, yes," she answered readily.

"Is that what you think is best right now?" I continued.

She hesitated just a bit, no doubt remembering what life had been like back at home, and responded, "I don't know . . . I'm not sure." This was such a critical time; the outcome would affect her for the rest of her life.

But how do you tell a young girl who has all the normal longings for a loving family that it might be best for her to be away, to remain in an institutional setting for the time being? Long ago I had come to rely heavily upon the words in Proverbs 3:5, 6. "Trust in the Lord. . . ." I knew my trust had brought me to this place, to this encounter with this child. I also knew she must come to have that same trust and acknowledge God in her life . . . or her life would most likely take the same direction as her mother's. "Lean not on your own understanding. . . ." Understanding? Why do bad things happen to good people, especially innocent children? We can't hope to understand in our limited reasoning. But God understands.

Linda hasn't gone back home yet. Her mother hasn't given up the drug habit that made her incapable of caring for her three children. But in this atmosphere of love—this love for God that manifests itself in care and concern—Linda has blossomed. She can giggle now—play a joke now and then. She can smile and even give me a hug. Can it be that she is learning to acknowledge God in her life? To trust in His plans? O Lord, let it be so! And, Lord, may I have childlike trust in You so that You may direct my paths.

REMEMBER TODAY: When we commit our inner being, our intellect and our will to God, He promises to give us direction in our lives.

Ann Roberts
Tampa, FL

Related Scriptures
Acts 1:8; 1 John 4:7, 8;
Philippians 4:7

March 7
2 Timothy 1:7

*For God hath not given us the spirit of fear; but of power,
and of love, and of a sound mind* (2 Timothy 1:7).

LIVE IN DAILY PEACE

One by one I flipped through the cards, reading what the children in my Bible class had written. These boys and girls are only 8 to 11 years old. How could they have so much fear in their lives?

The lesson was 2 Timothy 1:7. I had given out cards and asked each child to write down his or her fears. My heart was moved with compassion for each child as I continued reading:

"Fear of the war . . . if I got kidnaped or raped . . . If my Mom and Dad get divoresed. . . afrade that the Lord will not accept me when I die . . . afrade of the dark . . . scard of being alone . . . of robbers and burgerors, kidnappers . . . My dad is pretty old and I am afraid he will die . . . afraid that my family won't have enough money to pay bills. . . ." The list continued.

I was amused by the children's spelling but overwhelmed with their honesty and saddened by their fears. I asked myself, *What would the cards say if I had passed them out to adults?* Fear of cancer, fear of dying, fear of losing a spouse, fear of financial ruin, fear of divorce? Would the list be so different from that of my students?

Peace engulfed me as I quoted 2 Timothy 1:7 and realized that the message is for anyone willing to receive. The power given is the same power as that referred to in Acts 1:8; the same love as that in 1 John 4:7, 8; and the same sound mind as that in Philippians 4:7. I perceived these Scriptures were saying that we have the Trinity working for us against fear, through the power of the Holy Spirit, through the love of God and through the mind of Christ within the believer. No wonder I felt such peace!

REMEMBER TODAY: The believer can live in peace daily, knowing that perfect love casts out all fear.

Jewell W. Hammons   **Related Scriptures**   **March 8**
Winston, OR   Genesis 42:36; Ruth 1:14-17; 4:13-17;   Romans 8:28
       Esther 4:14

*And we know that all that happens to us is working for our good
if we love God and are fitting into his plans* (Romans 8:28, *TLB*).

HOW CAN THIS BE GOOD?

After we gave our lives over to God, every month seemed to bring a different crisis. I questioned, "Why? Do I not have enough faith?"

We had never had these kinds of problems when we were living in sin. I was always questioning God or asking for help. Sometimes I wondered if God even heard me. Year after year, situation after situation arose. We survived each one! Still, I had no answers. With self-pity I questioned, "Why is God letting all this happen?" And I prayed, "God, don't You care that I'm suffering? What are we doing wrong? People will think we're not living right! I'm doing all I know to do."

Then after my husband accepted the call to preach and our ministry began, I began to understand. Over and over again we found ourselves ministering to people who were going through similar circumstances. People wanted to hear someone who had been there say, "I know how you feel." It's difficult to receive from someone who has never experienced the problem when she tries to tell you how to deal with yours!

Sharing from personal experience makes a difference. When others saw the joy of the Lord in our lives, they had a desire for the same joy. Was the Lord preparing us? Think about Jacob's words before he knew Joseph was alive: "All these things are against me" (Genesis 42:36). Remember Ruth and Esther and the events in their lives that led to the time God used them in fulfilling His divine purpose. You may not be called into the ministry per se, but if you're a child of God and love Him, there is a plan for your life.

I am becoming more conscious that things happen for a reason. Yes, we still have crises arise, but our faith has grown stronger from all the exercise.

Remember, the Master Designer knows the pattern He has for your life. When we don't even know how to pray, the Holy Spirit can plead for us in harmony with God's will. Trust Him for the finished product.

REMEMBER TODAY: Surely the Creator whose hands hold this universe can be trusted to do what's good for you and me.

Evaline Echols
Cleveland, TN

Related Scriptures
Isaiah 40:31; Psalms 27:14; 40:1

March 9
Psalm 37:9

But those that wait upon the Lord,
they shall inherit the earth (Psalm 37:9).

PATIENCE TO SOAR

Someone has said that patience can wait because it knows there is a divine clock that has wings where man's clock has hands. Charles H. Spurgeon once said, "When we cannot trace God's hand, we can always trust His heart."

Life does have its holding patterns when there is nothing to do but wait. Sometimes the preparation to get us out of our holding pattern comes with crises that force us to get in touch with where we are and who we are and, more importantly, who He is. Many times God closes some doors to get us to notice the ones He has standing open for us.

When life falls apart in one area, perhaps God is giving us an opportunity to grow in another area of our life. We grow and we learn, not when things come our way instantly but when we are forced to wait and "be still" (Psalm 46:10). It is then that we begin to hear His footsteps in the winds of adversity and to feel the gentle breeze of His grace.

When I went through a dark tunnel in 1981 (a divorce after 25 years of marriage), I received a letter which I considered to be inspired. Excerpts from this friend's letter are as follows: "You have been squeezed into a narrow channel that is going to bring loneliness, but this is for a purpose. . . . In this period of aloneness you are going to gain new resources, strength one never knew you had, and you will emerge into broad fields of opportunity and accomplishment. . . . How long He will allow you to be alone will be determined by how successfully you grow in your period of aloneness. This 'school of aloneness' will teach you to lean upon Him and upon your inner resources. But you have to be patient now."

When we develop our "wings of patience," we have no desire to look backward. We will soar above the clouds of despair and disappointment into the realm of hope and joy.

REMEMBER TODAY: Patience is character that God is building in you.

Nancy A. Neal	**Related Scriptures**	**March 10**
Cleveland, TN	Matthew 10:29, 30	1 Peter 5:7

Cast all your anxiety on him because
he cares for you (1 Peter 5:7, *NIV*).

I'M GONNA TELL GOD*

At first Marie was tickled by the exclamation of her young son. But the longer she thought about it, the better the idea sounded.

Four-year-old Michael and 9-year-old Paul were arguing, typical behavior for two boys restricted by the confines of riding in a car together for more than 15 minutes. Amid the ruckus Michael suddenly declared, "Paul, I'm gonna tell God on you!"

Actually, that's not such a bad idea.

How often have we been hurt, misrepresented, misunderstood? Sometimes it seems like there's nothing we can do to rectify a situation. Nobody understands. No one believes our side of the story. Nobody really seems to care about the pain we're experiencing. Sometimes others seem immune to seeing beyond their own set of circumstances.

But . . . we can tell God.

Suppose someone really grates on your nerves. Tell God. Nine times out of 10 it's likely that He will change you and not the other person. Either way, you'll come out on top.

Suppose someone falsely accuses you. This happened to me. Regardless of what I tried, I simply could do nothing right in the eyes of one individual I served with in an administrative capacity. More stories were concocted about things I allegedly said than I could count. I finally reached the place I could sincerely ask the Lord to bless her and love her (Matthew 5:44). I confess it wasn't easy to begin with, but I persisted. Eventually I felt better. Furthermore, I remembered that "blessed and happy and enviably fortunate and spiritually prosperous . . . are those who are persecuted for righteousness' sake (for being and doing right), for theirs is the kingdom of heaven!" (Matthew 5:10, *Amp.*).

Scripture reminds us to cast all our care—anxieties, worries, concerns—on Him (1 Peter 5:7). Why? Because He's interested and watches over us with great affection. I'm naive enough to believe God really means for us to bring the seemingly insignificant things to Him along with the crises. Why else would He have taken time to remind us in His Word to do so?

*Adapted from "I'm Gonna Tell God," *Church of God Evangel*, June 1990.

REMEMBER TODAY: If you're suffering from hurt feelings or have been misrepresented or misunderstood, say to yourself, "I'm gonna tell God."

Beverly Usherwood
Fort Washington, MD

Related Scripture
Romans 12:9-13

March 11
1 Peter 4:9, 10

*Be hospitable to one another without grumbling. As each one has
received a gift, minister it to one another, as good stewards
of the manifold grace of God (1 Peter 4:9, 10, NKJV).*

WORN HOSPITALITY

"Oh, yes, we would love to come by for dinner. We had planned to go back today, but we can't miss a chance to have fellowship with you." That was our response to the same invitation we had received many times from our friends over the past 18 years. Although we didn't see one another often, it was almost as if we had never been apart when we did get together.

As we sat at the dinner table, everything had been immaculately prepared and served fit for a king. Entertainment had not changed. There was the same wonderful time of joking around the table that brings laughter and joy. How great it was to laugh and relax!

At first I thought nothing had changed. But as I took a closer look, I found that some things had changed. The living- room furniture was worn; the carpet was torn; the kitchen floor was discolored from years of mopping and waxing; the appliances in the kitchen also showed signs of wear. This house was worn out. But I could still hear the laughter from years of entertaining college students who had lived there while attending college, of missionaries who had passed through in need of rest, of church members at Christmas parties. Oh, yes, I could still hear the laughter of God's children in this home. No one ever saw the pain on the faces of our hosts or the struggles that existed over the years. We only saw the joy of their giving.

Lord, what kind of people are these? I know You give strength, and I know You give joy. But when I see such never-ending dedication and commitment to serve, I see You. I see Your hand that never stops opening the door, inviting people to come in. I began praying in my heart, "O Lord, may their rewards be even greater in heaven." As I prayed, I could almost hear the thundering claps of heaven for these servants who had worn out everything in their service for God.

REMEMBER TODAY: In reaching out to others, we are always ministering the love of Christ.

Linda Lemons	**Related Scriptures**	**March 12**
Cleveland, TN	Isaiah 43:2, 3; Philippians 4:6	John 14:1

Let not your heart
be troubled (John 14:1).

HOUNDED BY WORRY

"Let not your heart be troubled." That's not easy to do—especially if you are a parent, a wife, a sister, a friend. The list goes on and on. There is always something to worry about. But I can't relax in God's protection as long as I keep worrying.

Isaiah 43:2, 3 states, "When thou passest through the water, I will be with thee; and through the rivers, they shall not overflow thee: when thou walkest through the fire, thou shalt not be burned; neither shall the flame kindle upon thee. For I am the Lord thy God." I enter those troubled waters, but God accompanies me. I'm not alone. Illness in the family, a spouse out of work or a troubled teenager are burdens bigger than I can handle. God does more than just tell me not to worry. He also tells me that I don't have to face anything alone.

REMEMBER TODAY: Worry will only make you feel bad; it will never solve anything.

Patricia Miller
Cocoa, FL

Related Scriptures
Proverbs 3; 14:12; Psalm 23;
Romans 1:16-32

March 13
Matthew 7:13, 14

Enter ye in at the strait gate: for wide is the gate, and broad is the
way, that leadeth to destruction, and many there be which go
in thereat: Because strait is the gate, and narrow is the way, which
leadeth unto life, and few there be that find it (Matthew 7:13, 14).

WIDE ROADS AND NARROW PATHS

A group of singers was invited to sing at a little country church in the hills of St. Andrew, Jamaica. After the performance, they were invited to lunch at the home of their friend's aunt. They were to travel a steep rocky path, which wound its way downhill to the small cottage. After some deliberations, the group chose the road instead of the path.

Sixty-five minutes later, they arrived—tired, hot and frightened. The road turned out to be a death trap for pedestrians. The friend's aunt, looking at their disheveled appearance, said, "Though the pathway is steep and rocky, the singing of the birds, the breeze from the trees and the flowing of the stream make the 20-minute hike a pleasant experience. More important, my son was waiting to guide you along." The singers could only shake their heads, thinking of the trouble they could have saved themselves. They had trusted their own wisdom and paid dearly for it. How often is this the fate of Christians?

Because God's way is not ours (Isaiah 55:8), we may not always understand the path He chooses for us. But we can be assured of His promise. "'I will never leave you nor forsake you'" (Hebrews 13:5, *NKJV*).

Proverbs 3:5, 6 tells us, "Trust in the Lord with all thine heart; and lean not unto thine own understanding. In all thy ways acknowledge him, and he shall direct thy paths."

REMEMBER TODAY: May we all try God's way because He said, "I am the way, the truth, and the life" (John 14:6).

Sherry B. Lee Cleveland, TN	**Related Scripture** 1 Peter 1:8	**March 14** John 20:29

Jesus said to him, "Because you have seen Me,
have you believed? Blessed are they who did
not see, and yet believed" (John 20:29, NASB).

HEALING . . . BOTH KINDS

"Seeing, then believing" is a way of thinking prevalent among Christians today. I personally have desired miracles. There have been periods of time when nothing short of an instantaneous finished product would appease my desire for the concrete evidence of God's supernatural intervention on my behalf.

God has intervened, miraculously, in my circumstances. At the age of 19, I was instantly healed of a speech problem—stuttering—which had plagued me since childhood.

Recently I experienced another healing miracle. This healing was not seen by others. In fact, only my husband and I knew about it. It did not happen instantaneously. I'm not really sure when the healing began and when it ended. I do know that I prayed earnestly for this inner restoration over a long period of time. I do know that the results I desired lay beyond my human capacities. At times I grew tired of asking and believing.

Individuals with whom I pray and counsel often ask me, "What's wrong? I have prayed and prayed, and I can't see any changes." In John 20 Jesus speaks to this point. He expresses the value of "seeing, then believing" but exalts the higher principle of "believing *without* seeing." It is this kind of faith, believing, without seeing, which refuses to despair but exercises patience until the miracle-work is accomplished.

Healing miracles are not always instantaneous. The cripple who springs from the bed of affliction is no more or less healed than the one who first uses a crutch to steady his weak legs. The results are the same.

How many times I, the cripple, stumbled and fell. How I dreamed of leaping and running. Days of exercising that numb limb passed, endless hours of praying, "Lord, make it whole." I can now leap and run. I know about miraculous healing, both kinds.

REMEMBER TODAY: All healing, whether instantaneous or progressive, comes from our only source of health and wholeness, God the Father. Keep asking Him.

Joan May
Cleveland, TN

Related Scriptures
1 Corinthians 3:1-3; Galatians 5:22, 23;
Ephesians 4:11-16; Hebrews 5:11-14; 1 Peter 2:2

March 15
Ephesians 4:15

*But speaking the truth in love, may grow up into him in
all things, which is the head, even Christ* (Ephesians 4:15).

GROWING UP IN CHRIST

Don't you just love little babies? They are soft and cuddly—such bundles of joy! Sometimes even their naughtiness can be overlooked because they are so adorable. On the other hand, there is nothing uglier than a grown-up acting like a child. I fear that even among Spirit-filled believers, we have adults who act like spiritual babies.

Each of us matures spiritually according to our own efforts and desires. Along the way there are crisis points and testing grounds that stunt our growth or add to our maturity.

Spiritual growth can be measured by comparing the Christian's actions to those of small children. Some are selfish and insensitive to the needs of others. Some are impatient, never understanding the words, *no, later* or *maybe*. Some have tantrums. Everyone gets angry, but only immature Christians have tantrums. Babies need to be carried. They can't care for themselves. There is a period of time when the young Christian needs to rely on the strength and counsel of a mature Christian. But there is a time to grow up in the Lord and look to Christ for direction.

The problem child is disobedient and rebellious. There are even those who refuse to grow up. They want only the "milk" of the Word rather than a balanced diet. Hebrews 5:11-14 instructs us to eat as adults. Then we can reason what is good and evil.

In some cases we have babies caring for babies. This results in hurting, bruised and starving spiritual babes.

How will you react today? Will you be the spiritual baby, expecting others to care for you, or will you be the mature Christian, responding in love, joy, peace, patience, kindness, goodness, faithfulness, gentleness and self-control? It's time to measure your spiritual maturity by God's Word.

REMEMBER TODAY: To grow in Christ we must allow Christ to grow in us.

Marsha J. Moore
Muscatine, IA

Related Scriptures
2 Corinthians 2:14-16; Psalm 34:8

March 16
2 Corinthians 2:14

*But thanks be to God, who always leads us in triumphal
procession in Christ and through us spreads everywhere the fragrance
of the knowledge of him (2 Corinthians 2:14, NIV).*

THE AROMA OF CHRIST

Certain smells from my mother's kitchen always produce a pleasant aroma. Even now I can almost smell them—the combination of Southern-fried chicken, homemade vegetable soup, beef soup, macaroni pie and fried corn bread. My mother-in-law's kitchen yields pleasant aromas of pinto beans, fried cabbage, collards, beef roast and chocolate cake. When we are able to travel the thousand miles to sit at their tables, we anxiously taste of the aromas lingering in our memories. These "memory" aromas have created a longing for the actual taste.

The fragrance of a flower lingers in my memory during the winter months. I long for the actual fragrance to be more than a memory. Then spring comes. I am excited when the fragrance becomes a part of the present!

I am reminded that as a child of God I am to be an aroma, a fragrance of beauty of the knowledge of Christ, to those with whom I come in contact. I ask myself, "What are they smelling?" Is it a pleasurable fragrance? Does the fragrance of my life cause another to desire to "taste and see that the Lord is good"? (Psalm 34:8).

May we, as His children, breathe the fresh fragrance of His Spirit daily. We then can be the aroma of Christ to the world.

REMEMBER TODAY: Perhaps the greatest "cup of cold water" we can give in the name of Christ is a fragrant life!

Debra Ballard
Arvada, CO

Related Scripture
Philippians 4:13

March 17
2 Corinthians 3:5

*Not that we are adequate in ourselves to consider
anything as coming from ourselves, but our adequacy
is from God* (2 Corinthians 3:5, *NASB*).

I CAN'T

I can't, I can't, I can't. These two words are the best "excuse" for not reaching potential. Until recently, these words were prominent in my vocabulary. If I didn't know how to do a task, or if I was afraid to pursue the task because of what I felt was "lack of adequacy," I would give up on the task or not even attempt. However, I longed to be a useful tool for the Lord. But how can one be a useful tool if she is afraid to be used? It's impossible.

I thank God for this scripture: "Not that we are adequate in ourselves to consider anything as coming from ourselves, but our adequacy is from God!" What a comfort!

God did not intend for us to be afraid to do His work or to be a sedentary tool for His kingdom. Instead He wants us to be willing; He will provide the adequacy. We need not be fearful to do God's work with His adequacies covering our inadequacies. When we present the Lord with an empty and willing vessel, He will fill it to overflowing with His love and give us the abilities to do the work He has called us to do.

When I read this scripture, I am encouraged to know I was not created to be adequate in myself. Rather, I was created for God's adequacy, which is perfect, to flow through me.

REMEMBER TODAY: We were not created to be perfect but to allow God's perfection to shape and flow through us.

Katherine Lankford	**Related Scriptures**	**March 18**
Bramalea, Ontario	James 4:14; I Thessalonians 4:17;	Philippians 1:21
	Proverbs 22:6	

For to me to live is Christ, and
to die is gain (Philippians 1:21).

NO WAY TO LOSE

Thirty-seven years ago our home was blessed with our second son, Woody. It seemed only yesterday that I was rocking him to sleep, cuddling him in my arms and watching him grow in the church. Playing his saxophone and singing in the choir, he was a real joy to us and we were so proud of him.

When he accepted the call to the ministry, we celebrated with him as he left Bible school and went to a new mission in New York. We rejoiced as we watched his church grow. What a pleasure to listen to his sermons and songs on cassette tapes! Then on March 18, 1987, we received a call saying Woody had leukemia. Our world seemed to stop. No, not our baby! For the next three years and seven months we learned that God is able to give victory, even over the fear of leukemia. Woody entered Sloan Kettering Cancer Center in New York on August 16, 1990, for a bone marrow transplant. He subsequently developed pneumonia and went to heaven on October 27.

Woody left two testimonies that reveal his faith and have been a source of inspiration. When he knew he might not survive the transplant, he wrote a song to his mom and dad: "I dreamed I went to heaven and you were there." The chorus says, "Thank you for giving me to the Lord. I am a life that was changed. I am here today because you gave me to the Lord. Thank you for giving me to the Lord."

His second testimony was found on the first page of his hospital diary. The day he entered the hospital he wrote, "DIARY OF MY HOSPITAL VICTORY: FOR ME TO LIVE IS CHRIST AND TO DIE IS GAIN—NO WAY TO LOSE."

REMEMBER TODAY: Live or die, you cannot lose if you dedicate your life totally to Jesus Christ.

Billie I. Jones   **Related Scriptures**   **March 19**
Augusta, GA   Psalm 147:3; Jeremiah 17:14   Jeremiah 8:18

My sorrow is beyond healing, my heart is
faint within me! (Jeremiah 8:18, *NASB*)

WOUNDED AND HURTING?

When my marriage of 37 years ended in divorce, I had no idea how much pain, humiliation, rejection, sorrow and hurt I would experience. It was a nightmare! Not only was my marriage gone, but also my 31-year ministry as a pastor's wife.

What would people think of me? I had been taught by godly parents that marriage is "till death do you part." I had counseled many couples who were facing divorce, not knowing it would happen to me. I prayed, "God, show me what to do; help me to hold my head up and smile through my tears."

God opened new doors for me—a new home in another state, a new church, a better job, many new friends. I tried to be happy, but inside I was hurting. I could not let go of the pain and the memories. I attended church regularly, played the organ, sang in the choir, did everything I felt God wanted me to do. But inside I was crying.

I was invited to a special service at a church I did not usually attend. Reluctantly I went, not knowing that the Holy Spirit had ordained my being there. Following are highlights of the message the Holy Spirit gave me that night:

> "There is no denying your heart breaks. There's no denying you
> are a wounded soldier indeed. But liberty only comes when you
> lay it all down and surrender to Me. Hurt and grieving will
> destroy you; you must come to Mount Moriah and yield it to Me.
> Out of the ashes I will bring beauty for thee; out of the brokenness I
> will bring healing; out of the emptiness I will fill you; out of the
> grieving I will bring joy. But I can only do with what you yield
> unto Me."

God healed my broken heart that night. Healing came when I fully yielded to Him and stopped trying to figure out why this had happened to me. He gave me peace and a balm that I had not known. Of course He did not erase all the memories, but He replaced the bad memories with joy, happiness and contentment. What more could I ask for?

REMEMBER TODAY: There is a balm in Gilead—there is a Great Physician there!

Tina M. Rightnour
Carson City, NV

Related Scriptures
Psalms 100; 121:1,2; 34:15;
1 Peter 5:7

March 20
2 Chronicles 20:21

*And when he had consulted with the people, he appointed singers
unto the Lord, and that should praise the beauty of holiness, as
they went out before the army, and to say, Praise the Lord; for
his mercy endureth for ever* (2 Chronicles 20:21).

VICTORY THROUGH PRAISE

A few years ago I was going through what seemed to be the greatest trial of my life. It seemed as if everything that could go wrong did. I had financial problems, car problems and health problems—just to name a few.

I had carried the weight of these problems until I could no longer bear them. In my spirit I began to cry out, "God, why?"

Then one day as I was working around my house, I began to audibly cry out to God. With tears streaming down my face, I heard God speak to my heart. He said, "If you will praise Me and worship Me, I will give you strength and victory." Immediately God placed a song in my heart.

As I began to raise my hands to the Lord, the bands began to break and the load lifted. I received glorious victory and was assured that God had it all under control. I learned a valuable lesson that day. We may not feel like praising God for the problem, but the true secret of victory is to praise through the problem.

When we praise Him, God gives us victory. When it seems no one understands or even cares, God understands and He cares. "Casting all your care upon him; for he careth for you" (1 Peter 5:7).

The word *cast* means "to throw upon, part with, to shed or drop, to let go." When the trials and problems come, cast them on the Lord and just praise Him.

REMEMBER TODAY: There is victory through praise.

Rachel B. Weir
Bessemer, AL

Related Scripture
Psalm 46:1, 2

March 21
Philippians 4:13

I can do all things through Christ
which strengtheneth me (Philippians 4:13).

OUR UNSHAKABLE STRONGHOLD

On March 21, 1991, my husband of 54 years passed away. The cause of death was pneumonia and empyema, both diagnosed on March 2, 1991.

We were married in 1937, during the Great Depression. Material things did not seem important to us. We had accepted Christ as teenagers. During stressful times our faith carried us. The key to our long marriage and serving God was working together as a team. My husband was blessed with friends from all walks of life.

In 1969 my husband was diagnosed with Parkinson's disease. At this time we were approaching retirement age and planned to travel and do all the things retired people do. Needless to say, God had other plans, perhaps to test our faith. At first the physical changes came slowly. He was able to garden, keep our grass cut and help with household chores.

As the care giver, I retired from my job and adjusted all my activities in order to be able to give him daily care. "I can do all things through Christ which strengtheneth me."

We continued attending Sunday school and church; however, as his disease progressed, I curtailed all activities other than caring for him. With the help of doctors and medication, he never became bedridden. In fact, for several years prior to his death he was able to cut our grass and our neighbor's.

During these years I was conscious of God's presence. When I felt stressful, I cried out to God. He was with me in the good times and the bad.

Shortly before Christmas 1990 my husband lost his balance and fell down the steps, breaking seven ribs. His body was not strong enough to handle this along with all the other complications. He went to be with the Lord at 7 a.m., March 21, 1991.

There are no words to express my feelings at this time. Psalm 46:1, 2 comforted me: "God is our refuge and strength, a very present help in trouble. Therefore we will not fear, though the earth be removed, and though the mountains be carried into the midst of the sea" (*NKJV*).

Losing your lifetime partner is not easy. I have focused on the steadfast faithfulness of God.

REMEMBER TODAY: He is an unshakable stronghold and our source of strength.

Flo Petry
Folsom, LA

Related Scriptures
Hebrews 6:15; 12:11

March 22
Romans 15:5

May the God who gives endurance and
encouragement give you a spirit of unity among yourselves
as you follow Christ Jesus (Romans 15:5, NIV).

ENDURANCE

It seemed like the more Chuck tried to do right at home and at school, the deeper he got into trouble. His grades weren't improving at all. I constantly encouraged him to hold on and not quit. "Don't give up, Chuck. It takes endurance. You can do it!" Goals were set, and endurance enabled him to take his problems one day at a time.

When it came to sports, Chuck could endure anything. He would force himself to lift an extra pound or run an extra mile. He would do anything to stay on the football team.

Difficulties face all of us in this world. Maybe a loved one said a harsh word or a child is giving us a hard time. But God enables us to endure no matter what the obstacle is. He is our source of strength. He gives us the endurance to face our many problems one day at a time. Chuck obtained physical endurance by exercising every muscle in his body, even when it hurt. Our spiritual endurance requires the same discipline. We must trust God in all things and allow Him to have complete control of our lives.

REMEMBER TODAY: Endurance is the power to bear anything. The source of endurance is God!

Ulna B. Black	**Related Scriptures**	**March 23**
Makati, Philippines	Isaiah 11:5; Psalms 36:5; 119:90	Luke 12:37, 38

It will be good for those servants whose master finds them watching when he comes. . . . It will be good for those servants whose master finds them ready . . . (Luke 12:37, 38, NIV).

OVERCOMING DISCOURAGEMENT

After 44 years of sharing my husband's ministry, we moved to a foreign land as missionaries for the first time. More than once I had said to him, "Honey, if you ever feel a call to the mission field, you'd better be sure it's from God, because I'd probably be scared to death!" But soon after we were asked to pray about going to the Philippines, we both knew it was His will.

Our involvement in Christian education in Manila has been taxing but rewarding. We have had to adjust to a new culture—to find ways to accomplish routine tasks in a setting where our ways are not necessarily effective. The people are warm, loving and receptive; but being far from home we have had to search for new ways to do old things. Communication was sometimes difficult at first, and sometimes I became confused and discouraged.

Shortly after our move I attended a conference for Christian women. On the platform was a large banner that said "Great Is Thy Faithfulness." The Lord seemed to tell me that this theme had a personal significance for me. I felt He was showing me that my strength would come through faithfulness—that my name (Ulna) was part of this word *faithfulness* ("Uln" plus *a*) and that His faithfulness to me would see me through every situation that came my way. Major things or minor things—He's always there!

Do you have times of confusion or discouragement? I think so. But His faithfulness is the "sash around his waist" (Isaiah 11:5, *NIV*), it reaches to the skies (Psalm 36:5), and it "continues through all generations" (Psalm 119:90, *NIV*). We can wear our sash of faithfulness every day. His faithfulness is for our generation and for generations to come. We can depend on it. It is His promise, and He is faithful.

REMEMBER TODAY: Expect Him to meet your needs—every need—as you wear the sash of faithfulness every day. Be watching, be ready, and be faithful.

Sharon Echols
Atlanta, GA

Related Scriptures
Proverbs 3:5, 6; Hosea 2:6, 7

March 24
2 Corinthians 12:7-9

> *There was given me a thorn in my flesh. . . . Three times I pleaded with the Lord to take it away from me. But he said to me, "My grace is sufficient for you, for my power is made perfect in weakness"* (2 Corinthians 12:7-9, *NIV*).

WHAT IS YOUR THORN?

We sometimes identify our thorns as those area's where we are weakest. But when we call on God, He provides for us His guidance. He wants us to experience real peace through His Holy Spirit, even when we have no explanation for our thorns.

The Word never reveals exactly what Paul's thorn in the flesh was. Perhaps the reason it was not specified is that the Lord does not want us to focus on just one event, as in Paul's case, but to relate this scripture to a multitude of circumstances in our lives.

No doubt, most of us carry some type of "thorn" we believe to be a hindrance in our lives—a hindrance that limits us from doing all we would like to do for God. The Lord can turn these "hindrances" into hedges—hedges of protection.

" 'Therefore I will block her path with thornbushes; I will wall her in so that she cannot find her way. She will chase after her lovers but not catch them; she will look for them but not find them. Then she will say, "I will go back to my husband as at first, for then I was better off than now" ' " (Hosea 2:6, 7, *NIV*). God transforms those thorns into a hedge of protection to keep us close to Him. There we can learn to trust Him for direction.

God, in His love and infinite wisdom, provides the thorns in our lives to enable us to grow in our Christian walk. What once was a thorn of hindrance becomes instead a hedge of protection.

REMEMBER TODAY: Do you allow your thorn to be a hindrance or a hedge?

Barbara A. Weaver   **Related Scriptures**   **March 25**
Sanford, NC   Luke 10:30-37; James 2:12-16   Matthew 5:7

Blessed are the merciful: for they
shall obtain mercy (Matthew 5:7).

BEFRIENDING THE UNFORTUNATE

Every time I attend a mission service, I get called to be a missionary. Well, not literally, but the stories of needy people makes the yen to serve in another country arise in me. However, I have not been called to be a missionary abroad, but I want to stay in tune with the needs of hurting and helpless people.

Compassion is a combination of love, care and the desire to help. Sometimes we think we have compassion just because we pity someone who is less fortunate than we. But compassion goes beyond pity. If we are truly compassionate, we will be willing to get involved. If the Good Samaritan hadn't been willing to help, the poor man on the roadside would have lain there and possibly have died. "If you have a friend who is in need of food and clothing, and you say to him, 'Well, good-bye and God bless you; stay warm and eat hearty,' and then you don't give him clothes or food, what good does that do?" (James 15:16, *TLB*).

What if the Good Samaritan had said, "Well, hello, sir; I see you've had a little misfortune today. I hope you get to your destination so you can carry on your business." That man knew he had been robbed and beaten, that he had met with misfortune but wasn't able to help himself. That's the plight of many hurting people today. They are aware of their circumstances and possibly can't understand how they got into such an unfortunate condition, but they don't know how to help themselves.

What could possibly be worse than to be hungry but with no food? This was the plight of Margarita and Anita, beautiful Indian twins who live at Casa Shalom, a home for children in Guatemala, run by my sister and her husband, Rick and Jan Waldrop. When these little girls were brought to the home, they were underfed, listless and generally unhealthy. Now they are happy and usually eat a second helping at each meal. I may never see Margarita and Anita, but my monthly contributions will help to provide good physical care and a good education. Every time I look at their pictures in my office, I am reminded that I am helping to make a difference in their lives.

REMEMBER TODAY: Ask yourself this question: What could be more important in this life than to know you have befriended someone and made a difference in his or her life in this world and in the world to come?

Judy Lowdermilk   **Related Scriptures**   March 26
Tryon, NC   Psalm 37:25; Matthew 6:25; 7:11   Exodus 14:14

The Lord shall fight for you, and ye
shall hold your peace (Exodus 14:14).

HAVE YOU FORGOTTEN THE RED SEA?

While reading the Book of Exodus, many times I wondered how God's chosen people could have so often doubted that He would provide for them in every situation. Each time a new problem arose, they seemed to have forgotten all about the crossing of the Red Sea, along with all the other miraculous events God performed in their lives.

I was judgmental and self-righteous, thinking I could never be like these people. Then one day I realized I too had often forgotten the Red Sea. During times of trials I murmured and complained. I tended to readily recall the times I thought God had not answered the way I thought best and then forget the numerous times God provided just what I needed. There have been times in my life when it seemed God could not be reached, but He could. He appeared to be unfair, but He wasn't. It was difficult to believe He loved me, but He did.

I had often made the statement "Just when we seem to be getting ahead financially something always happens." Then one day I turned the situation around and thought, *What if the crisis occurred before we were financially able to handle it? This time God just provided our needs in advance.* God's timing is always best.

When tough times arise, we reveal the source upon whom we rely. It is in the valley that we prove whether or not we can be used of God. Many of us are often ready to give up.

Frequently we travel in the wilderness of despair because, like the children of Israel, we have forgotten what God has done in the past and is able to do now. If God can part the Red Sea, there is no problem we encounter that is too difficult for Him to solve.

REMEMBER TODAY: Remember the Red Sea. He can do it again!

Belinda West   **Related Scripture**   **March 27**
Newburg, MO   John 14:26   Zechariah 4:6

Not by might, nor by power, but by my
spirit saith the Lord of hosts (Zechariah 4:6).

A POWERFUL CHEERING SECTION

Comforter—one who comes alongside, gives aid and assistance in time of need.

This definition reminds me of several years ago when my oldest daughter, Christy, was in the fifth-grade track meet. She had trained long and hard for the 220 event. On the day of the meet, the girl who was to run the mile did not show up. After competing in her event, the coach told Christy, "You will run the mile. Go get ready." Slowly, Christy walked to her position. She thought, *This can't be so bad. But I've never run the mile in a race. . . .*

"Bang!" The gun sounded and they were off. After two laps Christy began to fall back, getting slower and slower. Her dad was in the stand cheering and saw the discouragement on her face that seem to say, "I can't make it." He ran down the bleachers and across the field until he reached Christy. On the grass beside the track, he ran along with Christy. In a strong, clear voice he repeated over and over again, "You can make it, Christy. I'm right here."

At the beginning of the third lap, she began passing a few competitors along the way. On the final lap, the ribbon was broken, and Christy came in second place. More importantly, she realized the love of her father. She knew her dad was there beside her.

We all realize Dad has his human limitations, but our heavenly Father has no limitations.

REMEMBER TODAY: When you're ready to drop out of the race, remember you are not alone. You have a powerful cheering section.

Ginger Sanders	**Related Scriptures**	**March 28**
Cleveland, TN	Matthew 22:37-40; Ephesians 6:24	Revelation 2:4

*"Yet I hold this against you: You have
forsaken your first love"* (Revelation 2:4, *NIV*).

THE BALLOON IN THE CORNER

It was a sunny spring afternoon outside and in my heart as well. Things were great in my life. I had achieved my first 4.0 grade-point average in college, had an active social life and was dating a wonderful guy. All of these things happening at one time was a miracle!

This particular afternoon found me preparing a little package of balloons and candy for a special friend. My mind raced with anticipation of his response . . . a tender kiss, a bouquet of flowers or just that special smile would be reward enough to make my special efforts all worthwhile.

However, my temporary drift to dreamland was interrupted by the sweet but corrective voice of the Lord. "What about Me?" My joy and anticipation were crushed into humility and sorrow. I suddenly realized I had become like the church in Ephesus. Everything new and exciting in my life had replaced my first love. I dropped to my knees and fell in love with my Lord all over again. He became exciting anew.

When I arose from my position of prayer and praise, I put my boyfriend's balloons aside and, with tears of love and joy streaming down my face, I wrote a love note to my Savior. I placed it in a balloon, blew it up and purposefully put it in the corner of my room where it would remind me continuously of my first love.

I don't believe our loving Savior is asking for balloons, roses or candy (although an occasional note of love would bring a smile to His face). I do know, however, that He does desire our first priority to go to Him—our first love.

Sure, my priorities occasionally get out of order. But when they do, I think back to a balloon in the corner of my room and write another note of love to my Lord.

REMEMBER TODAY: Make a conscious effort to do something personal for the Lord. When we draw near to God, He will draw near to us.

Oneta Smith
Beckley, WV

Related Scriptures
Exodus 38:8; 2 Samuel 24:24;
Matthew 22:36- 40; Mark 14:3-9

March 29
Romans 12:1

I beseech you therefore, brethren, by the mercies of God, that
ye present your bodies a living sacrifice, holy, acceptable
unto God, which is your reasonable service (Romans 12:1).

DREGS OR POLISHED BRASS

One week into my daughter's senior year, she became sick with a sore throat, accompanied by feelings of fatigue. However, since the basketball team of the Christian school she attended was involved in a week of tournament games and since she was a cheerleader, she dragged herself out of bed to go cheer for her team. Each morning I tried to get her to stay home, but she insisted they needed her. When Saturday came, I breathed a sigh of relief, hoping she would spend the day in bed in order to recover. To my surprise, she announced she had a date and couldn't refuse because he was the cute boy she had been wanting to ask her out.

But Sunday morning was a different story. She couldn't drag herself out of bed and insisted she was too sick to go to Sunday school. I responded, "You just give God the dregs!" Not so with the ladies in Exodus 38:8. They loved God so much they were willing to part with their valued polished-brass mirrors in order to meet a need for God's house. Their sacrifice takes on more meaning when we realize they were in the middle of the wilderness and could not run to a nearby store to replace those mirrors.

Are you more like my daughter or the ladies who gave their mirrors?

REMEMBER TODAY: Examine your heart today to see if you are giving God the dregs of your life or your best.

Kitty Shelton
Brighton, MI

Related Scriptures
Romans 6:22; 8:2, 3; Galatians 5:1

March 30
John 8:36

So if the Son sets you free, you
will be free indeed (John 8:36, *NIV*).

THE LESSON OF THE QUARTER BOX

On a clear spring day when I was 13, my Mom gave her usual request, "Kitty, run to the store for me while I finish with this customer." Her home beauty shop was busy, so I headed for the buffet, which held the box of quarters. She called out, "Take four quarters and get bread and milk. And hurry!" I went casually and picked up four quarters. I was halfway to the alley before I realized I had actually taken only four!

I suddenly understood what my experience the previous day at the altar really meant. I had prayed a sinner's prayer and was assured that all my sins were forgiven. As I arose from the altar, a dear lady told me, "You're free. You don't need to be held by your sins any longer." In my childlike faith I believed her but had not understood what she was trying to teach me.

God used this object lesson to give me assurance. You see, the "quarter box" had always been a temptation for me. I had cried many times on my way to the drugstore because I was unable to quit stealing from my mom. That day, through no effort of my own, the sway of sin was finally gone!

Now 23 years later, I remain free from the tyranny of sin's grip. God's mercy has kept me free. How grateful I am that in His kind way, God has always taught me—sometimes through object lessons, sometimes through His Word.

REMEMBER TODAY: I'd rather have Jesus than anything this world offers.

Kim Hathaway
Mobridge, SD

Related Scriptures
Psalms 31:3; 33:20; 43:3; 71:5;
John 16:13

March 31
Psalm 25:4, 5

*Show me your ways, O Lord, teach me your paths; guide
me in your truth and teach me, for you are God my Savior,
and my hope is in you all day long* (Psalm 25:4, 5, NIV).

NEW AND BETTER PATHS

One beautiful spring day my family went to the lake for the afternoon. As my husband fished and my two older children played, I took our 13-month-old son, David, on a rocky path that led to the lake. Not too far from the path was a dirt road which appeared to be smoother for David's little feet. So I took him there.

As I held his little hand and walked down the road, David wanted to go back down the familiar path. I took him back to the path, and he was satisfied.

After some encouragement we walked down the road again. This time we went further before he was ready to turn back. After doing this several times, no longer was he apprehensive but rather enthusiastic about going down the new path.

As Christians we become familiar with the path where God has been leading us. Then when God begins to lead us down a new path, we too become apprehensive. We find ourselves leaning toward the more familiar path. However, with the gentle tugging of the Holy Spirit, we can be encouraged to go down the new path God is taking us.

Just as my son trusted me to lovingly show him a new and better way, so can we trust our Savior and allow Him to lovingly lead us down new and better paths.

REMEMBER TODAY: When our hope is in God, we can trust His guidance in new paths of truth.

NOTES

Vicki Stewart
Tucson, AZ

Related Scriptures
Matthew 6:26-29; 10:29-31;
Luke 12:24-47

April 1
Matthew 10:29

*"Are not two sparrows sold for a cent? And yet not
one of them will fall to the ground apart
from your Father"* (Matthew 10:29, *NASB*).

APRIL FOOL REALIZATION

It was early in the morning on April 1 when this verse ministered to me. I was changed and blessed with a new awareness of our heavenly Father's care for His children.

This was my fifth morning in the hospital, since having a bilateral mastectomy. As a 27-year-old mother, I felt I had been forsaken and abandoned—hopelessly victimized. The pain I felt on the outside could not compare to the pain I had on the inside. The agony of facing reality prevented me from even verbalizing a prayer.

In the midst of stinging tears I answered the phone, expecting the early call from a well-wishing saint from my husband's congregation. Instead I heard the voice of my 8-year-old son, Jon. "Mom," he said, "I have chicken pox and can't go to school today." After a groan from me and a giggle from him, he gleefully shouted, "April fool!"

He proceeded to tell me, "Remember, Mommy, two sparrows are worth a cent and God knows when they fall, and we are much more important than they are."

That evening he brought me a paper with that very same verse on it. He wrote it down so I could have a reminder. God did care about me and my situation. He was there. He loves His creation and takes care of us all of the time! What a lesson to learn from the lilies and sparrows . . . and my young son's April fool joke. What a joy to know we are of more value than many sparrows.

REMEMBER TODAY: God's Son paid such a price to buy us that it is the Father's good pleasure to keep us!

Gail L. Price   **Related Scriptures**   April 2
Geneva, IL   Matthew 5:5; 1 Peter 5:5, 6   2 Chronicles 7:14

> *If my people, which are called by my name, shall humble*
> *themselves, and pray, and seek my face, and turn from their*
> *wicked ways; then will I hear from heaven, and will forgive their*
> *sin, and will heal their land* (2 Chronicles 7:14).

IN THE POTTER'S HANDS

This particular segment of 2 Chronicles focuses on a topic we usually avoid—humility. We do not ponder the fact that as Christian believers we are to have a meek and quiet spirit. Attitudes of humility and meekness are totally against the human nature; it is a constant battle for us. The old nature wars against all God intends us to be. It is only through complete and daily submission to God that He is able to bring humility to our hearts.

Notice in this passage of Scripture that the believer receives an absolute direct line. The Bible clearly records, "If my people, which are called by my name." Therefore, the Word refers directly to the saint, not the sinner. It relates to those who have made a decision to serve Christ, walk in His ways and keep His statutes. It addresses the blood-washed, whose lives are to imitate Christ.

Humility is difficult. Our egos are so enlarged that humility cuts against the grain. It is a part of the old nature to desire our own way and respond to criticism and unfair treatment with our fists up and our mouths in motion. The old man desires to retaliate, but the Lord says, "If only my people would humble themselves!"

Deep within each of us is a self-seeking human nature that must be crucified daily with Christ. It is natural for us to be selfish, greedy and arrogant, gratifying ourselves at another's expense. However, it is not spiritual. God can do more within us when we are willing to humble ourselves.

Many times we must be brought to a place of brokenness before we can be molded and shaped like clay in the hand of the potter. And it is a sad commentary that many of our dreams must crumble and a lot of our successes fold beneath us before we are willing to look to the Lord for our help. We seem to think we have all the answers. We lean toward the concept that we can make it alone. But the bottom line is, we cannot.

REMEMBER TODAY: If we hope to be part of the kingdom of God, we must set aside human pride and totally depend on Christ.

Naomi Hancock
Baltimore, MD

Related Scriptures
Ephesians 6:12; 2 Chronicles 20:15

April 3
Isaiah 54:17

*No weapon that is formed against thee shall prosper; and every
tongue that shall rise against thee in judgment thou shalt condemn.
This is the heritage of the servants of the Lord, and their
righteousness is of me, saith the Lord* (Isaiah 54:17).

FIGHT BACK!

"If you don't hit her back the next time she picks a fight with you, I'm going
to whip you!" These words were yelled at me by my older brother when I was
in the second grade. Frances would pick on me, pull my hair and hit me every
time I went outside. After I realized I had my big brother on my side, I became
brave! The next time I went out, Frances started pulling my pigtails and I
fought back—hitting, scratching and kicking. Frances ran crying to her mother.
She never bothered me again!

During my spiritual walk, I have often encountered similar experiences. At
one time the devil kept picking on me, making me have recurring negative
dreams. Finally, I realized I was bigger than he because of my Elder Brother—
Jesus. I simply said to him, "Devil, I know where these dreams are coming
from, and they are a lie. Now, I never ever want to have another one!" The bad
dreams ended!

Often the Enemy picks a fight with us over our children, saying they will
never serve God. Oh, we might have a tug-of-war, but God is on our side and
our children are a heritage of the Lord! During our battles, if we will keep in
mind that we "wrestle not against flesh and blood, but against principalities,
against powers, against the rulers of the darkness of this world, against
spiritual wickedness in high places" (Ephesians 6:12) and learn to fight with the
sword of the Spirit, we will certainly be able to put down those tongues that
rise against us. Surely this is our heritage as His children.

REMEMBER TODAY: Do not be afraid, nor dismayed. The battle is not
yours—it's God's! (2 Chronicles 20:15).

Sherry B. Lee	**Related Scripture**	**April 4**
Cleveland, TN	Psalm 46:1-7	Isaiah 4:6

And there will be a shelter . . . and refuge and protection [a hiding place] from the storm and the rain (Isaiah 4:6, *NASB*).

THE STORM

The tornado came without warning. It appeared suddenly, seemingly coming from nowhere, and loomed angrily over the northern hillside of the horizon. Having time to act only upon existing wisdom, I ran to the centermost section of my small home, the hallway, where there were no windows and many strong door casings. I knelt and called upon the only source of help during a storm.

The roar of the destructive winds was deafening. I pulled over my kneeling body the afghan I had grabbed instinctively from the sofa. I gripped the hall closet doors and began to quote, "For I am convinced that neither death, nor life, nor angels, nor principalities, nor things present, nor things to come, nor power, nor height, nor depth, nor any other created thing shall be able to separate . . . [me] from the love of God, which is in Christ Jesus our Lord" (Romans 8:38, 39, *NASB*).

The sounds of the surrounding terror overwhelmed my weak, quivering voice. Darkness engulfed me. The whole house trembled as it absorbed the beating of the wind, the rain and the flying debris. Windows shattered, doors banged, furniture toppled, lightning splintered, thunder clapped. Time was suspended. I dangled between life and death.

When I could hear my voice again, I was screaming, "I will not be afraid of the terror by night . . . of the destruction that lays waste at noonday . . . a thousand may fall . . . ten thousand . . . but it shall not approach me. For I have made the Lord, my refuge . . . The Lord will be with me in trouble . . . He will rescue me." (See Psalm 91, *NASB*.)

Calm now—unbelievable, deafening calm! Slowly I arose from my knees. I walked resolutely back into life and began clearing away the fragments of my shattered world, repeating softly to myself, "No weapon formed against me shall prosper. . . . I can do all things through Christ who strengthens me. . . . His grace is sufficient for me. . . . All things work together for good to them that love God and are called according to His purpose."

Where do you go and what do you do when storms beat upon your house?

REMEMBER TODAY: Storms are inevitable. How we respond is indicative of our trust and confidence in God.

Brenda Gunter
Baton Rouge, LA

Related Scriptures
Exodus 4:2; Joshua 6; Judges 15;
1 Samuel 17

April 5
Colossians 3:17

*And whatsoever ye do in word or deed, do all in
the name of the Lord Jesus, giving thanks to God and
the Father by him* (Colossians 3:17).

WHAT IS THAT IN YOUR HAND?

Sometimes we may feel unskilled and useless in God's kingdom. But as Christian women we can look to God's Word for our instruction, example and encouragement.

However, we must be willing to use what we have today—not daydreams of what we can do tomorrow when we are wiser, stronger, more capable or richer. Small, unimportant things surrendered to God become important. Take, for example, our hands.

Examples of people in the Bible can give us encouragement and strength today. Rahab's scarlet cord, which she held in her hand, resulted in salvation and safety for her and her family. Joshua used seven rams' horns to bring down the walls of Jericho. What did David do with just one stone and a slingshot? Samson picked up the jawbone of an animal and killed a thousand enemies. Dorcas used a needle and made clothes for the needy. A little boy shared his lunch with Jesus and fed a multitude. The widow had just two mites but gave all she had in the name of the Lord.

Get the idea? We are unique people in unique places. Let's stop counting our days and make our days count! You never know how a simple deed can make a difference in someone's life.

What is that in your hand?

REMEMBER TODAY: He made a worthy vessel with one small piece of clay. *Lord, use it in Your power today!*

Anita L. Allen
Freehold, NJ

Related Scriptures
Psalm 119:105; John 15:7; Acts 1: 8

April 6
Matthew 6:33

*But seek ye first the kingdom of God, and his righteousness;
and all these things shall be added unto you* (Matthew 6:33).

FIRST THINGS FIRST!

The very life and ministry of our Lord Jesus Christ was characterized by the challenge to seek the kingdom of God first. This challenge was given not as an option but rather as a spiritual mandate. It is absolutely vital for us as Christians to maintain proper priorities.

"But seek ye first the kingdom of God, and his righteousness; and all these things shall be added unto you." For both spiritual prosperity and Christian maturity, we should put into practice the following biblical truths:

Read faithfully. "Thy word is a lamp unto my feet, and a light unto my path" (Psalm 119:105). God's Word provides nourishment, direction, counsel, strength and comfort. Make it a priority!

Pray believing. "If ye abide in me, and my words abide in you, ye shall ask what ye will, and it shall be done unto you" (John 15:7). What a beautiful dimension to our relationship with our Lord! It is a great privilege and comfort to communicate with our heavenly Father. Make it a priority!

Witness regularly. "Ye shall be witnesses unto me" (Acts 1:8). We are all ambassadors of Christ and His representatives. True service to Him will be characterized by frequent witnessing and constant sharing of the gospel. Make it a priority!

REMEMBER TODAY: Keeping first things first will establish the child of God in his faith.

Yvette S. DeHaney
Winnipeg, Manitoba
Related Scriptures
Deuteronomy 4:29; Joel 2:12

April 7
Hosea 10:12

> *Sow for yourselves righteousness, reap the fruit of unfailing love, and break up your unplowed ground; for it is time to seek the Lord, until he comes and showers righteousness on you* (Hosea 10:12, NIV).

IT'S TIME TO SEEK THE LORD

"Lord, send a revival! Lord, renew us! Lord, pour out Your Spirit on us!" How many times have we heard Christians praying for these things? I know I've prayed this prayer.

As I was reading these scriptures, I realized that as good and as commendable as it is to ask God for these things, before God will send a revival, before He will renew us or pour His Spirit upon us, we need to seek Him—just Him. Not what He has to offer, nor what He can do for us, but simply seek Him to know who He really is so we can build an intimate relationship with Him.

As we earnestly seek Him, He will reveal Himself to us and we will see ourselves as we really are. He will show us those unplowed areas in our lives that need to be broken up. We will also see what He wants us to be.

God is calling us as individuals and as the church collectively to seek Him. Only after the church sincerely begins to seek God will He send showers of righteousness upon us. He will pour out His Spirit abundantly, and we will be empowered for service . . . His service!

REMEMBER TODAY: To receive from God, we must first seek Him.

Nancy A. Neal
Cleveland, TN

Related Scriptures
Proverbs 17:17; Ecclesiastes 4:9-12;
John 15:17; 1 Corinthians 13; 1 Peter 1:22; 3:8, 9

April 8
John 15:13

*Greater love hath no man than this, that a man
lay down his life for his friends* (John 15:13).

THE HIGH COST OF CARING

One of my two closest friends died. No dirge was played. No minister spoke words of comfort. No flowers marked her grave. She didn't die a physical death. Rather, she just walked away from our friendship one day. For a while I clung to the hope that she'd return to that special friendship we'd shared.

But my friend remained distant, and our friendship faded. I felt the pain of death. Bereft and betrayed, I cried.

In my cries of grief, I heard echoes of friends in Scripture who wept over their separation from each other: David and Jonathan (1 Samuel 20:41), Paul and the Ephesian elders (Acts 20:36-38), Jesus at the tomb of Lazarus (John 11:35).

Created for deep relationships, we need some friends who are more meaningful than others. Jesus illustrated this. Of His 12 close friends, only three were permitted with Him in His most revealing moments; one was called "the disciple whom Jesus loved."

In the Garden of Gethsemane the disciples left Him alone. Though He probably cried when they deserted Him, He did not turn away from them. Instead, even in His darkest hour, He chose to continue to love those friends to whom He'd given much but from whom He received nothing in His time of crisis.

Commitment is the most important quality in a close-friend relationship. Commitment means sticking by when your friend is preoccupied, is in difficulty or has failed. It means hanging in there when you are not getting what you want, or even deserve, out of a relationship. It means being faithful when the well of spontaneous affection seems nearly dry.

The quality that made separation from my friend so costly was our shared intimacy. An intimate friend is the one we have taken into the deepest chamber of our heart, into the most private and vulnerable place we have.

The model of intimacy is found in the relationship between the Father and the Son: "I am in the Father, and the Father in me" (John 14:11). We know we are intimate with God if we walk as Jesus did (1 John 2:6). Jesus made Himself vulnerable. His love for His friends cost Him His life. Though we will likely not be required to give our life for a friend, caring as Jesus did will cost us.

REMEMBER TODAY: God allows us to go through difficult circumstances, but He provided a close Friend to help see us through those times (Proverbs 18:24).

Marie Leonhardt
Charlotte, NC

Related Scripture
Psalm 23; John 14:1-6

April 9
Matthew 28:20

Lo, I am with you alway, even to
the end of the world (Matthew 28:20).

JESUS, WHERE ARE YOU?

When my granddaughter, Amanda, was 4 years old, she and her new baby brother were visiting us for a few days. One evening at dusk she decided she wanted a doll she had left upstairs in the bedroom. Since I was busy preparing the evening meal, I told her to go get it for herself.

To get to the lighted foyer and the stairs, she would have to go through the dark dining room. She walked over to the doorway and hesitated, peering into the darkness. Realizing her apprehension, I saw my chance to drop a pearl of great wisdom. In my most grandmotherly tone I said, "Honey, you don't have to be afraid of the dark room; Jesus will go with you."

She edged a little closer, stuck her head into the room, looked to the left and to the right and then shouted, "Jesus, where are You?"

On today's date my brother, Roy, three years older than I, went home to be with the Lord. After a massive heart attack two weeks before, he hesitated at the door of the "dark room." He saw the light on the other side and his victorious testimony was "Though I walk through the valley of the shadow of death, I will fear no evil, for Thou art with me. If it is God's will, I'm ready to go home." It was . . . and he did.

Can you imagine the utter desolation Jesus' disciples felt as they sat in their starless midnight and thought their Messiah, their hope, was gone? Yet His words from a few days earlier, "Let not your heart be troubled," were still ringing in their ears. We only have to look a few days forward to see that their sorrow turned to blessed joy and their darkness into marvelous light.

Ah, it is an easy thing to trust God when the path is filled with sunshine and the room is well-lighted! The real victory of faith is trusting Him in the dark and through the dark, "even to the end," which, after all, is really the beginning.

REMEMBER TODAY: No matter how dark the night may look, Jesus is the eternal star of the morning—just across the vale.

Kay McEachin   **Related Scriptures**   **April 10**
Jeffersonville, GA 1 Chronicles 16:7-36; Psalms 51:12; 94:19; Nehemiah 8:10
       John 15:11; 16:22, 24

*"Do not grieve, for the joy of the Lord is
your strength"* (Nehemiah 8:10, *NIV*).

WHERE DOES YOUR JOY COME FROM?

Devoid of bitter tears
Yet within . . . the turbulent pool is rising
And the dam is straining from the pressure.
Swirling waters ready to gush at a gesture!
Physical pain would be much kinder to endure—
Medical remedies could surely cure!

This intimate stanza is from a poem titled "Pain," which I wrote during an extremely difficult time in my life. It had left me with one burning question: "Will it always hurt?" Heartfelt joy had disappeared from my Christian service. Circumstances had taken control of my battered feelings.

Are your feelings dictated by the circumstances surrounding you? My religious service had become a prodigious burden to me. It was no longer a spontaneous joy. Isn't that what happened to weary Martha in Luke 10:38-42? The demanding conditions caused her to become unhappy with all she was having to do to serve the Lord. She forgot to focus first on her relationship with Christ, her source of true joy.

As I lost my vision of Christ, I lost my joy. As I lost my joy, I lost my desire to praise Him. And as I lost my desire to praise Him, I lost my ability for effective service.

Yet Paul and Silas didn't allow the depressing circumstances of prison to rob them of their Spirit-born joy. Because of their clear vision of Christ, they could still praise Him unrelentingly (Acts 16:23-34).

My pleading prayer became "Lord, 'restore unto me the joy of thy salvation.'" Through it all, I have learned no *thing* and no *one* can take my joy from me, no matter how crushing the situation or intolerable the person may be. I am the only one who can lose it! And there's not any *thing* or any *one* that can give joy apart from Jesus Christ. A worked-up worship service or an overexuberant preacher may give you a brief high, but if that's all it is, it will last only the distance from the church door to your car door.

Our joy is found only in Jesus. Heavenly joy transcends the world's assaults that seek to devastate God's children. I now know where my joy comes from.

REMEMBER TODAY: Don't allow circumstances to control your feelings. Keep your eyes on Jesus, and the *joy* of the Lord will be *your* strength.

Donna Luna
Sierra Vista, AZ

Related Scriptures
Acts 14:22; Romans 4:20;
2 Corinthians 5:7

April 11
Hebrews 11:1

*Now faith is the substance of things hoped for,
the evidence of things not seen* (Hebrews 11:1).

BUILDING BLOCKS
AND EMBROIDERY THREAD

Building faith is a lot like toddlers learning to stack building blocks. By trial and error and, most of all, perseverance, they stack the blocks into a tower. In this same way we must persevere in our walk with the Lord. We must learn to pick up those spiritual blocks and keep restacking them until we complete our faith lesson.

Likewise, the embroiderer cannot see the finished pattern when beginning a new canvas. It's only after working with all of the tangled mass of threads on the underside that the beautiful pattern begins to appear.

Sometimes it's difficult to see past the tangled threads of this canvas of life God is creating. Faith in Christ Jesus and in His promises turns the tapestry of our lives into a beautiful piece of art.

Believing that God is in control of our lives is the foundation of our faith. As we trust in Him, we build our faith just like the toddler with his blocks and the embroiderer with her needlework.

REMEMBER TODAY: Belief in Jesus enables us to overcome life's trials and tribulations.

Judy Y. Watson	**Related Scriptures**	**April 12**
Bridgeport, IL	Matthew 7:24-27; 2 Timothy 3:16	Psalm 127:1

Except the Lord build the house, they
labour in vain that build it (Psalm 127:1).

GOD'S GUIDE TO LIVING

Have you ever tried putting a do-it-yourself kit together without reading the instructions? How about cutting out a dress without using the pattern's guide sheet? For me it is a disaster! So it is in our Christian walk. We need guidelines. The Word of God gives direction from Jesus Christ—our Master Builder.

The earthly gadgets we buy come with basic instructions for use, care and important safeguards. The Bible, the Word of God, is our instruction for living. The Word gives us assurance, guidance and direction for our lives.

Jesus told the story of a wise man and a foolish man who both built houses. Of course, only the wise man's house stood, because it was founded upon a rock. Jesus said we are like the wise man if we allow our lives to be guided and directed by His words (see Matthew 7:24-27). We can build morality, faithfulness, character, decision making and all the virtues of Christian living upon the Rock.

The Christian life is characterized by a lifestyle of constant fellowship with God, thus we walk in harmony with God and others. How encouraging it is to know that God is with us each step of the way! Complete surrender to God's will enables us to build a lasting structure for eternity.

REMEMBER TODAY: God has a plan for our lives, but we must read the instructions. His plan will guide and direct us in all we do.

Charlene Gray	Related Scripture	April 13
Weatherford, TX	Romans 8	Romans 8:18

*For I consider that the sufferings of this present
time are not worthy to be compared with the glory
which shall be revealed in us* (Romans 8:18, NKJV).

FAITH FOR TODAY, HOPE FOR TOMORROW

One aspect of being a pastor's wife that brings great joy to me is visiting others with my husband. Recently we were in the home of a lady caring for her terminally ill mother. In spite of 25 years of suffering with cancer, Sister Mayda Funchess has been an active member of the North Main Church in Weatherford, Texas, and a prayer-group leader for many years. However, a few months ago her activities slowed down dramatically.

Friends and family sensed that her death is near. This saint of God, filled with the Holy Spirit for 56 years, listened as her pastor read Romans 8 in its entirety. Although she obviously was in pain, faith began to rise in her heart as she received the Word of God. Her steadfast trust and hope became evident to all of us as she began to praise the Lord in tongues as the Holy Spirit gave the utterance. We were encouraged and blessed by her expressions of worship.

Sister Mayda accepted Romans 8 as her message from God for that day. Then in a beautiful act of giving, she looked into the face of her granddaughter kneeling beside her chair and said, "I transfer this to you."

Your circumstances may look bleak, but you can say with the apostle Paul and Sister Mayda, "Neither death, nor life, nor angels, nor principalities, nor powers, nor things present, nor things to come, nor height, nor depth, nor any other creature, shall be able to separate us from the love of God, which is in Christ Jesus our Lord" (Romans 8:38, 39).

REMEMBER TODAY: Regardless of what you are facing today, absolutely nothing can separate you from God's love.

Mamie Alice Barwick
Kenly, NC

Related Scriptures
Jeremiah 18:1-6; Job 14:14;
1 Corinthians 15:51, 52; 2 Corinthians 3:18;
Philippians 3:20, 21

April 14
Jeremiah 18:4

And the vessel that he made of clay was marred . . .
so he made it again another vessel (Jeremiah 18:4).

ALTERATIONS: MODIFY OR TRANSFORM

"This suit is exactly what I want, but these buttons must go!" "The dress fits beautifully, except it is too long." "The seams are large enough to let out, thank goodness!" Oh, the joy of finding a bargain that needs minor alterations! Occasionally a purchase is justifiable, although a major make-over is necessary. While some shops offer alterations free with purchases, others charge for this service.

Aunt Ora was gifted, possessing that rare couturiere ability to take your measurements, look at an illustration and create an excellent—and I do mean *excellent*—garment. Never can I remember seeing her rip out a seam in a garment she had cut out; however, I remember seeing her skilled hands at work altering or remodeling ready-to-wear clothing. My sister, Barbara, and I enjoyed the fruits of her labor.

The difference in Aunt Ora's alterations and others I have seen is that hers never looked made-over! She taught me that if a project is worthy of my time, effort and money, it should be excellent work. Putting her example into practice, I have learned the fine art of altering before cutting and have salvaged some off-the-rack purchases.

Today's scripture presents an excellent example of a "make-over." He did not discard the material; rather, he completely altered the marred clay.

God's grace has already transformed our sinful natures to Christlike natures, and He continues to modify us with His gentle long-suffering. But like Job and Paul, we eagerly await our final transformed state!

REMEMBER TODAY: Whether alterations to our character are minor modifications or drastic transformations, our Father performs thoroughly, yet lovingly!

Jan Wright	**Related Scriptures**	**April 15**
St. Louis, MO	Proverbs 12:18; 18:4, 21; 25:11; Isaiah 50:4	Proverbs 16:24

*Pleasant words are as an honeycomb, sweet to the
soul, and health to the bones* (Proverbs 16:24).

THE POWER IN OUR SPOKEN WORDS

It was raining and the sky was gray. The thunder cracked loudly in the sky. Our neighborhood, which usually flourished with activity, was desolate today. My oldest son was already off to school and my husband at work. Josh, my 3-year-old, and I were homebound for the day. He begged me to read his favorite books.

We pulled out his favorite dinosaur blanket and began to snuggle underneath it. Looking at me with his brown eyes dancing, he said, "You're a good mommy, I yuv you." I was immediately flooded with intense love.

There was power in those simple words, spoken so sincerely. I could suddenly see that ray of sunshine I desperately needed. What had changed? My circumstances and surroundings were exactly the same, but my attitude and perspective had been transformed. Why? Proverbs 16:24 reminds us that "pleasant words are as an honeycomb, sweet to the soul, and health to the bones." God had used Joshua to bring health to my ailing spirit and life to my weary soul. There is power in our words, when spoken from the heart.

What will you do today? Will you consciously decide to let your words be instruments of healing and encouragement to someone? "The Lord God hath given me the tongue of the learned, that I should know how to speak a word in season to him that is weary" (Isaiah 50:4).

We face many weary people in the world around us. And what about our families and the pressures they face daily? You possess the tool that can bring them spiritual health. "Death and life are in the power of the tongue" (Proverbs 18:21).

REMEMBER TODAY: It was with the spoken word that God brought the world into existence. Encourage someone with your words today!

Lorna V. Gosnell	**Related Scriptures**	**April 16**
Beckley, WV	Judges 6; Psalm 122:7; Isaiah 48:18; Daniel 10:19	Mark 4:39

*And he arose, and rebuked the wind, and
said unto the sea, Peace, be still. And the wind
ceased, and there was a great calm* (Mark 4:39).

PEACE, BE STILL

Traumatic times—we've all been there! How do we face them? Let me share my response when the doctors told me I might have cancer of the thyroid gland. At first I felt my world was falling apart. Others may immediately rely on the Lord, but for a while I listened only to my own thoughts. I seemed to forget I had Someone I could talk to about my fears.

Then one day I took time to listen to my heavenly Father. I stopped fretting long enough to hear His calm, loving voice say, "Peace, be still!" Who can describe that feeling? I felt like a pool of warm water had flooded my heart. From that point I knew everything was all right.

Have I ever doubted this peace? Yes, but only when I refused to hear my Father's powerful and majestic voice saying, "Peace, be still!"

Look to Christ, even when you fail Him, whether in word, deed or faith. Let Him smooth out the rough places and make you into something grand!

REMEMBER TODAY: Listen to your heavenly Father whisper those soothing words to you today, "Peace, be still!"

Sharon L. Perry   **Related Scriptures**   **April 17**
Mallory, WV   Psalm 51:10; 2 Peter 3:18   2 Corinthians 5:17

*Therefore if any man be in Christ, he is a new
creature: old things are passed away; behold, all
things are become new* (2 Corinthians 5:17).

A PERSONAL SPRINGTIME

Spring is my favorite time of the year. Everything seems so fresh, vibrant and new! Spring is a time of awakening, renewal, and growth of all the wonderful and beautiful things God has created on earth.

As His children we can participate in a spiritual springtime. To accomplish this, however, we must awaken to a time of refreshing in our relationship with Him.

The psalmist implored, "Create in me a clean heart, O God; and renew a right spirit within me" (51:10). This can be a time of renewal and spiritual growth for us as we receive new strength and draw closer to Him through prayer, fasting and reading His Word.

Just as the warmth of the sunshine and the fresh spring rains bring strength and new life to the plants and trees, so will a time of praise, meditation and closer communion with God bring a personal springtime to us.

So, arise and take action! Our days, like spring, quickly pass. "But grow in grace, and in the knowledge of our Lord and Saviour Jesus Christ. To him be glory both now and for ever. Amen" (2 Peter 3:18).

Ask God to help you have a personal springtime with Him by simply praying, "Lord, cleanse me afresh; renew me with your Holy Spirit."

REMEMBER TODAY: Just as the sap rises in the trees each spring, giving them fresh life, so does the Spirit of God renew our lives in Him.

Jeanette A. Vance
Greenville, SC

Related Scriptures
Job 35:10; Psalm 77:6; Isaiah 30:29;
Psalm 30:5

April 18
Psalm 42:8

*Yet the Lord will command His lovingkindness
in the daytime, and in the night his
song shall be with me* (Psalm 42:8).

HIS SWEET NIGHT SONG

Visiting hours were over at the St. Francis Hospital in Greenville, South Carolina. Mom was relatively free of pain and resting comfortably. Earlier in the week she had undergone a modified radical mastectomy. I gently kissed her on the cheek and said, "I love you, Mom. Rest well, and I'll see you early in the morning."

As I made my way from the hospital room and down the long corridor, my mind wandered over the events of the past week. I recalled the doctor's piercing words, "The tumor is malignant." I thought, *Can this really be happening again?* Three years earlier I had watched as my dad suffered the pain of a malignant tumor. I remembered the endless hours we spent in the hospital and my feelings of helplessness.

Approaching the large, front doors of the hospital, I found myself literally running through the parking lot. I had tried to be so brave in Mom's presence, but now the tears were flowing freely.

I unlocked the door of the car, leaned over the steering wheel and began to scream, "God! Where are You?" It was at that moment, in my captivating darkness, that I felt a divine presence. The Holy Spirit began to sing through me. Before long, I recognized the song as God's sweet night song—written, orchestrated and directed especially for me. The blackness of the night could not silence His song. I sang this divine melody over and over, and I experienced the joy of His sweet communion.

Early the next morning I entered Mom's hospital room. The attending physician was there. "Good news!" he said. "The surgery was the cure. The tumor has not spread, and there will be no need for any follow-up treatments." Mom and I began to cry and laugh simultaneously. Oh, how we thanked the Lord for His steadfast love!

On two other occasions His sweet night song has returned to me. Each time I have recognized this divine melody and awaited the dawn and the miracle that morning would bring.

REMEMBER TODAY: Many times our night experiences become our passage into the light of all His promises.

Esther Witcher	Related Scriptures	April 19
Forrest City, AR	Matthew 28:2; Hebrews 1:13, 14	Mark 16:3, 4

They said among themselves, Who shall roll us away the stone from the door of the sepulchre? And when they looked, they saw that the stone was rolled away: for it was very great (Mark 16:3, 4).

STONE-REMOVAL SERVICE

Mary Magdalene, Mary the mother of James, and Salome had a problem they couldn't handle as they made their way at sunrise on Sunday morning to anoint the body of their beloved Lord after His death. Their conversation focused on this concern: "How in the world can we get that stone moved from the door of the tomb so we can enter?" The weight of the stone would require at least four strong men to move it, and how would they find and recruit four strong men this early in the morning? They did have a problem, didn't they?

But when they arrived, they saw that the stone was already moved from the tomb entrance! Discussing their concern, these women realized that their obstacle—their worry, their problem—was gone! And we know the secret, don't we? "The angel of the Lord descended from heaven, and came and rolled back the stone from the door" (Matthew 28:2).

Rest assured that Jesus knows about our impossible situations, our "stones" which must be removed before we can finish our tasks. He can even command angels to do for us those jobs that are bigger than we can handle! So many times we worry about problems we fear facing only to find that when the time comes to deal with the problem, it's not even there!

Since we know how the problem was solved for the women, we know where we can go for solutions. Let's look to our Problem-solver, our Stone-remover, for miracles when we need them.

❦

REMEMBER TODAY: Instead of worrying about "stones" you cannot move, look to the One who can move them for you!

Dora Bonilla
San Antonio, TX

Related Scriptures
Matthew 5:16; Isaiah 52:7

April 20
Jeremiah 1:12

Then said the Lord unto me, Thou
hast well seen . . . (Jeremiah 1:12).

A BAREFOOT SERMON

I was preoccupied because the color of the shoes I was wearing didn't match my dress.

It was time to collect the missions offering. As the ushers deposited it on the altar, my attention was drawn to an elderly, feeble lady holding a small bag which she laid with great devotion on the altar. Then she knelt down to pray. With tears in her eyes she thanked God for the privilege of being able to participate in expanding God's kingdom. This dear lady had been saving all year to bring her offering. She had deprived herself of essentials, even food.

As I watched her returning to her seat, I noticed she was also barefoot! I asked the Lord for forgiveness over and over again. I had been preoccupied by the color of my shoes, and she didn't even have shoes!

God does not see the color of our shoes, but He does see "the beautiful feet that carry the good news" (see Isaiah 52:7). She preached a sermon to me with her bare feet. She covered the feet of some missionary to go where she was not able to go.

REMEMBER TODAY: Lord, anoint my eyes that I may see beyond my personal ambitions.

Katherine Lee Cantrell
Cleveland, TN

Related Scriptures
Psalms 40:1-3; 69

April 21
Ephesians 5:18, 19

*Be filled with the Spirit, speaking to one another in psalms
and hymns and spiritual songs, singing and making melody
in your heart to the Lord* (Ephesians 5:18, 19, NKJV).

A SONG IN THE RAIN

One night I dreamed I was sitting on a set of bleachers outdoors when it began to rain. I stood up and began to sing the familiar tune "Singing in the Rain." Others joined in. I was facing a group of people, directing them in the song. One woman in particular was smiling broadly as she stood there singing in the pouring rain.

The Christian walk has some rainy days. The Lord encourages us to sing our way through them. Ephesians 5:18, 19 admonishes us to "be filled with the Spirit, speaking to one another in psalms and hymns and spiritual songs, singing and making melody in . . . [our] heart to the Lord" (*NKJV*).

The psalms of David let us know that he had a song in the rain. Psalm 40:1-3 and Psalm 69 speak of miry clay, floodwaters and deep waters. This gives us an image of grounds saturated from heavy rains. Relating this imagery to his life, David felt "saturated" by his troubles—as if he were drowning: "I have come into deep waters, where the floods overflow me. I am weary with my crying" (Psalm 69:2, 3, *NKJV*). Yet, in the same passage, David called on God to deliver him, then proclaimed, "I will praise the name of God with a song" (v. 30). Psalm 40:3 reads, "He has put a new song in my mouth—praise to our God" (*NKJV*).

These scriptures reveal the rainy days of David's life. We read also of the constant song in his heart to the Lord. When we carry a song in our hearts regardless of the circumstances, we are an inspiration to others. Jesus said, "'In the world you will have tribulation; but be of good cheer, I have overcome the world'" (John 16:33, *NKJV*).

When your rainy days come, find deep in your heart that song of praise to the Lord. Before you know it, the rain will stop and the sun will shine again!

REMEMBER TODAY: We can have a song in our hearts regardless of the weather in our lives.

Lori Libby
Scarborough, ME

Related Scripture
Romans 12:1-8

*Just as each of us has one body with many members, and these members
do not all have the same function, so in Christ we who are many form
one body, and each member belongs to all the others. We have different
gifts, according to the grace given us* (Romans 12:4-6, NIV).

STONE SOUP

Are you familiar with a French tale by Marcia Brown called "Stone Soup"?
In the story, peasants of a village see three soldiers journeying home from war.
Knowing the soldiers will be hungry, the villagers hasten to hide what little
food they have. The soldiers enter the village and find no one willing to offer
them a meal. They decide to help these folks out by making them stone soup.

All that is required for the soup is a large iron pot, water and three round
stones. Simple enough. But how much better the soup would taste if it had
carrots. One of the peasant folk hurries home for a few carrots. Then one
soldier mentions that a good stone soup should have cabbage. Again someone
runs home for a cabbage or two. On and on the story unfolds until many
vegetables are added, and delicious soup is enjoyed by all.

This is such a simple tale, yet it portrays a great truth. No one villager had
enough food, but when everyone contributed, they all had plenty. The apostle
Paul taught this same principle in Romans 12. We are all members of the body
of Christ. We have all received gifts according to the grace given us. If we
faithfully use our gifts, all the needs of the body will be met.

Paul listed some of the gifts: prophesying, serving, teaching, encouraging,
contributing to the needs of others, leadership and showing mercy. So often we
feel like the French villagers—what little we have is not enough. We forget that
David had only a little sling. And what about the nameless lad whose lunch
fed 5,000 people? Christ's plan is for everyone to work together.

REMEMBER TODAY: Use what you have today for the glory of God.

Frankie Powers
Bradley, IL

Related Scripture
Psalm 118:24

April 23
Deuteronomy 11:13

Hearken diligently unto my commandments which I command
you this day, to love the Lord your God, and to serve him with
all your heart and with all your soul (Deuteronomy 11:13).

WHOLEHEARTEDNESS

My 7-year-old daughter recently made a cute but insightful statement to her dad: "Daddy, I wish I had a rewind button on my body like a VCR, and when I've had a good time playing with my friends, I could just push rewind and do it over again."

The psalmist wrote, "This is the day which the Lord hath made; we will rejoice and be glad in it" (118:24). Our text says, "Hearken diligently unto my commandments which I command you this day, to love the Lord your God, and to serve him with all your heart and with all your soul."

We must not grow weary in well doing. We can become so busy working for God that we forget to take time to know Him, to commune with Him and let Him speak to us. What a wonderful formula for a victorious life—to carefully obey the word that God has given today and to love the Lord and serve Him with all our heart and soul.

How nice it would be to have a rewind button on our bodies to push whenever we neglect to make the most of our day. Today is within our grasp—not yesterday nor tomorrow. There is truth in the observation that yesterday is past and tomorrow never comes.

❦

REMEMBER TODAY: Let us dedicate this day to our Lord, serving Him with our whole heart.

Aurelia Johns
Hoover, AL

Related Scriptures
Acts 5:31; Ephesians 1:7

April 24
1 John 1:9

*If we confess our sins, he is faithful and just to forgive us our
sins, and to cleanse us from all unrighteousness* (1 John 1:9).

SETTLING OUR ACCOUNT

I received a letter the other day that stated: "I am delighted to inform you that you have been preapproved for a credit card. That means all you have to do to get your credit card is complete the acceptance certificate below, sign it and mail it back. There are no long applications to fill out, and we cannot turn you down."

I'm sure we have all received letters like this in the mail. Most of us use credit cards. But what about the credit we use without a credit card—that is, the blessings of God we receive on credit?

Sure, we have been preapproved at Calvary. All we have to do is repent, confess and accept Christ as our Savior. There are no long applications to fill out, and we cannot be turned down.

When we obtain things on credit, we receive a statement for payment. God doesn't send us a statement, but He does expect us to do our part. When we do all we know to do in obedience to God, He will take care of our sin debt.

REMEMBER TODAY: Since we have been preapproved, why not take advantage of the opportunity to be part of the family of God?

Wilma Carter
Knoxville, TN

Related Scripture
Proverbs 3:5, 6

April 25
Proverbs 16:9

A man's heart deviseth his way: but the
Lord directeth his steps (Proverbs 16:9).

DON'T TURN BACK

On a beautiful April morning I wound my way up Ski Mountain en route to Himmel Haus, where I would meet my friend, Wanda, and several ladies from Lee College. It had been almost two years since I had seen many of them.

After many hugs, tears, prayers and a beautiful devotion, we left the chalet to shop in nearby Pigeon Forge, Tennessee. As Wanda and I made our way back down the mountain, we chatted about the events of the past two years. I shared my deepest thoughts with her concerning the roads Charlie and I were pursuing which all seemed to point to a dead-end sign.

Suddenly, I realized we had taken a wrong turn, so we turned around to retrace our path. Only a mile or so down the road, we again realized that this road too was unfamiliar. The only answer was to go back to where we started and begin again.

This time we chose the road we had taken the first time—only we went farther down the road. Upon reaching the markers that read "Pigeon Forge," I remarked, "Wanda, we were on the right road the first time; we just didn't go far enough."

Surprisingly, my own words resounded in my ears as the Lord whispered to my spirit, "You are on the right road; just keep going and don't turn back." What renewed hope sprang up as we laughed and cried, rejoicing over this message of encouragement!

Now I can wait with anticipation to see what destination the Lord has for me and Charlie at the end of this winding road we began to travel two years ago.

REMEMBER TODAY: The Christian life is a winding road, but when we keep our eyes on God, it always ends at the right destination.

Jean C. Stines
Eden, NC

Related Scriptures
Matthew 4:23; Luke 9:11;
Philippians 4:4-8; James 5:14-16

April 26
Exodus 15:26

I am the Lord that
healeth thee (Exodus 15:26).

STANDING ON HIS PROMISES

There was no audible voice or visible sign. The miracle of healing could have escaped those praying nearest me, but it happened. There was a quiet awareness that all was well, a gentle peace settling within my innermost being, a knowledge that I was healed.

Many prayers had been offered in my behalf by my family, minister and church family. I do not know who was instrumental in praying the prayer of faith. The biblical directives in James 5 were followed, and the Lord Jesus Christ healed me. I am grateful to those who prayed and thankful to the Lord for His saving and healing power.

When I returned home, I disposed of the medication, not as an act of faith but because I knew I was healed and made whole. I experienced no problems. During my next visit to the doctor, he stated, "I knew something had happened to you when I saw you in the waiting room." Then he dismissed me.

I cannot explain why some do not receive healing. I can only testify that I was healed. I find it a great comfort to know that we can stand on the promises of God written in the pages of His Word. I have found that He does hear and answer prayer, according to His will. Whatever your need, take it to the Lord in prayer. Take hope in His Word.

REMEMBER TODAY: Healing is provided for all in the Atonement.

Val Sovdi   **Related Scriptures:**   **April 27**
Moose Jaw,   Psalms 4:4; 37:4, 46:10;   Isaiah 7:4
Saskatchewan   Isaiah 30:15; 55:8, 9

Take care, and be calm, have no fear and
do not be fainthearted (Isaiah 7:4, NASB).

PRESUMED RIGHT: POSSIBLY WRONG

"I'll just get my feelings out in the open—confront him and tell him my thoughts, then I will have resolved this conflict."

It sounded like a reasonable resolution—the right thing to do in this situation. As a counselor I had encouraged others to express themselves, to be open and honest with their feelings. My own background was a mixture of being told that I shouldn't express all my feelings (women were not supposed to be too outspoken) and of being encouraged to get everything out in the open without considering whom I might be hurting. Now as I asked the Lord to sanction my expression and help me to be fair and respect the other person, I felt a nudge by the Holy Spirit. The words of Isaiah stood bold before me. I felt the Holy Spirit leading me in a new direction.

"Take care, and be calm, have no fear. . . ." I was being instructed to wait and not presume or assume I was right in this particular instance. Along with this came the words of Psalm 4:4: "In your anger do not sin; when you are on your beds, search your hearts and be silent" (*NIV*). I wondered if I was angry and needed to do some soul-searching first. This was a different viewpoint. I had presumed that getting everything out in the open was always right, but I didn't have the complete picture this time. I could not have known what the other person was facing. This was not the time to express; it was a time to be silent.

We become accustomed to doing things the same way. But we must remind ourselves that God's ways are higher than the prescribed or usual way, and His counseling is beyond our understanding (Isaiah 55:8, 9). What is required of us is a greater openness and honesty to the voice of God and to the counsel He gives.

Whether it be with our husbands, friends, fellow workers, or brothers and sisters in the Lord, we should not be so eager to presume we are right but should subject our understanding to God's infinite wisdom, listening to the voice of the One who knows best.

REMEMBER TODAY: In every aspect of our lives we need to seek personal relationship with Christ and submit our ways to Him.

Kathy Isaacs
Birmingham, AL

Related Scriptures
Psalm 37:4; Isaiah 61:10

April 28
1 Thessalonians 5:16

Be joyful always
(1 Thessalonians 5:16, *NIV*).

HAPPY IN THE LORD

"I don't know if I'm going to make it. Things have never been this bad before." How many times had I heard this from my friend Cindy! Every time I asked, "How are you doing today?" this was her response.

One day I asked, "Are your problems too big for God?" She seemed surprised at my question. Cindy is not the only one facing this problem.

Too many times we live beneath our privileges as God's children. We carry life's hurts and disappointments around with us instead of giving them to the Lord: "Cast your cares on the Lord and he will sustain you" (Psalm 55:22, *NIV*). Notice we are told to *cast*. We must make the effort. We must release everything to Him! Only then can we experience real joy.

Psalm 37:4 says, "Delight yourself in the Lord" (*NIV*). Delighting in the Lord is much more than an outward action. It is an inner attitude toward God. It means saying to God, "No matter what I'm going through, no matter what I'm facing, I know You are there." We must remember that He is in control. In 1 Samuel 30:6 we read that "David encouraged himself in the Lord his God." "At midnight Paul and Silas prayed, and sang praises unto God" (Acts 16:25). Even though they were in very trying circumstances, they knew the key to deliverance was to delight in the Lord.

REMEMBER TODAY: Your happiness is affected by what happens around you, but your joy is secure in the Lord Jesus Christ.

Nancy Peterson
Manhattan, KS

Related Scriptures
Exodus 3:1-6; 13:21, 22; Isaiah 6:1-8

*"'The fire must be kept burning . . . continuously;
it must not go out'"* (Leviticus 6:13, *NIV*).

SPIRITUAL FIRE

We recently moved into a house with a wood stove. With great anticipation of keeping warm and saving money, we learned how to properly tend the fire. In our zest to become "comfort" experts, we discovered the following principles:

1. It is much easier to keep a fire going than it is to get it started.

2. The more wood we put into the fire, the bigger it gets and the warmer it is.

3. The fire must be tended regularly.

4. If the ashes are not cleaned out regularly, they will snuff out the fire.

When God gave Moses the regulations for the priest, He used an absolute when He referred to the fire: it must not go out. If we expect to be effective workers in God's kingdom, we must tend to our spiritual fire with the same concern. Simply attending church once or twice a week will not keep us "hot." Sporadic prayer and reading will not keep us in the "comfort zone." Allowing sin to stay in our life will quench our fire. As we do our work in the Lord's ministry, our light will shine to all as we continually keep the fire burning in our hearts.

Lord, show me how to gather wood in my life so that I might be effective in Your work. Show me the ashes that need to be cleaned out of my life. As my fire begins to grow larger, use me in a way that I might spread warmth to those around me. Amen.

REMEMBER TODAY: The warmth of His fire must be shared with those around us.

Freeda May   **Related Scriptures**   **April 30**
Cleveland, TN   James 5:14; Mark 2; Hebrews 11:1   James 5:15

And the prayer of faith shall save the sick, and
the Lord shall raise him up; and if he have committed
sins, they shall be forgiven him (James 5:15).

THEY PRAYED AGAIN

My husband, O.L. May, our son, Danny, and I moved from Georgia to pastor the Church of God in Warren, Arkansas.

We had been there a few months when a tornado swept through the town leaving destruction in its path. Forty-six people were killed and over 300 injured. Our church and parsonage were completely destroyed, and we were blown over the top of two houses and landed in the backyard of the third house. O.L. and I received minor injuries, but Danny was safe in the arms of his daddy, held there by the help of the Lord.

My parents came and took Danny and me home with them to Marked Tree. We had been there two days and nights, and I had rested very little because of a sprained wrist. In the afternoon of the third day, I asked my daddy to get the doctor. He said, "Honey, let me get the pastor to come and pray one more time." The pastor, his wife and another couple came and prayed, but I was still suffering. I thought, *When they leave, Daddy will get the doctor and I'll get better.*

They prayed again, and the Holy Ghost ministered in a wonderful way. My mother danced over to my bed. She interceded for me in tongues, laying her hands on me. The Spirit flowed through my body, and I was healed instantly.

I'm thankful they prayed until victory came. I was too weak to pray and have faith for myself, but they had faith for me. The Lord knew my heart and could see that I had faith enough to know He could heal me but not faith enough to believe He would at this time.

I've been healed many times and know that His healing power is real.

REMEMBER TODAY: Jesus Christ is the same yesterday, today and forever, and by His stripes we are healed.

Martha D. Mecum	Related Scripture	May 1
Gastonia, NC	Nehemiah 8:10	Matthew 6:28, 29

Consider the lilies of the field, how they grow; they toil not, neither do they spin: And yet I say unto you, That even Solomon in all his glory was not arrayed like one of these (Matthew 6:28, 29).

WOMEN—GOD'S FLOWER GARDEN

"Flowers are in the world of nature what women are in the world of humanity—they concentrate in a small space so much energy, so much life, and such an ecstatic combination," said Paslo Montegazza.

To me, nothing is more beautiful than a bouquet of freshly cut flowers arranged by one with artistic ability. Each flower is unique in its creation. They come in all shapes, sizes and colors. Different flowers thrive in different environments.

Like flowers, women come in all shapes, sizes and colors. Different personalities adapt to and thrive in different areas of ministry. We can learn much by a closer study of various flowers.

The lily symbolizes beauty and purity. Our lives must be pure and holy before we can bring joy to others or praise to God. A daffodil makes me think of happiness and laughter. If we have the joy of the Lord in our hearts, it will shine to others. "The joy of the Lord is your strength" (Nehemiah 8:10).

The daisy looks as though it has the sun as its center with white rays spreading around it. The Sun of Righteousness must shine in our hearts so that rays of goodness and purity can spread around us, reflected from the light of heaven within us.

John Keats called the violet the "Queen of Secrecy." If we are to influence others, we must be trustworthy. How wonderful to have a sister to confide in without fear of betrayal! Let us be that kind of sister.

The rose is a symbol of love—unassuming love. The love of God dwelling in us will reach out to others. We will not only suffer with them and mourn with them, but we will rejoice with them during victories and success.

REMEMBER TODAY: As we enjoy the fragrance and beauty of flowers, let us reflect the beauty of Christ and give forth the fragrance of a submitted spirit.

Monte L. Ratchford
Mauldin, SC
Related Scriptures
Colossians 2:1, 2; 1 Corinthians 14:31;
Romans 1:12; Hebrews 13:3
May 2
Isaiah 43:2

*"When you pass through the waters, I will be with you; and
when you pass through the rivers, they will not sweep over
you. When you walk through the fire, you will not be burned;
the flames will not set you ablaze"* (Isaiah 43:2, *NIV*).

ENCOURAGE ME, LORD

Encourage means to inspire with courage or hope. We all feel like we've walked through troubled waters and blazing fires at some time in our lives. No one is exempt from difficulties. We need courage and hope to sustain us.

In the Book of Acts, Barnabas was known as the Son of Encouragement. He kept the early church encouraged. He gave them hope when circumstances were difficult. Maybe you've just returned from the funeral of a loved one or you've just heard the prognosis of the surgeon—"It's only a matter of time." You cry out, "Encourage me, Lord."

The old spiritual says, "It's not my brother, nor my sister, but it's me, O Lord, standing in the need of prayer." The murky waters of affliction and the hot fires of testing have caught up with me. I'm the one who needs encouraging. It becomes very personal when problems and cares of life overtake us. David cried out in Psalm 69:1, "Save me, O God, for the waters have come up to my neck" (*NIV*). So along with David, the outcry is *"Encourage* me, Lord."

"Praise be to the Lord, to God our Savior, who daily bears our burdens" (Psalm 68:19, *NIV*). He is the Sovereign One; He is the Omnipotent One; He is the One who sees all, hears all and understands all. All our cares can be cast upon Him for safekeeping; He will not betray our trust. He is the great I Am. Encourage me, Lord!

REMEMBER TODAY: In times of distress, heartaches and problems, there is a strength that only comes from our heavenly Father, encouraging us to hope in God.

Betty J. Proctor
Harrisburg, IL

Related Scriptures
Proverbs 3:12; Isaiah 28:10

May 3
Proverbs 4:13

*Hold on to instruction, do not let it go; guard
it well, for it is your life* (Proverbs 4:13, *NIV*).

FOLLOW INSTRUCTIONS

After several revivals, we had returned home for a few days. The laundry was done, the house freshened up, and I was ready to enjoy my kitchen.

I had never made an angel food cake, but I decided to get out my cookbook and try one. I meticulously followed the instructions. The cake was a beauty and tasted great!

I was so pleased that in a few days I tried to make a second one. This time I did not look at my cookbook. I put the cake together, and when I took it from the oven, it was picture perfect. However, when I cut the cake, I was stunned! It had large holes in it! I forgot the last step—cut through the batter before baking.

I asked myself, *Why is it so difficult for me to follow instructions?* I concluded that it was hard for me to listen, take time and submit to authority.

I shall never forget the day my dad told me not to talk to a young man who was much older than I (13 years). At first I was furious and rebellious. I avoided Dad for a few days. Then I realized how much he loved me and how concerned he was about my well-being. I followed his instructions and loved him for giving me direction.

No longer do I have my earthly father, for he is with our heavenly Father. Therefore I am grateful for the precepts (prescribed rules of conduct) our heavenly Father has given us. And how great will be our reward if we hold on to His instructions and pass them on to future generations!

REMEMBER TODAY: Submission to God's authority is restful.

Phyllis Crissey	**Related Scriptures**	**May 4**
Smithsburg, MD	Psalm 37:4; Galatians 4:19;	Genesis 30:1
	1 Corinthians 3:1; 1 Thessalonians 2:7;	
	1 Peter 2:2	

Give me children,
or else I die (Genesis 30:1).

DESIRING MOTHERHOOD

I bore my first child, a beautiful daughter, when I was only 18. She was healthy—I thought. But two and a half months later I lost her to crib death. Pregnancy became an obsession.

I craved a child. When I learned I was pregnant again, I was elated! In my third month of pregnancy, I lost the baby. The experience was traumatic; I desperately wanted a child. Soon after the second loss, I was overjoyed to hear the wonderful news that I was pregnant again. I carried the baby full term and delivered a healthy girl—the child of my dreams. Again, at age 2 months the death angel knocked and I experienced another crib death. I thought my world had ended. Every waking moment was spent dwelling on bearing a child. I longed for children. As Rachel prayed in Genesis 30:1, so I prayed: "Give me children, or else I die."

God granted me the desires of my heart. I now have three beautiful gifts from God for which I am truly thankful. As I relate the natural desire for children to the spiritual, I must ask myself, "How important is childbearing for His kingdom? Are we bearing spiritual children for the Master?" How many times do we pray, "Give me children, or else I die" in reference to spiritual childbirth?

Motherhood is a wonderful gift from God, and we can be mothers—spiritual mothers—if we're willing to pay the price. Are you bearing spiritual children for the Master? The psalmist David said, "Happy is the man [woman] who has his [her] quiver full of them" (127:5, *NKJV*).

REMEMBER TODAY: If we desire spiritual children, we must have an intimate relationship with the Father, who gives a spiritual harvest.

Wanda Griffith
Cleveland, TN

Related Scriptures
Revelation 3:19, Proverbs 3:11, 12

May 5
Hebrews 12:6

*For whom the Lord loves He
chastens* (Hebrews 12:6, *NKJV*).

DISCIPLINE

Before a scolding or spanking, Mother would always say, "Wanda, this hurts me much more than it hurts you." This was really difficult for me to understand until I became a parent and disciplined my own child. Only then did I learn that when you love your child, you must discipline him, and it does hurt.

When writing my thesis for my master's degree, I began with an over-abundance of confidence. The first chapter was a breeze, or so I thought! I whipped out 15 pages and mailed it to my major professor at the University of Tennessee. When it was returned a few days later, I was devastated. The professor's ruthless red pen had slaughtered my wonderful introduction and first chapter. However, the impact of that experience was not easily forgotten as I began rewriting the paper. I learned quickly from his suggestions. Anxious to gain his approval, I checked the work over again and again before submitting it. I wanted to learn from previous mistakes and not repeat them once I had been corrected.

This experience held a spiritual lesson for me. My heavenly Father desires the best for me, just as my major professor did. He does not want to see me fail, so He corrects me. If I can learn from each lesson in life with the same enthusiasm to please Him and seek His approval as I did my professor, then I will see growth in my Christian walk. His discipline will be for my benefit, not my detriment.

REMEMBER TODAY: "No pain, no gain." He wants us to experience spiritual growth with each chastening.

Bobbie Lauster
Naples, FL

Related Scriptures
Ephesians 2:4-7; Revelation 20:6

May 6
Ephesians 2:4-6

*But God, who is rich in mercy, for his great love wherewith he loved us,
even when we were dead in sins, hath quickened us together with
Christ . . . and hath raised us up together, and made us sit together
in heavenly places in Christ Jesus* (Ephesians 2:4-6).

YOU ARE SOMEONE IMPORTANT

Whether it was Ringling Brothers, Barnum and Bailey, or Holiday on Ice, our family usually had to take poor seats because the better seats were more expensive. In some of the old opera houses and theaters of Europe are private boxes and alcoves from which the magnificently bejeweled and bewigged noblemen and heads of state enjoyed the performances.

It is also an honor to be invited to sit at a head table. But most people will go through life without ever having even this experience.

A friend invited me to a Philharmonic performance at the Fine Arts Center recently. Throughout the program I kept glancing toward the private boxes. How pleased the occupants looked as they enjoyed the performance, enclosed with family and friends. Because it takes so much money to rent or own a private box, I realized that it isn't probable that I'll ever belong to that privileged class. I will no doubt always be viewing the performance from the cheapest seats in the house.

As I was musing thus, I concluded there must be an almost universal cry of "Tell me I'm not just another face in the crowd, a John or Jane Doe, a boring statistic on someone's poll!"

The Word of God invaded my reverie and the unimportant was sheared away. God brought to my remembrance the many times I have experienced spectacular things while seated with Christ in heavenly places.

REMEMBER TODAY: If the bitter sting of snobbery attempts to steal your joy, reject it by asserting yourself as one so important to God that He places you beside Christ in heavenly places.

Peggy Decanter
Blytheville, AR

Related Scriptures
1 Peter 5:7; 1 John 4:4

*There shall no evil befall thee. . . . For he shall give his angels
charge over thee, to keep thee in all thy ways* (Psalm 91:10, 11).

THE LORD CARES FOR MY CHILDREN

My heart sank when that great big yellow school bus "swallowed up" my two small daughters. In September 1973 we pastored Sharpe Chapel Church of God near Wynne, Arkansas. In order for my girls to get to the Vandale Elementary School, they had to travel over a narrow, curvy gravel road. I was so afraid of that road.

One day as I was watching the bus leave with my most prized possessions on board, I began praying for their safety. I earnestly prayed, "Lord I can't protect my girls, even if I were on the bus with them, but You can!"

The Lord did protect my girls and continues to bless them now 18 years later, and I continue to pray for them. Tena is in Lake Charles, Louisiana, 10 hours away, and Teresa, the mother of two, lives in Magee, Mississippi, six hours away. Though I am helpless and powerless to take care of my family, Jesus loves them even more than I. And He protects them.

The Word encourages us, "[Cast] all your care upon him; for he careth for you" (1 Peter 5:7) and "Ye are of God, little children, and have overcome them: because greater is he that is in you, than he that is in the world" (1 John 4:4).

REMEMBER TODAY: We can trust the Lord to care for the most important ones in our lives—our family members.

Joyce Miles
Salisbury, NC

Related Scripture
Revelation: 5:1-14

May 8
Revelation 5:12

Worthy is the Lamb that was slain
to receive . . . honour . . . (Revelation 5:12).

HONORS NIGHT

Every year at East Coast Bible College, we set aside one night right before graduation which we call Honors Night. On this night we faculty members give special recognition to those students who have excelled. This year during Honors Night, my mind raced forward to a very special "Honors Night" that will occur in heaven. On this night Jesus, the Lamb of God, will be the honored guest.

I want to be there when Jesus is declared the only one in heaven, on earth or under the earth who is worthy to open the book which He takes out of the right hand of Him who sits upon the throne. I want to join the four beasts and the 24 elders as they fall before the Lamb with their harps in their hands. I want to sing along in the new song of praise to the Lamb, saying, "'You are worthy . . . for You were slain, and have redeemed us to God by Your blood out of every tribe and tongue and people and nation'" (Revelation 5:9, *NKJV*).

I want to join the heavenly voices numbering "ten thousand times ten thousand, and thousands of thousands," who with a loud voice say, "Worthy is the Lamb that was slain to receive power [over my life and over the universe], and riches [for He has given me material blessings], and wisdom [for He has granted me wisdom in difficult times], and strength [for His joy has been my strength], and honour [for He has honored me by giving His life for me], and glory [for His glory has been revealed to me], and blessing [for my life has truly been blessed by Him]" (v. 12).

Finally, I look forward to joining the four beasts as they say, "So be it! Amen."

REMEMBER TODAY: We can start today giving honor to the Lamb, for He is worthy.

Marianita Moreno
San Antonio, TX

Related Scriptures
Matthew 5:14-16; John 8:12

May 9
Ephesians 5:8, 9

Live as children of light for the fruit of the light consists in all
goodness, righteousness and truth (Ephesians 5:8, 9, NIV).

WE ARE THE LIGHT

When I was 8 years old, I fell in love with the sun. I loved the way the sun shining down made my face feel. That tingling sensation exhilarated me. I loved the way the sun burst through my bedroom window. I decided that the sun would be my constant companion, my friend. It did not matter if the day was dark, dreary or rainy, my companion would soon be shining through. All the windows in my home are covered with sheer curtains that allow the sun to shine through. At night I close the blinds for privacy, and in the morning, even with the blinds closed, my companion comes peeking through.

Have you ever visited a home during the summer when the drapes were drawn and darkness filled the room? When you left the dark and came into the light of day, it's as if you had just left a cold, dark tomb and returned to the living.

The sun reminds me constantly that Christ wants us to be the light of the world. He wants us to shine so that He can be glorified through us (Matthew 5:14-16). Christ is the Light of the World and we, His children, are children of light. Shine for Him today.

REMEMBER TODAY: Open the drapes of your life and let the light of Christ shine through.

Linda Joy Fox
Bayshore, NY

Related Scriptures
Psalms 127:3-5; 103:13;
Matthew 19:13, 14

May 10
Psalm 127:3

*Lo, children are an heritage
of the Lord* (Psalm 127:3).

TOMORROW'S MEMORIES

"Mom, Ryan is such a burden," said my 10-year-old son, Timothy.

Those startling words made me realize I must be giving my children the impression that our new baby is more work than enjoyment. I replied, "No, he is no more burden than you and your older brother. Our new baby is a precious gift but a big responsibility."

Sometimes we get so caught up in our role of serving our families that we forget to enjoy them. Although those early years can be stressful, we must realize that weeks roll into months and months into years. Before we know it, our children are grown and gone. The spills and muddy sneakers will someday no longer be imprinted on the kitchen floor. That baby who clings to you all day and night will someday cling to other people and interests. Each day that goes by is tomorrow's memory. Instead of becoming frustrated by unfinished chores, untidy bedrooms and unvacuumed floors, I've learned to treasure each moment I spend playing a game with my older boys and teaching my 10-month-old how to play peekaboo.

God has given us children to enrich our lives. What an honor it is to mold a human life—the life of a child!

REMEMBER TODAY: Lord, give me patience to live each day thanking You for the awesome responsibility You've entrusted me with—being a mother!

Linda Lemons
Cleveland, TN

Related Scriptures
Psalms 27:5; 57:1

May 11
Psalm 91:1, 2

He that dwelleth in the secret place of the most High shall abide under the shadow of the Almighty. I will say of the Lord, He is my refuge and my fortress: my God; in him will I trust (Psalm 91:1, 2).

A MOTHER'S FAITH

Several years ago, quite unexpectedly, my mother was told she had cancer. My mother, the strong one, faced the biggest battle of her life. After a year of treatment, she seemed fine.

Within five months of the five-year "cured" period, the cancer reoccurred. The battle was difficult the first time, but what do you do the second?

An acquaintance asked her, "Why aren't you crying? The tears wouldn't stop if it were me." Mother responded, "I could cry and even pound the floor, but when that's all finished, I'd still have cancer."

Instead of despair, all of her family saw the determination that was characteristic of her. She took the treatment, continued to work almost every day and faithfully attended church.

Her strength came from her faith, not her family. We loved her, but she needed more than our love. She turned to Psalm 91:1, 2. These verses were the constant reminder of God's faithfulness and love for her. "He that dwelleth in the secret place of the most High shall abide under the shadow of the Almighty. I will say of the Lord, He is my refuge and my fortress: my God; in him will I trust."

After trusting her God and following the treatment prescribed by her doctor, Mother recovered. Today she is still well and still trusting God.

REMEMBER TODAY: You can trust God for the big things as well as the small things.

Dorothy Hilton   **Related Scripture**   **May 12**
Springdale, AR   Matthew 5:16   Matthew 5:14

*Ye are the light of the world. A city that is
set on an hill cannot be hid* (Matthew 5:14).

SHINE YOUR LIGHT

When I gave my life to the Lord, I wanted to be something for the Lord. As a new Christian I watched others in our church, and I chose a role model to imitate. I felt I was a failure, because I could never measure up to that person.

One day the Lord showed me there are different kinds of lights. Light bulbs of different sizes have different uses. Long neon lights will not fit in a table lamp, nor will a normal light bulb fit inside a refrigerator. Yet, all these lights work well in their own places.

I began to let the Lord use me where He wanted me. As I grew in the Lord, I found joy and contentment serving in the place He assigned me. I try to become all He intends for me to become.

REMEMBER TODAY: "Let your light so shine before men, that they may see your good works, and glorify your Father which is in heaven" (Matthew 5:16).

Judith S. Isaacs	**Related Scriptures**	**May 13**
Gastonia, NC	Psalms 18:35; 125:1; Mark 4:39;	John 10:28, 29
	Romans 8:38, 39	

And I give unto them eternal life; and they shall never perish, neither shall any man pluck them out of my hand. My Father, which gave them me, is greater than all; and no man is able to pluck them out of my Father's hand (John 10:28, 29).

GOD'S PROTECTING HAND

The storm was raging all around us. Trees were bending double in the wind, the waves were rough and high, rain was beating against the house, and water was coming in around the windows. The beach house was swaying on its pillars. Thirty-two ladies were gathered together for a retreat! It had been a perfect day, and the Lord had blessed.

The storm had come suddenly—spawning numerous tornados as it moved toward the coast. The weather forecasters changed their forecast from warm and sunny to severe storms throughout the weekend. Several of the ladies became frightened, and everyone was disappointed that our plans for the next day would be canceled.

As the lights flashed off and on, we gathered together, joined hands and prayed. While the storm raged all around us, a message came from the Lord: "Fear not, My little children, I have you safely in the hollow of My hand, and nothing can harm you." Suddenly the storm ceased and all was quiet. We lifted our hands in praise to God for calming the storm and quieting the ocean. The next day was beautiful, and the weather forecasters were amazed.

Often the storms in our lives cease suddenly. Sometimes they subside slowly. Regardless, we always have the assurance that our Lord is in control, so we need not be afraid.

REMEMBER TODAY: God is protecting and watching over us. He is the Master of our storms.

Betty J. Hockensmith
Northport, AL

*Fear thou not; for I am with thee: be not dismayed; for I am thy
God: I will strengthen thee; yea, I will help thee; yea, I will uphold
thee with the right hand of my righteousness* (Isaiah 41:10).

FEAR NOT

The shrill ringing of the telephone pierced the stillness of the night. "I have bad news for you. Your son is dead. I'm sorry."

My heart began to cry out, "No, Lord. This can't be true!" Millions of questions rushed through my mind. There seemed to be no rational, logical or meaningful answer. Nothing!

For over 35 years I had trusted God as my source of strength. I had leaned on Him for answers. Now where was God? Why had this happened to me?

The Holy Spirit immediately brought a calmness to my spirit and this scripture to my mind: "'Do not fear . . . you are Mine! When you pass through the waters, I will be with you; and through the rivers, they will not overflow you. When you walk through the fire, you will not be scorched, nor will the flame burn you'" (Isaiah 43:1, 2, *NASB*).

Psalm 23:4 says, "Yea, though I walk through the valley of the shadow of death. . . ." Our Good Shepherd leads us through the valley. This does not mean we will die there, even though sometimes we'd like to! Our Shepherd goes before us . . . through our valleys.

I will not fear even in dark trials, in dismal disappointments or in distressing moments. Not until we have walked with Him through these situations do we discover He can lead us to find rest for our hearts and spirits. In the valley during the winter, the sheep and shepherd have a close, intimate relationship. Intimacy with the Good Shepherd brings a feeling of hope for today and tomorrow.

We discover that even in the dark, lonely valley, He is our source of strength and courage. Never will a shepherd take his flock where he has not been. Storms of life will come, predators will aggravate and possibly attack, but He has been there before and will lead us safely through.

Thank God that even in difficult times, even when we experience the death of our dear ones, we can be confident of His care. We can be assured that He is with us in the valley and has total control!

REMEMBER TODAY: Through times of adversity, frustrations and disappointments, He has said, "Fear thou not; for I am with thee."

Kathryn S. White
Cleveland, TN

Related Scripture
Philippians 2:15

May 15
2 Corinthians 3:18

*But we all, with unveiled face beholding as in a mirror the glory
of the Lord, are transformed into the same image from glory to glory,
even as from the Lord the Spirit* (2 Corinthians 3:18, *ASV*).

A PERFECT HEART

Who am I today, Lord? By the ring on my finger, I'm known as a wife, but the suit in my closet says I'm a businesswoman. By the Sunday school lesson on my desk, I'm known as a teacher, but the crib in the nursery says I'm a mother. So many roles to fill; so many counting on me. The media tells me I'm to be the perfect listener to my husband, watch my weight, keep a gleaming house, bring in a needed paycheck and have all of the answers for my children. In addition to all this, I am to participate in the ministries of my church, and remain cheerful at all times.

When I'm on the verge of being overwhelmed by all these responsibilities, I remember my mother, who filled many roles and kept a cheerful heart. She was special. Although she passed away before my own children knew her, I tell them stories about her life, her own journey in striving for perfection. Mother's specialness was characterized by her faithfulness, her steadfastness. No, she wasn't perfect. But people who knew her saw Christ in her life. She did what she could and kept her priorities straight. She didn't always please everyone, but never was there any doubt that Christ was the center of her life. What better role to play than to be a window for Christ to shine through?

REMEMBER TODAY: Who am I today, Lord? Whom do I want people to see when they see me? Lord, let Your perfection shine through me as a witness to those I meet.

Jane Thornton
Birmingham, AL

Related Scripture
Psalm 103:8

May 16
James 5:16

*The effectual fervent prayer of a
righteous man availeth much* (James 5:16).

THE EFFECT OF INTERCESSION

God is looking for holy men and women to intercede. By His very nature He is "merciful and gracious, slow to anger, and plenteous in mercy" (Psalm 103:8). He does not desire to inflict judgment but suffers long. It pleases God to supply our needs.

God sought Abraham to intercede for Lot and the cities of Sodom and Gomorrah. The significance of Abraham's intercession is seen as God continued to grant as long as Abraham prayed. Abraham's faith in God's mercy is seen as Abraham returned "unto his place" (Genesis 18:33) with no fear, knowing that all was in the hands of the Almighty. Intercessory prayer procures the ministry of angels.

Five times Moses interceded for Israel as they journeyed through the wilderness. In each circumstance God's judgment was stayed. He intervened when they built the golden calf at Sinai (Exodus 32:10-14); when they complained at Taberah (Numbers 11:1-3); when they believed the 10 spies concerning Canaan (Numbers 14:11-21); when Korah, Dathan and Abiram rebelled (Numbers 16:20-22); and when the people complained of the judgment of Korah, Dathan and Abiram (Numbers 16:44-48), Intercessory prayer can even appease God's wrath.

Job interceded for his miserable comforters. The inhabitants of Nineveh prayed, and God rescinded His decree against them. However, our supreme example of intercession is Jesus. He knew the time had come for Him to be offered, so He prayed an intercessory prayer for His own that are in the world. He is presently ever interceding for us in the presence of God (Hebrews 7:25).

Prayer secures for us the mercies of God. We do not deserve these blessings, for they are ours only through Christ's suffering. God's promises are sure, but to obtain these promises we must pray. God desires to give more than we desire to receive. The condition for receiving from God is prayer.

REMEMBER TODAY: Though we go through the flood and fire, when we pray, we do not drown, neither do we burn.

Joan Jones   **Related Scriptures**   **May 17**
Farmingdale, NY   Mark 5:1-20; Romans 10:14, 15   Mark 5:19

*Go home to thy friends, and tell them how great
things the Lord hath done for thee* (Mark 5:19).

SHARING CHRIST WITH OTHERS

There was a man in the country of the Gadarenes possessed with an unclean spirit. Crying out, he wandered in the tombs day and night. There seemed to be no answer or remedy for his plight. Then one day Jesus came to his land from across the sea. Seeing Jesus, he ran, fell down and worshiped Him. Jesus commanded the unclean spirit, "Come out of the man." The spirit came out and entered a herd of swine in the land. Later the man sat clothed and in his right mind, requesting of Jesus that he be allowed to stay by His side. Jesus said to him, "Go home and tell your friends what great things the Lord has done for you."

We who have received Jesus Christ as Lord and Savior can share our experiences with others. Our account may not be as dramatic as the account of the man of Gadara, but our lives have been touched and transformed by Christ.

The world around us needs to hear about the living Lord we serve. God has entrusted us with His message of salvation. We must share this good news, remembering that now is the day of salvation throughout the world. But "how shall they believe in Him of whom they have not heard? And how shall they hear without a preacher? And how shall they preach unless they are sent? As it is written: 'How beautiful are the feet of those who preach the gospel of peace'" (Romans 10:14, 15, *NKJV*).

REMEMBER TODAY: They will never know unless we "go home" to our world and share with them what Christ has done.

Kathy D. Watson Eldorado, IL	**Related Scriptures** Romans 12:2; Galatians 5:22, 23; Psalm 119:11	**May 18** Proverbs 31:28

*Her children arise up, and call
her blessed; her husband also,
and he praiseth her* (Proverbs 31:28).

JUST ANOTHER DAY!

How do you handle your daily routine? Is your day so power-packed that you are changing hats 15 times? Do your actions reflect a peaceful, calm temperament or that of a frazzled, worn-out, exhausted, bent-out-of-shape housewife/mom? Unless I totally lean on God each day, I inevitably take my frustrations out on the ones I love the most. How long has it been since you made it through one day without raising your voice to your family or feeling so stressful you thought you might explode?

Stop! Reflect on God's Word today before those frustrations build. Send those children off with a hug, a prayer, and words of love and encouragement. After all, as a woman of God you should set an example for those you love. You are God's reflection . . . or are you?

REMEMBER TODAY: Demonstrating God's love should start at home. Our home front should experience the fruit of the Spirit firsthand.

Marilyn E. Ward
Palm Beach Gardens, FL

Related Scriptures
Matthew 6:33; Psalms 37:25; 26; 50:10;
Malachi 3:10-12; Hebrews 13:5;
2 Corinthians 9:8

May 19
Philippians 4:19

*And my God will meet all your needs according to his
glorious riches in Christ Jesus* (Philippians 4:19, *NIV*).

SUPERNATURAL PROVISION

"The grace period for the car insurance expires tomorrow. I don't know how we will be able to go to church or school; there are no buses going either place," my husband said to me.

Newlyweds, my husband was pastoring a small church while attending college and I worked as a secretary. With no student aid available, it took every penny we earned to pay rent, tuition, payments on our old jalopy and other expenses. The $50 insurance premium was more than we could pay.

We had not told anyone of our need, partially because of embarrassment but primarily because my husband insisted that because we had been faithful in our stewardship, God would provide. It seemed easier for him to believe. As the son of missionary parents, he had experienced God's supernatural provision many times. I thought I had depended upon God, only to discover that I really had been subconsciously dependent upon my father's secure employment.

As the day ended, we prayed about the matter as we had many other nights. Early the next morning a friend came to our door and handed us an envelope. "Someone sent this to me and asked that I give it to you." Inside the envelope was the exact amount needed for our insurance.

Since that time, God has miraculously met much larger material needs for us, but I will never forget that first experience of trusting God for finances. He is indeed Jehovah-jireh—our faithful provider!

REMEMBER TODAY: Our loving Father really does know what you need, and He will take care of you!

Sherry B. Lee
Cleveland, TN

Related Scripture
Job 12:10

May 20
Acts 17:28

For in him we live, and move, and have our
being . . . for we are also his offspring (Acts 17:28).

WE ARE HIS OFFSPRING

The birth of a child is one of God's greatest miracles. Any mother who has experienced giving life to another human being will agree.

The joy of giving birth, however, is not only in the actual physical manifestation of the child but also in its daily formation, growth and preparation for life. For nine months I carry the potential promise of a whole new existence near my heart, feeling its first tremors of life, watching it literally grow from my own strength source. All of these fulfilling phenomena bring some of the highest feelings of purpose and meaning to me and others who have experienced life within.

The bringing forth of an entity after its own kind occurs constantly in our universe. Reproduction is God's idea, and only He could have set it in motion. God then used His own idea of birth as a spiritual concept. The term *born again*, although used quite flippantly in our age, was Jesus' way of expressing a spiritual change in one's parentage, character and quality of existence.

I do not believe physical manifestation of my new life in Jesus has yet begun. I believe that like the fetus yet in the stages of formation, I am daily assuming the qualities of character, the personality and the Godlike life of my heavenly parentage. I am nestled close to His heart "in Him," experiencing the first tremors of Kingdom life, drawing daily from His power source and being formed in His image.

One day I will be translated into His actual kingdom and will inherit eternal life. I will be His genuine daughter and heir. When I see Him, I shall be like Him. Until then, I will live and move and have my being in Him, for I am His offspring.

REMEMBER TODAY: We are in the process of being made into His likeness, being born again not after the flesh but after the Spirit.

Zelma LaFevor   **Related Scripture**   **May 21**
Birmingham, AL   Colossians 4:5, 6   Luke 19:3

*And he sought to see Jesus who he
was; and could not . . . (Luke 19:3).*

A TRUE PICTURE

Recently while visiting in my son's home, my daughter-in-law showed me a picture she had posted on the refrigerator. The picture was one my 7-year-old granddaughter, Lauren, had colored in Sunday school. I stood looking proudly at my granddaughter's art work. Then it dawned on me what I was supposed to see in this picture. The picture was of Ruth, but I hardly recognized her with her rosy cheeks, cherry-red lips and bright-red fingernails. This coloring was indeed an original, modern-day Ruth.

Days later a smile came to my face as I remembered the picture. I wondered about the origin of Lauren's concept of Ruth. I also wondered what concept of Jesus I leave with those with whom I come in contact. A glamorous Jesus? A professional Jesus in a three-piece suit? A taskmaster who is hard to please? The Good Shepherd, a lover of lost sheep?

Faces of family members, friends and people I hardly knew began to come to mind. What needs did I see in these faces—sadness, loneliness, despair, problems with no answers? I wondered if the frame on my picture was so ornate that it detracted from the picture. Perhaps the picture was blurred or had shadows. Was there a clear picture at all?

I said, "Lord, how can I show You to the world?" The Spirit seemed to speak to my heart and say, "Just a smiling face, a loving, kind spirit and conversation seasoned with grace." I began to pray, "Jesus, let Your image be clearly reflected through me."

REMEMBER TODAY: You can make a difference in a life today.

Ligia R. Ambriz
Houston, TX

Related Scripture
2 Corinthians 12:10

. . . who comforteth us in all our tribulation, that we may be able to comfort them which are in any trouble, by the comfort wherewith we ourselves are comforted of God (2 Corinthians 1:4).

COMFORT OTHERS . . . EVEN IN THE MIDST OF DIFFICULTIES

I remember the night in a youth convention when my husband and I received our call to the ministry. From that time, my life had a new meaning. Everything was new and refreshing as we set out to do the Lord's work in the pastorate. Even though I had been raised in a Christian home and had always been involved in church, I had never felt such fulfillment.

As time passed, however, we faced new challenges and I wanted to escape from it all. The difficulties and trials in the ministry began to feel greater than I could bear. Even my health began to decline, and the desire I had when I first began to serve the Lord ebbed, turning into doubt. I needed the comforting hands of God to renew me.

While visiting my home church one Sunday morning, a sister asked me to minister to a woman who was visiting. I had gone to the service to seek healing and strength for myself. How could I minister to someone else? Then I remembered that our Savior prayed for those who were crucifying Him. My trials could not compare to His sacrifice. Little did I know that in the midst of my own problems, God still wanted to use me. Guided by the Holy Spirit, I led this woman to Christ. Then I asked God to forgive me and renew me spiritually and physically. God's presence refilled me and healed me.

Since then I make it a point to minister to others when I have a need. When I am sick, I pray for the sick; when I am sad, I pray for those who are sad; when I feel troubled, I pray for those who are in trouble. God in His wonderful mercy helped me see that in every circumstance I needed to comfort others, just as He has always comforted me. Satan's plan is to destroy us through a trial. God wants to use our lives at all times to comfort a hurting world.

REMEMBER TODAY: God wants you to be a blessing to others, even in the midst of your own difficulties.

Elaine Lee
Noblesville, IN

Related Scriptures
Psalms 8:2; 9:14; 51:12

May 23
Psalm 50:23

"He who sacrifices thank offerings honors me,
and he prepares the way so that I may show
him the salvation of God" (Psalm 50:23, NIV).

PRAISE BRINGS SALVATION

All seemed quiet and peaceful in the house—all, that is, except me. I was restless and seemed to be at the end of my rope. I was weary in my role of leadership as a pastor's wife. Feelings of inadequacy and questions filled my mind. I even wondered, *Why did God make me the mother of two adorable little girls?*

Mentally, physically and spiritually exhausted, I entered my prayer closet. There I asked God to apply His living Word to my situation. He directed me to Psalm 51:12: "Restore to me the joy of your salvation and grant me a willing spirit, to sustain me" (*NIV*). He also showed me in Psalm 50:23 that I was to sacrifice thank offerings to God, which would pave the way for His salvation in my life.

I began to pray and thank God for restoring to me the joy of His salvation and for granting me a willing spirit. This God-given willing spirit would sustain me as a wife, mother and pastor's wife. Even though I didn't feel grateful, I began to thank God for the roles of ministry in my life. As I did, I began to receive cleansing and freedom. The Lord lifted my spirits and gave me the joy of His salvation.

We will experience times when we do not feel grateful. Those are our most important opportunities to give God praise and thanksgiving as a true sacrifice from obedient hearts.

REMEMBER TODAY: Give praise, worship and thanksgiving to God—especially when you do not feel like it.

Patrice Curtiss
Grand Rapids, MN

Related Scriptures
Psalm 37:23; Colossians 1:9, 10

*The fear of the Lord tendeth to life: and he that
hath it shall abide satisfied* (Proverbs 19:23).

THE IDEAL AGE

"Remember what it was like to be 18? I think that's about the perfect age."

"No, that's too young. I wish I could have stopped the clock at 30. I'd love to be 30 years old for the rest of my life."

"Hey, I'd be happy to settle for 40 and holding!"

Enjoying our coffee and fellowship after church, several ladies had a good time teasing each other about "getting old." Of course, we didn't really want to remain an "ideal" age. Yet, the anxiety we all felt about growing older was very real.

When we worry about the new wrinkles we've discovered or fret over the number of birthdays we've had, we should remind ourselves that "the fear of the Lord tendeth to life: and he that hath it shall abide satisfied." The Creator of the universe in His infinite wisdom is the designer and planner of our days on earth. Knowing Him is the very essence of life, and He brings us joy as we develop a mature relationship through life's varied experiences.

I would never exchange the precious years I have had walking with Jesus for the chance to be 18 again. He has made me the age I am, and that is the ideal age for me.

REMEMBER TODAY: As each day passes, we can obtain an everlasting treasure and true satisfaction in our Lord.

Oneta Smith
Beckley, WV

Related Scriptures
Deuteronomy 6:5-9; Joshua 1:8,
Psalm 78:1-8

May 25
Proverbs 22:6

*Train up a child in the way he should go: and when
he is old, he will not depart from it* (Proverbs 22:6).

TRAIN UP A CHILD

Even though we were not always successful, we made an effort to teach our five children to have daily devotions with the Lord. This was quite difficult, especially when their ages ranged from a toddler to a teenager. Our son at 3 years of age would bring the book *The Bible in Pictures for Little Eyes* and say in his childish voice, "It's time for bo-botions." I would say, "Devotions," and he would repeat "De-bo-botions."

We decided to give the children devotional materials when they reached the junior level, realizing their need to develop the habit on their own because they would eventually be away at college. We were so rewarded one Saturday night when we observed our son, who was then 12, kneeling by his bed praying. We automatically assumed he was having devotions and was retiring for the night. When we saw him still on his knees 30 minutes later, my husband decided to investigate. I heard a quivering voice say, "I want the Holy Ghost." What a blessed sound as I heard father and son join in praise and supplication to the Lord! The final result was an infilling of the Holy Ghost with the initial evidence of speaking in tongues.

Truly all our efforts to initiate the habit of daily devotions had been rewarded. Today our son is a youth pastor and is teaching other young people to dedicate their lives to the Lord while they are young.

REMEMBER TODAY: The home is the best place to teach a child how to build a relationship with God.

Deborah King	**Related Scriptures**	**May 26**
Waterville, ME	John 14:27; Philippians 4:7;	Isaiah 26:3
	Psalm 29:11	

*Thou wilt keep him in perfect peace, whose mind is
stayed on thee: because he trusteth in thee* (Isaiah 26:3).

GOD'S PEACE IS REAL

Where is your peace, Lord? I asked that question over and over as I went about the daily tasks and busyness of being a mother to two small children. Life seemed dull. I wasn't feeling the peace of God flowing in my life as I thought it should. I knew Christ as my personal Savior and was involved in church activities. Wasn't that enough to guarantee God's peace in my life? Having known the love of God and experiencing the baptism of the Holy Spirit, why was I now sinking into such a state of mental apathy?

As the pressures and frustrations of life oppressed me, I sank deeper into despair. Each morning I awoke with a sense of dread hanging over me. I cried out to God for months, but my prayers went no higher than the ceiling. I thought there must be something desperately wrong with me. Physical symptoms appeared, and yet the doctors could find no cause for my fatigue and loss of appetite. I needed a touch from the Master, for His Word to come alive in me.

With this resolve I set aside a quiet time to seek God. Shutting myself in a secret prayer closet, I started memorizing scriptures until they became a part of me. New life began to spring forth. The answers were there all the time. I must keep my mind on Him as I go about my daily tasks. I must sing to the Lord, give thanks for my beautiful children and a wonderful husband. God's peace overshadowed my darkness and oppression. Sunlight broke through the gloom; God's Word had not failed.

I still have struggles, but I have touched the One who gives peace. Whenever I feel I am losing that peace, I examine myself to see if my mind "is stayed" on Him. The promise is real. His peace is real.

REMEMBER TODAY: Keep your thoughts on Him. His peace surpasses all human understanding.

Rebecca J. Jenkins
Jackson, MS

Related Scriptures
Proverbs 3:5; 1 Peter 3:12

May 27
Proverbs 3:6

*In all thy ways acknowledge him, and
he shall direct thy paths* (Proverbs 3:6).

THE PROPER PATH

"She hasn't felt like talking tonight; she told me to talk to her while she rested her eyes," her husband said to us.

They took her early, so my husband and I didn't get to speak to our church member and friend the night minor surgery was performed. I phoned her the following day. The report was good; however, the moment I hung up the telephone, the dream I had one month earlier and had shared only with my husband came rushing to my memory. I knew it was necessary to drive 30 miles to see her that night, even though my husband planned to see her the next morning.

She opened her eyes, smiled and didn't stop talking for the entire visit. I left the hospital feeling better; however, the following morning the call came . . . cardiac arrest.

It was humbling to be privileged to bring her joy during her last evening on this earth. I sensed God's love for her. Later I learned there was a dual purpose: it was for my benefit as well. I have held tenaciously to this experience. It continues to serve as tangible evidence of His directing my path during times I cannot see where the path is leading nor feel His mighty hand.

REMEMBER TODAY: If times are tumultuous, close your eyes. Let His Word, along with your own God-given personal experiences, speak to you and bring a smile to your face. Never doubt that He directs your paths and that He knows where you are today.

Barbara Fulbright
Cleveland, TN

*This is the day which the Lord hath made; we
will rejoice and be glad in it* (Psalm 118:24).

OBLIGATED TO REJOICE

When taking my youngest daughter to preschool, we always sang a chorus, said a few Scripture verses and had prayer. She was at the time memorizing a verse of Scripture for each letter in the alphabet. One day after we had sung our chorus, I said to her enthusiastically, "Abigail, this is the day the Lord has made!"

She looked at me and confidently said, "Mother, every day is the day the Lord has made!" In her young mind, that fact was unquestionable. We didn't even need to discuss it.

My mind was drawn to Psalm 8:2: "You have taught the little children to praise you perfectly. May their example shame and silence your enemies!" (*TLB*). Oh, if I could only walk in that same faith as my 4-year-old daughter!

I had to agree and explain to her how we are responsible for the second part of Psalm 118:24: "We will rejoice and be glad in it." God gives us the day. He has made it for our benefit, but what we do with each day is our responsibility. Regardless of our feelings, we are obligated to rejoice.

Since that morning I've had days that seemed long and lonely and I didn't feel like rejoicing. There are days when troubles seemed to be in the forefront of my life. But my mind goes back to a 4-year-old's conception of scriptural truth. This is the day the Lord has made. I have no choice but to rejoice.

REMEMBER TODAY: Regardless of the circumstances, God has made this day for me to rejoice.

Bertha Rogers	**Related Scriptures**	**May 29**
Shippensburg, PA	2 Peter 1:19; Psalm 30:5	Acts 27:29

*Then fearing lest we should have fallen upon rocks, they
cast four anchors . . . and wished for the day* (Acts 27:29).

CAST FOUR ANCHORS

Fear! What an awesome enemy! How many times fear cascades like ocean waves over our souls, creating a darkness blacker than night. We are awakened from sleep. A cold sweat and a pounding heart convince us that we will surely crash upon the rocks this time. We arise, pace the floor and wish for day, hoping that daylight will bring peace from the storm.

But wait! We have forgotten something. "They" in the biblical account did something else before they wished for day. They cast four anchors: *hope*—that "maketh not ashamed" (Romans 5:5); *faith*—that "worketh by love" (Galatians 5:6); *love*—that "never faileth" (1 Corinthians 13:8); and *obedience*—that is "unto righteousness" (Romans 6:16). The ship that is moored by these anchors will overcome the waves of fear! Morning is when the light drives away the darkness. Morning is when His mercies are renewed.

Through the long nights of Calvary, the women at the cross desired the dawn of the first day of the week. They were not disappointed! Very early they came and found an empty tomb. He who is victor over death, hell and the grave is also the victor over fear. He tells us again and again, "Fear not; I have overcome!"

Peter proclaimed that he did not depend upon "cunningly devised fables" but had "a more sure word of prophecy . . . a light that shineth in a dark place, until the day dawn, and the day star arise in your hearts" (2 Peter 1:16, 19). Cast these four anchors in your heart and wish for day. The daystar will arise for you!

REMEMBER TODAY: "Weeping may endure for a night, but joy cometh in the morning" (Psalm 30:5).

Wanda LeRoy
Bushey Heath, England

Related Scriptures
Psalms 33:18-22; 91;
1 Corinthians 10:13

May 30
Psalm 33:18

*But the eyes of the Lord are on those who
fear him, on those whose hope is in his
unfailing love* (Psalm 33:18, *NIV*).

GOD'S PROTECTION

The moon shone like a bright ball in the dark sky, casting an eerie silvery glow on our backyard. My familiar playground had been transformed into a strange, frightening world filled with grotesque shadows.

"Go on, now," Mother said. "I'll wait here at the door for you."

Trembling, I hesitantly began what seemed to my 7-year-old mind an impossible, endless journey. Earlier that day I had disobediently taken my beautiful little wooden chair into the yard and left it there. Now I was being sent to retrieve it.

Every step I took away from the safety of Mother and the door seemed fraught with danger. Unusual shapes and sounds surrounded me. At any moment, I felt something would grab me from behind or that arms would reach out from a shadow and engulf me. When I finally reached my chair, I snatched it up and ran back to Mother, who had remained faithful to watch me.

Many times in my adult life I have thought about that night. When faced with difficult tasks, I have remembered the feelings of fright and loneliness associated with unfamiliar surroundings, but I have also remembered the watchfulness of my mother. This memory has helped me to understand the principle of God's loving care.

Just as Mother would have rescued me from any real danger, so God stands ready to protect us, His children. Although at times we seem to be completely on our own, He is never far away. Sometimes the dangers we face are imagined ones, and God lets us walk on under His watchful eye. However, when we encounter real dangers, such as the traps of Satan or the shadow of death, He is quickly beside us to be a present help in our time of need.

REMEMBER TODAY: We are never without the protection of God's watchful care.

Alma Kelley **Related Scripture** **May 31**
Cleveland, TN Philippians 4:13 Psalm 19:14

Let the words of my mouth, and the meditation
of my heart, be acceptable in thy sight, O Lord,
my strength, and my redeemer (Psalm 19:14).

YES, I CAN

How many times have you said something that once the words were out of your mouth you wished you had thought before you said them? Words once spoken can never be taken back.

I can remember as a child how other children were so cruel with their words toward me. I've had a weight problem all my life, and their words about my heaviness hurt. If they had given me a chance, I could have become their friend.

In our daily devotion to Him, may we pray, "Lord, as I meet the world today, may I have You speaking through me that I may find favor in Your eyes."

If there is someone you feel a need to speak to or to do something for (perhaps someone you really don't feel comfortable around), don't push that feeling away. It may be that this person is praying for God to send someone by to help, to touch, to bring love or to pray with them.

Just remember our verse for today: "May my spoken words and unspoken thoughts be pleasing even to you, O Lord my Rock and my Redeemer" (Psalm 19:14, *TLB*).

REMEMBER TODAY: "I can do all things through Christ which strengtheneth me" (Philippians 4:13). Can I do it? Sure you can!

NOTES

Judith S. Isaacs
Gastonia, NC

Related Scriptures
1 Peter 5:7; Psalm 55:22;
Jeremiah 32:27

June 1
Isaiah 45:2

I will go before thee, and make the
crooked places straight (Isaiah 45:2).

STRAIGHT PATHS

My life was in turmoil. My youngest child was getting married, I was experiencing health problems, I was working a part-time job, my husband and I were building a house, I was deeply hurt by a longtime friend, and church responsibilities were piling up.

I was like a drunk staggering from one side of life's road to the other, feeling that at any time I would fall. Each day I tried to cast my cares on Him, but at the same time I was asking myself if God cared for me.

One day while in prayer about a speaking engagement I had that night, I thought of the problems of others—death, sickness, layoffs, rebellious children, troubled marriages. I felt God was leading me to change subjects and minister to people who were hurting—people like myself. The topic would be "Making Our Crooked Places Straight Again."

I rushed home, gathered my study materials and wrote quickly as God spoke to my heart. It was a message of hope and encouragement; it challenged and promised victory. I took that outline along with the one I had prepared several weeks earlier, prayerfully asking for God's guidance. As I sat in the service meditating on the two messages, God revealed to me that the first message I had prepared was for the congregation. The second message was for me. I was struggling with cares, staggering from side to side. Then Jesus appeared and lifted my load, bandaged my wounds, took my hand and helped me walk down a straight path. From that minute the load was lighter; I was relaxed and at peace in the arms of my Lord.

REMEMBER TODAY: When we are burdened with the cares of life, we need to stop and remember that He can make our paths straight.

Joan May
Cleveland, TN

Related Scriptures
Genesis 2:1-8; Galatians 5:22, 23;
Colossians 3:10-17

June 2
Genesis 2:8

*And the Lord God planted
a garden . . .* (Genesis 2:8).

A SPIRITUAL GARDEN

When I was an 11-year-old girl, we moved into a new neighborhood. I was delighted when I discovered a small flower garden in our backyard. The previous owner had planted the garden, but the house had remained empty. The garden was overrun with weeds and thistles.

"This is mine!" I proclaimed and immediately took ownership. I began clearing and pulling weeds from my garden. I took great pride in my effort as a garden began to emerge from the miniature jungle. The flowers now had room to grow—some tall, some bushy. I did good!

Our lives are much like a garden. They can become overrun with weeds and pests if there is no caretaker. The Bible teaches that if we submit our wills to Christ, we become like Him. He begins to cultivate us as a gardener cultivates his flower bed.

He deeply plants a little kindness and humility. He'll add a row of meekness and long-suffering. He'll pull up weeds of hurt, bitterness and anger so that forgiveness, love and understanding will flourish! He rains down peace that passes all understanding. When He warms our life with the light of His Word, thankfulness begins to spring up like flowers.

Is your life being overrun and choked by Satan? Is it out of control and growing wild like a jungle? Give it to God for cultivation. Let your life be God's garden where nothing grows except the beauty He plants.

REMEMBER TODAY: As we submit our will to God, our life becomes a spiritual garden full of Christlike attitudes and actions.

Carolyn L. Poitier	**Related Scriptures**	**June 3**
Leesburg, FL	Hebrews 11:1, 8; Isaiah 41:10; 43:1, 2	2 Corinthians 5:7

*For we walk by faith, not
by sight* (2 Corinthians 5:7).

STEPPING INTO NOWHERE

"Mommy, is it time for Daddy to come home?" my 3- and 4-year-old daughters would inquire. "Almost," I would reply. With that answer, the girls would run hurriedly to the family-room window to await their father's arrival.

Our home was located on a small hill. To enter the family room from the carport, you had to climb three or four steps. The carport's driveway was roughly constructed with concrete, stone and pebbles. Because of this, I constantly cautioned the girls to be careful when walking on the stairs.

As soon as the hum of the Volkswagen could be heard, the girls would shout, "Daddy's home, Daddy's home!"

After parking the car, my husband would rush to station himself in front of the family-room door. Our youngest daughter would open the door and jump into her father's arms. She was oblivious to the height of the stairs or the roughness of the pavement below. She was confident that when she jumped, her father would catch her.

This is the same type of blind faith we must have when trusting our heavenly Father. It is the Enemy's desire for us to focus our attention on the rough places, billows and torrential storms of this life and declare, "There is no hope!" God forbid! But "we walk by faith, not by sight" Therefore, regardless of our Enemy's tactics, let us go to the window of our mind and wait for the Father. When we see Him, let us open the doors of our hearts and jump into His arms, knowing that when we jump, He will be there with outstretched arms waiting to catch us.

"Fear not. . . . When thou passest through the waters, I will be with thee; and through the rivers, they shall not overflow thee: when thou walkest through the fire, thou shalt not be burned; neither shall the flame kindle upon thee" (Isaiah 43:1, 2).

REMEMBER TODAY: Walking by faith and not by sight is like stepping into nowhere, knowing that our heavenly Father is everywhere.

Carolyn M. Hodges
Greenville, SC

Related Scriptures
James 1; 1 Peter 1:7; 4:12-16;
2 Corinthians 4:8-10; Romans 5:3-5

June 4
Philippians 1:6

Being confident of this, that he who began a good work in you will carry it on to completion until the day of Christ Jesus (Philippians 1:6, *NIV*).

SMOOTHING THE EDGES

It was summer. I was traveling alone to Tennessee for a visit with my family. The narrow, winding road was bounded on the right by a bank of rocks and small trees. On the left a creek was flowing. The rocks in the creek bed were clearly visible because the dry summer had caused the water to be low. As I looked at those smooth rocks allowing the water to flow so gently over them, I wondered how jagged and rough those rocks were many years ago. But through the years, perhaps even centuries, the continual flow of the creek waters had caused the rough and jagged edges to become smooth and rounded.

I began to reflect on a painful situation I was facing at the time. I could not understand why I was being tested in this manner, especially since I was certain that God knew I was totally committed to Him and that nothing could cause my faith in Him to waver. Then the Holy Spirit pricked my heart. Are there some rough edges in my life that need to be smoothed out? Do I need to allow the Holy Spirit to flow over and through me to change something in my life that is displeasing to my Lord?

Is there a lesson to be learned or a strength to be gained through this ordeal?

As I pondered these questions, I began to ask God to help me to be patient as He worked His will in my life. I asked the Holy Spirit to flow over me, to remove any rough edges, to make me a smooth, clean child of God. Incredible! I had traveled that road many times; I had watched the flow of that creek and had seen those stones in all seasons of the year; yet, God chose this day to allow me to see it all in a new perspective.

REMEMBER TODAY: God sees what we will become if we will allow Him to do His work in us by the Holy Spirit.

Sarah Glover	**Related Scriptures**	**June 5**
Sumiton, AL	Psalms 91; 27:5; 46:1	Psalm 91:15

I will be with him in trouble; I will deliver
him and honor him (Psalm 91:15, *NKJV*).

OUR HELP IN TROUBLED TIMES

The elevator door opened. As my husband and I started to step out, three frantic young people screamed: "Danny has drowned!" Frantically I ran six blocks to the beach of San Juan, Puerto Rico.

The youth choir I directed was invited to sing at an international conference, and in less than 24 hours after our arrival, tragedy struck. A young man in our choir, wading along the edge of the water, was pulled out to sea by an undertow. Three other choir members and a policeman tried to save him but were unsuccessful.

Where was God that day? I became aware of His presence in several ways. First, there seemed to be an indescribable strength undergirding me, helping me to think straight and holding me together when I wondered, *How on earth am I handling this?* Then there were some precious "angels" who stood with us through that five-hour wait on the beach while we waited for the body to be picked up. These angels were Christian men and women who helped us understand the wonderful reality of being a part of the family of God. One even sang gently to us in the Spirit. Also, scriptures from God's Word constantly flooded my mind. The Holy Spirit was so real I realized my strength was not my own.

No one is exempt from tragedy, but God promised to be "a very present help in [time of] trouble" (Psalm 46:1). In Psalm 91:15 He promises to be with us in trouble. That promise is to those who dwell "in the secret place of the Most High" (v. 1, *NKJV*).

We do not need to live in fear of trouble or danger. When trouble comes, I can assure you that if we live in the pages of Psalm 91, we can claim verse 11: "For He shall give His angels charge over you, to keep you in all your ways" (*NKJV*).

REMEMBER TODAY: God has promised to be with us through every trial as we walk with Him and trust Him daily.

Alicia A. Dotson
St. Louis, MO

Related Scriptures
Philippians 4:13; 2 Timothy 1:12;
Hebrews 2:18; 7:25; Jude 24

June 6
Ephesians 3:20

*Now to him who is able to do immeasurably more
than all we ask or imagine, according to his power
that is at work within us* . . . (Ephesians 3:20, *NIV*).

NO QUESTIONING GOD'S ABILITY

"God is able to meet your need." Many times I have heard those words spoken to encourage someone in a difficult situation. I have heard ministers preach from the pulpit that same message of hope. Why haven't I been able to accept this truth for myself during moments of dark desperation? Why do I even allow myself to plunge into the pit of total despair before finally turning to the Word of God?

My husband and I began our full-time ministry almost five years ago in the inner city of St. Louis. We knew we were where God wanted us to be, but right away we encountered events and situations that made questions surface. Could the Scriptures we held dear to our hearts sustain us? Could God really work all things together for our good?

Guess what! We discovered His Word was applicable for every situation. When we questioned the validity of our salvation, we found God able to "save completely" (Hebrews 7:25, *NIV*). When we questioned the trials, we realized that Jesus "learned obedience from what he suffered" (Hebrews 5:8, *NIV*). When we questioned our stability, we discovered God was able to keep us from falling (Jude 24).

We will have more questions. But now turning to the Word of God awakens me to the freshness of God's desires for me and gently reminds me that I am His child. As His child, I can boldly approach Him with my questions because He has the answers.

REMEMBER TODAY: Memorize this acrostic based on Philippians 4:13. I am
A-Able   B-Because the   L-Lord   E-Enables.

Loretta C. Huffman
Smithfield, NC

Related Scriptures
Matthew 9:22; 18:1-6; Mark 9:29;
Acts 1:14

June 7
Matthew 7:7

*Ask [and believe], and it shall
be given you* (Matthew 7:7).

THE MIRACLE

The last few days had been exhausting. As I awoke that morning and arose from the little cot where I had lain the last few hours, I looked into the face of a gravely ill 7-year-old boy. His big eyes were closed, and he was very still.

Our son had been diagnosed with rheumatic fever. He was in the hospital 33 days and then sent home for complete bed rest. Four days later he started having convulsions, one after another. I sent for my husband from work, and we immediately rushed him back to the hospital. The doctor met us there.

"We must take him off the medicine," the doctor said. "He seems to have had a reaction." For days he lay in a coma. When he finally awoke, he didn't know anyone. We prayed as we had never prayed before. The doctors told us he wouldn't live. Then they said if he lived he would just be a vegetable. We continued to pray. Oh, how the devil fought us, but we kept on praying.

That morning as I freshened up, I heard a small voice singing, "I know the Lord, I know the Lord, I know the Lord has His hands on me." I couldn't believe my ears. Was this my son? I dashed to the bedside, and he was singing this little song we taught the children in church. I started crying. He looked at me and said, "Hey, Mother, what are you doing here?"

I cried, I jumped up and down, I hugged him and screamed, "He knows me, he knows me, he knows me!" The nurses heard me and, thinking he had died, ran into the room. When they saw what had happened, they cried also.

He is alive today and is preaching the gospel. We gave him to the Lord when he was a baby. When he was so sick, we asked the Lord to let us keep him, but we still wanted His will done. When God says He will answer prayer, He means it. Trust Him for your needs today. When you know of nothing else to do but pray, pray. Prayer changes things and it changes people.

REMEMBER TODAY: Nothing is too hard for God.

Sharon DeFino
Holiday, FL

Related Scripture
Song of Solomon 1; 2

June 8
1 Peter 1:8

And though you have not seen Him, you love Him, and though you do not see Him now, but believe in Him, you greatly rejoice with joy inexpressible and full of glory (1 Peter 1:8, NASB).

HAPPILY EVER AFTER*

The love story in the Song of Solomon can be likened to the story of a Shulamite girl whose cruel brothers put her in charge of the vineyards and flocks. She had no time to beautify herself. In those days girls who were fair and fragile were considered lovely, but she felt ugly because although she was comely, she was tanned by the sun (Song of Solomon 1:6).

One day a stranger whom she perceived to be a shepherd spoke to her. Embarrassed, she apologized for her looks; but he told her how beautiful she was to him (1:8, 9, 10, 15). They fell in love, and he asked her to be his bride but said he must go away for a while, promising to return. She believed him and waited with anticipation for her wedding day.

When the day arrived for his return, there was a great cavalcade of beautiful horses and body guards. The grand procession stopped right by the lowly shepherd girl (Cinderella), and as she looked into the coach, she looked into the face of the king himself. She realized it was the shepherd for whom she had been waiting. He took her into the chariot, and they rode off to live happily ever after.

There are times we feel ugly, unloved and mistreated. At those times the Good Shepherd, Jesus Christ, will come and tell us how beautiful we are to Him and how much He loves us. We need to take time to fellowship with Him. He has promised to return someday and take us from this place of cares and woe. We must believe, keep ourselves pure and watch for Him. He will come for us in all His glory as the King of Kings. But we must know Him as the Shepherd of our life before we can go with Him as our King.

*Adapted from *The Song of Solomon*, by H.A. Ironside (Loizeaux Brothers, Inc., 1933).

REMEMBER TODAY: You are beautiful to Jesus. He loves you and will keep His promise to return and take you to be His bride.

Debbie Burdashaw
Wichita, KS

Related Scriptures
Matthew 5:14-16; John 8:12; 9:5;
Ephesians 5:8

June 9
1 John 1:7

*But if we walk in the light, as he is in the light, we have
fellowship one with another, and the blood of Jesus
Christ his Son cleanseth us from all sin* (1 John 1:7).

THE TRANSFORMING LIGHT

When my husband accepted a pastorate in the Midwest, I was not excited. This was new, unfamiliar territory. The flat, desolate plains with tumbleweeds and extreme weather were in sharp contrast to the lush green countryside and mild seasons I was accustomed to. I found out that real cowboys do exist! Besides the culture shock I was experiencing, we were a thousand miles from family. I immediately decided I wouldn't like it here. I would be a good pastor's wife and fulfill my obligations, but that was it! I would not love these people; I would merely be here if they needed me.

We moved in on Saturday, and after unloading the household goods from the truck, we made our way to the church to unload my husband's library. I took my first look into the sanctuary. It was a lovely sanctuary with red carpet and padded pews, but it was dark and the windows were colorless.

The next morning we left for church much earlier than usual. I wanted to be waiting for the people, rather than having them wait for me. As I entered the sanctuary, I gasped. The stained-glass windows which were dark and colorless the night before were now illumined by light from outside. They transformed the sanctuary, filling it with radiant colors. *O God*, I thought, *what a contrast! Please do the same for me.*

Immediately I asked God to forgive me and change my attitude. I wanted His light to shine through me and to those around me just as His light was shining through those windows.

My negative, discontented life was being transformed into one of love and contentment. That morning I was able to greet the people as they arrived and tell them how truly glad I was to be here and to be a part of them.

REMEMBER TODAY: The transforming light of Jesus Christ can flow through your life and shine on the lives of others if you are willing to be a "window." Let Him shine through you!

Nancy A. Neal
Cleveland, TN

Related Scriptures
Psalm 46; Lamentations 3:22-36;
2 Corinthians 12:9, 10

June 10
Psalm 46:10

Be still, and know that I am God (Psalm 46:10).

HE SPEAKS IN A QUIET MOMENT

I took advantage of the final morning of a much-needed vacation to go in search of seashells and last-minute photo opportunities. As I ambled along on the beach before 8 o'clock, I marveled at how calming were the sound of the ocean, the squish of wet sand between my toes and the call of the pelicans. Though waves tumbled onto the shore, a stillness pervaded. I expressed my thankfulness to God for His creation.

As I bent to select another tiny shell for my collection, I fleetingly wondered if anyone ever found a sand dollar. I had walked only a few steps when I casually glanced to the left and saw my first "real" sand dollar—without a chip or crack anywhere! It seemed to be a sign.

Legend has it that the sand dollar tells of the birth and death of Jesus. Upon close examination, we see four nail holes and a fifth one made by a Roman's spear. On one side is the Easter lily, its center the star that appeared to the shepherds and led them to the Christ child. Etched on the other side is the Christmas poinsettia, reminding us of His birthday. Legend says that breaking open the sand dollar releases five white doves waiting to spread good will and peace.

That quiet morning on the beach I was reminded that God has invited us to "be still and know" Him. The word *still* in this passage means "to loosen your grip, to let go." God wants us to let go of our tight hold on things—job pressures, financial worries, faulty relationships, chronic illness, wayward children—to be able to hold His mighty yet gentle hand. Best of all, He wants to hold our hand. He wants to lift us up. He longs to show us His love. But we can't hold to His hand if we're gripping careers, finances, relationships.

The hum of my computer, the phone ringing, the blowing of the air-conditioner and the voices in the hallway outside my office as I write are all reminders of a busy, noisy world that wants to grab hold of me. On the gulf shore of Florida, though, I did not have to hold on to anything but the hand of the Savior. It was "just Jesus and me" talking together while the waves splashed in the background. Even the pelicans paused from their flight on a worn pier. The "still" moment was memorable, though too short. But my sand dollar reminds me of that special moment during a difficult point in my life and the nail-pierced hand to which I can cling.

It's not easy to let go, for we're taught early on to "hang on for dear life." But there's comfort in taking the hand of Jesus. Be still and know God. Experience His presence in everything you do. Take those things that are a constant bother, that you grip daily, and let go of them—even if only for a few minutes.

REMEMBER TODAY: God longs to hold your free and open hand. Learn to be still and let God!

Ina Boling
Little Rock, AR

Related Scriptures
Deuteronomy 28:6; Psalm 37:23

June 11
Psalm 121:8

*The Lord shall preserve thy going out and thy coming in
from this time forth, and even for evermore* (Psalm 121:8).

THE TWO CARDS

I awoke in a strange bed at a strange house surrounded by boxes. After 15 years of pastoral work, my husband had been assigned to a state position. The change had been sudden and dramatic. In less than a week we had packed, said our goodbyes and traveled several hundred miles to our new location. My emotions were in as much chaos as the rooms of our new house. I opened a box and began the task of settling into our new surroundings.

As I worked through the morning, I tried to find some excitement in our new life. Yet my mind kept wandering back to the people we had left. God had given them to us to nurture in His Word, and we had spent the last five years watching them grow and mature in the Lord. I couldn't help wondering what would happen to them now. I had known that this move was God's will, but shadows of doubt began to creep into my mind. By the time my husband arrived home for lunch, I was on the verge of depression. We talked together and prayed for God's peace, but doubts still lingered.

Checking the mail before returning to his office, my husband brought two cards and placed them in my lap. The first one I opened was from a member of our former church. It brought a flood of memories and a tug of homesickness. I turned to the verse and read the words. They spoke of love and friendship. A personal note told me how much we were missed.

Struggling to fight back the tears, I opened the second card. It was from a minister's wife in our new state. A warm and cheerful welcome flowed from its pages.

As I sat looking at the two cards, the Lord brought to my remembrance Psalm 121:8. God had kept us when we pastored; He had blessed our efforts and prospered our plans. Now He would keep us as we entered into a new field of labor. I returned to the task of unpacking my boxes with peace in my heart. A warm feeling began to surround me. It was the feeling of home.

REMEMBER TODAY: Our place in the work of the Lord is what really matters, not our location.

Joann McIntire
Fort Worth, TX

Related Scriptures
Philippians 1:21; Hebrews 6:19

June 12
Hebrews 10:23

Let us hold fast the confession of our hope without wavering,
for He who promised is faithful (Hebrews 10:23, *NKJV*).

ANCHORED IN CHRIST

I have three anchors that keep my boat secure in any storm: (1) I have a purpose. (2) My failures are not fatal. (3) My death is not final.

Jonah's purpose was to preach the gospel at Nineveh. He chose to disobey God, was tossed overboard and landed in the belly of a whale. God gave Jonah another chance. His death was not final in the belly of the whale. The great fish spit him up. He obeyed God, went to Nineveh, and the city repented. Through God's mercy, his failure was not fatal.

We too have a purpose—to reach the lost for Christ. It may not always be easy, but we must have our faith anchored in Christ during the storms of our lives. "Let us hold fast the confession of our hope without wavering, for He who promised is faithful." The storms that rock our spiritual boat will soon pass. We must stay anchored to the rock of purpose, and the captain, Christ Jesus, will cause the winds to cease.

All of us have failed at one time or another in our walk with God. We fail to witness to the lost or comfort the hurting and brokenhearted. But God forgives us and gives us another chance. "For all have sinned, and come short of the glory of God" (Romans 3:23).

If we are faithful, anchored in Christ, our final destination will be the shores of heaven. We, like Paul, must have a perfect resignation to face the future— whether service with Christ on earth or living in heaven with our heavenly Father. We must gladly accept whichever God chooses for us! Paul wrote in Philippians 1:21, "For to me to live is Christ, and to die is gain."

REMEMBER TODAY: God is the God of every tense—past, present and future. He is the help of our past, the hope of our future and the Great I Am of today!

Virginia Eure Norfolk, VA	**Related Scriptures** Leviticus 26:6; Isaiah 12:2; 59:19; 1 Peter 5:7	**June 13** 1 John 4:18

There is no fear in love; but perfect love casteth
out fear: because fear hath torment. He that
feareth is not made perfect in love (1 John 4:18).

PEACE IN TROUBLED TIMES

When we experience stress or fear, our bodies react and destroy our tranquillity. Symptoms of these reactions may include shortness of breath, moist palms and disorder in our thinking. It is true, we don't know what life will dish out to us. But it is also true that we have been invited to cast all our care upon the Lord, for He cares for us (1 Peter 5:7). When we are in a desperate situation, we don't mumble or whisper our needs; we *boldly* go before the Lord as a child would go to his father. We cry out for the deliverance and peace that is freely ours.

Even in these times of anxiety and uncertainty, the love of God supplies peace. Fear destroys; peace enables. Peace brings joy and freedom from worry.

A story is told of a worrier. His brow was furrowed. He never smiled; he just worried. He soon became known as The Worrier. One day a friend saw the worrier approaching him. The worrier was smiling and there was no furrow in his brow.

"Why are you smiling, Mr. Worrier?" asked the friend.

"I hired me a worrier," he replied.

"Hired you a worrier?" repeated the amazed friend. "And how much do you pay him?"

"A thousand dollars a week," responded the worrier.

"A thousand dollars a week? Where do you get that much money?" "That's his worry!" answered Mr. Worrier.

We may not all be able to hire a worrier, but we can all go to our Savior, who will take our worries, bear our burdens and give us peace of mind in these troubled times.

REMEMBER TODAY: Peace cannot be purchased. Freedom from fear cannot be purchased. But God's love and peace are available to all who ask.

Eleanor S. Sheeks	**Related Scriptures**	**June 14**
Cleveland, TN	Psalms 37:23, 24; 139:7-10;	Psalm 139:10
	Isaiah 41:10; Exodus 33:22	

Your hand shall lead me, and your right
hand shall hold me (Psalm 139:10, *NKJV*).

HIS HANDS

I had not known what to expect of my emotions. This was my first experience with the death of a parent. As I stood viewing my father's 90-year-old expired body for the first time, I found myself totally absorbed with his hands.

Perhaps it was because I had never seen his hands folded like that. Dad was extremely industrious. He classified laziness and idleness right up there with murder and adultery! Perhaps it was because these hands were smaller and whiter and more well-manicured than I had experienced them. The hands I remembered were big, loaded with strength and skill. I remembered them bronzed by the sun, roughened and toughened by the elements and hard work, usually bearing proof of a long day's work on the farm. I remembered hands that, combined with his good head, could do whatever any situation demanded.

As I stood there with my eyes fastened on those hands, a lifetime of memories tumbled through my mind . . . the childhood growing-up times at home, the college era, the adult years. I remembered some times when I'd be home for a visit and Dad would get my attention and give me a familiar hand gesture that meant "Leave the group—come with me." When he did this, I never knew where he would lead me. It might be to see a weird-shaped vegetable he had grown, a crazy cartoon he'd clipped and saved just for me, or maybe a check he'd written in advance for "a little nest egg." There was infinite variety, but I always knew that the "Come with me" gesture meant special moments with my father.

So much had flowed through Dad's hands to me—discipline, protection, provision, constant blessing. I realized again in a fresh way the tremendous benefits of a good father's hands.

We have a heavenly Father whose hands will never be folded. His hands are at work in the everyday unfolding of our lives. His hands are big hands—hands of discipline, protection, provision and constant blessing. And sometimes His hand motions us away from the crowd for special times and precious relationship with Him.

REMEMBER TODAY: The power and resources I need are mine today from a heavenly Father who loves me and whose hands uphold and cover me.

Pat Daugherty	**Related Scriptures**	**June 15**
Charlotte, NC	James 4:2; Matthew 7:11	Hebrews 10:25

*Not forsaking the assembling of
ourselves together* (Hebrews 10:25).

MY FATHER'S HOUSE

"Not forsaking the assembling of ourselves together" is our Father's way of saying to, His children, "Don't forget to come home often." This command is not given so much for His benefit as for ours. We are not told to go to His house just so He will not be angry with us. There is a blessing awaiting us at the Father's house.

In April of 1990, while living in Baton Rouge, I felt a strong tug in my heart to fly home to south Georgia to visit my mom and dad. It was a brief visit, and the three days passed quickly. Several times during the visit my dad and I had serious father-daughter talks. Finally, on the morning I had to leave, my parents walked me to the porch. My dad said to me, "Honey, is there anything around here you need?" I answered, "No, sir, I can't think of anything." There was no doubt in my mind that whatever I had asked for, if it had been possible, my dad would have given it to me.

On the flight back to Baton Rouge, I replayed those words over and over, for they seemed to be so special. I reflected on the love of my heavenly Father, who wants me to come to His house often so that while I am there in worship, He can ask me, "Is there anything you need or want?"

Little did I know when I stood on that back porch that those would be the last words my dad would ever say to me. A cardiac arrest on May 28 was his invitation to go to his Father's house.

Scripture supports the desire of our heavenly Father to give good gifts to His children. "Ye have not, because ye ask not" (James 4:2). Matthew 7:11 says, "How much more shall your Father which is in heaven give good things to them that ask him?"

REMEMBER TODAY: When you are in the Father's house, listen for Him to ask, "Is there anything you need or want Me to do for you?"

Samara Stanfield
Mercersburg, PA

Related Scriptures
Psalm 55:22; 2 Corinthians 12:9;
Hebrews 4:16

June 16
Psalm 46:1

God is our refuge and strength, a very
present help in trouble (Psalm 46:1).

GRACE ENOUGH FOR ALL OUR NEEDS

What a comforting realization when we fully accept the fact that we are never alone! In the good times and in times of adversity, He is always there. With this assurance we can feel a calmness, even when our heart is breaking.

I was able to witness one of the greatest examples of this abiding peace when my husband and I were ministering in Montana. One of our ministers and his wife were blessed with a beautiful little girl. Soon after birth it was discovered the baby had cystic fibrosis. Knowing there was no known cure for this disease, the parents never wavered in their confidence that God's grace was sufficient in all situations.

Little Margaret lived to be 6 years old. During these years, her parents stayed in close fellowship with the Lord. Even in their sorrow, they were able to minister an abiding peace to others in need.

Friend, God is also watching over you. In your time of need, He sees you as if you were His only child in the whole world, and He offers you His help. Oh, what a Savior!

> There is sufficient grace,
> For each trial we face.
> It doesn't matter if it's large or small,
> He's always there to answer your call.
> —SS

REMEMBER TODAY: Our needs + His grace = Success

Patty Stallings
Rapid City, SD

Related Scriptures
Jeremiah 17:7, 8; Ezekiel 47:12

June 17
Psalm 1:3

He is like a tree planted by streams of water, which
yields its fruit in season and whose leaf does not wither.
Whatever he does prospers (Psalm 1:3, NIV).

LIKE A TREE

We most often think of a tree as being isolated—dependent upon itself, standing alone in its own particular place. However, Lowell Ponte in an article titled "What Good Is a Tree?" tells that trees are connected and communicate in unseen ways.

Ponte notes that chemical ecologist found that when a willow tree is attacked by web worms or tent caterpillars, it is capable of releasing a chemical that alerts nearby willows of the danger. The neighboring trees then respond by pumping more tannin into their leaves, making them more difficult to digest by the insects.

As Christian women, when we build relationships and communicate openly, we help one another fend off the attacks and hazards we all face.

Ponte also reported that when the roots of two trees touch, a battle for dominance begins. However, tiny organisms can change all that. They not only reduce competition between the trees, but they actually link together the roots of trees of the same species or even different species. The result is an amazing network of sharing. In one experiment, seedlings were grown with these organisms present to join their roots. The scientists then cast shade over one of the seedlings. The shaded tree began to draw missing nutrients from the sunlit tree through the linkage between them. Thanks to these tiny microorganisms, an entire forest can be linked together like a community. If one tree has access to water, another to nutrients and a third to sunlight, the trees share with one another.

If we allow God to act as the agent that links our hearts together, rather than competing, we can share with one another the things God has provided in our lives. Your life can nourish a broken heart, a hurting spirit, a weary soul. In turn, your life will be refreshed, just like a tree planted by streams of water.

REMEMBER TODAY: What has God provided in your life to share with others? Could it be there is someone waiting to hear your words of encouragement, comfort or wisdom? Perhaps it is simply a smile someone needs. Refresh someone today.

Joyce R. McGlamery
Cleveland, TN

Related Scriptures
Ecclesiastes 3:1, 2, 4; 1 Peter 5:7

June 18
Proverbs 15:13

*A happy heart makes the face cheerful, but
heartache crushes the spirit* (Proverbs 15:13, *NIV*).

SMILE

Do you remember the first time your child smiled while you were encouraging him or her with baby talk? Etched in my memory is the love and warmth that filled my heart when my son first smiled at me. That smile erased the pain and agony I experienced during the long ordeal of childbirth.

Has your child ever brought home a paper from school with a smiley face? Returning from an ordinary day at school, my daughter proudly brought home her first smiley face. She had been rewarded for work well done.

Have you ever had a stranger pass you on the street and just smile? This greeting simply said hi without speaking a word. When your friends smile, they are indirectly telling you that your friendship is important. Do you realize when your mate gives you that certain smile, he is nonverbally telling you that he loves you?

But what about the times you don't feel like smiling? This is the time to turn to the Holy Spirit for renewed cheerfulness.

With the sudden passing of my mother in 1986, I wondered if I would ever smile again, because of my broken heart. A minister friend said, "Joyce, you will now know the Holy Spirit in a way you have never known Him before."

Depending upon the prayer support, words of encouragement and, yes, smiles from friends, my heart began the healing process. Once again I began to smile, because "there is a time for everything, and a season for every activity under heaven: a time to be born and a time to die . . . a time to weep and a time to laugh" (Ecclesiastes 3:1, 2, 4, *NIV*).

So when you do not feel like smiling, let the Holy Spirit comfort you. Learn to smile through Him by "cast[ing] all your anxiety on him because he cares for you" (1 Peter 5:7, *NIV*).

REMEMBER TODAY: Let the Holy Spirit smile through your face to someone today.

Mildred Taylor	**Related Scriptures**	**June 19**
Decatur, IL	Isaiah 1:18; Hebrews 1:3; 1 John 1:7	Psalm 51:7

*Purge me with hyssop, and I shall be clean: wash
me, and I shall be whiter than snow* (Psalm 51:7).

WHITER THAN SNOW

What a beautiful scene! I found myself going frequently to the glass doors to watch the sparkling snowflakes as they fell so quietly and peacefully. Soon the snow began to accumulate and cover the small shrubs at the edge of the patio. While observing the small mounds of fresh snow and admiring their glowing whiteness, I asked myself, "How can anything be whiter than this?" Immediately I thought, *Oh yes, God's children are made whiter than snow.* I was reminded of David's prayer in Psalm 51:7: "Wash me, and I shall be whiter than snow."

It is said that snow gives forth a perfect image of purity. In the natural, a nurse's white uniform symbolizes cleanliness, and a bride's white dress symbolizes purity. But a nurse's uniform and a bride's dress may not always be the ultimate in white.

In the spiritual, we are cleansed from all our sins and made pure by the sacrificial blood of Jesus Christ. Our hearts are washed through and through by the blood; all stains, spots, blemishes and gray areas are removed. All impurities are washed away. We are then whiter than snow. Whiter than snow is the ultimate degree of whiteness! What a miracle!

I am grateful to the Lord for this earthly illustration to remind me again of His precious blood and the power it has to cleanse hearts and lives and make them whiter than snow!

REMEMBER TODAY: God does a marvelous work in the hearts of people through the blood of His Son, Jesus Christ!

Holly K. McIntosh
Belfast, ME

Related Scriptures
Psalms 91; 107:6, 13; 1 Peter 5:7

June 20
Psalm 91:2

I will say of the Lord, He is my refuge and my
fortress: my God; in him will I trust (Psalm 91:2).

HELP IN DISTRESS

One quiet summer evening my husband and I were sitting at our kitchen table drinking coffee and watching our 4-year-old daughter, Kay, playing in the yard on the swing set. Suddenly she ran across the yard shrieking, "Daddy, Daddy, a sneak, a sneak!" (*Sneak* was her term for snake!)

Immediately, her father checked out the situation. I followed to see how Dad was going to handle it. We carefully made our way to the swing set, looking for any signs of the snake. Spotting a piece of rope on the ground, I asked Kay if that was the snake. Unfortunately, it wasn't. Daddy asked what color the snake was, and Kay replied that it was yellow and brown.

All of a sudden, Kay began pointing under the swing set and yelling, "There it is!" As we approached the swing set, we realized Kay's "snake" was a fuzzy caterpillar.

As I reflected on this incident, I was reminded of God's care for us. We can run to Him with our problems, our fears and our cares. Just as Kay trusted her father to help her in a time of distress, how much more can we trust our heavenly Father to protect us, help us and deliver us from all our troubles and fears!

REMEMBER TODAY: In our times of distress, we can run to the Lord Jesus Christ for help.

M. Joyce Pennington
Kenova, WV

Related Scriptures
Matthew 7:7-11; John 1:11-13;
Romans 8:14-17

June 21
1 John 3:1

*Behold, what manner of love the Father hath bestowed upon us, that
we should be called the sons [or daughters] of God: therefore the
world knoweth us not, because it knew him not* (1 John 3:1).

DADDY'S GIRL

Looking into the clear blue sky, I breathed a child's prayer of thanks before
climbing into the wagon beside my daddy. He was going to dig a well for a
neighbor. The youngest of 10 children, I was thrilled at the thought of being
alone with him, even if it meant riding six miles in a horse-drawn wagon.

Daddy moved over so I could sit on the rough board beside him. He
snapped the reins and called, "Giddap." With a sudden jerk we started down
the road. I stretched as tall as I could and tried to look very important.
Everyone for miles knew my daddy, and I was his daughter.

We bumped past several wheat fields. I counted the fence posts as they
passed by and watched the cattle. They seemed to share in my happiness. I
moved closer to my dad, and we rode along in silence for a while. Soon we
turned into the neighbor's lane with a long row of beautiful evergreen trees on
each side.

After eating lunch my daddy started digging the well. Mr. Cann marked the
spot, and Daddy centered the auger. Holding it tightly, he twisted it to the
right. I climbed into the white swing on the porch and watched him work. In a
few minutes he was lifting the black earth out of the hole. Suddenly, he raised
up and winked at me. My heart leaped, and I burst into singing. I was the
happiest girl in the whole wide world.

I will always cherish the memories of my father's love; however, 1 John 3:1
says, "Behold, what manner of love the Father hath bestowed upon us, that we
should be called the . . . [daughters] of God." I have learned that my earthly
father's love was limited, but my heavenly Father's love is unlimited. It
pleased my daddy when I snuggled close to him; I felt warmth and protection.
God, our heavenly Father, yearns for us to move closer to Him—close enough
to feel His warmth and security.

REMEMBER TODAY: Do you want to draw closer to God? He is waiting for
you.

Marge M. McClain
Cleveland, TN

Related Scriptures
Psalms 118:5, 24; 119:92; 1 Peter 5:7

June 22
Psalm 30:5

*Weeping may endure for a night, but
joy cometh in the morning* (Psalm 30:5).

JOY . . . IN THE MORNING

What an inspiration and thrill it is to walk out into the fresh morning air! Night has passed and we are refreshed. A new day has dawned, and the opportunities of the new day are limitless.

Psalm 118:24 tells us, "This is the day which the Lord hath made; we will rejoice and be glad in it." But it is hard to rejoice when you have wept all night. Perhaps you are going through a black, nighttime experience when joy and laughter and rejoicing seem far removed.

Perhaps it is the black experience of losing someone you love dearly through death or suffering rejection from a divorce. Maybe it is the blackness of a financial reversal or a lingering disease or sickness and you just can't seem to touch God. This was my experience when I was pronounced incurably ill several years ago. Each day was a living death, until my night experience ended when Jesus touched me!

As a parent maybe you just learned your unmarried daughter is expecting a child or your son is addicted to alcohol or cocaine. One of my sons was addicted to alcohol and drugs for 13 years, but today he is free, born again and filled with the Spirit. My long, dark night has ended, and my morning of joy is here! To God be the glory!

Don't despair or lose hope! Weeping may endure for the night, and tears may soak your pillow, but *joy* comes in the morning!

REMEMBER TODAY: God will turn your tears to laughter and your weeping to joy, and He has promised that your joy will be *full*.

Denise Hacker
San Antonio, TX

Related Scriptures
Psalms 37:23; 139:5

June 23
Proverbs 16:9

A man's heart deviseth his way: but the
Lord directeth his steps (Proverbs 16:9).

THE RIGHT PLACE AT THE RIGHT TIME

"How's the fishing? Getting any bites?" asked the tall soft-spoken gentle-man.

"I haven't caught any today, so I guess they're not biting," I said. I was a young child then and loved to go to my favorite spot on the river to fish.

The man and I began to talk about fishing, and I imagined he thought it strange that a little girl would enjoy this sport so much. Our conversation went from one topic to another. Then we began talking about my family. I told him my father had been ill, and he expressed concern. Something was different about this man.

A few days later he and his wife visited my home. They began visiting quite frequently, and we became friends. They prayed for us and gave tremendous support to my father.

It was not until after I married and became a Christian that I realized God had placed that wonderful Christian man (who was also a Pentecostal preacher) on that same riverbank where I was fishing many years ago. So often we can look back and see that God has been in total control of our lives. He places people in our paths for a reason.

REMEMBER TODAY: Nothing happens by chance! God places us in the right place at the right time.

Linda Hayes
Milwaukee, WI

Related Scripture
1 Samuel 1:24-28

June 24
Exodus 2:3

But when she could hide him no longer, she got a papyrus basket for him and coated it with tar and pitch. Then she placed the child in it and put it among the reeds along the bank of the Nile (Exodus 2:3, NIV).

LETTING GO

After the service ended and we said our goodbyes, the big question was "Who will ride home with Daddy in the new car?" My husband said he would take two of the children, so I grabbed my 4-year-old's hand and began to cross the busy street to my own car. "But Daddy said that was mine and his new car. I want to go with him," she screamed as she let go of my hand and ran. I managed to grab the back of her coat.

"No," she cried. "I want Daddy! I want to ride in my new car." She tore away from me. I almost panicked as I saw two headlights coming.

"Sara, STOP!" I screamed as the car screeched to a halt. Shaking inside and thinking what might have been, I held her tight.

I found myself in a situation I could not control. It was out of my hands. I imagine this was the same panic that Jochebed felt as she laid the baby Moses in his waterproof basket and placed him into the Nile River. Pharaoh had ordered that every newborn Hebrew son be killed. After hiding him for three months, she placed him in a basket. She knew that the future of her son was in God's hands and that she must trust Him and let go.

There comes a time when we must all realize that our children's future and safety are in God's hands. We train them and love them; but no matter what age they are, they are not truly ours—ultimately they belong to God.

REMEMBER TODAY: God is in control. Let us do our job by trusting Him and letting go!

Betty Mickovich	**Related Scriptures**	**June 25**
Farmingdale, NY	Psalm 139:1-18; Isaiah 49:16	Acts 10:5, 6

And now send men to Joppa, and call for one Simon, whose surname is Peter: He lodgeth with one Simon a tanner, whose house is by the sea side: he shall tell thee what thou oughtest to do (Acts 10:5, 6).

EVERY DETAIL

As I read Acts 10:5, 6, I suddenly realized how very detail-oriented God is. It also reminded me of what my husband always told our congregation, "Hey, God knows where you live!"

This scripture tells me that God is mindful of everything in my life. As I pray, seek, listen and obey (even when it seems like a crazy idea), God brings about marvelous things—when I act in faith.

Because of Peter's faith and trust, doors were opened to the Gentiles. Even he was amazed at the results. It was a whole new ball game of spiritual revelation—Jesus came to save all people. The darkness of religious bigotry was shattered by the light of truth!

How comforting to know that God knows where I live. He is mindful of me and He hears me. If necessary, He will send the answer I need miraculously. He can even send me to help someone else in need. He knows, He hears, and He works out every detail—even leading us to a current street address. Is anything too hard for God?

Our witness team was passing out tracts stamped with the church's name, address and phone number at a stadium in Orlando, Florida. A few weeks later we received a letter from a man in Illinois. This man owned a small store. He was sweeping one day and picked up one of our tracts, which had fallen to the floor. He wanted to know more about Jesus and where he could find a church in his area.

Praise God, He knows our address, our phone number and our occupation. Is He not a personal Father?

REMEMBER TODAY: God is in control of your life. He's got every detail in the palm of His hand!

Lois J. Garrison
Winterville, NC

Related Scriptures
Mark 11:22-24; Romans 12:3;
Hebrews 11:1

June 26
Mark 11:24

*What things soever ye desire, when ye pray, believe that
ye receive them, and ye shall have them* (Mark 11:24).

A MIRACLE THAT CONTINUES TO BLOSSOM

"Yes, your pregnancy test is positive. According to the test, your baby will be due in May." I had waited for these beautiful words for over 17 years. I had always prayed and dreamed of having a little girl. I was 35, and because of a disease called Crohn's, which required many medications, including steroids, I was almost ready to give up. In a Sunday service I was given a prophecy by our pastor concerning our ministry and our family—we would be blessed with a child. We were elated! Now this prophecy was being fulfilled.

My pregnancy went great! A patient with Crohn's disease is considered high risk. It is a miracle to hear of such a patient getting along well without continuing to take prednisone and other drugs. I felt better than usual and was able to continue teaching and traveling with Delbert while he was evangelizing. On June 26, 1986, my miracle was granted. But we had many battles with the Enemy during the first few days of our baby girl's life.

During delivery I heard the doctor call Code Blue. Both of us were dying. The baby was lodged in the birth canal. As I was being sedated, I could faintly hear Delbert say, "If you want this little girl, you need to pray and help us!"

In a few hours I was told that I had a baby girl who had gone through a very traumatic birth. She was alive thanks to the extraordinary power of our God. I was overwhelmed with thanksgiving. My tears flowed. She weighed 9 pounds 10 1/2 ounces and was placed in the neonatal unit because of medical problems which needed constant attention. We called our church prayer chains to pray.

In the following days, God lived with me as a constant friend. The devil presented battle after battle to test our faith in God. Many complications occurred, but as I reached through the protective oxygen tent, I declared her God's property. Immediately I felt a hot rushing wave of love and peace flow through my body. I knew she was going to make it. I remembered Philippians 4:13: "I can do all things through Christ which strengtheneth me." As new problems surfaced, we simply turned them over to God and continued to pray and trust in Him. On the fourth day great news finally came—she would be moved to the regular nursery. She had been healed day by day, problem after problem.

We went home together on July 4, 1986. We named our baby Jacquelyn Faith because prayers and *faith* were the keys that brought her home. We are thankful for this precious gift God has given us. Faith, now a bright 5-year-old helps us evangelize. We feel the Lord has something special for her to do for His kingdom. She is our miracle that brightens our lives each day.

REMEMBER TODAY: "Every good gift and every perfect gift is from above" (James 1:17). Never lose your faith that all things are possible with God!

Wanda Martin
Cleveland, TN

Related Scriptures
Mark 11:24; 1 Timothy 2:8

June 27
Luke 12:27

Consider the lilies how they grow: they toil not, they spin not; and yet I say unto you, that Solomon in all his glory was not arrayed like one of these (Luke 12:27).

THE GARDEN OF PRAYER

A lifetime friend and "second mother" to my husband has always been acclaimed for her beautiful flower gardens. They spread from the top to the bottom of the hillside in her backyard, which is in full view of half the town.

It would be foolish to enclose this profusion so no one could see it, but even more foolish, perhaps, to hide it from her own view. Such gardens should be shared, providing flowers for the table, the hospital or the church. She would never consider hiding or refusing to share this beauty with others. Many people, however, do hide their gardens—not their flower gardens but a special kind of garden, the garden of prayer.

Prayer is not like a four-leaf clover or rabbit's foot, only to be used to ward off evil. Nor is it a fire extinguisher for emergencies. Prayer is talking to God. In the Garden of Eden, God established the principle of prayer, His unchangeable desire to talk with man. Those who love God desire to talk with Him, whether it be while washing dishes or performing data entry, whether in church or in a secret closet. To talk with Him is to know Him better, to love Him more, to understand how He desires for us to help others. Keeping open the gate of the garden of prayer is to let its fragrance and beauty fill our lives and the lives of those around us.

REMEMBER TODAY: God's Garden of Prayer is comprised of a great variety of prayers from many petitioners. And He responds to each one. "Lord, teach us to pray."

Shirley Wilson	Related Scriptures	June 28
Lakeland, FL	James 1:19, 26; 3:5-11; Ephesians 4:15;	Psalm 34:13
	Proverbs 15:1; 1 Peter 3:10.	

Keep thy tongue from evil, and thy
lips from speaking guile (Psalm 34:13).

POISON CONTROL FOR THE TONGUE

My friend cares for children in her home and teaches them Scripture verses corresponding to the alphabet. She uses the referenced verse for the letter K. Recently, one 3-year-old quoted it this way: "Keep thy tongue from sticking out." For most of us the tongue has always been a source of trouble.

As children we've all shown displeasure by sticking out our tongues at the enemy. Adults often communicate the same principle when they speak.

Words spoken by the tongue have power. Words can cut, abuse, slander, blaspheme and sow discord. However, words also have power to soothe, comfort, encourage, praise, heal and bring peace. James said, "The tongue is a fire, a world of iniquity . . . an unruly evil, full of deadly poison" (3:6, 8). What a sobering description! He further revealed that an uncontrolled tongue produces vain (empty) religion (1:26). Christians have a poison-control center for the tongue.

God's Word is replete with "control" formulas: "Be . . . slow to speak" (James 1:19). "Speaking the truth in love" (Ephesians 4:15). "A soft answer turneth away wrath" (Proverbs 15:1). Whom have we poisoned with our words? Perhaps harsh words were spoken to a child today or sharp words addressed to a companion. Was rudeness displayed to the clerk or salesman who called? Let's allow the Holy Spirit to search our hearts and sanctify our tongues, that we may glorify our Father. Speak comfort today with a word. Encourage someone with sincere praise. Someone's happiness, including our own, may depend on it. The Bible offers a happy life formula to all keepers of the tongue: "For he that will love life, and see good days, let him refrain his tongue from evil, and his lips that they speak no guile" (1 Peter 3:10).

REMEMBER TODAY: There is power in the tongue to soothe or sting.

Anita Hughes Cleveland, TN	**Related Scriptures** Psalms 127; 128	**June 29** Psalm 127:3

*Lo, children are an heritage of the Lord: and the
fruit of the womb is his reward* (Psalm 127:3).

LITTLE BLESSING

At 7:39 p.m. on Saturday, June 29, 1991, Jared Scott Gregory was born. I stood spellbound in the birthing room as I watched the miracle of life unfold right before my eyes.

A little over nine months before, Jared had not been conceived or even imagined. Bright-eyed and innocent, he came into this world and was placed in the arms of his mother. The pain that accompanied childbirth was soon forgotten as she gazed into his face.

So many thoughts raced through my mind. I wondered, *How can anyone see a newborn and not believe there is a God, the Master Designer of all life?* His tiny fingers and toes, bright eyes and button nose—all were perfectly formed. How could anything this perfect, this miraculous, just evolve? With the controversy over abortion, I cannot understand how there could be any choice other than that of life.

I was also reminded of what a blessing children are and what a gift from God they are to us (Psalm 127:3). They are placed in our keeping for such a short time, ours to nurture and guide into adulthood. They are given to us only to be given back to God in dedication.

Along with the awesome responsibility of raising children comes the joy and the blessing. Jesus tells us in Matthew 18:5, "And whoso shall receive one such little child in my name receiveth me." As we receive these "little blessings" into our lives, we do so as unto the Lord. He is the One who bids, "Suffer little children, and forbid them not, to come unto me: for of such is the kingdom of heaven" (Matthew 19:14).

REMEMBER TODAY: Count your "little blessings" as gifts from God.

Brenda Pettyjohn	**Related Scriptures**	**June 30**
Locust Grove, OK	Luke 4:4; 1 John 1:1; John 6:67, 68	Luke 5:5

And Simon answering said unto him, Master, we have
toiled all the night, and have taken nothing: nevertheless
at thy word I will let down the net (Luke 5:5).

AT THY WORD

"Daddy, please help me!" These words dug deep into my heart as my husband and I sat nursing our son who had been hospitalized for almost six weeks after having been diagnosed with leukemia. The initial treatment for leukemia bombards the body with intense doses of chemotherapy. Our son's little 7-year-old body was barely able to suffer the effects of these treatments.

During one of the many times his father and I stood over his bedside, washing his weathered face after he had become violently ill from a treatment, he looked into his father's eyes and desperately pleaded, "Daddy, please help me!"

At that moment we felt as the disciples did when Jesus had asked them to launch out into the deep and let down their nets again. They had fished all night and had nothing to show for it. Would one more time make a difference? Was the Lord able to help them now after all their work?

We had been toiling six hard weeks, praying and expecting, but to no avail! Now, with our only son longing for an answer, were we truly able to help him?

Yet, through all our questioning we could hear Simon's reply to the Lord, and we also replied, "Nevertheless, at Thy word."

There will never be a time convenient for us to give up! At our deepest, darkest hour God's Word speaks to us with the ever-present help we need. Just like the miraculous healing of our son, through God's Word we can find answers for all of life's questions.

REMEMBER TODAY: We can always rely on God's Word.

Freeda May	**Related Scriptures**	**July 1**
Cleveland, TN	Romans 8:37; 1 Corinthians 10:13; 15:57	2 Corinthians 12:9

*And he said unto me, My grace is sufficient for thee: for my
strength is made perfect in weakness* (2 Corinthians 12:9).

GRACE FOR EVERY NEED

I was raised by Christian parents and was taught at an early age to trust the Lord and to believe that His grace was sufficient for all our needs. A trying experience in my life proved beyond any doubt that there is grace for every need.

I had gone to the library to pick up some books for my son, Danny, and me. One of the members of our church came into the library with her daughter-in-law while we were there. As we were leaving, she began accusing me of something that wasn't true. She was talking loudly, and suddenly I felt pity for her and her lack of direction. I told her I wasn't going to argue with her and started to walk away. This made her angry. She approached me from behind and slapped my face. Then she said, "And the Bible says to turn the other cheek." She then slapped the other side, scratching my face and neck. The grace of God restrained me, or I would have slapped her back. The Lord helped me feel pity for her instead of anger.

I took Danny by the hand and walked down the street, with tears streaming down both our faces.

My husband came home later and wanted to know what had happened. He knew it wasn't my nature to accept this kind of action with meekness, but he was thankful that I had.

God's grace is sufficient in times of trials. He sees our pain and sorrow and heals our hurt. He is right by our side when we need Him. Trust Him and He will never fail you.

REMEMBER TODAY: He doesn't let us fight our battles alone but is by our side fighting for us.

Ruth Starnes Craven	**Related Scriptures**	**July 2**
Greenwood, SC	Deuteronomy 6:7; 1 Thessalonians 4:9	Psalm 71:17

O God, thou hast taught me
from my youth (Psalm 71:17).

HALLOWED REMEMBRANCES

Fireside remembrances are hallowed moments, where tender love from parents pour forth in rapturous note. We learn through the tender care of loving parents that God is a heavenly Father who watches over us.

I can recall my early childhood in a little town where everyone knew everyone else's business. Our English teacher lived down the street, and it was not uncommon for her to visit us. On holidays everyone participated in social gatherings. We had homemade ice cream and cookies, and all the young people competed in games. During summer evenings the children gathered under the lampposts to catch lightning bugs or swap stories, while the adults rocked comfortably on the front porches. Even now, the laughter of children, the pungent smell of fresh-baked bread and the fragrance from daffodils blooming in the yard all spark pleasant memories in my heart.

In those days there were no drugs, robberies or Satan worship to fear. We seldom locked our doors. On Sunday church bells tolled, beckoning us to gather for worship in God's house. The public school also participated in church affairs. How proud we were at Easter time to dress up in costumes, march down the aisle at church behind the American flag, recite poems and join together in singing patriotic songs! It is so different now, but I am thankful for the memories.

REMEMBER TODAY: It is up to us as parents to cultivate hallowed memories for our children.

Evelyn Roset
Moose Jaw, Saskatchewan

Related Scriptures
Hebrews 12:2; Jude 24

July 3
Hebrews 2:10

For it became him, for whom are all things, and by whom are all things, in bringing many sons unto glory, to make the captain of their salvation perfect through sufferings (Hebrews 2:10).

THROUGH THE STORM

"We will bite the bullet and go in." This was the captain's voice coming over the speakers on our flight from Toronto, Ontario, to Charlotte, North Carolina.

My trip began from Regina, Saskatchewan, to Toronto, and now we were nearing our destination. An hour earlier the captain informed us that a storm was passing through Charlotte Airport and he could not receive clearance to land. We would be circling about 75 miles outside of Charlotte over Virginia for 15 to 20 minutes. The message was repeated two more times before he received clearance to land. He said the storm hadn't passed and we would have a rough ride as we went down, but "we will bite the bullet and go in."

Somehow it seemed impossible that a storm was raging. We were flying above the billowy white clouds in the sunshine at 8 p.m. in July. But as the plane descended, darkness covered us. Lightning flashed, the rain poured, the air was turbulent. With the captain's skill and our heavenly Father's care, we landed safely.

We are on the journey of life with heaven as our destination. It would be so nice and comfortable to go through life without a single storm, dark cloud or any frustrating delays. But we have no need to fear when we have Jesus, the captain of our salvation. He is able to guide us through the storms of life and see us safely home.

When things look dark, let us "bite the bullet" by sinking our spiritual teeth into the living Bread and go through with our captain, the Lord Jesus Christ.

REMEMBER TODAY: Through sufferings, Jesus purchased our salvation that He might bring us safely to the Father.

Sharon Powell
Baton Rouge, LA

Related Scriptures
Proverbs 8:14; Colossians 3:23

July 4
Philippians 4:13

I can do all things through Christ which strengtheneth me (Philippians 4:13).

THROUGH HIS STRENGTH

On July 4, 1975, the Lord spoke to my husband at the North Georgia Camp Meeting and called him to preach. Our daughter was 4 years old, and we were expecting our second child. We owned a beautiful home and had a successful career. According to society, we had it made!

When my husband came home from camp meeting that evening, he told me the Lord had called him into full-time ministry. I became apprehensive and said, "Oh no, let's pray." I was a quiet, bashful and timid person. I immediately thought, *Lord, I can't do this.* I honestly felt God had called the wrong couple. At that point, I fell on my knees and began to intercede. During that hour of prayer, God spoke to my heart and said, "Daughter, you are called too. I will give you peace that passes all understanding."

I then turned to my husband and said, "With God, all things are possible."

Since that day God has blessed our ministry abundantly. We have pastored for 16 years and presently are pastoring the Villa Del Rey Church of God in Baton Rouge, Louisiana. During those early years of ministry, God changed me from a quiet, bashful and timid girl to a woman with godly boldness.

The writer of Philippians 4:13 says, "I can do all things through Christ which strengtheneth me." Whatever you are called to do, stand on this scripture, for our strength comes from the Lord.

REMEMBER TODAY: Do everything as unto the Lord, for He is your strength.

Margaret W. Lackey
Mount Holly, NC

Related Scriptures
Matthew 21:22; John 14:13; 16:24;
Ephesians 3:20

July 5
Matthew 7:7, 8

Ask, and it shall be given you; seek, and ye shall find; knock, and it shall be opened unto you: for every one that asketh receiveth, and he that seeketh findeth; and to him that knocketh it shall be opened (Matthew 7:7, 8).

THE VALUE OF PRAYER

As we drove to church on Sunday evening, dark heavy rain clouds hung in the distance, giving an eeriness to the beautiful blue summer sky behind us. Suddenly, without warning, rain was beating in torrents upon our car.

Our 3-year-old son, Reed, buckled in the armrest between my husband and me, yelled, "Turn it down, it's raining too loud, turn it down!"

"Honey," I responded, "God sends the rain. We have no control over it. We can't turn it down."

Without hesitation, Reed looked straight up into the sky and called out, "God, please turn it down. It's raining too loud!"

We drove immediately out of the rain.

Reed smiled a confident grin, stretched out his little hands to gesture his approval and announced, "See, I just telled Him to turn it down, and He stopped the raining."

This may sound like a mere coincidence, a typical summer rain into which one could drive in and out in a matter of minutes, but it was more than that to me. It proved to a 3-year-old the reality of God's promise, "Ask, and ye shall receive" (John 16:24).

That promise was instilled in me as a child, and through the years I have learned to trust it. Prayer is one of the most valuable assets in life. Answers do not always come as quickly as Reed's. Some are years in coming. Sometimes God says, "Wait a while." Other times, He says, "No, I have a better plan for you." Reed asked Him to turn down the rain, and He brought the sunshine. Sometimes He gives us more than we ever hoped for or dreamed could be possible. But always He answers prayer.

REMEMBER TODAY: God longs to fill the empty places in our lives. All He requires is faith and obedience.

Pat McBride
Grand Rapids, MN

Related Scriptures
2 Thessalonians 3:13; Matthew 5:44:
Ephesians 6:10; Romans 12:2: 8:37

July 6
Galatians 6:9

*Let us not be weary in well doing: for in due
season we shall reap, if we faint not (Galatians 6:9).*

VICTORY IS YOURS!

Have you ever wanted to give up? Have you ever reached the point that you felt being the good guy wasn't producing fruit and you wanted to throw in the towel? Well, you are not alone.

Persistence is the key, so don't give up. In the midst of all opposition and circumstances that would conform us to this world, we are admonished in Scripture to hold fast to our confession of faith, to live a godly lifestyle, and to do good to those who persecute us and speak falsely against us.

"Be strong in the Lord, and in the power of his might" (Ephesians 6:10). You are not in the battle alone. You are more than a conqueror through Jesus Christ. The victory is yours.

REMEMBER TODAY: It is not by might nor by power, but by the Holy Spirit that we are able to stand (Zechariah 4:6).

Dione A. Clagg
Caldwell, ID

Related Scriptures
Matthew 10:31; 1 John 4:18

July 7
2 Timothy 1:7

God hath not given us the spirit of fear; but of power,
and of love, and of a sound mind (2 Timothy 1:7).

"FEAR HATH TORMENT"

The tree branches brushing against the outside of our wood- frame house caused my imagination to run wild. Peeking out from under the quilts on my bed, I suspiciously watched the shadows on the wall by the streetlight outside. This fear attacked again and again in the dead of night, always leaving me terrified under my blankets. I tried to shrink in my bed so I would not be seen by an intruder.

Sound familiar? Many times, however, unresolved childish fears follow us into our adult years. Women especially seem prone to attacks of fear and un-explained panic. I have marveled at how many people experience tormenting fears and accept it as a normal circumstance of life. The passage in 2 Timothy 1:7 says that fear is not given by God, but that God is the giver of power, love and a sound mind. He does not give us fear, nor does He want us to be controlled by these fears; therefore, He must have made provision for us.

Matthew 10:28-31 explains not one sparrow falls that God does not know and that we are more valuable than the sparrows. Because we are valuable, there must be a way we can counterattack these fears. The battle is in the mind; therefore, it can be combated in our minds with the knowledge and use of His Word.

I challenge all Spirit-filled women to study God's Word for answers to fear and other life problems. We are made overcomers by the blood of the Lamb and by the word of our testimony (Revelation 12:11).

REMEMBER TODAY: You are an overcomer! No weapon formed against you can prosper, whether instituted by Satan or man (see Isaiah 54:17).

Hazel P. Landreth
Tifton, GA

Related Scriptures
Psalm 34:19; Isaiah 43:2;
2 Corinthians 4:17; 12:9; 1 Peter 4:12, 13

July 8
Romans 8:28

And we know that all things work together
for good to them that love God, to them who are the
called according to his purpose (Romans 8:28).

NOTHING HAPPENS BY CHANCE

Take a look at a jigsaw puzzle. In the puzzle is quite a mixture of different parts—different colors, ugly shapes, odd sizes. Any one of these pieces, or any group of these pieces, without the entire number is of no value. If one piece is lost, the entire puzzle is useless. On the other hand, if all the different colors, ugly shapes and odd sizes are pieced together, they can form a beautiful picture.

So it is in our lives. All things that happen to us are not good, beautiful or just exactly what we want. Many times we have some tragic, unfortunate, disappointing, hurtful and distasteful things come our way. When all these things are put together—good and bad, beautiful and ugly, joyful and sorrowful—they work for our good.

If any one of these unfortunate things were left out, regardless of how bad, ugly or sorrowful, our lives would not be complete and all the other situations that have come our way could not work completely for our good. Remember, in the final analysis all that touches our lives will be blended together for our good.

The Bible says *all* things work together for our good because we love God and are called of Him.

REMEMBER TODAY: The promises of God are true, and He says, "I will never leave thee, nor forsake thee" (Hebrews 13:5).

Mary E. Graves	**Related Scripture**	**July 9**
Birmingham, AL	John 21:15-17	Song of Solomon 1:8

If thou know not, O thou fairest among women, go thy
way forth by the footsteps of the flock, and feed thy
kids beside the shepherds' tent (Song of Solomon 1:8).

"FEED THY KIDS"

My mother, a beautiful, dedicated and committed lady, had six children in addition to me. My father was the only medical doctor in the village and also in over half of the county. Consequently, they were very busy people. Early in life we learned that the church was all-important in their devotion to Christ. It was understood in our home that as long as we lived there, we would attend regularly and would give our services, our time and our money to the church. We were never allowed to criticize the minister or the members. We were taught, "They are the Lord's people; He will teach them and us."

As we grew older and began to make plans to leave home for higher education, jobs and marriage, mother gave us this verse from the Song of Solomon. She would interpret it like this: "'Go thy way forth by the footsteps of the flock' means to walk with the church (the flock). To 'feed thy kids beside the shepherds' tents' means to stay close to the church. When you have children, feed them by the shepherds' tent, or the church, where they will be fed God's Word and His truth."

My husband and I have brought up our three children with this same understanding. We have kept them close to the church. Through the years when I have ministered away from our home church, I have taken my three children with me. They have learned to love the church and its people. Now as they too are leaving home, I advise them as my mother advised me, "Stay close to the church. In it are the best friends you will ever have. Be a friend to those you meet in the church, and together Jesus will be the friend to all."

REMEMBER TODAY: Friends made among God's people are the dearest, truest, sweetest people in the world.

Evaline Echols	**Related Scriptures**	**July 10**
Cleveland, TN	Psalm 37:23; Philippians 3:13, 14	Psalm 23:1-3

*The Lord is my shepherd; I shall not want. He maketh me
to lie down in green pastures: he leadeth me beside the
still waters. He restoreth my soul (Psalm 23:1-3).*

LIFE'S TURNING POINTS—
GOD'S MEETING PLACES

In July 1978 I faced a major turning point in my life. Because of an automobile accident, I found myself lying in the hospital with a broken leg and hip. Twelve years later I realize that this turning point was preparing me for some steep curves in the road ahead.

One day when I was preparing to speak on "Life's Turning Points," I turned on the radio and heard Chuck Swindoll speaking on the same topic. He said that turning points have four characteristics: (1) They occur in the normal routine of our lives; (2) they are usually sudden and unexpected; (3) they impact the lives of others as well; and (4) they prompt changes in us that surprise others.

When we face a major turning point in our lives, we must not waste our time and energy looking back. In my time of devotion one morning, the Lord impressed me with this thought: "If I am looking back, I could miss the next turn in the road." In Philippians 3:13, 14, Paul admonishes us, "Forgetting those things which are behind, and reaching forth unto those things which are before, I press toward the mark for the prize of the high calling of God in Christ Jesus."

The turning point in my life became God's meeting place. When I was lying in the hospital, He spoke to me through Psalm 23. He said, "Evaline, I made you to lie down in green pastures. I am leading you beside the still waters. I am restoring your soul."

In retrospect I recognize that this turning point in my life—a time when I suffered physical pain—helped to prepare me for a sharp turn in the road about three years later when I would suffer emotional pain. After the dissolution of a marriage of 25 years, I learned that a broken leg heals faster than a broken heart. But I also learned that God meets us at every turn in the road.

REMEMBER TODAY: Life's turning points can become God's meeting places.

Brenda Combs	**Related Scriptures**	**July 11**
Taylor Mill, KY	Proverbs 3:5, 6; Matthew 6:25-34; 1 Peter 5:7	Psalm 37:5

Commit thy way unto the Lord; trust also in him;
and he shall bring it to pass (Psalm 37:5).

CHOOSE TO TRUST

The young child stared in wide-eyed wonder as I picked him up from the portable carrier. For several minutes I cuddled, played with, and talked to that small, beautiful bundle of life. To my delight, he did not cry or indicate any displeasure. He seemed pleased with the attention, occasionally rewarding me with laughter.

As I returned the child to the carrier, I was suddenly stricken with the knowledge that in those few minutes I had wielded absolute control over someone who was helpless to protest. He was completely at my mercy, dependent upon my ability to preserve and protect him.

God, our heavenly Father, desires that we, His children, yield our lives completely to Him. His sovereignty dictates that He who has created us will surely perform that which is in our best interest. "And we know that all things work together for good . . ." (Romans 8:28).

Everyone is faced with the harsh realities of life—unforeseen circumstances, bitter losses, stinging reproof, certain disappointment, "screaming" demands, relentless pressures. This constant bombardment upon our lives often provokes us to undesirable attitudes and actions—maybe even to the point that we sometimes despair of life.

"Casting all your care upon him; for he careth for you" (1 Peter 5:7). What assurance! What consolation! We can approach a loving God who will accept us as we are, with all the baggage that accompanies us. In childlike faith we commit to Him our wills, our needs, our cares, knowing our God is sufficient and will supply the need as we trust in Him. "Trust in the Lord with all thine heart" (Proverbs 3:5).

REMEMBER TODAY: Be confident that God is working His will for your life this very day.

Deborah W. Childers
Doraville, GA

*Ponder the path of thy feet, and let all
thy ways be established* (Proverbs 4:26).

THE SCENIC OVERLOOK

We were traveling through the beautiful Smoky Mountains of Tennessee, winding our way up a steep mountainside. The curves of the road were sharp and treacherous; visibility was limited. As we neared the top of the mountain, a sign read "Scenic Overlook." We pulled in and got out of our car to enjoy the view. It was a beautiful sight . . . how different the winding curves and deep crevices appeared from the height of the overlook. The road no longer looked dangerous but was part of a spectacular view! The scenic overlook was an option for us as motorists. If we had not stopped, we might have reached our destination sooner, but we would have missed the beautiful view.

What do we as Christians gain from stopping for the "scenic overlook"? First, we alleviate tension and tiredness, giving ourselves time to refresh and reflect. Isaiah 40:31 says, "They that wait upon the Lord shall renew their strength." Second, we expand our view. Our visibility is no longer limited to what's immediately in front of us. Third, we can look back over the road we just traveled, gaining new perspective about where we came from. Finally, we can share the beauty of our surroundings with others who are traveling with us.

In your Christian journey, have you taken time to stop at a scenic overlook to look back over the road you've traveled? Taking time to "ponder the path" we have traveled helps us to see more clearly how God has established our way. Psalm 37:23 says, "The steps of a good man are ordered by the Lord: and he delighteth in his way."

REMEMBER TODAY: Taking time to stop for the "scenic overlook" helps us gain a new perspective on our life's journey.

Lexie Golden
Joliet, IL

Related Scriptures
Philippians 1:6; Hebrews 11:6;
Romans 8:28

July 13
1 Thessalonians 5:24

*Faithful is he that calleth you, who
also will do it* (1 Thessalonians 5:24).

IN HIS SERVICE

We met a lady who had just prayed and received salvation. We invited her and her children to ride our church bus to Sunday school. She expressed concern for her family needs and wanted to learn more about how to be a Christian wife and mother. She began by having studies in her home.

Weeks went by and she remained hopeful but somewhat skeptical until God revealed His power through an accident in her own yard. As I was leaving her home one day, I heard her say, "Watch out for the hole we dug." Too late! We both heard my ankle bone crack, as if it had broken.

I sat there in pain as she inquired, "What are you going to do now, Teach?"

The implications of the question seemed to be testing my faith, so I said, "Pray with me." In God's mercy, He answered. We both heard my ankle bone crack again as if going back in place. I walked out of the hole! Immediately the pain left, and I was able to return to work as if the accident had never happened.

The new convert was overwhelmed and rejoiced to see God's miraculous power manifested before her eyes. She talked about it for days! Her doubts were weakened and her faith grew stronger. She began to believe God for other needs. Her husband, children and other family members were saved. The last report I heard, she was still believing God and teaching a Sunday school class!

He who had called me to share the things I knew about God had been faithful to do it!

REMEMBER TODAY: God calls every Christian into His service; allow the Spirit to use your life to bless another.

Ellen B. French	**Related Scriptures**	**July 14**
Cleveland, TN	Psalm 37:23; Proverbs 3:5	Proverbs 3:6

In all thy ways acknowledge him, and
he shall direct thy paths (Proverbs 3:6).

SUBMITTING TO GOD

In the summer of 1941 my husband and I, together with our two small sons and an infant, had passage to sail from San Francisco aboard the *S.S. President Harrison* for the Orient. The purchasing and packing were well in hand, and we were eager to begin ministry in the land of our calling: India. "Lord, direct every aspect of our lives as we make this move" was our constant prayer.

Shortly before we were to leave for the West Coast to board, two unexpected things occurred. First, the State Department announced that because of tensions with Japan, passports for women and children would soon be invalid for travel to the Far East. Second, the Missions Board notified us that our departure for India would be postponed.

My husband hurried to Cleveland to plead that we be allowed to go to India while we could or that he be permitted to go ahead, with the family to follow as soon as possible. When his requests were denied, he returned home crushed in spirit. The *President Harrison* sailed without us.

We wrestled with the larger question: Why—so near to our goal—were we denied the opportunity to go forward? We had prepared for years for this moment. Eventually, however, we committed the unanswered questions to a loving Father, who guides His own into paths of His choosing.

At times in our Christian walk, guidance is given to us personally by the Holy Spirit; at other times, guidance comes from those who are over us in the Lord. And at those times, the Word says, "Obey . . . and submit yourselves: for they watch for your souls" (Hebrews 13:17).

Can you imagine our state of mind when we learned that the *President Harrison* had been bombed and sunk in the China Sea the day after Pearl Harbor, with all lives lost? With what perfect hindsight we could now understand and thank God for overruling our own wishes!

In God's time we went to India and from there continued a lifetime of ministry spanning 55 years—all because our Father directed our paths, even in ways we did not understand at the time.

REMEMBER TODAY: I will submit myself to God's guidance, even if I do not fully understand, and I will praise Him continually, knowing that to trust Him in the darkness is the highest expression of faith in His perfect will for me.

Sharon K. Bass   **Related Scriptures**   **July 15**
Anchorage, AK   Philippians 4:19; Psalms 23:1; 24:1; 50:10   Matthew 6:8

"Your Father knows what you need
before you ask him" (Matthew 6:8, NIV).

GOD WILL SUPPLY

We were pastoring a small church in a rural town in southern Illinois. I was soon to give birth to my second child. My husband and I were experiencing financial difficulty. Many people in our congregation were losing their jobs.

I shared with my husband that I needed a new gown for my stay in the hospital. Uncomfortably, he walked toward me and said, "We just don't have the money."

I tried to pretend I didn't need one after all, but because of the emotional stress I was experiencing, the tears began to flow. I should have trusted Jesus to supply my need as He had done many times before. But I was going through a time of questioning. My husband quickly changed the subject and said, "Well, why don't we have breakfast? I want some pancakes." I told him we didn't have the ingredients to make pancakes. So he drank a cup of coffee and left. He was going to visit a couple who didn't attend our church but had requested a visit.

It wasn't long before he returned with grocery sacks in his arms and an envelope in his hand. The couple he visited said the Lord spoke to them to share their groceries. The first thing they gave him was a box of pancake mix and a bottle of syrup. On his way out the door, the lady called him back and handed him an envelope that contained 20 dollar bills.

He handed me the envelope and said, "Let's go get that new gown." It was then I realized God's Word is true. "God will meet all . . . [our] needs according to his glorious riches in Christ Jesus" (Philippians 4:19, *NIV*).

❦

REMEMBER TODAY: No matter how great or how small, God can meet your needs.

Gladys Thomas
Weatherford, TX

Related Scripture
Isaiah 55:8

July 16
Mark 14:36

Abba, Father, all things are possible unto thee; take away this cup from me: nevertheless not what I will, but what thou wilt (Mark 14:36).

USE ME, LORD!

I am only what I am and I cannot add stature to my height nor a hair to my head. I cannot change my life and make it what it once was, but I can daily offer my vessel to the Lord, submitting it to Him for His purpose each day.

I am a vessel, a temple or a dwelling place for the Lord, and I offer Him this house to abide in. He used a raven to feed a man of God, and He even used a rooster and a donkey to speak His truth. He also used a little squirrel to speak to me when I was frustrated and questioning, "Why, Lord?"

Following brain surgery and many complications, my husband could no longer pastor. He had been a caring and compassionate pastor for over 26 years. Suddenly I found myself sitting under the pastoral leadership of other men in what I felt to be a strange land. It seemed the devil was out to devour pastors that year. I found fault with some of the pastors, especially in areas of compassion. At times they lashed out at people instead of staying in the Word.

One lonely day I carried a quilt to the backyard and made a pallet. The yard was surrounded by trees and vacant lots. I began to pour my heart out to the Lord. I knew He loved me; many good things had happened, and I could see His hand working. Yet, the frustration and questions poured from my lips. Suddenly I saw a little squirrel climbing a tree upside down. In his squirrel language he began to talk to me.

The tears stopped; all my attention was focused on the little critter. After 20 to 30 minutes of this visitor's sermon, I said, "Little squirrel, I wish I could understand you, but I don't understand anything you are saying."

Then the Lord spoke to me and said, "If I tried to give you an answer to all your questions concerning your husband's illness, you could understand no better than you do this little squirrel."

That day the Lord challenged me to a new commitment. I recognized His ways and His thoughts are far above mine. I am to be a yielded vessel for His use.

REMEMBER TODAY: Lord, fill us with Your goodness so that we may follow in Your great example of submission.

Barbara Henderson
Akron, OH

Related Scriptures
Matthew 6:33; 1 Corinthians 7:29;
Ephesians 5:16

July 17
Ecclesiastes 3:1, 2, 8

*To every thing there is a season, and a time to every purpose under
the heaven: a time to be born, and a time to die; a time to plant, and a
time to pluck up that which is planted . . . a time to love, and a time
to hate; a time of war, and a time of peace* (Ecclesiastes 3:1, 2, 8).

TIME

Sixty seconds make a minute. How much good can I do with it?
Sixty minutes make an hour. I'll do all that's in my power.
Twenty-four hours make a day,
Time for work and time for play.

—From an old school reader

In today's world time is valuable. It is a precious item. We all have the same
amount of it, but some people just seem to get more out of their 24 hours.

We live in a society where things are automatic—push-button and instant.
Yet we seem to have less time to get things accomplished than ever before.
When it comes to things for God and His kingdom, we have all heard, "I just
didn't have time." Time is precious, and we should be good stewards of it.

Matthew 6:33 says, "Seek ye first the kingdom of God, and his righteousness; and all these things shall be added unto you." Do we have our priorities
in order? In looking back over the days, weeks and years of my life, there are
some things I would do differently. But that is past. Time can never be
recalled.

In 1 Corinthians 7:29 Paul said, "But this I say, brethren, the time is short."
The time we spend with God and His Word is never wasted but invested. It
will bring forth good fruit in our lives so we can be a blessing to those we touch
each day.

GOD'S MINUTE
I have only just a minute;
Only sixty seconds in it,
Forced upon me, can't refuse it.
Didn't seek it, didn't choose it.
I must suffer if I lose it,
Give account if I abuse it.
But eternity is in it.

—Author Unknown

REMEMBER TODAY: Make time today for God and His Word in your
personal life, in your home, in your church and in your place of work.

Jewell Vaught   **Related Scriptures**   July 18
Cleveland, TN   Numbers 6:24-26; Psalms 16:11; 32:8   Psalm 119:165

Great peace have they who love
your law (Psalm 119:165, NIV).

MOVING DAY

Relocating a family is not an easy task. We had lived in the same town for 27 years. Our children were born in that area and grew up there with many friends, making it very difficult for us to make a decision to relocate. However, when the Lord says move, you move!

Sadness, rebellion, disappointment and loneliness were some of the emotions we had to deal with. On Sunday morning, July 18, 1980, we left our oldest daughter and her family, our youngest daughter's boyfriend, many precious friends, a beautiful home, and our youngest son's school in Minot, North Dakota. He was to enter his senior year of high school in August and was, understandably, very disturbed, since he was in the marching band, concert band, choir and other special activities. He had told us he was going to stay there and finish high school. With much persuasion, counseling and prayer, he came along with us. God honored his decision. He found that the Lord blesses His children when they obey Him.

Our trip to Cleveland, Tennessee, began early on that Sunday morning. I had visited Cleveland several times and did not feel I could be happy living in the fast lane. We had prayer before beginning the trip, asking the Lord to guide, protect and encourage each of us. We moved ourselves. My husband and oldest son drove a U-Haul truck, towing one car, and I drove the second car, accompanied by our two teenagers.

We were separated in St. Louis, Missouri. Believe me, we prayed for many miles that we would see the U-Haul along the highway. That didn't happen. Finally, in desperation, we turned the car around, watching with keen eyes hoping to catch a glimpse of them. The Lord answered our prayer! We found them at a truck stop eating lunch and anxiously waiting for us to arrive. They thought we were behind them. Our spirits were lifted because we knew God was with us.

Arriving at our new home and new community was an exciting time. Finding a new church home and meeting new friends was a blessing to each of us. Our children had been involved in school activities, in the church and in the community at our former location, and we were anxious to see them become involved again. This was our prayer that God would speak to their hearts and lead them in His path—which He did!

Now we can say that peace and joy can be found in following the Lord and loving His law. Our lives have been touched by many wonderful people, and it is our desire to be able to touch others for Him.

REMEMBER TODAY: God directs our paths and gives us peace, joy and understanding when we trust Him.

Mae Smith
Dublin, GA

Related Scriptures
Numbers 23:19; 2 Chronicles 20:20;
Luke 1:45; Romans 4:20, 21;
2 Timothy 1:12; Titus 1:2

July 19
Acts 27:25

*Wherefore, sirs, be of good cheer: for I believe God,
that it shall be even as it was told me* (Acts 27:25).

BELIEVING GOD

During the early days of our ministry, my husband and I learned to live by faith. As trials came, we triumphed by seeking God's help through prayer and fasting. God never failed us, though the trials did seem to get bigger each time they came. God was simply building our faith in Him.

One incident especially tried our faith and patience. We had a 2-year-old, I was pregnant with our second child, and my husband was pastoring his first church and going to college full- time. Together with the normal stress of such circumstances, a special need arose. As the battle raged, we prayed and asked others to pray. At one point I became so weary that I just wanted to go home and be with my family until the storm was over.

However, God reminded me of Paul's journey and his shipwreck, recorded in Acts 27. As I read the account, the points which really drew my attention were Paul's exhortation to "abide" on board and his encouragement to believe God. I clung to this through the remainder of the crisis. It wasn't long before God "whose I am, and whom I serve" (v. 23) moved in our behalf as He did for Paul and his shipmates. Now when trials come, I find tremendous comfort in knowing I am God's child, that I serve Him, and that His help is on the way if I will only abide in Him and believe His Word.

REMEMBER TODAY: The safest place to weather the storm is in Christ. His Word is trustworthy in all circumstances.

Diane Falco
West Babylon, NY

Related Scriptures
Genesis 22:1-14; Philippians 2:13;
1 Samuel 15:22, 23

July 20
Genesis 22:14

*Abraham called the name of that
place Jehovah-jireh* (Genesis 22:14).

THE LORD WILL PROVIDE

Everything seemed to be going along smoothly. My husband had become a believer, and we were finally becoming the Christian family I had always dreamed we would be. I had a large house in the suburbs, two beautiful children, and now a husband who loved Jesus and enjoyed taking his family to church.

Then something totally unexpected happened. After a routine checkup our 4-year-old son was diagnosed as having a hole in his heart. He had been born with a heart murmur, which was continually monitored. Now the doctor said if our son did not have surgery to close the hole, he would never be normal. Our pastor prayed, the church prayed, our Bible-study group prayed, but nothing seemed to change.

Then at an altar service one Sunday morning, the Lord spoke to our hearts as He had spoken to Abraham's in Genesis 22:2: "Take now thy son, thine only son . . . whom thou lovest . . . and offer him there for a burnt-offering. . . ." Offer our son for a burnt offering? How? Why? The anxiety, fear, doubt and confusion was overwhelming, but pleasing God was all that mattered. So my husband lifted our son up to the Lord in a sacrificial manner. God not only healed our son, but He also called my husband into full-time ministry.

In today's scripture, Abraham called that place where God supplied a ram for sacrifice "Jehovah-jireh," meaning "The Lord will provide." This name of God reveals His character: God knows exactly what we need and provides at just the right time. God himself provided the strength *after* we chose to obey.

God has given us salvation through the sacrifice of His Son on the cross. He wasn't looking for another sacrifice but another heart. When we face hard situations, God provides the power through the Holy Spirit for us to do what He asks. "For it is God who works in you to will and to act according to his good purpose" (Philippians 2:13, *NIV*).

How reassuring to know that when the tasks ahead seem overwhelming, the Lord will provide—Jehovah-jireh. "I know that thou fearest God, seeing thou hast not withheld thy son, thine only son from me" (Genesis 22:12).

REMEMBER TODAY: Don't be afraid to give God everything; where God guides, He provides.

Sherry B. Lee
Cleveland, TN

Related Scripture
Ephesians 4:8

July 21
Ephesians 4:11, 12

*And he gave ... for the perfecting [equipping] of the
saints, for the work of the ministry* (Ephesians 4:11, 12).

TOOLBOX ANSWERS

Flashing lights had been visible for some distance as our family auto sped down the long, flat Florida highway. Visibility of the accident increased as our car drew closer.

We were separated, however, from the actual scene by a long line of detained motorists who had spread themselves and their vehicles the width of the two-lane road. Most appeared to have been waiting for some time. People were on the grass, on top of cars, some laughing, some scowling.

As our car slowed to a stop, one idle motorist pointed to my left front tire and yelled, "Your tire is going flat."

Within minutes my husband and 11-year-old son evaluated the situation and began unpacking a week's worth of vacation luggage to reach the little spare stored in the trunk.

We had never changed a tire on this new car with all its modern equipment and those beautiful spoked hubcaps. Out came the instruction booklet! "The wrench may be found in the glove compartment to unlock the hubcaps," the instructions read. The search was made. Twice. No wrench. The locked hubcap seemed to grin at us. We wondered how we would ever figure our way out of this one.

A friend and his family joined the waiting line a few cars behind us. He immediately came to offer assistance. "For some reason, the Lord put it in my heart to pack my toolbox before I left home," he said.

Within minutes the formidable hubcap lay dismantled. The little spare was mounted, and we were ready to ride.

How many times in life have I sought answers to apparently insurmountable difficulties! With my head buried in the pain of the problem, I couldn't see God's toolbox, just lying there ... waiting ... available to me.

God has equipped each of His saints for life and the work of ministry. He has a tool for every situation needing "fixing." Our responsibility is to keep the tools sharpened, available, ready for the testing time.

REMEMBER TODAY: God will provide the tools if we will do the work of the ministry.

Emeline Gayle
Brooklyn, NY

Related Scriptures
Psalm 62:8; Luke 1:37

*And all things, whatsoever ye shall ask in prayer,
believing, ye shall receive* (Matthew 21:22).

SEEKING GOD THROUGH PRAYER

Everyone faces a crisis sometime in life. The outcome of such a problem depends on the help available to us. God's power can be released through prayer if we rely on Him through His Word. "Trust in . . . [the Lord] at all times; ye people, pour out your heart before him: God is a refuge for us" (Psalm 62:8).

In 1979 my world began to fall apart when my doctor diagnosed that I had cancer in the second stage. Knowing the devastating outcome of this disease, I realized my only hope was in God. Each day as my need became more urgent, the fervency of my prayer became stronger. I could not allow my faith to waver. The Lord comforted my heart with these words: "For with God nothing shall be impossible" (Luke 1:37). I held on with faith.

During surgery a test was done, which revealed there was no trace of cancer. I knew God had come through for me.

Seeking God through prayer is an important part of life; therefore, we should not wait until we have a crisis before we seek Him. Twelve years have passed, and I am still praying and praising my God for answering prayer.

REMEMBER TODAY: Jesus offers sweet peace and comfort amid the storms of life.

Brenda A. McGarity	**Related Scriptures**	**July 23**
McCalla, AL	1 Chronicles 28:9; Psalms 19:14; 26:2;	Philippians 4:8
	2 Peter 3:1	

Finally, brothers [sisters], whatever is true, whatever is noble, whatever is right, whatever is pure, whatever is lovely, whatever is admirable—if anything is excellent or praiseworthy— think about such things (Philippians 4:8, *NIV*).

"BEEP"—THINK AGAIN!

When I was acquiring computer skills, I would sit at the keyboard practicing for long periods of time. There were times when I tried to key in data or a particular function I wanted performed and the computer would "beep" at me. There were instances when I received a beep every time I pressed a key. Sometimes the beep would be followed by the question "Are you sure you want to do this?"

The brain of the computer was trying to tell me it had not been programmed to comprehend what I was trying to key in or that I was about to do something I might regret. I was being warned to think again!

As Christians we are equipped with a warning system, a beep, to warn us that we have permitted Satan to key in something we have not been programmed to think on.

Paul instructs us to think, to program our hearts and minds, with those things that are true, noble, right, pure, lovely and admirable. He says we should think on the excellent things that rise above the ordinary things of this world and have eternal value and on those things that have God's approval and are pleasing to Him.

We have the power to govern our thoughts and thus are responsible for them. We should program our minds with the study of the Word and think on good things.

REMEMBER TODAY: A "beep" should sound a warning when we are tempted to dwell on a thought that is contrary to what our Christian training has programmed us to think!

Alice Thomas
Cleveland, TN

Related Scriptures
Psalms 16:11; 36:9; 27:1

July 24
James 4:14

Whereas ye know not what shall be on the morrow.
For what is your life? It is even a vapour that appeareth
for a little time, and then vanisheth away (James 4:14).

LIFE'S CANVAS

Let's call an artist and ask him to paint a picture of our lives. What size canvas will he need to depict our deeds? What colors and hues will he use? Will he use dark, stormy colors, or will he use soft, gentle ones? All this will depend on the way we have lived and the things we have done. What is our choice?

Do we choose to serve God? His Spirit invites us to choose Him, but we are never forced. We make our life what it is. "Thou wilt shew me the path of life" (Psalm 16:11). How beautiful to know that Jesus walks with us, guiding our footsteps.

"For with thee is the fountain of life" (Psalm 36:9). How refreshing is a cool drink of water when we are thirsty! A touch of the Master is as refreshing to the soul as cool water to the body. He is the fountain of living water.

"The Lord is the strength of my life; of whom shall I be afraid?" (Psalm 27:1). Nations are striving for power in order to control the world. Satan constantly tries to gain control of our lives. He has many ways to buffet our souls, but God is our strength.

According to God's calendar, life is short. It is compared to the wind, a vapor or the grass of the field. What kind of picture does the artist have on the canvas? Does it depict a life of restless turmoil, disobedience, careless ways? Or is it a faithful, peaceful life with beautiful hues of joy, love, kindness, patience, devotion and serenity?

As God looks at the canvas, may He be pleased and say, "Well done, faithful servant."

REMEMBER TODAY: The way we live each day will determine where we will live in eternity.

Donna Moore	**Related Scriptures**	**July 25**
Arleta, CA	Ezra 4:1; 13, John 17:15	Ezra 5:3

Who hath commanded you to build this
house, and to make up this wall? (Ezra 5:3).

BY WHOSE AUTHORITY DO YOU BUILD THIS HOUSE?

The adversaries of Judah and Benjamin had observed that the city was being rebuilt and the walls erected again. Jerusalem's walls were torn down, the Temple was destroyed, the houses were in confusion. Only the altar stood.

Daily offerings were sacrificed on the altar and there was great desire to rebuild the Temple. But there was also great opposition. It didn't happen overnight. Rebuilding the Temple took almost 20 years. Their enemies even sent a letter to King Artaxerxes saying that if the walls were rebuilt, the people would not pay toll, tribute and custom to the king (Ezra 4:13).

As parents we must build our house, making it safe and secure. Too often children are not protected and are subjected to the influences of this world. They are exposed to all kinds of "kings"—crime, drugs and gang violence, to name a few.

In our society we cannot escape exposure to such, but we can keep our home in good repair and surround it with a wall of love, understanding and an open channel of communication. Then our youth will not be tempted to pay toll, tribute or custom to the kings of this world. As Jesus prayed in John 17:15, "I pray not that thou shouldest take them out of the world, but that thou shouldest keep them from the evil."

Just as King Darius came to the rescue of the Israelites, One greater than he will give us the wisdom to build our house and reset the walls. His name is King Jesus, the greatest authority of all time.

REMEMBER TODAY: Of all our earthly possessions, our families are our greatest asset. Let's claim them through the power and authority of Jesus Christ.

Monica Stewart   **Related Scriptures**   **July 26**
Boise, ID   Proverbs 3:5; Philippians 1:21; 4:13;   1 Corinthians 15:55
                                                    John 11:25; 14:27

O death, where is thy sting? O grave,
where is thy victory? (1 Corinthians 15:55).

TO DIE IS GAIN

It was a beautiful July morning in Dallas. As I gazed from the hospital window, the sun was shining brightly against the tall skyscrapers downtown.

The doctor told my husband and me not to worry or be concerned about this type of heart surgery; she was a strong 15-year-old. While we waited patiently for the doctor's report, I filled my mind with the Word of God. As the doctor entered the waiting room, our hearts were gripped with fear. In the ministry, we had seen that look many times as a doctor came to speak with a family. He could not look directly into our eyes. With his head held low, he explained to us that he had made a mistake and damaged our daughter's heart. "She is still alive," he said, "but very critical. You may see her shortly in the Intensive Care Unit."

As her daddy entered the room, her eyes became filled with tears. She could not speak because of the tubes in her throat. As he held her hand, she began writing things in the palm of his hand: "I love you, Daddy, and I love Jesus." Tears filled his eyes as he leaned over her and said, "I love you too, Sugar."

I stood beside her bed and gently stroked her beautiful brown hair. Putting my face very close to her face so that she could hear me, I began reading from the Word of God until she peacefully fell asleep.

Our hearts were breaking. We prayed, "Oh, God, what can we do? How can we go on if something should happen to one of our children?" The Word of God again became alive in my spirit. "Trust in the Lord with all thine heart" (Proverbs 3:5). Our beautiful daughter, Tammy Renee Stewart, went to be with Jesus, July 27, 1989. ". . . To live is Christ, and to die is gain" (Philippians 1:21).

If there is an empty chair at your table, a missing face in your family portrait, let me leave these words of comfort with you as my Comforter, Jesus, left them for me: "Let not your heart be troubled" (John 14:27). "I am the resurrection, and the life" (John 11:25).

REMEMBER TODAY: No matter what trials and tribulations come our way, we have God's Word: "I can do all things through Christ which strengtheneth me" (Philippians 4:13).

Pat Brock	**Related Scriptures**	**July 27**
Hamilton, OH	Isaiah 26:4; Jeremiah 17:7; Nahum 1:7	Proverbs 3:5

Trust in the Lord with all thine heart; and lean
not unto thine own understanding (Proverbs 3:5).

MEMORIES

The brain is a marvelous organ. In many ways it is like a colossal computer with unlimited memory recall. Every bit of incoming data has been stored in files of our memory, ready to be recalled at a moment's notice.

Sometimes a memory file jumps to the active window, even if we have not loaded it intentionally. However, most of the time a memory becomes active because we have "called it up." The dictionary tells us that a memory is the ability or power for retaining or reviving in the mind past thoughts, images and ideas. There are two ways to retrieve a memory.

Remembrance is the act of having events and things come to mind again. Recollection is the voluntary effort and detailed remembering of an event or thing.

Memories . . . I know what it is to deal with the good and the bad. Have you ever felt like you have had the very best that God could bless you with but experienced at the same time the worst that could come to you in life? We handle the good memories and blessings from our heavenly Father with great pride and joy! But for the bad memories, we let them steal our joy and sometimes damage our trust in God.

July 27, 1986, will always be that time of bad-memory recall for me. It was on that day that my energetic, fun-loving, handsome, black-haired, brown-eyed, 16-year-old son, who loved God with all his heart, was killed on his way home from church by a 19-year-old drunken driver.

Often I have quoted Proverbs 3:5, "Trust in the Lord with all thine heart; and lean not unto thine own understanding." So many times my human understanding asks why this happened. But we cannot torture ourselves with the good or bad memories.

REMEMBER TODAY: With our memories, good or bad, we must trust Him completely and lean heavily only on our Savior, the Lord Jesus Christ.

Wedis Webber
Alexandria, VA

Related Scripture
Luke 12:32, 34

July 28
Revelation 4:3

He who sat there was like a jasper and a sardius stone in appearance; and there was a rainbow around the throne, in appearance like an emerald (Revelation 4:3, *NKJV*).

TREASURES IN THE RAINBOW

I was in my late teens, married with two small children, and I felt my life was complete. In fact, I knew I had grasped the golden ring and found the treasure at the end of the rainbow.

After three and a half years, the glow began to fade from my life. Many things were going wrong, sometimes all at once! The golden ring began to tarnish, and the treasure lost its luster. Something was terribly wrong with me. I did not have all I thought I needed. In the midst of all this discontent, my precious mother was stricken with cancer.

Then Sister Johnson, a sweet child of God who was instrumental in leading me to Jesus Christ, crossed my path. She told me that if I would accept Jesus as my Lord and serve Him, He would heal my mother.

At this point, I had nowhere else to turn. I accepted Jesus as my Savior and turned my life over to God. Mother was healed and remains healthy to this day (see Isaiah 53:5; James 5:13-15).

At age 20 I preached my first revival. In a short time, the Lord saved my husband, called us into full-time ministry and brought spiritual unity into our marriage (see Acts 16:31). Throughout the years we have seen God pour out His treasures upon us as we have served Him.

Truly I have found that He is the treasure in the rainbow. All I need is found in His glory. To all who seek Him, He shall be found (Luke 11:9).

REMEMBER TODAY: It is His good pleasure to give you the Kingdom (Luke 12:32).

Barbara Fulbright
Cleveland, TN

Related Scriptures
Psalm 130:5; Isaiah 40:31;
Lamentations 3:25; Romans 8:24, 25;
2 Thessalonians 3:5

July 29
Psalm 27:14

*Wait on the Lord: be of good courage, and he shall strengthen
thine heart: wait, I say, on the Lord* (Psalm 27:14).

PATIENCE IN WAITING

As a high school student my greatest desire was to attend Lee College. I had studied hard and had favor with my teachers, but as time was winding down during my senior year, finances were not available for me to attend college. One night as I was agonizing with God about my hopeless situation, I fell down on my bed with tears streaming down my face thinking all my efforts had been in vain. Even though I was a good student, I would not be attending college in the fall.

As I concluded my "pity party," I noticed my Bible was lying open on the bed. My eyes fell on Psalm 27:14: "Wait on the Lord: be of good courage, and he shall strengthen thine heart: wait, I say, on the Lord."

Was God trying to tell me something? Was I—as usual—trying to take matters into my own hands and rush God? I prayed and asked God to forgive me and help me to trust Him for His will for my life. As I opened my eyes, I had a peace that whatever the outcome, everything was going to be all right. When my faith grew weak and I began to doubt, I would open my Bible to Psalm 27, read the entire chapter and feast on the 14th verse. "Wait on the Lord," I would tell myself. Surely God will provide. Wait, wait, wait. Since I was not a patient person, waiting was a difficult task.

Within a short period of time, I was awarded scholarships that covered my tuition, room and board for the first year. I also discovered that while waiting on the Lord, my hope was placed in His Word and my strength was renewed.

REMEMBER TODAY: Waiting may not come easy, but when we wait upon the Lord, our strength will be renewed.

Beatrice Burroughs
Baton Rouge, LA

Related Scriptures
Psalms 23:4; 30:5; 37:39

God is our refuge and strength, a
very present help in trouble (Psalm 46:1).

WHEN WINDS OF SORROW BLOW

July 30, 1966—a day I shall never forget. While I was teaching piano lessons on this Saturday morning, the phone rang. My daughter, Annette, answered the telephone and screamed, "My daddy has been in an automobile accident!" Shortly I heard the saddest news of my life: my husband had been killed.

At first I felt as though the world should stop turning. I didn't feel I could go on living without my companion, my spiritual guide, my best friend. During those next few days and weeks—making funeral arrangements, moving out of a parsonage I had called home for years (with no furniture of my own), and learning to live alone (since my daughter and sons were married)—I felt I would drown in my tears. For almost a year I couldn't hear the birds sing or smell the roses.

Raised in a minister's home, I had learned as a small child to love God and to lean on Him. The time had come for me to seek refuge in His loving care. I'll never forget how the Holy Spirit comforted me: "Weeping may endure for a night, but joy cometh in the morning" (Psalm 30:5). These words of comfort were like applying a salve of His anointing oil to my broken heart and wounded spirit.

Through the prayers of many friends and the support of a loving family, one day I walked out on the porch and said to myself, "The sun is shining again, and I can hear the birds singing." God was saying to me, "I am with you. I am your refuge from the storm. I am your strength."

I must admit during those first years I wanted to ask, "Why, God?" But I have learned that through sorrow we are brought closer to Him. I have had more sorrow since then, but I have also experienced much joy. I can honestly say I do not regret a mile I have traveled as a minister's wife, even those miles when the road was rocky. God has been with me every step of the way.

REMEMBER TODAY: He is our refuge when the winds of sorrow blow.

Marilyn Daugherty	**Related Scriptures**	**July 31**
Vanceburg, KY	Psalms 37:23; 139:1-18	1 Chronicles 16:22

Touch not mine anointed, and do my prophets no harm (1 Chronicles 16:22).

FULFILLED HOMEMAKER

I had formed a bad habit of staying up late. In those quiet hours I reflected on the day and took a little too much time thinking about my own personal problems. Watching TV had become a late-night habit.

All the beautiful career women seemed to be eternally young. Looking at my own reflection in the mirror wasn't encouraging. My skin no longer had that youthful glow, my hair was turning gray, and I had gained extra weight, the result of two babies. I began to beat myself up mentally. You're a slob! You're unfulfilled! You're wasting your life!

But was it really that bad? Didn't God love me? Didn't He have some special purpose for my life? Just because I'm a woman and a homemaker doesn't mean that my life has no value. When Abraham and Sarah were wandering in the wilderness, they faced many dangers. God later gave an admonition to all the kings and people to "touch not mine anointed, and do my prophets no harm."

Was Abraham the only one who was anointed? No! Sarah was anointed as well. She was to be the mother of a great nation. What a calling! God's calling! She was anointed and in the will of God by being exactly what He intended for her to be.

So what if I wasn't a doctor, a lawyer or even a TV personality! I was what God had intended for me to be—a good mother. Sure, I still have imperfections. My hair is still gray, I'm still overweight and still growing older, but I can live out my life knowing I am important. I am fulfilled. I am anointed of God!

REMEMBER TODAY: No matter how unimportant we may seem to this present world, we are of infinite worth to God—so much so that He gave all He had that we might live.

NOTES

Anna L. Pratt
Cleveland, TN

Related Scriptures
Matthew 2:7; Galatians 6:10;
Mark 1:15; Ecclesiastes 3:1-8

August 1
2 Corinthians 6:2

I tell you, now is the time of God's favor, now is the day of salvation (2 Corinthians 6:2, *NIV*).

USING OUR TIME WISELY

We are given 86,400 seconds, 1,440 minutes or 24 hours each day.

We can do what we want with this daily allotment: spend it, use it, waste it, kill it, invest it or just ignore it. But whatever we do with it, when the day is over, our time for that day will be gone. There is no way to save any of it. Someone has said, "Life is like a coin—you can spend it any way you want to, but you can spend it only once."

Whenever the New Testament writers referred to clock or calendar hours, they used the word *chronos* (Matthew 2:7). Scripture also speaks of another kind of time that is harder to calculate. *Kairos* means a certain period that is usually linked to an event or opportunity. As Paul wrote in Galatians 6:10, "Therefore, as we have opportunity [*kairos*], let us do good to all people" (*NIV*). Jesus began His public ministry by saying, " 'The time [*kairos*] has come. . . . The kingdom of God is near' " (Mark 1:15, *NIV*).

As we deal with our 86,400 seconds each day, we must think about both kinds of time. *Chronos* questions include "How can I be efficient? How can I be sure I am on time?" *Kairos* questions ask, "How can I be effective? How can I seize the opportunity and be timely?"

> *There is a time for everything, and a season for every activity under heaven: a time to be born and a time to die, a time to plant and a time to uproot, a time to kill and a time to heal, a time to tear down and a time to build, a time to weep and a time to laugh, a time to mourn and a time to dance, a time to scatter stones and a time to gather them, a time to embrace and a time to refrain, a time to search and a time to give up, a time to keep and a time to throw away, a time to tear and a time to mend, a time to be silent and a time to speak, a time to love and a time to hate, a time for war and a time for peace* (Ecclesiastes 3:1-8, *NIV*).

Even a casual glance at these contrasts reveals that life is full of opportunities. It is up to us to be aware of them and to use them wisely.

REMEMBER TODAY: Use your time wisely.

Joyce Bouschard Wingo   **Related Scriptures**   **August 2**
Lemont, IL   Proverbs 18:9; 21:20   John 6:12

*When they had all had enough to eat, he said
to his disciples, "Gather the pieces that are left over.
Let nothing be wasted" (John 6:12, NIV).*

ME? WASTEFUL?

I had read the miracle of the loaves and fish many times, but recently the principle of "Let nothing be wasted" was brought to my attention.

God strongly impressed me that Christians strive for excellence in every area of their lives, including wise stewardship of all resources, at home or on the job. I began hearing sayings like "If you watch the nickels and dimes, the dollars will take care of themselves" and this old Amish motto: "Use it up. Wear it out. Make it do, or do without." This began my conscious effort to follow the example of Christ and sincerely try to waste nothing.

When choosing dresses or casual clothing, my family and I have learned to grade our selections. If we can't give the dress an *A* or *A+*—we don't buy it. No matter how good the price, we know it would be worn only once or twice and result in money wasted.

Frequently we have food left after a meal. Leftover roast or chicken becomes barbecued sandwiches or enchiladas. Mashed potatoes become potato rolls or fried potato patties. When leftover quantities are small, they are packed into lunches or saved for the occasional end-of-the-week smorgasbord.

I have learned that adding water to an empty shampoo bottle will give me three or four more shampoos. This also works for conditioners and detergents.

Preventive maintenance pays big dividends. Having young children wash their hands when coming indoors and after eating helps keep the walls clean. Changing into slippers or clean shoes when entering the house, as well as vacuuming once or twice a week, eliminates the need for shampooing the carpet and extends its beauty. When we sold our 15-year-old home with 15-year-old carpets, the buyer said she selected our house "because the carpets were new."

Incorporating this principle into my life, along with others in God's Word, has resulted in basketfuls of blessings.

REMEMBER TODAY: Gather all the pieces that nothing be wasted.

Wanda Turner
Anchorage, AK

*Weeping may endure for a night, but joy
cometh in the morning* (Psalm 30:5).

REJOICING IN SORROW

During my father's illness, I spent many nights on a cot beside his bed in the hospital. These nights were long and filled with uncertainties. I slept very little, anxiously waiting for morning to come. At the first sign of dawn, my anxieties began to subside and my hope was renewed that the new day would bring something better. I wanted to believe some miracle of healing would take place in Dad's body so my family and I could be joyful again.

I was with Dad through his last night on this earth. It was long and difficult, but the morning found him passing on to be with his heavenly Father. For me, the morning brought sorrow and weeping—not the joy I had waited and hoped for. In my grief, however, God comforted me with the assurance that Dad had endured the night and his joy had finally come.

Living in Alaska, I have found that the summers bring long, beautiful days with very little night. Winters are just the opposite, bringing long, cold nights and short days. How wonderful it would be to always live in the summertime of our life, without experiencing the wintertime. These are the nights when we endure extreme sorrow and weeping, waiting for a new day and a new hope. We can be assured, however, these nights last only for a season. They will pass, bringing us new reason to rejoice. John 16:20 tells us that even though we may be sorrowful, our sorrow will turn to joy.

REMEMBER TODAY: No matter how long or difficult the night, the new day brings with it a promise of renewed hope and reason for rejoicing.

Ruth R. Bordeaux
Petal, MS

Related Scriptures
Matthew 28:20; Hebrews 13:5

August 4
Isaiah 55:9

*For as the heavens are higher than the earth, so are
my ways higher than your ways* (Isaiah 55:9).

HIS HIGHER WAYS

The flowers on the wallpaper and the swirls on the ceiling were as familiar to me as my own hands and feet. For over two months I had been confined to bed awaiting the birth of the child God promised me. I also reminded Him of the three miscarriages and difficult pregnancies I had experienced and asked Him to please let this one be simple and healthy. I felt that only silence greeted my request.

These thoughts, as well as relief that the pregnancy was over and our baby was alive, were going through my mind as I waited in the recovery room. Reacting to the strain of the last two months of isolation and total dependence, I panicked when my legs started jerking uncontrollably as the epidural began to wear off. I begged the nurses to bring my husband to me. Alone, I awaited death as I heard the nurses calling out that they could not get a blood pressure reading and that other signs were failing.

Despair gripped my heart as I thought of my precious husband being left alone to care for our young son and a premature daughter. My mind groped for answers. Then I felt God's presence. "Jesus!" my heart cried out. The jerking stopped, and I heard the nurses report the return of my vital signs.

Proverbs 18:24 assures us that there is a friend who sticks closer than a brother. No matter how difficult the circumstances, we can trust God's promises, His presence and His higher ways.

REMEMBER TODAY: True peace comes when we learn to fully trust in His higher ways.

Myrtie Lee	**Related Scriptures**	**August 5**
Lebanon, TN	1 Kings 10:1-13; Jeremiah 29:13;	Hosea 6:3
	Matthew 12:42	

Then shall we know, if we follow on to know the Lord: his going forth is prepared as the morning; and he shall come unto us as the rain, as the latter and former rain unto the earth (Hosea 6:3).

A DETERMINED JOURNEY

The trappings on the silver bridles glistened in the sun as the camels slowly prodded across the burning sands. On one of the animals rode the queen of the nation; others carried her servants and the gifts she was taking to present to the king. The journey was long and painful. No doubt the only relief from the hot scorching sun was to have the servants rub her skin with oil many times a day.

The threat of robbers seeking the treasures she carried was constant. In addition, she had left her kingdom behind for others to oversee. They might create an insurrection; however, she was going. She had to go!

When the queen of Sheba reached the palace of Solomon, she was overwhelmed. She cried in ecstasy, "'Not even half was told me'" (1 Kings 10:7, *NIV*). She watched in awe as he worshiped, she saw the way he ruled his kingdom, and she listened to his great wisdom. In response to her curiosity and devotion, he gave the order that she could have whatever her heart desired. The great King Solomon would not allow his guest to give more than he gave.

In this great adventure of faith, we often feel that our journey is endless and the traveling is through barren desert sands. How wonderful to have the Holy Spirit come and bathe us in the oil of gladness, enabling us to reach our goals! Heaven seems far away, but I have heard of the King who rules in all of His glory, and I must see Him. I must see for myself this wonderful Kingdom. On the way I have encountered the robber who would like to steal the gifts I am carrying to present to Him, but I know the toils will seem as nothing when I see Him. I know my gifts will seem small compared to the riches of His kingdom. All my heart's desires will be mine, for truly One greater than Solomon is here!

REMEMBER TODAY: Determine to complete the journey.

Marlette Finger   **Related Scriptures**   **August 6**
Olympia, WA   1 Peter 2:2; Psalm 62:1, 5;   Psalm 95:6
       Isaiah 8:17; 40:31

O come, let us worship and bow down: let us
kneel before the Lord our maker (Psalm 95:6).

FAST-FOOD FIX

What will it be? McDonald's, Wendy's or Burger King? No, not another fast-food meal! My stomach begins to churn. The thought of one more hamburger or deep-fried something is more than I can bear. Grab a bite here, snatch a candy bar there. Just enough to get by. Squeeze in a bite between appointments, errands, car pools, ball practice, prayer meetings and Bible studies—that fast-food fix.

What about the kids? Are they getting what they really need? Whatever happened to the four basic food groups? I faintly remember those from high school home economics class.

I do the same to the Lord. I pull up to the spiritual drive-thru. "I would like some meat, Lord. You will have to put it between two slices of bread because I have to eat it on the run." That same attitude prevails as I go to church. *Hurry up, everyone. Let's get on with this. There is more to my agenda today.*" I may not say these things verbally, but I communicate them by my actions. My prayers boil down to "Quick, Lord, I need another spiritual sandwich. I'm on the run again."

What about those nutrients that come from feasting on the Word, the real meat? What about dining, sitting down and enjoying each bite?

We recently took our two young sons to a fine restaurant. They were dressed in suits and ties (no jeans and T-shirts for this event). They had a hard time not expecting instant food. Appetizers, salads, bread and butter, the main course, and dessert were all brought with ample time allowed between each course to savor and enjoy.

There is life beyond instant. I want to dine. The drive-thru is old, and all the food tastes the same. I must sit, converse and enjoy the Lord's presence. How sad the Lord must feel after preparing a feast for me that contains everything I need to grow, mature and be the best I can be, when I say, "Sorry, no time; make it a sandwich, please."

REMEMBER TODAY: A constant fast-food spiritual diet will result in an anemic, weak Christian. "They that wait upon the Lord shall renew their strength" (Isaiah 40:31).

Brenda Short
Chattanooga, TN

Related Scriptures
James 4:7; John 10:10

August 7
Matthew 6:33

But seek ye first the kingdom of God, and his righteousness;
and all these things shall be added unto you (Matthew 6:33).

THOSE LITTLE HINDRANCES

Today is the day. I am going to pray and study the Word of God. Nothing is going to stop me. But first I must clean out the closet. Oh, the phone is ringing. Now back to the closet. What started out as a small job ended up being an all-day project.

This kind of thing has happened to most of us. The desire to be alone with God was sincere, but "little foxes" stole our valuable time.

As Christians we realize the importance of spending time with our heavenly Father. He is interested in our problems, needs and desires. When we pray we are communicating with God. As we wait before Him, He speaks to us. God will talk to us, but we must be willing to listen. As we read and study His Word, He speaks to us through the Scriptures. This is when we receive fresh ideas, new direction for our lives and the assurance that He has everything under control.

Jesus knew the importance of spending time with the Father. He prayed in the early morning hours, receiving strength to minister throughout the day. When Satan came against Him, He would speak the Word. The Bible says in James 4:7, "Submit yourselves therefore to God. Resist the devil, and he will flee from you."

Time alone with God is valuable. Guard it. In John 10:10 the Word says, "The thief cometh not, but for to steal, and to kill, and to destroy: I am come that they might have life, and that they might have it more abundantly."

Abundant living is spending time with God and receiving all the benefits of His Word.

REMEMBER TODAY: Don't let "things" steal your time with Him.

Virginia Beaty
Cleveland, TN

Related Scriptures
Malachi 3:16, 17; Psalms 8; 86:8-13;
1 John 5:1-4

August 8
Malachi 3:16

*Then those who feared and loved the Lord spoke often of him to each other.
And he had a Book of Remembrance drawn up in which he recorded the names of
those who feared him and loved to think about him* (Malachi 3:16, *TLB*).

A BOOK OF REMEMBRANCE

What woman, at some period in her life, has not kept a diary or journal to record the thoughts and deeds she cherishes and wishes to remember? She often confides to her diary the thoughts she cannot or does not wish to share with anyone else.

Isn't it interesting to know that the God of this vast universe also keeps a "Book of Remembrance"! Women are uniquely like their Creator in this respect. In diaries, teenage scrapbooks, wedding albums, baby books and picture albums, we store memories of our lives.

The Scripture verse tells us that God records in His "Book of Remembrance" the names of those who feared Him, loved Him and loved to think about Him. Let us look at the things we should do to be inscribed in His book.

First, we must have a reverential awe that leads to adoration and worship. Like the psalmist, we will sing hymns of praise when we consider the works of His hands.

We must also have a love that leads to obedience and service. In 1 John 5:3 we read, "This is love for God: to obey his commands" (*NIV*). If we do not obey, we do not love. When we love Him, we love to think about Him and will find time to meditate on Him from the Word often.

"Then those who feared the Lord talked with each other . . . " (Malachi 3:16, *NIV*). We will witness to each other proclaiming His love and faithfulness. Malachi 3:16 continues, ". . . And the Lord listened and heard" (*NIV*). How wonderful to know that God listens and heeds our testimony of praise and is so pleased He causes it to be recorded in His presence! "They shall be mine," says the Lord Almighty, "in that day when I make up my jewels" (Malachi 3:17).

REMEMBER TODAY: God is aware of us today and is inscribing His jewels in the Book of Remembrance.

Paulita M. Rodriguez
San Antonio, TX

Related Scripture
Matthew 28:20

August 9
Joshua 1:9

*Be not afraid, neither be thou dismayed: for the Lord thy
God is with thee whithersoever thou goest* (Joshua 1:9).

THROUGH THE STORMS OF LIFE

I was already running late when I found myself in the midst of heavily congested traffic. I was scheduled to be at the women's retreat, where I was scheduled to serve as a group counselor, by 5:45 p.m. I felt sure I wasn't going to make it.

As soon as I left the heavy traffic behind, I was engulfed by rampaging winds that lashed at my truck, rocking it from side to side. Like fog creeping over a city, my anxiousness slowly began to mount. After several minutes the winds diminished, then gave way to a ravaging rainstorm. The windshield wipers did not work properly, and I could not see more than 10 feet ahead. I wanted to turn back but realized that doing so would be self-defeating. I was in the middle of the storm, and going back would be just as bad as going forward. I thought about pulling over to the side and waiting, but that too would keep me from getting to the retreat on time. I decided not to give up and kept going. As I drove up the hill, my eyes beheld the most beautiful scene.

The rain abruptly stopped. The vast blue sky merged with a radiant bluish-purple horizon. On each side of the hill were tall trees majestically standing, and fields of buttercups, Indian paintbrushes and bluebonnets swayed back and forth.

"Lord," I exclaimed, "how great You are! Through my ordeal You have given me a vivid contrast of the Christian's life." We live in the midst of a congested world that has tremendous pressures. When we survive one storm, we are overcome with even greater circumstances—sickness, problems and sorrows that can cause us to deviate from His righteous way. But if we persevere, we will discover that He is a faithful God who is always near, holding us by the hand and tenderly guiding us through the storms of life.

REMEMBER TODAY: Let us not be dismayed when the storms of this world engulf us, for God is always near.

Wanda R. Porter
Douglas, GA

Related Scriptures:
Hebrews 10:23-25; Romans 14:19;
Proverbs 12:18, 25; 15:23

August 10
Hebrews 10:24

*And let us consider one another to provoke
unto love and to good works* (Hebrews 10:24).

ENCOURAGEMENT

As our boys grew up, their dad was their constant teacher. He taught them how to walk, play ball, ride a motorcycle, drive a car. Many hours were spent in repetition, instruction, encouragement and demonstration. I often heard him say, "That's good. Do it this way. That's better. Wow, that was outstanding!" Never once do I ever remember hearing my husband ridicule or criticize the boys as they endeavored to accomplish a goal. He was constantly encouraging them.

We all need encouragement from others as we travel life's journey. We are living in a day when discouragement and depression are prevalent. Wouldn't it be wonderful if each of us looked for ways to encourage (put courage into) one another and considered the needs of others? If we focus on the needs of others, we take the focus off our own needs.

We might be surprised to know how many people are on the brink of defection. Life often gets tough; things don't always go as planned. Difficulties are all around us—physical illnesses, financial setbacks, marital problems and disappointments in relationships. An encouraging word could make the difference in an individual's stability. Just the words "I care about what happens to you" or "I believe in you" can cause a person to stand up spiritually and press through the detours of life.

Our confidence is in Jesus, the One who saved us. He is our help. He constantly encourages us through His Word; therefore, let us think of ways we can encourage one another to love and do good deeds.

REMEMBER TODAY: The wise man Solomon said it this way: "Heaviness in the heart of man maketh it stoop: but a good word maketh it glad" (Proverbs 12:25).

Margaret K. Tioaquen
Hilo, HI

Related Scriptures
Matthew 18:19; 1 Thessalonians 5:18;
Proverbs 3:4

August 11
Jeremiah 42:11, 12

Be not afraid of the king of Babylon, of whom ye are afraid; be not afraid of him, saith the Lord: for I am with you to save you, and to deliver you from his hand. And I will shew mercies unto you, that he may have mercy upon you, and cause you to return to your own land (Jeremiah 42:11, 12).

DEPLOYED

On the morning of August 11, 1990, while in San Antonio, Texas, for the Church of God General Assembly, the telephone rang in our hotel room. We had planned that our next stop would be El Paso for 18 days to visit our son and his family. Little did we know that our plans for the next day (August 12) would be uncertain.

Our son and his wife were on the other end of the line. Their voices were trembling. He had just received word that he might be deployed to Saudi Arabia any day. We prayed, "O God, it can't be. We're so close to seeing him tomorrow. We've traveled so far, and we are only one day's journey away. Please, Lord, don't let him have to leave; just let us be able to see him."

We called our home church in Hilo. Relaying the message of Tommy's pending deployment, we asked the church to stand with us in agreement. We felt strength and peace as our church family joined us in prayer. Matthew 18:19 tells us, "If two of you shall agree on earth as touching any thing that they shall ask, it shall be done for them." We had more than two in agreement. We had our whole congregation! We came together in the Spirit, knowing that our God is able!

God granted our heart's desire. Our son remained in El Paso all of the 18 days we were there! He was not deployed until the last week in September. Isn't the Lord good? In 1 Thessalonians 5:18 we read, "In everything give thanks."

Today we are praising the Lord for protecting him and returning him to us.

REMEMBER TODAY: "So shalt thou find favour and good understanding in the sight of God and man" (Proverbs 3:4).

Geri Henson
Cleveland, TN

Related Scriptures
Romans 2:4; 9:23; Ephesians 1:7

August 12
2 Corinthians 8:9

> *For ye know the grace of our Lord Jesus Christ, that, though*
> *he was rich, yet for your sakes, he became poor, that ye*
> *through his poverty might be rich* (2 Corinthians 8:9).

YOU CAN BE RICH

Sounds like one of those 30-minute, late-night, buy-real-estate-with-no-money-down commercials, doesn't it? Well, it isn't. This is for real. You can be rich, and it is offered to you as a gift.

Perhaps everyone has fantasized about getting rich and living the lifestyle of the rich and famous. No doubt, every boy has thought, *Someday I will hit the big bonanza*, and every girl has dreamed of meeting and marrying a rich man. Scripture says clearly that through Christ Jesus our Lord we can be rich—not with money but with the true riches of life. Money is far too elusive, temporary and sometimes tainted to be associated with the true riches of Christ. Let's notice the riches He refers to.

The riches of His goodness (Romans 2:4). There is no meagerness in God's goodness. When we begin to count the blessings of His goodness—family, friends, home, shelter, liberty and freedom, and too many social comforts to mention—we want to exclaim, "I am rich in God's goodness!"

The riches of His grace (Ephesians 1:7). If the riches of His goodness leads us to repentance, then surely the riches of His grace provides us redemption and forgiveness. His grace should be labeled "rich," especially in light of the price the Father paid for us to experience it.

The riches of His glory (Romans 9:23). The great surprise of life is that God is willing to share His riches with us. He shares the riches of His goodness with us through nature and the riches of His grace through Christ, and now He informs us that the riches of His glory await us in heaven. We are truly rich with wealth that moth and rust cannot corrupt, nor can thieves break through and steal.

REMEMBER TODAY: It is God's goodness that leads us to Him, not His wrath or judgment.

Peggy Scarborough
Rochester Hills, MI

Related Scriptures
Exodus 15:26; Matthew 8:17;
Proverbs 4:20-23; Psalm 118:17

August 13
Matthew 15:13

*Every plant, which my heavenly Father hath not
planted, shall be rooted up* (Matthew 15:13).

HEALING IS FOR YOU

"Don't get your hopes built up about a thing in this world" was the abrupt conclusion by a specialist in Pontiac, Michigan. I had a mammogram that said, "Slight thickening in the left breast. X-ray again in six months." The gynecologist, as a precautionary measure, had sent me to see a specialist. He looked at the lump and immediately diagnosed it as cancer. Out of my spirit rose the words, "I will not have cancer." I felt at that moment I had to verbally state my faith. He did a needle biopsy, and the fight was on!

Within a few hours the phone rang. The doctor said, "It is cancer." Immediately I realized I could not lean on the arm of the flesh. The Word became my survival. I began to "attend to it" by the hours. This was the first time in my life I decided that I would not listen to the doctor's statistics. Was healing a biblical truth or not? I walked the floor quoting the healing verses. I played tapes with the healing scriptures. "Every plant, which my heavenly Father hath not planted, shall be rooted up" became a word from the Lord to me.

When the many frightening tests began, my friend Barbara said, "Peggy, just walk it through." That's what I did. I walked it through and found God to be faithful to His Word. I asked the doctor to remove only the lump and lymph glands. When I went into surgery, I wrote Matthew 15:13 on my hand along with other scriptures. The anesthesiologist said, "What does that say?" When I told him, he smiled and showed me the Bible in his pocket. Then I really felt covered.

Through this ordeal I learned that cancer has three spirits: infirmity, fear and bondage. But disease is reversible. "Himself took our infirmities, and bare our sicknesses" (Matthew 8:17).

Accompanying the surgery were many fears—especially terrors by night. I learned to speak to my body. I commanded fear to leave. I prayed, "I thank You, Jesus, that You are my healer. With Your stripes I am healed. You're healing me now." God's prescription for life and health is "Attend to my words; incline thine ear unto my sayings. Let them not depart from thine eyes; keep them in the midst of thine heart. For they are life unto those that find them, and health to all their flesh" (Proverbs 4:20-22).

REMEMBER TODAY: If you are sick, stay away from sympathizers. They will kill you. Quote the Word: "I shall not die, but live, and declare the works of the Lord" (Psalm 118:17).

Margaret W. Lackey
Mt. Holly, NC

Related Scripture
Proverbs 3:5

August 14
Isaiah 40:31

*But they that wait upon the Lord shall renew their strength; they
shall mount up with wings as eagles; they shall run, and not be
weary; and they shall walk, and not faint (Isaiah 40:31).*

HIS GLORY REVEALED

I stood in the midst of a heap of broken, shattered dreams. Day after weary day I fought bitterness, confusion and loneliness. Inside I struggled to cling to the promise I'd been given as a child: "Trust in the Lord with all thine heart . . ." (Proverbs 3:5).

But where did I go from here? Where did I fit in? One night during one of my private pity parties, I scribbled these words:

> "It just takes time," I've heard so many say,
> But the hardest part is waiting for the time to go away.
> One day ends, and I'm thankful it's gone.
> I wish my life away, and time moves on.
> One moment I'm happy, but the next one I'm sad.
> One day things look brighter,
> The next day they look bad.
> Sometimes I sit and worry and feel so blue.
> I ask myself the question, "What can I do?"
> Why does life have to be this way? Why is this my fate?
> Then I remember that time heals all wounds.
> So what I must do is wait.

Days turned to weeks and weeks to years. One day at a time I faced the struggles, knowing "they that wait upon the Lord shall renew their strength" (Isaiah 40:31).

Seven years later God picked up the broken, shattered pieces of my life and started putting them back together. And the picture He painted for me is more beautiful than I could have ever imagined. I've been viewing this scene for more than 14 years.

At times during the waiting I became impatient. I was more than willing to tell God exactly when and how to work things out for me. What a mess I would have made! I'm so glad I waited for Him.

Have you been waiting a long time for an answer? Don't give up. In His time, God does all things well. In your lowest moments, He will renew your strength. Then one day you will soar as an eagle, and in that flight to victory, you will see the glory of God.

REMEMBER TODAY: If you're willing to wait on the Lord, His glory will be revealed in your life. He does all things well.

Debra Rivers Boutwell
Jackson, MS

Related Scriptures
2 Corinthians 2:14; Hebrews 10:23;
Isaiah 41:10; 45:2; Philippians 3:14

August 15
Habakkuk 3:19

The Lord God is my strength, and he will make my feet like hinds' feet,
and he will make me to walk upon mine high places (Habakkuk 3:19).

THE HIGH PLACES

As I watched my cat, Baby Biskett, climb his favorite tree, I noticed his tenacity to go higher and higher. He gracefully walked on branches that seemed too small for his weight, yet he never noticed. His claws sank deep into the bark as he sought his goal for a higher place. His attention was solely on his venture and not on the prospect of a fall.

Our Father tells us He will make our feet like hinds' feet in order for us to climb the mountains of life and walk upon the high places. He does not want us to focus on our inability to achieve but rather on His ability to always cause us to triumph.

As my cat held on firmly with all his might, "let us hold fast the profession of our faith without wavering." When it seems we cannot go another step for fear we will fall, let us rest assuredly in the One who holds us in His hand. Jesus will uphold us with the right hand of His righteousness, so let us step through this life with faith in Him who has trodden the path before us. He has gone ahead of us in order to make the crooked places straight. Let us follow our Lord as He gives us the strength we need to reach the high places He has set before us.

REMEMBER TODAY: Let us "press toward the mark for the prize of the high calling of God in Christ Jesus" (Philippians 3:14).

Joan Swank
Monroe, MI

Related Scriptures
Mark 5:36; 1 John 4:18

August 16
Psalm 127:1

Unless the Lord protects a city,
sentries do no good (Psalm 127:1, *TLB*).

GOD'S PROTECTION

I have always been afraid to be alone at night. Since my husband is a minister, he is sometimes called to the hospital in the early-morning hours.

We pastored one church where the parsonage was completely isolated. When my husband was called to the hospital, I stayed up as usual and locked the door behind him. Then I made another round, checking all the locks on each door. I would sit down for a few minutes and then make my rounds again, checking the doors and praying, "Please, Lord, protect us and take care of us."

After repeating this routine six times, it seemed as if the Lord spoke to me and asked, "Don't you trust Me?" I immediately said, "Yes, Lord." Then I realized that no, I was not trusting Him when my actions proved differently. If I trusted Him, I would go back to bed after checking the doors once and asking His protection for my family.

Now I do not fear. Instead I trust the words Christ said to Jairus concerning his daughter: " 'Don't be afraid. Just trust me' " (Mark 5:37, *TLB*).

REMEMBER TODAY: "Perfect love casts out fear" (1 John 4:18, *NKJV*).

Ina Boling
Little Rock, AR

Related Scriptures
Psalms 40:3, 4; 42:8

August 17
Jeremiah 17:7

*Blessed is the man [woman] that trusteth in the
Lord, and whose hope the Lord is* (Jeremiah 17:7).

BECAUSE HE HAS A SONG

I was standing at my door one morning several weeks ago listening to one of my favorite sounds—the lovely early songs of the birds. I always enjoy their beautiful tunes. No vocalist has ever been able to match their notes, because they reflect a special praise for the Creator.

But how could they be so cheerful this early in the morning? I thought. And in that moment God spoke to my heart.

"Maybe," He said, "it is because they have spent a night of restful sleep free from worry and fret of what tomorrow will bring. They have learned the secret of the peace which comes from complete faith in My provisions for their needs."

If we could ever learn that secret, we too would be able to awake with a song in our hearts and praise on our lips.

REMEMBER TODAY: The bird sings not because he has the answer but because he has the song.

Joy A. Vanoy
Winchester, KY
Related Scriptures
Deuteronomy 6:6-9, 25; Jeremiah 1:5
August 18
Psalm 127:3-5

Lo, children are an heritage of the Lord. . . . As arrows are in the hand of a mighty man; so are children. . . . Happy is the man that hath his quiver full of them (Psalm 127:3-5).

DANDELION BOUQUETS

As my teenage daughter was helping her preschool sister get ready for Sunday school, a moment of nostalgia came over me. Wasn't it just yesterday that I ran out of time just when the last ponytails and ribbons were in place? I had little time then to spend on myself.

I have taken each stage of motherhood seriously. My children were all born in different parts of the world, wherever our ministry was at the time. I was blessed to be able to put my teaching career on hold while they were young. But now, as my youngest looks forward to going to school with her sisters, I often take time to read and reflect on a plaque that has meant a great deal to me through those hectic but precious days.

DANDELION BOUQUETS

The baby is teething.
The children are fighting.
Your husband just called to say,
"Eat dinner without me."
One of these days you'll explode and shout to the kids,
"Why don't you grow up and act your age?"
And they will.
Or,
"You guys get outside and find yourselves something to do.
And don't slam the door!"
And they won't.
You'll straighten their bedrooms all neat and tidy,
Toys displayed on the shelf,
Hangers in the closet, animals caged.
You'll yell, "Now I want it to stay this way!"
And it will.
You will prepare a perfect dinner with a salad that hasn't had all the olives picked out and a cake with no finger traces in the icing, and you'll say,
"Now this is a meal for company."
And you'll eat it alone.
You'll yell, "I want complete privacy on the phone.

No screaming. Do you hear me?" And no one will answer.
No more plastic tablecloths stained with spaghetti.
No more dandelion bouquets.
No more iron-on patches.
No more wet, knotted shoelaces, muddy boots, shoes all over the house or rubber bands for ponytails.
Imagine: A lipstick with a point.
No baby-sitter on New Year's Eve,
Washing clothes only once a week.
No P.T.A. meetings or silly school plays, where your child is a tree.
No car pools, blaring stereos or forgotten lunch money.
No more Christmas presents made of library paste and toothpicks.
No more tooth fairy.
No more gigglers in the dark.
No wet oatmeal kisses, scraped knees to kiss or sticky fingers to clean.
Only a voice asking: "Why don't you grow up?"
And the silence echoes: "I did."

—Author Unknown

REMEMBER TODAY: Our children will grow up all too quickly. Make today count—don't miss the dandelion bouquets.

Marilyn Rushing Lewistown, PA	**Related Scriptures** Hebrews 12:2; Acts 2:28	**August 19** Psalm 16:11

Thou wilt shew me the path of life: in thy
presence is fullness of joy; at thy right hand there are
pleasures for evermore (Psalm 16:11).

A SPECIAL KIND OF JOY

What is joy? Is it laughter and happiness? It can be. But I believe the fullness of joy the psalmist spoke of is satisfaction in knowing we are in the presence of the Father, who has the answers to every problem we encounter. It is the assurance that we are safe under the shadow of His wing.

I learned a valuable lesson about this kind of joy. On August 19, 1985, my husband and I had to give up one of the most precious gifts the Lord had given us. Our son, Michael, lost his life by an act of violence on another man's part. Michael was 28 years old. He was a very handsome young man who brought joy to the hearts of his parents. It would have seemed impossible to experience fullness of joy in that situation. If joy were measured by laughter and excitement, there was none. Thank God, He revealed to us a fullness of joy like we had never known before and could not have known from any other source.

One of the first things I felt God speak to my spirit that fateful night was "I understand your sorrow. My Son suffered at the hands of another also, and He was without sin." In that moment, I began to experience that special kind of joy that can only come from a personal encounter with God himself. This joy is available to all who know the Lord as personal Savior. Christ himself felt joy in His heart as He neared the time He would give His life for the sins of the world. "Who for the joy that was set before him endured the cross" (Hebrews 12:2).

REMEMBER TODAY: To experience fullness of joy we must be acquainted with the Joy-giver.

Charlotte Hurst
Stonington, ME

Related Scriptures
Isaiah 64:8; John 3:30; 2 Timothy 2:20, 21

August 20
2 Corinthians 4:7

But we have this treasure in earthen vessels, that the excellency of the power may be of God, and not of us (2 Corinthians 4:7).

GOD'S VESSEL

As I cared for my mother who had terminal cancer, I had to do many things I knew I couldn't do in my strength alone. Many times I repeated the beautiful words of Scripture, "I can do all things through Christ which strengtheneth me" (Philippians 4:13). I came to fully realize I could do nothing in my own strength, but when I submitted myself to Christ, He could then shine through me.

A lump of clay is a lifeless, useless object. (That's what we all are in the beginning.) God takes the clay, molds it and shapes it into a vessel, smoothing the edges. He then puts it in the fire for a while. After the fire He takes it out to cool, slowly so it won't shatter. But it is still fragile, untried.

The shape is lovely, but there is no luster, no shine. It is a dull, plain vessel— a little more useful than before but still not quite what the Potter has in mind.

God then coats the clay with a beautiful glaze of love. Still dull and untempered, it is once again put into the fire. This time the fire is a little hotter and the time a little longer. Again, the vessel is allowed to cool slowly.

Finally, a beautiful, sturdy vessel covered with a glowing glaze of heavenly beauty lovingly displays His handiwork. This vessel can be proudly used wherever He wishes. But most importantly, the clay can no longer be seen.

REMEMBER TODAY: In our own strength we cannot become a vessel God can be proud to use. But through His tender love and mercy, we can withstand the heat of trials and tribulations.

Evaline Echols
Cleveland, TN

Related Scriptures
Matthew 5:7; Psalm 57:1; Isaiah 43:2

August 21
Psalm 37:21

The righteous sheweth
mercy, and giveth (Psalm 37:21).

BLESSED ARE THE MERCIFUL

God's mercy is concealed within every storm, and His grace flows beneath every crosscurrent. Out of every disappointment there is to be gleaned some treasure.

Without mercy, Calvary would have become a symbol of condemnation rather than of forgiveness. When Jesus expressed His mercy toward His enemies, He provided us an example of how we should show mercy to those who hurt us. "Blessed are the merciful: for they shall obtain mercy" (Matthew 5:7).

When Joseph was sold by his brothers unjustly and put into prison for a crime he did not commit, he did not react; he responded. He responded by trusting that God was in control and by leaving revenge in the hands of God. So must we.

A few years ago when I was preparing an article on the topic of mercy, I was sorely tested to show mercy. How do you show mercy when you know a person is a bad influence on someone you love dearly? How do you identify with a teenager who is reaching out for love and acceptance? To bring it closer to home, what if this is your own daughter? Who wants to show mercy in a situation like this? I didn't.

But one morning in my devotions, God spoke to me through a message on a cassette tape from the Mount Paran Church of God: "I the Lord your God call upon you this day that you will go forth into the harvest field to reconcile—to show mercy. For I am raising you up in this hour that you might minister to those who are in need. Accept those whose faith is weak. Accept those who struggle, and I the Lord will give to you strength that you might bear them up and that you being strong might bear the infirmities of the weak."

I felt somewhat like I believe the psalmist must have felt when he wrote, "Horror hath taken hold upon me because of the wicked that forsake thy law. . . . The earth, O Lord, is full of thy mercy: teach me thy statutes" (Psalm 119:53, 64).

REMEMBER TODAY: We are covered with His goodness and mercy, which shall follow us all the days of our lives (Psalm 23:6).

Alice Lynd	**Related Scriptures**	**August 22**
Hill City, KS	Psalms 8; 19:1	Psalm 8:3, 4, 9

When I consider thy heavens, the work of thy fingers, the moon and the stars, which thou hast ordained; what is man . . . that thou visitest him? . . . O Lord our Lord, how excellent is thy name in all the earth! (Psalm 8:3, 4, 9).

GOD'S HANDIWORK

I stepped outside one summer night to quietly worship God. The stars were splashed lavishly against the night's dark, velvet blue curtain, and in the distance I could hear a coyote howling. A soft breeze brushed my face as I stood amazed at the splendor of this beautiful God-given scene.

How can anyone ever doubt the existence of our great Creator? I thought. *Here is the evidence of a well-planned, well-organized and beautiful display of His handiwork.*

Then the Spirit spoke softly, saying, "What is that in your hand?" I wanted to pick up a rock, a stick—something—but I had nothing. I slowly opened the palms of my hands and whispered, "I have nothing, nothing, my Lord." I could almost feel His hand brush the tears from my face as He whispered back to me, "Daughter, I can use your 'nothing' if it really belongs to Me."

REMEMBER TODAY: God will use what you perceive as "nothing" when He truly has your all. You too are His handiwork.

Florence Clawson
Simpsonville, MD

Related Scriptures
Isaiah 50:4; Proverbs 12:18, 25;
Ecclesiastes 10:12

August 23
Proverbs 25:11

A word fitly spoken is like apples of
gold in pictures of silver (Proverbs 25:11).

A WORD FITLY SPOKEN

One morning I telephoned a lady to tell her I was thinking about her and to ask how she was getting along. This was such a simple gesture. However, the next time I saw her, she expressed her appreciation for the call and even said, "It made my day."

When I was a child, I used to hear the little ditty "Sticks and stones may break my bones, but words can never hurt me." This is just not true. The words we speak are extremely powerful. They have the capacity to bless and encourage or to curse and destroy, to build up or to tear down. Words can be sharp enough to cut and pierce, yet kind enough to comfort and console.

In James 3:2 we are told, "If any man offend not in word, the same is a perfect man." Even the words we speak to family members at the beginning of a day can literally determine their mood for that day. "Pleasant words are as an honeycomb, sweet to the soul, and health to the bones" (Proverbs 16:24). In Proverbs 15:1 we read, "A soft answer turneth away wrath: but grievous words stir up anger."

Once a word is spoken, it cannot be retrieved. We are warned in Proverbs 18:19 that a brother offended is harder to win than a strong city. Realizing the truth of this, our daily prayer should be, "God, please help me and 'let the words of my mouth, and the meditation of my heart, be acceptable in thy sight, O Lord, my strength and my redeemer'" (Psalm 19:14).

REMEMBER TODAY: God is able to give us the wisdom and help we need to say only words that bless and benefit others.

Ethel Ray Brummett
Calhoun, GA

Related Scriptures
Matthew 10:29; Psalm 35:28

August 24
Psalm 146:5, 6

Blessed is he whose help is the God of Jacob, whose hope
is in the Lord his God, the Maker of heaven and earth,
the sea, and everything in them (Psalm 146:5, 6, NIV).

IN GOD'S CARE

My 3-year-old son lay in the hospital fighting for his life. He had just been diagnosed as having the same dreadful disease that had taken the life of my father. The prognosis of this young life was promising, but I knew all too well the daily struggle of insulin shots, balanced with a carefully selected diet. I also knew that as a diabetic, this child would face numerous physical difficulties as he grew older. Grief and fear swept through me, but the strength of the Holy Spirit undergirded me and God's Word encouraged me: "The very hairs of your head are all numbered. Fear ye not therefore" (Matthew 10:30, 31).

As is so often the case in times of grief and pain, I also drew encouragement from God's creation. The earth had been bathed in heavy rains, and the bright morning sun shone upon the greenery of early spring. The countryside was echoing with the voices of birds singing—rejoicing in different tones and rhythms. My heart was lifted in praise and thanksgiving to God for life and for the beauty of His creation. I joined creation in praising and blessing the God who made it all. "My tongue shall speak of thy righteousness and of thy praise all the day long" (Psalm 35:28).

Oftentimes we marvel as we watch God move in a situation, but there are also times we cannot see His work. God is our Creator, and He knows our needs. He is always there when we need Him, whether we see Him or not.

REMEMBER TODAY: In our lowest moments God is always there. When we look for Him, we will find Him.

Wilma Amison
Cleveland, TN

Related Scriptures
Matthew 25:34-40; Luke 10:30-37;
John 15:13

August 25
Romans 5:8

*But God commendeth his love toward us, in that, while
we were yet sinners, Christ died for us* (Romans 5:8).

"I WAS A STRANGER . . ."

While on a mission in Europe in his work with Ministry to the Military, my husband, Don, was traveling by train from Germany to Norway. He observed a frightened young man—little more than a boy really—trying to escape the blows of a larger, stronger man.

He hadn't watched long before he was out of his seat and, moving swiftly down the aisle, had restrained the attacker from behind. He fastened the angry man's arms behind him with his own arms and further immobilized him with a leg lock.

At that point several other men came forward and secured the attacker in one of the train's compartments until he could be turned over to the authorities, who had been notified of the trouble aboard the train and were waiting at the next stop. Whether the man was drug-crazed or otherwise psychologically disturbed, my husband never learned.

Another traveler, a young Scandinavian man with whom my husband had been talking earlier, asked if he was a law enforcement officer, so efficient had been his maneuver. Of course, he is not! What actually happened was he saw in the young man being attacked a picture of our own son. He imagined him in a similar predicament and knew he would want someone to come to his rescue. His reaction after that was so instinctive he hardly thought at all. Perhaps laying his own life on the line, he went to the rescue of a stranger. We are told in Romans 5:8 that "God commendeth his love toward us, in that, while we were yet sinners [strangers to Him], Christ died for us."

However, God extended His love to us not as strangers but as His children and friends. Only through eyes of love could He visualize what we had the potential of becoming rather than the unlovable strangers we were when He came to rescue us from the attacks of Satan and eternal death.

REMEMBER TODAY: "Now, therefore, you are no longer strangers and foreigners, but fellow citizens with the saints and members of the household of God" (Ephesians 2:19, *NKJV*).

Patty D. Rains	**Related Scriptures**	**August 26**
Mesa, AZ	Matthew 9:36; Romans 8:38, 39	1 Peter 5:7

Casting all your care upon him;
for he careth for you (1 Peter 5:7).

I KNOW ALL ABOUT IT, DAUGHTER

Years ago a young lady gave birth to her second child—a darling little girl with black curls and brown eyes. She was just what her parents had ordered, except the baby was born almost blind, and because of a difficult delivery, had an injury to the spine.

The little baby demanded almost all of the mother's time. She went through the motions of praying and attending church, but the mother carried a heavy load deep in her heart. When the baby was a year old, the young lady finally ran to the Lord and cast all her care on Him! He listened while she poured out her heart, and then He gently said, "I know all about it, daughter!"

Oh, the sweet peace that came with that knowledge! She had someone to share her load. That sweet peace still abides today. You see, I was that young mother! The circumstances did not change, but I did. His words seemed to say I was chosen for this special child and together we could handle the situation.

The doctors warned us that my daughter would never be well and would only live to be about 16. She was 42 in October. She is a happy person. She loves the Lord and enjoys good health.

Richter wrote, "The burden of suffering seems a tombstone hung about our necks, while in reality it is only the weight which is necessary to keep down the diver while he is hunting for pearls."

REMEMBER TODAY: Lord, please help us to lean upon You rather than the present circumstances.

Rachel Corley Wiggins
Winchester, KY

Related Scriptures
John 14:27; Colossians 3:15

August 27
Philippians 4:7

And the peace of God, which transcends all
understanding, will guard yourhearts and your minds
in Christ Jesus (Philippians 4: 7, *NIV*).

TO GUARD YOUR HEART

True peace, the high and abiding peace that passes all understanding, is experienced not in retreating from the battle but only in the thick of the battle.

My oldest brother, Bobby, though reared in a Church of God minister's home, had wandered away from the faith. Mother prayed faithfully for Bobby's salvation. At age 35 Bobby was killed in an automobile accident! Our family was devastated. I was deeply troubled about Bobby's salvation but could find no peace.

One night I dreamed Bobby and I were swimming in the ocean off the coast of Florida. I dreamed we were on a raft when Bobby turned and said to me, "Sis, you swim to shore and save yourself. I'm too sick to swim." In the dream I took Bobby's hand under my arm and swam for shore.

Upon reaching the beach, I dreamed I grabbed the sand, and as the water sifted the grains through my fingers, I realized we had barely made it to shore. It was then God spoke to me and said, "Bobby is safe with Me." Jesus gave me the peace I so desperately needed. I know death is not the end. Death, for the child of God, is the beginning of new life!

This peace that God has given me concerning the death of my brother is beyond human understanding, but through the years it has "guarded" my heart against the attacks of doubt Satan brings against it.

REMEMBER TODAY: Only Jesus can give you peace—true peace, lasting peace!

Jennifer Vassell
Brampton, Ontario

Related Scriptures
Matthew 6:25-34; Philippians 4:19;
1 Peter 5:7

August 28
Philippians 4:6

*Be careful for nothing; but in every thing by prayer
and supplication with thanksgiving let your requests
be made known unto God* (Philippians 4:6).

GOD EVEN PROVIDES TIRES

Since I became a Christian, I have read this verse over and over, and each time I am blessed. But this day I was depressed; I needed a miracle from God. In my distress I heard a testimony that brought Philippians 4:6 back to my mind. The story was told by a camper at our annual youth retreat.

"On a lonely road one cold wintry night, I saw a miracle happen," Chris said. "There were 15 kids on our bus traveling to the Church of God youth retreat. We were late leaving for the retreat, but we hoped that we would arrive in time for the night snack. To our surprise, we had a flat tire and there was no spare tire on our bus. The closest repair shop was over 50 miles away."

He continued, "In the midst of this crisis, God was just waiting to give us peace. Instead of giving in to panic, we prayed and began to thank God. When the bus finally stopped, we realized that we were in the middle of nowhere. There were no street lights, no houses and no other vehicles around. Actually there was nothing—just darkness, open field . . . and the Lord. Then in the darkness, someone on the bus looked across the open field and saw a brand-new tire. The tire was filled with air and was the right size for the van. We replaced the tire, got back on the bus and arrived at the retreat with shouts of praise."

As I listened to Chris' testimony, my burdens were lifted and my faith in God was increased. Why? When I saw how God provided a tire for the bus, I was convinced He could supply my need.

A few days later the answer came, and my needs were met. God will provide if we just cast all our cares on Him and take Him at His word.

REMEMBER TODAY: Where there is trust in Jesus, cares disappear and miracles appear.

Pauline James	**Related Scriptures**	**August 29**
Lemmon, SD	Isaiah 55:6-13; Psalm 23; 2 Timothy 2:1-13	Isaiah 55:8, 9

"For my thoughts are not your thoughts, neither are your ways my ways," declares the Lord. "As the heavens are higher than the earth, so are my ways higher than your ways and my thoughts than your thoughts" (Isaiah 55:8, 9, NIV).

THE WAY OF SORROW

While we were sitting in a hospital waiting room, the doctor delivered the shocking news that our son's 25-year-old wife had ovarian cancer in the third or fourth stage. They had been married only four years and were beginning a new career in the Air Force chaplaincy.

During the five-hour surgery, I found myself weeping before the Lord in the hospital prayer chapel. First, I cried, "No, God, this cannot be! This should not be happening to us!" Then I prayed, "Why, God, why? For what purpose?"

These were my thoughts and prayers for many days. Over a year later the Holy Spirit made travailing intercession through me as I prayed with my daughter-in-law. The peace God gave me was a precious gift. He also lifted the fear of death from my daughter-in-law.

My daughter-in-law believes that no matter what the future holds, God is ultimately in control. She is comforted by David's psalm, "Even though I walk through the valley of the shadow of death, I will fear no evil, for you are with me" (23:4, NIV).

The road has been long and hard, but we are reminded of the One who went before us down another long, hard road to Calvary. The Scripture says, "If we suffer, we shall also reign with him" (2 Timothy 2:12).

Through this school of suffering we have learned deep dimensions of love. Pain and suffering are not oversights or accidents but part of the eternal plan of God.

REMEMBER TODAY: God wants us to trust Him no matter what the circumstances.

Aurelia Brewer
Cramerton, NC

Related Scripture
Psalms 148; 150:6

August 30
Psalm 148:12, 13

Both young men, and maidens; old men, and children: let them praise the name of the Lord: for his name alone is excellent; his glory is above the earth and heaven (Psalms 148:12, 13).

PRAISE YE THE LORD

Small children often teach adults great lessons in life. Such was the case one Sunday morning recently when Ashleigh, a 2-year- old from our congregation, joined in the praise time by clapping her hands and lifting them up. She caught the attention of the choir, choir director and others. What pleasure it must bring to God when His saints catch His attention with praise and uninhibited worship!

In Psalm 148 we are reminded that God is great and worthy to be praised. The psalm declares that He is praised by the angels. He is praised by the beauty of the earth. He is praised by the high and low, the young and old. While God is praised by the whisper of the wind, the song of the bird, the glory of a sunrise, the ripple of the brook, He rejoices most in "the praise of all his saints . . . a people near unto him" (v. 14).

REMEMBER TODAY: Praise the Lord today—not only by the things you say but by the attitudes you display and the life you live. "Let every thing that hath breath praise the Lord" (Psalm 150:6).

Delta Schrade	**Related Scriptures**	**August 31**
Arvada, CO	Psalm 119:97-106; Proverbs 3:5-7, 11, 12;	Jeremiah 29:11
	Luke 11:11-13; Hebrews 12:9-11	

"For I know the plans I have for you," declares the Lord,
"plans to prosper you and not to harm you, plans to
give you hope and a future" (Jeremiah 29:11, NIV).

THE GOODNESS OF OUR HEAVENLY FATHER

One of the most cherished stories I remember hearing as a young girl depicts a small boy disobediently playing with his mother's most valued vase. After the boy's hand had been caught in the vase, the child frantically alarms his father, "Daddy, Daddy, this mean ol' vase swallowed my hand and won't let go."

The two tried every method the father could possibly imagine to free the imprisoned hand. With each unsuccessful attempt, both grew more and more anxious about the possible results. During a final attempt, the father discovered that the boy's hand was drawn up in a fist.

"At last," the father sighed. "This isn't going to be as difficult as it first seemed."

The father reached into his pocket and pulled out a big, shiny silver dollar. "I will give you this coin, Son," the father said with hopeful anticipation, "if you will simply open up your fist."

With tear-filled eyes the boy looked from the silver coin to his father's face. "But, Daddy, if I do as you ask and open up my hand, I'll drop the nickel I lost in the vase."

Don't we as God's children do the same thing? We cry, "Father, O Father, fix it please!" He offers us a perfect plan of escape. Then, with the same torn spirit as this child, we say, "But God, that's not how I wanted to escape" or "You mean I can't have both the nickel and the shiny silver dollar?"

Our heavenly Father lovingly responds, "My daughter, don't you see, it's My pleasure to give you good gifts. Not only do I have this shiny silver dollar, but I also have more nickels if that is really what you want. Child, allow Me to let you in on a little secret. Once your hand is freed from the vase, all we need to do to retrieve the nickel you dropped is to turn the vase over."

REMEMBER TODAY: Since our understanding is limited, we must relinquish our will to His unlimited wisdom and trust that His fatherly thoughts toward us are good.

NOTES

Wanda Landreth Rice	**Related Scriptures**	**September 1**
Hamilton, OH	Proverbs 17:17; 27:10; Luke 10:27-37	Proverbs 18:24

A man [woman] that hath friends must shew himself [herself] friendly:
and there is a friend that sticketh closer than a brother (Proverbs 18:24).

AM I REALLY YOUR FRIEND?

Someone said that if in your lifetime you find one true friend, you have found a rare and priceless treasure. Why do we avoid opening ourselves to offer genuine and selfless friendship when there is such an overwhelming demand and limited supply?

In Luke 10 Jesus described the attributes of a true friend in the story of the Good Samaritan. Loving selflessly requires giving of yourself and your time, expecting nothing in return. And sometimes, it hurts severely. Yet nothing is more rewarding than the fulfillment of true friendship.

I have been blessed with several genuine and loving friends. In my darkest times, those special people have helped "carry" me. Several years ago, a young lady made such an impact on me that I wrote the following poem:

MY VERY SPECIAL FRIEND
If with quill and ink words could be penned
To tell the meaning of a special friend,
A book could not express a single thought
Or fully tell what an act of love has wrought
In many lives who needed a helping hand—
And you, my special friend, met that demand.
There's never been a time when you've restrained
To share the joys and laughter, tears and pain.
Though oftentimes you've borne much grief and care,
Not once were you unwilling to be there.
For when others never seemed to understand,
God placed a healing balm within your hand.
I know when Christ looks down from heaven above
And sees the endless flow of selfless love,
His heart must burst within with pride and joy;
Thus, all attempts of Satan He'll destroy.
Yes, with every step you take, He holds your hand—
He's leading you, my very special friend.
So never feel you've lived thus far in vain
For you have the gift of easing the deepest pain.
A channel of God's love you've been to me.
A reflection of Christ's image I can see.
(So seldom will one find a friend so true.)
My very special friend, I really love you!

Have you been that kind of friend to anyone? Are you ready to accept the challenge?

REMEMBER TODAY: Be a friend. The cost of genuine caring does not begin to compare with its rewards.

Beth D. Lirio	**Related Scriptures**	**September 2**
Lancaster, PA	Psalms 103:1-5; 106:1, 2	Psalm 103:2

Praise the Lord, O my soul, and forget
not all his benefits (Psalm 103:2, NIV).

A NO-CALORIE MOTIVATOR

Some people rely on coffee to wake them every morning or energize them throughout the day. Others drink soda or eat sweets when they are feeling low. My personal favorite is chocolate. However, I have discovered a new, far safer motivator to rely on when my spirits wane. It is inexpensive, easily accessible and contains absolutely no calories!

The psalmist David reminds us of the many works God performs for us. He forgives us our sins, heals our diseases, redeems us from the pit, crowns us with love and compassion, satisfies our desires with good things, and renews our youth (Psalm 103:3-5). Verse 2 directs us to praise God for his numerous benefits to us.

Resolve today to thank God specifically for your family, house, job, church, friends and material blessings. Call out individually the many benefits He has given you. You might say, "Thank You for my son's new shoes" or "Thank You for the good communication I had with my mother this morning." Do it silently as you go about your daily tasks. You will be amazed how that specific praise to your Maker will rejuvenate you. He loves to receive our praise, and He restores those who offer Him thanksgiving. Certainly the lift you will receive is greater than the finest French-roast coffee or Swiss chocolate can ever offer.

REMEMBER TODAY: As you praise God continually, He will replenish your soul.

Dorothy H. Sibley
Jacksonville, FL

Related Scripture
Galatians 5:22, 23

September 3
Colossians 1:10

*That you may have a walk worthy of the Lord, fully
pleasing Him, being fruitful in every good work and
increasing in the knowledge of God* (Colossians 1:10, NKJV).

FLOWERS IN GOD'S GARDEN

How is your life being manifested spiritually? Are you fruitful in every good work? Are you blossoming beautiful flowers of love, joy, peace and patience? The Christian lifestyle should be fruitful in every good work.

In the Bible we read about flowers of the field and of the flowers appearing on the earth in the springtime (Psalm 103:15; Song of Solomon 2:12). Even specific flowers are named in the Bible—the lily and the rose. Genesis 2:8 refers to God planting a garden, the Garden of Eden. Metaphorically, we could interpret the garden as the church. The owner of the garden is God, Jesus Christ is the planter, the Holy Spirit is the caretaker, and we are the flowers in this beautiful garden.

If you had your choice, which would you be—the lily, which symbolizes purity; the violet, which symbolizes humility; the marigold, which symbolizes obedience; the orchid, which symbolizes wisdom; or the rose, which symbolizes patience?

Are we blooming for Jesus in all seasons of life? Whatever garden of life you are in, demonstrate God's love and bloom for Him. Let us send forth fragrances of the fruit of the Spirit, among which are love, gentleness, joy, peace, long-suffering and faith. Our fruitfulness depends upon our relationship with the Lord.

REMEMBER TODAY: We are planted in God's garden to bless and help others.

Ruth Hampton
Doraville, GA

Related Scriptures
2 Corinthians 6:2; Ephesians 5:16;
James 4:13

September 4
Proverbs 27:1

*Boast not thyself of to morrow; for thou knowest
not what a day may bring forth* (Proverbs 27:1).

PRACTICAL LIVING

Where do you live? No, I am not referring to your physical dwelling address. I'm referring to your mental address.

I was once located on "When" Street. As a mental resident there, my thoughts seemed to be one-track and my happiness determined by thoughts such as *when* I graduate, *when* I get a job, *when* I get married, *when* I have children, *when* they are potty-trained, *when* we get a larger house, *when* we get out of debt, *when* the holidays are over, *when* the children are older— the list goes on. You can certainly make contributions to the "when" list if you are a present or former resident of "When" Street.

One day I realized I was allowing life to pass me by. I was not appreciative enough of the daily provisions with which God had blessed me. I was waiting for tomorrow, next week, or month, or year, when "things" would make my life "just right."

Proverbs 27:1 was the U-Haul that appeared from God's Word to move my mental attitudes: "Boast not thyself of to morrow; for thou knowest not what a day may bring forth." God taught me to live day by day. To hope, plan, dream or wish is perfectly in order as long as you are content with today.

My new mental residence was also in God's Word. James 4:13 says, "Go to now." In other words, live *today* today! *When* poses a question; *now* affords an answer. *When* waits for action, *now* offers results. *When* causes anticipation; *now* produces certainty.

Now is the time to enjoy life, love and honor our spouse, cherish our children, enjoy the holidays and make them a celebration, and turn our houses into homes. Now is the time to worship God, to give thanks to Him, for you have become a resident of "Now" Avenue. Welcome!

REMEMBER TODAY: Now is the only time available to you. Use it wisely.

Iris Vest   **Related Scriptures**   **September 5**
Cleveland, TN   1 Kings 3:1-10; 2 Corinthians 2:3; 10:2   Galatians 5:10

*I have confidence in you in
the Lord* (Galatians 5:10, *NASB*).

THIS MATTER OF TRUST

We all struggle with this matter of trust. Some people we trust and some we don't. Some people we trust up to a point. With others, the "point" is definitely located closer in. The truth of the matter is, the whole matter of trust presents us with a certain dilemma. Let's examine it.

We are to trust God explicitly. There is no exception here. He is God . . . sovereign . . . almighty . . . perfect in character . . . worthy of trust—both willing and capable of keeping every promise.

Naturally it follows that there is a certain sense in which we trust God exclusively, meaning we would never trust any man in the same sense and to the same degree. Man is finite, human, frail, incapable of doing many things and often unwilling to do even those things he can do.

We can solve a lot of problems with a conscious, prayerful effort to control and shape our attitudes toward one another. For example, Solomon surely remembered things both good and bad about his father, but he chose to dwell on David's strength and his relationship to God rather than on his sins and failures.

Note Solomon's words: "Thou hast shewed unto thy servant David my father great mercy, according as he walked before thee in truth, and in righteousness, and in uprightness of heart with thee; and thou hast kept for him this great kindness, that thou hast given him a son to sit on his throne, as it is this day" (1 Kings 3:6).

Solomon could have blamed his father for some of his problems, but he was more interested in finding direction for the future than in placing blame for the past.

We often look for the worst in people rather than the best. William Barclay said, "We are sent into the world to love one another. Sometimes we live as if we were sent into the world to compete with one another or to dispute with one another or even to quarrel with one another. But the Christian is sent into the world to live in such a way that he shows what is meant by loving fellow-man."

REMEMBER TODAY: A lack of trusting relationships between members of the body of Christ will always blunt the effectiveness of the church.

Willie Lee Darter
Iowa Park, TX

Related Scriptures
2 Corinthians 6:10; 1 Thessalonians 5:16-18

September 6
John 15:11

These things have I spoken unto you, that my joy might
remain in you, and that your joy might be full (John 15:11).

THE WELLSPRING OF JOY

Do problems throw you? Which faces reflect joy in the line at the supermarket? What about your own? The lack of joy in our lives bears the same fruit in our homes. If we try modulating our voice to reflect joy and buoyancy, our children will quit whining too. Despondency is not for Christians.

Television programs are filled with laughter minus joy. This kind of laughter is artificial. Joy does not depend on material things; it depends on a right relationship with God. Only then can we experience the true meaning of joy.

When we suffer the sorrows of life, we don't shout "hallelujah" every few minutes, but in spite of the pain, the joy of the Lord abides in our hearts and becomes our strength. We can have joy in spite of circumstances, not because of them. Stanley Collins, in his book *Joy All the Way*, reminds us that God is the author of joy, the One who brings it into the world and into the human heart.

When asked the secret of her consistently overflowing joy, the late Mrs. R.P. Johnson said, "I've never gotten over the wonder of it all, the wonder that Jesus loves me." Her life of radiant joy influenced my life as an early teen more than that of any other Christian. Joy is our Christian privilege and the best advertisement for the gospel.

REMEMBER TODAY: Joy has its springs deep down inside, and that spring never runs dry, no matter what happens (Samuel Dickey Gordon).

Loretta C. Huffman
Smithfield, NC

Related Scriptures
Matthew 6:25-34; Luke 12:22-32; Romans 8:28

September 7
Philippians 4:19

*But my God shall supply all your need according to his
riches in glory by Christ Jesus* (Philippians 4:19).

HIS STOREHOUSE IS FULL

As my first grader prepared for school, I was in the kitchen trying to decide what I could prepare for breakfast with only a small portion of rice. We had been going through a recession, and everyone seemed to be suffering. I finally prepared the rice and called him to eat.

When he looked at the rice, he said, "But, Mother, I don't like rice for breakfast. Can't I please have something else?" I told him we didn't have anything else to eat right now, but if he would eat the rice, by the time school was out we'd have something very good to eat. I did not know where I was going to get food that day, but I knew what God had promised in His Word. I began to pray and ask God to supply our needs and supply food for the children.

Shortly, the phone rang. A lady told my husband she did not know us personally, nor did we know her, but that she had seen us at a fellowship meeting. While she was praying that morning, God had told her we were in need. He had instructed her to assist us.

She asked my husband what we needed. At first, he was a little hesitant. He disliked sharing with others how badly we were in need. Our church was small, and everyone seemed to be suffering lack in some area. Finally, he told her that a family with children could always use food. She told him that was all she wanted to know. She and her husband would be over shortly with groceries for us.

When my little boy came in from school and saw all the food, he exclaimed, "Mother said we would have some good food tonight if I ate that rice this morning!"

That morning the hope for food looked dim, except for the fact that we serve a Savior who never lets us down. Even if He has to move on the hearts of strangers, He will supply all our needs when we trust Him.

REMEMBER TODAY: God's storehouse is never empty. All we have to do is trust Him for our needs.

Julie Trusty
Livonia, MI

Related Scriptures
Psalm 16:11; Galatians 5:22;
John 15:4-11; Colossians 2:6

September 8
John 15:4, 11

"Take care to live in me, and let me live in you. For a branch can't produce fruit when severed from the vine. Nor can you be fruitful apart from me. . . . I have told you this so that you will be filled with my joy. Yes, your cup of joy will overflow!" (John 15:4, 11, *TLB*).

THE WAY OF JOY

God desires His children's joy to be full. In order for this to occur, a process must take place. This process begins by abiding in Christ and allowing Christ to abide in us. Then, as we grow, the pruning process begins.

How exactly does one abide in Christ? Abiding means to align your life with God's Word. This comes by studying God's Word and continuing in prayer. God doesn't just zap you with fruitful branches and fullness of joy. These characteristics occur as you walk in accordance with His Word and spend time alone with Him. It's then that you begin to produce fruit and walk in joy.

In John 15 God says He wants you to abide in Him and to bear fruit. It's a mandate for every believer. He reemphasizes in verse 11 that the reason He desires this for His children is so their joy will be full. In other words, no abiding, no fruit: no fruit, no joy.

Sometimes in the process of fruit bearing, it becomes necessary for God to prune the branches. This process is not always pleasant, but it is necessary! Many times it is even painful and difficult to understand why. But if we are truly abiding in Him, we will accept God's will above our own. Our heavenly Father finds it necessary to cut away things that hinder the formation of His likeness in us. Even the finest Christian must be willing to submit to the discipline of a loving Father.

God expects the life of Christ to be reproduced in you and in others through you. When He scans the earth, He recognizes His children by their remarkable likeness to Jesus. It is not enough to make a good impression, be attractive, appear mature or have a wide influence. God is looking for those who are bearing fruit. This fruit is not manufactured or developed by human ingenuity. Neither does it mature overnight. It is a life process. It isn't enough to possess good qualities, we must be capable of conveying Christ's love through our lives.

Pruning by the Father produces fruit, which in turn produces joy. On the other hand, a fruitless life is in danger of being severed from the vine, resulting in despair.

REMEMBER TODAY: The choice is yours—fruit and joy or fruitlessness and despair. Walk in the way of joy today.

Mary A. Smith
Elaine, AR

Related Scriptures:
Proverbs 22:6; Luke 15:11-32

September 9
Luke 15:24

For this my son was dead, and is alive again; he was lost, and is found. And they began to be merry (Luke 15:24).

THE PROMISE

"Mom, I've decided I want to live with Daddy" were the words my oldest daughter, Marie, used when she thought she didn't want to live with me any longer. I'll never forget those words.

Marie's father was not a Christian, so I knew he would not take her to church and teach her about the Lord. Her decision to leave our home brought grief and sorrow, and I remember spending much time in prayer over her decision. The Lord gave me the assurance that my daughter would be back home but that first she had to learn some things.

My youngest daughter, Anne, could always tell when I was missing her sister. She would say to me, "Mom, I won't ever leave you. I'll always stay with you." Anne and I stayed busy doing things together and requested prayer for Marie at each church service we attended.

Days turned into months, the summer passed, and school was ready to start. I knew the Lord had promised that Marie would be back home with me, but I did not know when. That promise from the Lord is what kept me going each day. The Lord gives us strength to endure until our prayers are answered. I knew Marie would have to learn lessons I could not teach her.

I reminded the Lord how I had given Marie and Anne to Him when they were babies and how I had taken them to church and taught them about loving and serving the Lord. Now I had to trust that this teaching was not in vain; I had to trust God to bring her home again.

Then one night the phone rang. I answered it and the voice said, "Mom, I love you, and I want to come back home." Luke 15:24 came to my mind, and I knew my own prodigal was coming home. God is not slack concerning His promises but is faithful to keep His Word.

REMEMBER TODAY: The way we train up our children will determine the choices they make in life.

Jean Barnett
Fenton, MI

Related Scriptures
Psalm 91; Isaiah 41:10;
Matthew 10:29-31

September 10
Psalm 91:1

*He that dwelleth in the secret place of the most High shall
abide under the shadow of the Almighty (Psalm 91:1).*

IN THE FATHER'S SHADOW

"Calm down . . . stop screaming . . . remember the children," said the old lady as three bombs found their target from an enemy aircraft.

We were trapped inside a shelter with debris and darkness surrounding us. My father, a London fireman, was off duty that night. He found a way out for us and protected us from seeing the terrible scene where many of our friends died. All my family lost their homes that night, and we slept in a factory until we could stay with an aunt in the countryside.

This was just the beginning of a time when an 8-year-old girl's world was turned upside down. We had quite a number of adventures from this event until I was 13. Then, suddenly, it was all over. But my life didn't turn right side up until I was saved at the age of 17.

Looking back, I realize the love and protection our heavenly Father demonstrated toward my sister and me. Isaiah 41:10 says, "Fear thou not; for I am with thee: be not dismayed; for I am thy God." As a Christian I know that my life is hid with Christ in God and I can enjoy a wonderful relationship as His child.

REMEMBER TODAY: God is aware of you and sees you through His Son, Jesus.

Lee Kincaid
Brook Park, OH

Related Scriptures
John 16:7; Isaiah 51:12

September 11
John 15:26

But when the Comforter is come, whom I will send unto you from the Father . . . (John 15:26).

THE SCRIPTURE QUILT

Recently while visiting my two granddaughters, I noticed the oldest, Jenny, was wrapped in an unusual quilt. My daughter-in-law, Cheryl, said softly, "Do you remember that quilt? It is the one I wrapped her in when I came out of the parsonage fire!" She had washed it and kept it. That tragic day her husband, David, and baby, Jonathan, were killed. Now it was being used again to comfort my granddaughter in the cool South Carolina mountain air. Jenny is coming through her teen years, and I'm sure she will pass that quilt on to her little ones some day. The church where our son and his family pastored had made a Scripture quilt for them. All the families of the church made a square with their favorite scripture and names written on it to be sewn together to make the quilt.

Oh, how God's spiritual quilt works today! His Comforter, the Holy Spirit, keeps us warm in the coldness of this world's heartaches, sickness, burdens and trials. The comfort, love and concern that come from God's family reminds me of Grandma Frazier's beautiful old quilts made of Aunt Helen's dresses, Aunt Frances' coats, Uncle Lynie's blue jeans, and my coats and dresses. We loved to pick out our old pieces of clothing from that quilt. A quilt is a prized treasure that is often preserved in the bottom of a trunk. What a waste! It should be shared so others can enjoy the beautiful, precious memories.

REMEMBER TODAY: Allow God to wrap His Comforter around you today!

Mary Fisher
Cleveland, TN

Related Scriptures
Nehemiah 8:10; Proverbs 12:25;
Joel 2:21; John 13:17

September 12
Philippians 4:8

*Finally, brethren, whatsoever things are true, whatsoever things are honest,
whatsoever things are just, whatsoever things are pure, whatsoever things are
lovely, whatsoever things are of good report; if there be any virtue, and if
there be any praise, think on these things* (Philippians 4:8).

DON'T WORRY, BE HAPPY

"Tell Grandma the new words you have learned," said my daughter-in-law to our 2-year-old grandson during their visit with us.

"Don't worry, be happy," came his quick response.

"Where did he learn that?" I asked. "That's the title of a new popular song. Haven't you heard it?" she asked.

I had not, but the title made me wonder what it was all about. Since I wasn't in the habit of listening to popular music on the radio, several weeks went by and I still hadn't heard the song.

Then one day when my husband and I were eating in a restaurant, I noticed a jukebox. This would be a good time to hear the song. The restaurant was small, crowded, and folks were talking with one another. The waitress was busy helping her customers. But over the background noise I caught the gist of the words:

No one is exempt from trouble, but worrying only makes things worse. When we worry, it often spills over and makes others miserable too. Ususally, whatever is causing us to worry quickly passes anyway. So smile and don't discourage people. Don't worry, be happy!

When the song came on, I noticed most of the patrons stopped talking. The waitress started singing along with the record and even continued singing after it was finished. It was a catchy little tune that changed the atmosphere in that restaurant for a few minutes and no doubt lingered in some hearts for days to come.

The message of this song reminds Christians of what they have already learned from Scripture: " 'Do not sorrow, for the joy of the Lord is your strength'" (Nehemiah 8:10, *NKJV*).

REMEMBER TODAY: Do you want to spread a little sunshine today? Smile and hum a happy tune where people can hear you. You'll find it will pick up your spirits, too.

Sherry B. Lee
Cleveland, TN

Related Scriptures
Luke 21:19; Romans 5:3;
Hebrews 10:36

September 13
Hebrews 12:1

*Let us run with patience the race
that is set before us (Hebrews 12:1).*

PATIENTLY RUNNING

"Be careful how you pray for patience," the exuberant preacher warned. "You will surely get tribulation." It was one of those statements received from an authority figure which I, as a child, readily accepted as truth with no personal discernment or contextual understanding.

Young adulthood prompted me to evaluate, screen and organize life's truths into meaningful principles which could be used and lived. In regard to the virtue of patience, my mind said, "Leave it alone. The only way to get it is to suffer more tribulation. Don't you have enough difficulty already?"

My stunted growth in patience has become more evident recently. The necessity of this virtue to spiritual excellence is repeatedly emphasized in Scripture. In seeking personal illumination, the Father revealed to me that this quality is neither taught, caught nor sought. Knowing the how-to's are of no value.

Paul said, "Run with patience." The metaphor reminds me of modern-day marathon participants who practice physical endurance. They run until running is easy. They endure until they have become patient endurers.

How I desire to practice spiritual patience. I want to serve until serving becomes easy, give and go until I patiently give and go. After the second mile, the third will be the test of joyful endurance. I long to break through to the "second wind" of the Spirit and breathe the free air of total abandonment to God's purposes.

So, with reservation of flesh but hunger of spirit, I say, "Father, I desire patience."

He responds as I sensed He would, "Start practicing. Run."

REMEMBER TODAY: The third mile is the test of joyful endurance. Break through to the "second wind" of the Spirit. Run with patience.

Patty Stallings	**Related Scriptures**	**September 14**
Rapid City, SD	Romans 5:8; 8:35-39	Jeremiah 31:3

The Lord hath appeared of old unto me, saying, Yea, I
have loved thee with an everlasting love: therefore with
lovingkindness have I drawn thee (Jeremiah 31:3).

LOVE THAT JUST WON'T QUIT

Our culture tells us that love comes and goes. "I love you because you love me" or "I will love you if you do something for me." This is conditional love.

But God's love is not only unconditional, it is also unfailing, unlimited, unending and unaffected. God does not strike a bargain with us to love us only when we love Him in return. Romans 5:8 tells us the proof of God's amazing love is that while we were yet sinners, the enemies of God, Christ died for us.

We know there is nothing within us that could attract the love of God, who is perfect in holiness. There is no act we can do to earn His love. It is undeserved. If nothing on our part persuaded God to love us, then surely there is nothing that will prevent Him from loving us. God himself is the reason for the love shown us. He is love. It is the essence of His unchangeable nature. That is why Paul was able to tell us in Romans 8:38, 39 that absolutely nothing can separate us from the love of God that is in Christ Jesus. We could not stop God from loving us if we tried.

The verse in Jeremiah is God's message to wayward Israel. They were in Babylonian captivity, exiles in a foreign land. God had allowed this condition, in love, to turn their eyes back to Him.

Perhaps you feel forsaken in an unfamiliar place and have wondered where God is. Remember, He loves you with an everlasting love. Maybe your life has been invaded by the Enemy and your treasures have been carried away. God loves you with an everlasting love. You may be under the disciplining hand of the Lord. God loves you with an everlasting love.

REMEMBER TODAY: Wherever you are, whatever your situation, God loves you with a love that never ends.

Linda F. Bostic   **Related Scriptures**   **September 15**
Lindsay, OK   1 Corinthians 2:14, 15; Ephesians 5:2   1 Corinthians 2:15

For we are unto God a sweet
savour of Christ (1 Corinthians 2:15).

A SWEET SAVOUR

Isn't it refreshing to go somewhere you have not been before and smell something that reminds you of a pleasant experience? My daughter and I have entered certain stores and remarked, "This smells like Gran's house." A number of times I have heard my husband reminisce about coming home from school and smelling the clean floors and all the little throw rugs his mom had washed. These pleasant odors are refreshing.

Yes, the smell of fresh home-baked bread or squeaky-clean floors is pleasant. But even more important is that people can detect the aroma of Christ when they come into our homes. Wherever we are, do we emanate a fragrance of genuine love and a lack of prejudice for people who are different? Are our lives still as clean as when the Lord first came into our spiritual houses? Is there still a sweet savor? We should remember that God uses us to spread His knowledge everywhere like a sweet-smelling perfume.

REMEMBER TODAY: Are you fulfilling our Lord's last commandment to spread His love in all places?

Sonia Griffey
Cleveland, TN

Related Scriptures
Jeremiah 29:11-13; John 15:1-8;
Romans 8:28; James 1:2-4, 12; Philippians 1:6

September 16
Galatians 5:22, 23

But the fruit of the Spirit is . . .
meekness . . . (Galatians 5:22, 23).

MEEKNESS DURING TRIALS

How has God been dealing with you lately? Are the blessings flowing, or is it a time of trials?

If it is a time of trials, then meekness, one of the characteristics of the fruit of the Spirit, is what you need.

"Meekness?" you say. "How can that help? If it does, where do I get it?"

Meekness is often explained by the word *gentleness*. Gentleness, however, is more an outgrowth of meekness. Vine's *Expository Dictionary of New Testament Words* describes meekness as a characteristic relating first to our attitude toward God. It is accepting God's dealings within our lives, realizing that what God is doing is for our good and not quarreling or resisting His work, even when it seems difficult.

What a wonderful attitude to have! How can we get this acceptance and trust in God? Only from Him. We cannot produce this fruit by ourselves. John 15:4 says: "'Remain in me, and I will remain in you. No branch can bear fruit by itself; it must remain in the vine. Neither can you bear fruit unless you remain in me'" (*NIV*). When we seek Him, looking only to Him and allowing His Word to fill our lives, then He will produce the fruit.

How can I say this with such confidence? Because God is doing this in my life. As I write this devotion, my family is going through a difficult trial. There are times when I cry and question God, but He always brings me back to a trust in Him. God causes my spirit to say, "Lord, I do not understand, but You are faithful and I trust You. I accept Your dealings and I know everything will work together for my good. Your Word says so and I will believe it."

If I depend on my feelings or look to circumstances, I will doubt. When I choose to keep my eyes on Christ, realizing who He is and what His Word says, He produces the meekness, the trust, the faith.

God will do this for you also. He will produce meekness, the acceptance of His work in your life during your trial.

REMEMBER TODAY: Remain in Christ. He will produce the fruit.

Lynne Couzens **Related Scriptures** **September 17**
Gimli, Manitoba Isaiah 43:1-3a; Psalm 27:1; 5 Proverbs 3:5, 6

Trust in the Lord with all your heart, and lean not on your
own understanding; in all your ways acknowledge Him,
and He shall direct your paths (Proverbs 3:5, 6, *NKJV*).

A NECESSITY FOR TURBULENT TIMES

Trusting the Lord is not a luxury but a necessity in our everyday turbulent lives. How do we react when we are placed in a situation that is not of our choosing? Sickness, death and emotional suffering of varying degrees affect us all from time to time.

For the last year I have been sick, sometimes for months at a time, but then I would feel fine for a while. The doctors can't find anything wrong! How should I react when I'm well one night but the next morning I almost pass out when I get up?

Aren't you glad we don't have to figure out the whys and wherefores? God's Word says to "lean not on your own understanding" but to "trust in the Lord with all your heart." God doesn't require us to understand or reason through these situations; He only asks us to obey His directions and *trust* Him for the results. God is interested in all aspects of our lives, including our physical well-being, but He is more interested in our spiritual health. Often for our benefit He chooses paths we would not have chosen.

He has instructed us, "In all your ways acknowledge Him." To "acknowledge" God means to recognize Him. Often we do not recognize Him in our circumstances but instead yell, "God, get me out of this!" If we truly believe God is in control, we must willingly submit to the circumstances and people He allows in our lives. Psalm 37:23 says, "The steps of a good man are ordered by the Lord." This does not mean we should not recognize Satan and stand against Him. It means that having done all to stand, we then submit to the will of God, for "all things work together for good to them that love God, to them who are the called according to his purpose" (Romans 8:28).

Lord, how are You going to use my situation for good? Are You going to draw me closer to You by teaching me important lessons I would not learn any other way? Perhaps You will save souls that would otherwise have been unreached. Lord, use me in the way You choose!

REMEMBER TODAY: God is in control; He knows all things and He loves you!

Linda Lippolt
Amityville, NY

Related Scriptures
Proverbs 11:30; John 4:14

*Like a trampled spring and a polluted well, is a righteous man
who gives way before the wicked* (Proverbs 25:26, *NASB*).

A VESSEL OF HONOR

Have you ever been so thirsty that you almost lost your sense of rationale? Most of us have at some time become so thirsty we could not think about anything else.

I remember one incident where a friend and I traveled four hours to visit a family who lived on a farm. When we arrived, we were tired and thirsty. I recall sitting in the kitchen almost wishing I could rush through all the greetings and small talk so I could have a cool drink of water. Then, as a gracious gesture, I offered to help clear the dinner dishes. As I leaned over the sink and opened the faucet, a foul odor was emitted from it.

I was careful not to reveal my shock; however, they were accustomed to informing all the new guests about the water. The water was OK to drink; the odor was caused by an overabundance of minerals. Later, they brought us some special spring water to drink, which also had a strong odor.

The next day my friend and I went to town and purchased some bottled water. Although the odor may have been only superficial, it overpowered our thirst. The cleansing, refreshing and purifying characteristics of the water were spoiled by the odor. Perhaps it tasted fine, but neither of us was willing to find out.

This reminded me of the scripture in Proverbs 25:26, which tells us that the righteous are like wells of water. If our lives are tainted with compromise, the refreshing well or spring will become foul. Not only is water essential for life, but it is also refreshing.

In the same way, we have been commissioned by the Lord to refresh the souls of the lost—to bring life and cleansing through the gospel and our examples.

People who recognize the light in us and realize their need will come to us. We must be careful to keep our lives and hearts pure so the water they receive will be what they are seeking. Jesus said to the woman at the well, " 'Whoever drinks of the water that I shall give him shall never thirst" (John 4:14, *NASB*).

REMEMBER TODAY: The vessel that the Lord wants to use must be a clean one!

Jimmi N. Campbell
Aiea, HI

Related Scriptures
Psalm 139:10; Isaiah 51:16;
Jeremiah 18:6

September 19
Psalm 37:24

For the Lord upholdeth him
with his hand (Psalm 37:24).

HOLDING HIS HAND

"I like to hold your hand," said my little grandson as his big brown eyes looked up at me so trustingly. I replied, "That's because it's Grandmother's hand, and if you keep holding my hand, you won't get lost."

Suddenly my heart quickened as I thought, *God is holding my hand, and if I don't turn loose, I won't get lost either.*

Many times in my life I have insisted on going my own way. I could have gone astray or made a hasty wrong decision, but God was there guiding me ever so gently in His perfect way. He was holding my hand. When I needed strength, He made me strong. When I needed solutions, He gave me wisdom. When I needed courage, He gave me boldness. There is safety and security in holding His hand.

"Lord, I like holding Your hand."

REMEMBER TODAY: As we face each new day, our sustaining strength is the knowledge that He is holding our hand.

Lou Beaver
Shreveport, LA

Related Scriptures
Isaiah 65:24; Luke 12:27-32

September 20
1 Peter 5:7

Casting all your care upon him;
for he careth for you (1 Peter 5:7).

WHEN I FAIL TO REMEMBER

My 17-month-old baby girl looked up at me, puckered her lips and said, "I 'ont Wosie [I want Rosie]." My heart began to tremble, and tears flooded my eyes as I realized that she didn't remember me! My husband and I had just returned from the Church of God General Assembly. Rosie, a loving mother of a 16-month-old baby girl had cared for Terrice while we were away. She had cared for her every need, whether she was happy and smiling or unhappy and fretful. We returned during her nap time, picked her up before she was fully awake and brought her home to resume our role as loving parents. But during the eight days we were away, she had bonded to Rosie, who had been her loving care giver during our absence. Even though it took only a short time for her to remember me, the impact of what happened was indescribable.

A powerful parallel came into focus, and my heart again trembled as tears flooded my eyes. I thought of the unconditional love and care that my heavenly Father gives me every day. Whether I am happy and smiling or unhappy and fretful, He meets even my smallest needs, often even before I ask (Isaiah 65:24).

Then I asked myself this question: "How does my heavenly Father feel when I fail to remember Him?"

REMEMBER TODAY: Our wonderful heavenly Father deserves our recognition in exchange for His loving and faithful care.

Wanda Griffith	**Related Scriptures**	**September 21**
Cleveland, TN	Joshua 6; 24	Revelation 12:11

And they overcame him by the blood of the Lamb,
and by the word of their testimony (Revelation 12:11).

RECALLING GOD'S BLESSINGS

Growing up in small churches in Alabama, I remember best some victorious Wednesday-night testimony services. My dad would announce, "Tonight we are going to recall what the Lord has done for us this week, last week or sometime in our past." And he would always end by saying, "Don't force me to call on you [and I knew he was inserting my name here] to stand and praise the Lord."

If Joshua were participating in a testimony service, I'm sure a recurring victory recounted would be the fall of Jericho. This conquest was unprecedented, not only because of the special and unusual instructions but also because Jericho was a fortress city located in a strategic position, forming a major gateway to Canaan (Joshua 6).

Joshua reminded the people that God had fought for them from the crossing of the Jordan to the day when the sun stood still. He knew that if the people kept in mind God's victories on their behalf and the blessings of the land He had given them, they would be less prone to wander (Joshua 24).

Standing and praising God for His blessings, miracles and victories has the same keeping, preserving effect today. Just as His Word promises, we too can be made overcomers by the words of our testimonies.

REMEMBER TODAY: Recalling our victories of yesterday builds our faith today.

Saundra Jennings Rose
Norcross, GA

Related Scriptures
Nehemiah 8:10; Psalm 146:1-6;
Proverbs 15:1-15, 30; 1 Thessalonians 5:16

September 22
Proverbs 17:22

*A cheerful heart is good medicine, but a crushed
spirit dries up the bones* (Proverbs 17:22, *NIV*).

HEALTH AND HAPPINESS

A recent article in *The Atlanta Constitution* stated, "Most people do not believe they will live to be 100. Perhaps that's why they won't. It apparently takes an optimistic attitude to get there." The article continued: "The high level of cheerfulness among centenarians is one of several surprises that researchers in the Georgia Centenarian Study have encountered."

This article provided an excellent description of my maternal grandmother, Stella Todd Miller, who is now 94 years old and, in her own words, is looking for the Lord's soon return or the year 2,000, when she will be 103—whichever comes first!

Recently she shared how one morning she was filled with so much joy thinking on the goodness of God that she could hardly contain it. Overflowing with thanksgiving, she went to the piano to play and sing praises to her Father. She was not surprised when she sensed that her daughter who lives across the street had entered the house and joined her in song as she had done in times past. However, when she turned to acknowledge her presence, there was no one visibly there. She immediately realized that she had been graced with a presence from another world that morning. What overwhelming love, joy and peace filled her heart!

When the words of today's text were penned, Solomon did not have insight into the knowledge we have today. Yet he understood that "a cheerful heart is good medicine." Medical research has confirmed that a cheerful individual, free from worry, stress and anxiety, will not be as likely to develop physical problems as the person who is always despondent, downhearted and depressed. Psalm 146:5 says, "Happy is he who has the God of Jacob for his help" (*NKJV*).

REMEMBER TODAY: A cheerful spirit brings health, healing and happiness to a heart who trusts in God.

Sandra Duncan
Jackson, MS

Related Scriptures
Hebrews 10; Hebrews 12; James 1:3

September 23
Hebrews 10:23

Let us hold fast the profession of our faith without wavering;
(for he is faithful that promised) (Hebrews 10:23).

IN TOUCH WITH THE PROBLEM-SOLVER

The silence of our "quiet" evening at home was broken by a bloodcurdling scream coming from our 4-year-old son's room. As my husband and I dashed into the room, we found an injured "Superman" with a sagging cape, rolling on the floor, cradling his left foot in his arms.

"I broke my foot! I broke my foot!" Scott was yelling. Being the concerned and professionally trained parents that we were, we carefully examined his foot, twisting it to see if he grimaced. After determining that it was nothing serious, we tucked "Superman" in bed. As he began his bedtime prayers, he asked us to pray that God would heal his foot. Early the next morning, my husband and I were awakened by Scott crawling into bed with us. As he settled in between us, he held up his foot and in a weak, pain-filled voice said, "Mommy, God didn't healed my foot; He just swolled it up."

How often do we feel this way? We sincerely pray about a problem, only to find that it seems to get bigger and bigger. This is when our faith is really put to the test. Physically, we feel worse; financially, we seem to be going under; emotionally, we are drained; spiritually, God seems to be on the back side of the moon. Yet we know, deep in our hearts, that God will never leave us nor forsake us. His Word promises healing—physical, financial, emotional and spiritual. We cannot afford to be sidetracked by our situations. God knows what we need and when we need it. The answer may not come as quickly as we wish, but rest assured—it will come. God may have to "swell up" our problems in order to get our undivided attention and draw us nearer to Him.

REMEMBER TODAY: No matter how big your problems are, don't lose touch with the Problem-solver.

Deana Landers
Dandridge, TN

Related Scriptures
Psalm 119:105; John 8:12; 1 John 1:5

September 24
2 Samuel 22:29

"You are my lamp, O Lord; the Lord turns my darkness into light" (2 Samuel 22:29, NIV).

REACH UP

It was almost dark, but I could vaguely see the light on the back porch. If only I could make it. . . .

When I was a small child, I lived on a farm in Juliette, Georgia. My four brothers and I had so many places to play and we often wandered off into the woods around the house. One of our places of adventure was down at the creek, where we would catch tadpoles and crawfish. Needless to say, I was a tomboy, always trying to keep up with my brothers.

One day my mom told me to get the boys for supper. It was almost dark, but I walked down to the creek calling their names. They weren't there, so I lingered at our favorite spot, playing in the water for a while. Suddenly I realized it was getting dark. I was afraid of the dark, so I began to run back to the house. I tried to stay on the trail to keep going in the right direction, but somehow I veered off and could not see the house for the tall grass surrounding me. I was so afraid.

My brothers were always telling me stories of panthers and bears and big snakes lurking in the dark. Suddenly in the distance I could see the light on the back porch of our house. I knew if I could make it to the back porch, I'd be OK. But between me and the light was darkness, tall grass and imaginary monsters waiting to grab me. With all the faith of a little child, I reached my hand up to the sky and in my imagination grasped the hand of God and pleaded, "Jesus, help me make it to the back porch!" Moments later I was rushing into my mother's arms beneath the warmth of the bright light.

Since then I have experienced many dark and scary places in my life, but I have always been able to reach up to the strong hand of my Father and let Him lead me back to the light.

REMEMBER TODAY: There is no place so dark that God will not provide the light when we believe.

Darla Hodges
North Pole, AK

Related Scriptures
Romans 12:2; Hebrews 12:11;
James 4:7

September 25
Romans 12:1

*Therefore, I urge you, brothers [sisters], in view of God's mercy,
to offer your bodies as living sacrifices, holy and pleasing to God—
this is your spiritual act of worship* (Romans 12:1, NIV).

THE PEACE OF SUBMISSION

"Practice, practice, practice! All I do is practice!" my 13- year-old son complained as I reminded him to practice the trumpet.

Practice is a learned discipline. Paul urged believers to "offer your bodies as living sacrifices, holy and pleasing to God." Presenting or submitting ourselves each morning to God frees His power to work in and through us. As we discipline ourselves to read the Word and pray, we become renewed vessels that glorify God. But submitting once in the morning isn't sufficient for the entire day because the devil is on the job, influencing the flesh to override the will of God. As we practice submitting ourselves immediately to the Lord in the face of difficulties, He enables us to resist the Enemy.

During a ladies Bible study and prayer meeting, I had been using the words *submission, discipline* and *alignment*. A lady who regularly attends is serving in the United States Air Force. She was accustomed to the frequent use of abbreviations and began to put into practice the subject of our discussion. On the following Sunday evening, the pastor asked for praise testimonies. She excitedly gave us the example SDI (Strategic Defense Initiative). By changing one letter she had composed her own abbreviation SDA (Submission, Discipline and Alignment), thereby formulating her own strategic defense against the Enemy. She began to apply it to every part of her life.

Submitting to God is a discipline worth developing. Then we can experience the peace that only God, the God of all grace, can give.

REMEMBER TODAY: Disciplining ourselves in submission to God brings us into alignment with His perfect will.

Lynda Pruitt
Alpine, CA

Related Scriptures
Exodus 31:3; 1 John 5:14

September 26
Proverbs 22:3

A prudent man foresees the difficulties ahead
and prepares for them; the simpleton goes blindly
on and suffers the consequences (Proverbs 22:3, *TLB*).

CAUGHT IN THE SNARE

In our early years of ministry I was sitting in a class of about 30 women at a seminar for women in ministry. I had come expecting to hear what the Lord had prepared for me that day. With three small children in diapers, my life was very full. In addition, I was in the process of organizing an active Ladies Ministries, playing the piano and helping my husband with his pastoral activities in our growing congregation.

I had just finished attending a class on the importance of properly maintaining a well-balanced diet for your family. This was an important class to me; however, I still felt overwhelmed with all the demands on my time. Then, as if awakening from a fog, I heard the speaker say, "Ladies, it's OK if your children are small. They're your ministry—minister to them while you can!"

That was it! So simple, yet I had been caught in the snare of getting my priorities in the wrong order. I asked the Lord to forgive me. Then I asked Him to help me to redirect my thoughts and actions into a more productive lifestyle.

REMEMBER TODAY: The Spirit of God gives us wisdom, understanding and knowledge. These are ours for the asking.

Mildred Cox	**Related Scriptures**	**September 27**
Rochester, NY	Romans 12:10; 1 Thessalonians 4:9	Hebrews 13:1

Let brotherly [sisterly]
love continue (Hebrews 13:1).

CHRISTIAN FRIENDSHIPS

Imagine what kind of influence Christians would have on the world if we modeled the ideal *permanence* of love in our relationships with one another rather than tossing the broken ones out and starting with new ones.

I recall a story I read some time ago about two birds in a nest pecking each other. Along came a little boy, who asked his older brother, "Why are the birds pecking one another?"

The older brother replied, "They are quarreling."

The little boy answered, "No! No! They can't be; they are brothers."

Are we much different from these birds? Quite often many of us find ourselves quarreling, moving as migrants from place to place. We try to escape the pressures of a relationship, when we should believe, trust and support one another. Remember, if God loves us and His mercy is a cloak that hides our shame, then our charity should be a veil before our eyes and the bond of sisterhood should abide.

The writer of Hebrews said, "Let brotherly [sisterly] love continue." My interpretation of this beautiful scripture leads me to believe that the love of a Christian sister should be a permanent obligation. We should allow the love of God to continuously flow through us.

REMEMBER TODAY: Christian friendships give us the opportunity to let sisterly love continue.

Shirley Strawn Walters
Cleveland, TN

Related Scriptures
2 Corinthians 12:9;
Philippians 4:7, 10-13, 19

September 28
Philippians 4:13

I can do all things through Christ which
strengtheneth me (Philippians 4:13).

FROM ANXIETY TO CONTENTMENT

We can have victory over anxiety. In every experience and lesson of life, along with victory, Jesus gives us contentment. I have learned I can be in a storm and still have peace. Through Christ I can adapt to any circumstance if I trust in God. He will give sufficient grace to keep and sustain me.

Through the death of my husband, remarriage, family problems, stepparent problems and heartaches, Jesus has given me sweet peace. I've adapted to many different situations in my life, and I have found God to be faithful and true.

Through the experience of losing a husband and father, our family actually lived on the premise that "I can do all things through Christ." I would awaken each morning repeating that verse. As I placed my sons on the school bus, we would say it together. We lived and breathed that wonderful scripture. Peace that passed all understanding swept over us.

God's grace is sufficient, and He will provide our every need in all circumstances. God brought scriptures alive to our hearts, increasing our faith and giving us strength for the day. We serve a faithful and loving God. His promises are being fulfilled constantly in our lives.

REMEMBER TODAY: He will never lead you where His grace cannot keep you. You can rejoice today in knowing God holds you in His hands. He is already making a way!

Myrtie Lee	**Related Scriptures**	**September 29**
Lebanon, TN	John 3:16; Matthew 6:25-34	Matthew 10:29-31

Are not two sparrows sold for a farthing? and one of them shall not fall on the ground without your Father. But the very hairs of your head are all numbered. Fear ye not therefore, ye are of more value than many sparrows (Matthew 10:29-31).

GOD MARKS THE FALL

The pair of robins fluttered anxiously above the fence. Although the bird appeared to be fully mature, it had not yet learned to fly. As I watched the anxious parents, I realized they were helpless in picking up the sibling and putting it back in the nest. I wanted to help, but I knew there was nothing I could do. At that moment I was reminded that God cared and He knew. He had marked the fall of that robin.

Tears of compassion rushed down my face as I remembered the parents in our church family who were anxious over their young. I have observed them trying so hard to put life back together after one of the children has fallen from the nest, only to see them discover there is nothing that can be done to make life exactly the same again. This often results in feelings of failure.

Learning to fly is painful. We want to soar into the air immediately without first spending long periods of time on the ground learning the mechanics of flying. With all our hearts we dream of our children being instant achievers in life; however, this is not usually the case. They are often scarred from wrecks along the way. God does not measure success only in soaring, but He marks the fall. It is often in these falls that we hear His voice and experience His loving concern. We think of discipline and judgment for the wayward one, but God extends love and restoration. Did He not say we are worth more than many sparrows? And one never falls to the ground without Him.

The robins I saw were doing all they could by bringing food to the fallen one. In the hour of crisis, you may not be able to make everything right, but do all you can and commit the rest to the heavenly Father.

REMEMBER TODAY: Nothing will happen today that my heavenly Father will not see. I will rest in knowing that He cares.

Ellen Treadway	**Related Scripture**	September 30
Dolton, IL	Philippians 4:7	Isaiah 26:3

Thou wilt keep him in perfect peace, whose mind is
stayed on thee: because he trusteth in thee (Isaiah 26:3).

PERFECT PEACE

The Sunday after Christmas 1986 my family and I were preparing to go to Ohio to visit my husband's family. My packing was interrupted by the ringing of the telephone. On the other end of the line was my mother with news that my sister had had surgery on Friday. What was to have been a simple lumpectomy turned out to require major surgery for a malginancy. The entire breast had to be removed along with several lymph nodes. The doctors assured us that they had gotten all the cancer and after chemotherapy she should not have any more problems.

During the Thanksgiving holidays of the next year, my sister and I were both visiting our parents. She showed me the markings on her chest where they were planning to give her radiation treatments. Cancer had developed where the breast had been removed. Immediately thereafter, cancer began to crop up all over her body.

During this period of time she, her husband and daughter moved to Birmingham, Alabama. I couldn't be with her, so I called her often. During the last month of her life, I called every day. I never ceased to be amazed at the peace that flowed from her.

Philippians 4:7 reads, "And the peace of God, which passeth all understanding, shall keep your hearts and minds through Christ Jesus." I don't think I had ever fully understood this scripture until I saw it in action in her life. I never heard her complain or feel sorry for herself. She only talked of her love for the Lord and His wonderful peace.

On September 30, 1988, Wilda went home to be with Jesus. At her funeral her favorite song was sung, "To God Be the Glory." The words so well expressed the love and thanksgiving she felt for our gracious heavenly Father. During times of crisis and difficult circumstances, I think of the peace she felt during a time far worse than anything I have ever faced. I know He has perfect peace for me too!

REMEMBER TODAY: God offers perfect peace to those whose minds are stayed on Him.

Nellie Thompson	**Related Scripture**	**October 1**
Albany, GA	Luke 10:38-42	Luke 10:42

But one thing is needful: and Mary hath chosen that good part, which shall not be taken away from her (Luke 10:42).

CHOOSING THE GOOD PART

"Mom, please come outside and play with me," my 5-year-old son pleaded.

"I just can't come right now," I responded. "I have to finish washing the dishes, and there are a hundred things I have to do."

As a busy pastor's wife, I felt justified in my "busyness." As he walked dejectedly out the back door, my conscience began to bother me. *Will anyone 10 years from now ever know if my dishes were washed?* I thought. *But time spent with my child will build lasting memories.* With that thought, I followed my son into the yard to spend special time with someone precious to me.

Many times in our daily lives God calls us aside to spend time with Him. Often we are so bogged down with "necessary" activities that communion with our heavenly Father gets squeezed out or is shortened. But we can follow Mary's example—we can choose "that good part."

Martha served—Mary anointed.

Martha cleaned—Mary was cleansed.

Martha cooked—Mary broke the box.

Martha hurried about—Mary sat at the feet of Jesus.

Martha worried—Mary worshiped.

Martha talked—Mary listened.

Martha wiped dishes with a cloth—Mary wiped Jesus' feet with her hair.

Martha received Jesus into her house—Mary received Jesus into her heart.

Both were sincere.

Both loved. Both served.

But Mary chose the good part.

REMEMBER TODAY: Let us be sure every day to make time in our busy schedules for the Lord and for those who are dear to us. That is vital—the good part.

Dorlene Harris
Tifton, GA

Related Scriptures
Psalm 92:12; Ephesians 4:11-15;
Philippians 1:6

October 2
1 Peter 2:2

*As newborn babes, desire the sincere milk of the
word, that ye may grow thereby* (1 Peter 2:2).

A HUNGER FOR SPIRITUAL GROWTH

Few Christians today really mature into the individuals God wants them to be. God desires for us to grow up in Him. Satan would like to stunt our growth by keeping us too busy to have time for the things of God. He crowds our minds and our lives with things that are insignificant to spiritual growth.

To grow in Christ, we must first realize whose we are. *The Living Bible* tells us in 1 Corinthians 6:20, "For God has bought you with a great price." Satan has no claim on us! God our Father is our owner. Just as an earthly father provides food for his children that they may grow physically, our heavenly Father provides spiritual food that we may be nurtured and grow spiritually.

Second, we need a healthy appetite. For children to grow properly, they must have the right foods. Children are immature in their thinking. They don't realize their need for a balanced, nutritious diet. My young daughter often thought that a nutritious meal consisted of a candy bar and Kool-Aid. Peter admonished us that as babes in Christ, we should have a sincere hunger for the Word of God. *The Living Bible* translates his words, "Long to grow up into the fullness of your salvation; cry for this as a baby cries for his milk."

If we are to grow into mature Christians, we must hunger for the food our Father has provided for us—His Word. When we do, we can be confident that our Lord will lead us daily as we grow in Him.

REMEMBER TODAY: Just as a growing child looks forward with anticipation to each new day, the growing Christian should look to each new day as one with new joys and exciting experiences in Christ.

Versell Wood
Scaly Mountain, NC

Related Scripture
Matthew 28:20

October 3
John 10:28

*"I give them eternal life, and they shall never perish;
no one can snatch them out of my hand"* (John 10:28, *NIV*).

PLACE YOUR HAND IN HIS

I listened intently as the children talked quietly on the front porch steps. The girls had recently attended the Kids Krusade I conducted, and they were discussing the Rapture and being ready to go to heaven.

Rhonda, 4, asked my 3-year-old granddaughter, "Christy, how in the world can you go up, up, up? I want to get saved and go to heaven, but I don't know how."

How will I ever make it simple enough for them to understand? I wondered, as Christy, who had asked Jesus to come into her heart during the crusade, responded, "Rhonda, that's easy. When you get saved, you just put your hand in Jesus' hand and never, never let go. Then when He gets ready to take you to heaven, He just lifts you up, up, up 'til you get there."

Rhonda had no problem with that. She accepted the explanation with no qualms or second questions.

What a simple gospel! Sometimes we make it so complicated. If only the world could see what Jesus did for us. His plan of salvation provided not only the grace and strength to live in this world but also eternal life. He promised never to leave us or forsake us, to be with us to the end of the world, and then to take us to heaven to live with Him.

Putting our hand in His means placing total confidence and trust in Him. In the bad times and the good times, He is there every step of the way, leading us all the way home.

REMEMBER TODAY: Jesus will be your constant companion. Place your hand in His, and He will lead you home.

Lucille Walker Cleveland, TN	**Related Scripture** Romans 5:1-6	**October 4** Habakkuk 3:18

Yet I will rejoice in the Lord, I will joy in
the God of my salvation (Habakkuk 3:18).

REJOICE IN THE LORD

Presenting a picture of famine that could come to Israel—no figs, no olives, no crops, dead flocks, empty barns—and painting a portrait of obvious despair and hopelessness, Habakkuk shocks readers with an unexpected response to this situation: "Yet I will rejoice in the Lord, I will joy in the God of my salvation." It is a testimony that God is faithful: you can count on Him in the darkest times, and He is worthy of our love and praise despite the worst of circumstances.

When my missionary-educator husband, Dr. Herb Walker, died suddenly, a dear friend sent me a parable that Habakkuk would have endorsed. It helped my spirit to rejoice in the Lord and to joy in God in the pain of my grief.

The parable is of a small boy whose sister was about to die. Hearing that just one leaf from the Tree of Life could bring healing and life, he knocked on the gate of heaven and requested a leaf from the angel who answered the knock. The wise angel responded, "I can't promise that your sister won't be sick again or will be spared from future heartache, troubles and sorrows." And, on purpose, the angel opened the gate of heaven just enough for the little boy to peep in. Amazed at the wonderful sight he saw, the little boy said, "It's OK about the leaf; forget it. Would you let me come with her?"

Yes, the goodness of God, His faithfulness, His forgiveness, the hope of eternal life in His presence all far excel the worst of life's circumstances.

REMEMBER TODAY: Thank You, God, that although we see through a glass darkly today, someday we shall see You face-to-face and understand that in all things You are good and worthy of our joy and praise.

Marge Bingham	**Related Scriptures**	**October 5**
Rome, GA	Psalm 95:2; James 4:8; John 14:27	Psalm 37:34

*Wait on the Lord, and keep his way, and he
shall exalt thee to inherit the land: when the wicked
are cut off, thou shalt see it* (Psalm 37:34).

WAIT PATIENTLY

When we think of waiting, our minds automatically ask, "How long?" Most of us do not like to sit and wait for someone. Our minds and bodies are geared to the do-it-now pace. But there are times when we must slow down and allow God to talk to us. After all, He is the One who has the answers.

Many times when I need an answer from God, I fall on my knees and begin to do what Psalm 95:2 says: "Let us come before his presence with thanksgiving." After getting lost in the Spirit with praises and thanking Him for His wonderful blessings, I can then bring my petitions before Him. Sometimes I receive my answer immediately, but other times I have to wait. It is through waiting that I learn patience and how to listen to God.

James 4:8 says, "Draw nigh to God, and he will draw nigh to you." The closer to God we get, the better we can understand what He is saying to us.

Knowing the Peacemaker brings peace that is not temporary but everlasting. "Peace I leave with you, my peace I give unto you: not as the world giveth, give I unto you" (John 14:27). Peace comes through prayer and thinking on good things. Only God can give true peace.

REMEMBER TODAY: Knowing the Peacemaker makes waiting a restful time and gives assurance that God is in control, regardless of the circumstances.

Joyce Miles	Related Scriptures	October 6
Salisbury, NC	Psalm 55:17; 1 Thessalonians 5:16-18;	Daniel 6:10
	Hebrews 4:16	

He kneeled upon his knees three times a day, and prayed, and
gave thanks before his God, as he did aforetime" (Daniel 6:10).

REGULAR PRAYER TIME

I used to wish I could pray more. Others were gifted at intercessory prayer, but not I. Others could pray for long periods of time, but not I. Others received answers to their prayers, but not I. I knew I needed to pray more.

Daniel gives us an example of what a life of prayer can mean when times of trouble and persecution come. Daniel prayed in the good times and in the bad times. He prayed humbly—on his knees. He prayed often—three times a day. He did not whine before his God—he gave thanks. He was persistent in his prayer life—even when Satan threw obstacles to prayer in his way. His praying paid off. God delivered him from lions, showed him the wonders of the future and used him mightily.

In the fall of 1989, God changed my prayer life by opening up a position for me as an instructor at East Coast Bible College. My job is 50 miles from my home, thus requiring me to drive two hours a day. My driving time has become a wonderful time of prayer. Like Daniel, I pray in the good times and in the bad times. Like Daniel, I have regular daily appointments with God. Like Daniel, I am delivered, I am shown wonders, and I am used of God. Like Daniel, I give thanks.

REMEMBER TODAY: Set aside time to pray on a regular basis. God will reward you.

Lala B. Bare
Earlysville, VA

Related Scripture
1 Corinthians 2:5

October 7
2 Corinthians 4:7

*But we have this treasure in earthen vessels, that the excellency
of the power may be of God, and not of us* (2 Corinthians 4:7).

THE RIGHT TIME

Opening the door, I quietly slipped into our room. My husband had been asleep for several hours. Hopefully, I could get ready for bed without waking him. I was wrong.

"What time is it?" he gently asked.

"About 2 a.m.," I whispered in the darkness.

"Have you been up 'til now?" he asked, with concern in his voice.

"Yes," I responded. "Dana came in from her date about 11:30 and wanted to talk. I have been listening."

There was a moment of silence. We both understood. Dana, our teenage daughter, was a beautiful young lady who loved the Lord. But like most teenagers, Dana did not talk on her parents' schedule. She picked her own times, which unfortunately were not always convenient times for us. God had given me understanding that when teenagers want to talk, it is time to listen. This was not the only night that my long day had been made longer by listening to the heart of a young person growing up in our world.

And the Lord has graciously multiplied this lesson in my life beyond our home. A knock on the door, the ring of a phone, a comment in passing—each may signal that a sister in Christ is ready to talk and it is time to listen.

Loving others is not always convenient. The Rescue Squad responds at night as well as by day. The time to listen is when others are hurting. The time to heal is when others are in pain. Need, not convenience, must be our call to service.

May the Lord ever teach us to be sensitive and available. We are earthen vessels, yielded for service.

REMEMBER TODAY: The Holy Spirit delights to use us as instruments of joy, peace and wisdom in the lives of others.

Carolyn Wiggins	**Related Scriptures**	**October 8**
Rocky Mount, NC	Psalm 116:15; 1 Corinthians 15:54-57	Romans 8:18

The sufferings of this present time are not worthy to be compared with the glory which shall be revealed in us (Romans 8:18).

MOTHER'S PRAYERS AND THE MIDNIGHT JOURNEY

"Your sister is dying. She wants you to come home and sing to her," Mother's words echoed through her tears. "Hurry. The doctor says the cancer is worse and she won't live long."

As I hung up the phone, I experienced a feeling of fear and loss as I questioned, "Why her?" She's only 36 years old, a young mother with so many unfulfilled dreams. I thought of her smile and the special way she had of making others laugh. We had believed God for her healing, but she only grew worse. Although we'd exercised faith, we weren't willing to pray, "Thy will be done."

Paralyzed completely and unable to talk, tears filled my sister's eyes as she slipped into unconsciousness just as we finished singing her favorite song, "Where No One Stands Alone." Somehow I knew her days of fear and loneliness were almost over.

At midnight, suddenly her eyes opened and a radiant smile swept across her face, as though she were welcoming a host of angels. She calmly laid aside this tabernacle of clay and began her journey home.

That same day she had given this testimony to Mother, "I thank God for His love, mercy and forgiveness. In planning my life and goals, I had forgotten Him. I don't want to die; my 3-year-old needs me. However, I have submitted to God's will. I can go home now, rejoicing in the Holy Spirit. Take care of my son. Tell him often how much I love him, and I'll wait for him in our new home. Thanks, Mom, for your prayers through the years of my rebellion and stubbornness. God has honored them, for I have found peace and hope for perfect healing."

REMEMBER TODAY: When midnight strikes and life has dashed our most cherished dreams to the ground, it could be a mother's prayer that takes us home.

Liz G. Jordan
St. Marys, GA

Related Scriptures
Psalm 85:8; Ecclesiastes 5:1;
Jeremiah 18:2

October 9
Psalm 46:10

Be still, and know that I am God: I will be exalted among
the heathen, I will be exalted in the earth (Psalm 46:10).

TOO BUSY TO LISTEN?

Do we become too busy to listen to God? I believe all of us do at some time in our lives. We become so wrapped up in our day-to-day existence that we lose the focus of our lives and those around us. A traumatic experience forced me to take a closer look at myself and my life.

The day after Christmas I thought I was having a heart attack. I honestly felt God was calling me home. I felt the blood swishing in my heart and heard it echoing in my ears. Later, I realized this was God's way of telling me I was too busy; I needed to stop and reevaluate my life.

There comes a time in life when we must realize that saying no is not bad. Sometimes saying no to people and placing God first in our lives is saying yes to God. I have found that I cannot be everything to everybody. I have to say no at times, even though I truly want to be helpful. I have to keep myself together to do God's will. It's time to stop and say, "Lord, You direct me . . . tell me how to handle this."

During my recuperation, I had a lot of time to evaluate my situation. I had no other choice but to listen to what God was saying. As a result, I was able to hear Him. I realized it had been a long time since I had listened to God.

Although I am on the road to recovery, I still find myself floundering and talking to my Lord constantly. I have set my priorities to include time to be with God and to listen to Him. Each day is different. New opportunities and new relationships develop, but without God's guidance and love, our time is meaningless.

REMEMBER TODAY: It is God's desire to direct our paths to a happier and more fulfilled life, but we must be able to hear Him.

Peggy J. Smith
Akron, OH

Related Scriptures
Psalm 68:1-6; Hebrews 1:5;
Matthew 6:26

October 10
Mark 14:36

And he said, Abba, Father, all things are possible unto thee; take away this cup from me: nevertheless not what I will, but what thou wilt (Mark 14:36).

CLIMB INTO HIS LAP

"Is your daddy bringing you to the school play?" asked my classmate.

I had never felt different from other children until I started first grade. Then I began to notice all my friends had dads to take them places, share fun things and, most importantly, take them to school activities. You see, my dad left my mom and me when I was 12 months old. He was a stranger to me. I only saw him four times in the first 12 years of my life.

When I was a small child, a Christian neighbor began taking me to Sunday school. Here I learned that God is my "Abba, Father." In simple, everyday language this means God is my "Daddy"—my Father. Anytime I need a daddy, I can climb into His lap and tell Him all my problems.

This early Christian training was valuable to me later on. It prepared me for coping with total rejection from my natural father a few years later. This type of rejection has caused young women to turn to drugs, alcohol, prostitution and other horrible escapes. Because of a Christian neighbor who cared enough to evangelize a neighborhood child, I was able to stand firm in my Christian faith.

Matthew 6:26 says, "Behold the fowls of the air: for they sow not, neither do they reap, nor gather into barns; yet your heavenly Father feedeth them. Are ye not much better than they?" I have learned that my heavenly Father loves me more than anything on earth. Because of His love I can face anything in life.

REMEMBER TODAY: God, our "Abba Father," is ready to take us in His arms, listen to our problems and love us.

Edith Bean
Brownfield, TX

Related Scriptures
Isaiah 53:5; James 5:14, 15;
Psalm 50:15

October 11
Luke 9:11

And the people . . . followed him and he received
them, and spake unto them of the kingdom of God,
and healed them that had need of healing (Luke 9:11).

THE GREAT PHYSICIAN

"After checking over your X-ray," the doctor said, "I'm afraid the bone has slipped out of place. We will have to rebreak the arm and put in a pin to ensure correct healing."

Those words sank deep into my heart. Rebreak? After all, I had already experienced a great deal of chiding because I, a 51-year-old grandmother, had broken an arm at a junior Sunday school skating party.

"At your age a broken bone will really give you trouble," they had said. "Arthritis and rheumatism will plague you the rest of your life," others had added. "It will look deformed if not corrected," the doctor had said.

My faith in God as my healer was strong, and I chose to leave the cast on as it was. I knew personally the One who had borne stripes on Calvary for my healing, and I trusted completely in Him to intervene. I went forward in the next church service to be anointed and prayed for as instructed in James 5:14, 15.

When the cast came off, my arm was as straight as the other one. I regained the strength in it, and today, several years later, I have to think back to remember which arm I broke. During the first year after the break, I went to my regular doctor for a physical. I told him I had broken my arm since I saw him. He looked at my wrist and said, "You must have had a good doctor." "Yes," I replied, "I had a Great Physician."

We serve a God who is still in the healing business!

REMEMBER TODAY: To those who come to Him, God offers healing for both the spirit and the body.

Delta Schrade
Arvada, CO

Related Scriptures
Isaiah 6:6-8; Luke 18:15-17

. . . whose hearts God had touched (1 Samuel 10:26, *NIV*).

THE SAVIOR'S TOUCH

One of the most effective methods of communicating is by touching. My husband can communicate to me a warmth of affection with a hug that comforts and assures like only he can. A strong guiding hand on my shoulder at the end of a service can communicate to me to end my conversations, so we can make our way out of the church and not detain the janitor any longer. His touch also relates the message "I am beside you." This message brings happiness, protection and security to me.

In the same way, our heavenly Father communicates with us. With the many trials and anxieties of life, we all reach the point when we need a touch from our heavenly Father. We need a time of communion, either in personal devotions or in a Spirit-filled altar where our loving Father wraps Himself around our aching souls to give us comfort and assurance. Through His loving touch He gives us direction or a slight push that says, "You've been here long enough; it's now time to move on with Me."

His touch can also remind us of His presence in our lives. When we think He has left us or given up on us, His touch reminds us, "My child, I am still with you. I've promised to never leave. I will continue to protect you. Take rest and security in Me."

REMEMBER TODAY: The arms of our Savior were once extended outward to die for us. Today His arms draw us into the life, peace, joy and rest He offers us.

Mary Sue Baker   **Related Scripture**   **October 13**
Champaign, IL   Proverbs 31:13-31   Ecclesiastes 9:10

Whatsoever thy hand findeth to do,
do it with thy might (Ecclesiastes 9:10).

HANDS IN SERVICE

Useful hands reflect hard work and productivity . . . the giving of a cup of cold water . . . a comforting and caring touch.

A reminder of the availability and usefulness of my hands came forcefully to me during a trip throughout South India. Riding along the bumpy road from Trivandrum to Paippard, India, I experienced for the first time the thrill of hands-on missions.

Life-size illustrations became vivid as I witnessed from the van window women working rice fields, roadside brick kilns and open-air butcher shops. The people's hands bore calluses and wrinkles from years of poverty, without hope of being elevated to another caste.

My heart filled with compassion as God spoke to my heart, "My hands were pierced for those hands. I desire those hands you see to be committed to Me."

My mind drifted back to childhood days when, at the tender age of 9, I began playing the piano. I didn't know my hands would one day minister in churches at home and around the world.

Through the years I've watched women serve who were specially endowed. Whether baking a chocolate cake for a neighbor, driving a senior citizen to town or holding a child's hand crossing the street—these simple activities are basic to the broader scope of caring for hurting people who need a touch from the Master's hand.

Ecclesiastes 9:10 reminds us that whatever work we find to do, we are to do it with all our heart.

❧

REMEMBER TODAY: Jesus Christ desires that you surrender your hands to Him.

R. Louise Douglas   **Related Scriptures**   **October 14**
Charlotte, NC   Genesis 3:1-6; 2 Samuel 24:10-14;   Joshua 24:15
       Book of Esther; Job 1; 2

*"But if serving the Lord seems undesirable to you, then choose for yourselves
this day whom you will serve, whether the gods your forefathers served
beyond the River, or the gods of the Amorites, in whose land you are living.
But as for me and my household, we will serve the Lord"* (Joshua 24:15, *NIV*).

CHOICES

From the abyss of Job's misery and despair comes a poignant question: "'Shall we accept good from God, and not trouble?'" (2:10, *NIV*). Job had lost everything he had except his disgruntled wife and his faith in God. At this point his plight would seem dismal indeed if we did not know what God was doing. Job made his choice to trust God even if he were slain.

Could we be like Esther when she was chosen as one of the virgins for King Xerxes? After she was brought to the palace, pampered and soothed with sweet oils, she obtained the king's favor and the royal crown. Mordecai suggested that perhaps she had " 'come to the kingdom for such a time as this'" (4:14, *NKJV*). Before approaching the king, uninvited, to request mercy for her people, Esther had made her decision in case things didn't work out: "If I perish, I perish" (4:16).

Oftentimes what we want and what we need are at opposite ends of the continuum. Much of what we experience falls somewhere in between.

The Israelites wanted more "gourmet" meals on the table; the manna was getting a bit boring. God gave them quail to eat but was displeased with them because of their complaints and sent a severe plague on them. Lot's wife wanted one more look at the burning cities; she became a salty monument of disobedience to God. Eve wanted to be "wise," as the serpent suggested, so she did the most foolish thing she could ever do and lost her good life.

I wanted a big, mountain retirement home. Why wouldn't God give it to me? He knew I didn't need it, and three months later, I didn't even want it.

When I pray, "Lord, I think I need that," if He says no, I try to make *no* my choice too. God will always give us what we need *when* we need it . . . but not before.

REMEMBER TODAY: It's much easier to make the right choices when we allow God to show us the way.

Siema Bailey Swartzel Phoenix, AZ	**Related Scriptures** Mark 9:33-36; Luke 9:46-48	**October 15** Matthew 18:3, 4

"I tell you the truth, unless you change and become like little children, you will never enter the kingdom of heaven. Therefore, whoever humbles himself like this child is the greatest in the kingdom of heaven" (Matthew 18:3, 4, *NIV*).

A CHILD OF GOD

"Joel! Mommy says NO!"

Frequently this cry can be heard as my toddler incessantly explores his surroundings, creating chaos. I'm quite sure I could not have believed how two little hands and feet can complicate the life of a young mother. My exasperation with my young son daily rivals my affection for his charm, exuberance and love of life. Even in the midst of a time of guidance and discipline, I find myself greatly admiring God's handiwork! I remember, through it all, that this sunny little fellow has become my joy, my laughter and the occasion for some of my most tender emotions.

In my own spiritual walk, while I am continually exploring and growing, I know my heavenly Father feels more love for me than He does exasperation. His love for me is inexhaustible, and His patience is unfathomable. I am forever a little one in His eyes. As I grow in His grace, He is guiding me and loving me through all my struggles.

Christ admonishes us to "change and become like little children. . . . Whoever humbles himself like this [little] child is the greatest in the kingdom of heaven." I am assured by these words that God will always be patient and loving toward me when I have a childlike attitude of trust and openness to His guidance and dependence on His Word. He helps me do His will.

I believe the key words in this passage are "change and become like little children." As we say yes to God's will and no to our own, we can submit to God's perfect guidance in our lives.

REMEMBER TODAY: As a child of God, I submit to His loving guidance. It is reassuring to know He can see the potential in me that others may not see.

Wilma Amison Cleveland, TN	**Related Scriptures** Matthew 6:33; Luke 12:32	**October 16** Luke 22:43

And there appeared an angel unto him from
heaven, strengthening him (Luke 22:43).

HAND IN HAND WITH JESUS

The house was quiet, the family in bed. Only she was still awake. She too was preparing for sleep when across the bayou came strains of angel music, though she didn't yet recognize the sound as such. She thought the faint melody came from a radio in the distance. It suddenly grew louder, and she thought someone had turned up the volume. Then there was no mistaking the music's source as it moved swiftly across the water, entered the room and encircled her. By now she was standing, arms raised over her head, the clothes she was removing covering her face.

She stood still, enraptured. She wished she could see her heavenly visitors; but cautious lest she dispel their presence, she moved not at all. She also longed to share this wondrous experience with her husband; but again, fearful lest they should leave, she did not call out. The angel choir sang in its entirety "Hand in Hand With Jesus," long before she knew the words of the song. Then as quickly as they had come, the angel choir was gone, the music fading as swiftly as it had filled the room.

Having been a Christian only a short while, she had heard the Bible-study teacher relate that she had heard the angels sing as she and her young daughter were walking home one day. And so, with the fresh faith of a babe in Christ, Mama Amison had prayed, "Lord, I know You don't love Sister Newsome any more than You love me. Would You let me hear the angels sing too?" And He had granted her simple request.

Some 46 years later she remarked to me, "God knew that with all the trials I would face throughout these years, I would need to walk hand in hand with Jesus."

REMEMBER TODAY: He and His angels are near us continually.

Sheila McLaughlan
Inverness, Scotland

Related Scripture
Psalm 121:8

October 17
Psalm 32:8

I will instruct thee and teach thee in the
way which thou shalt go (Psalm 32:8).

A SAVED LIFE

Having traveled from Inverness to London Airport, I was walking from one terminal to the other when a thought came to me to leave my luggage at the airport overnight. Never having done this before and because the luggage department was a long distance, I ignored the thought. The thought became so compelling that I turned around and went back to the other terminal.

All this cost me about 45 minutes. Then it seemed sensible to eat, since it would be another two hours' travel to the Leroy home, where I was spending the night.

Arriving on the railway platform about an hour and a half later, the guard informed me there had been a fire at King's Cross Station. Many had died in the fire and many others from the smoke in the underground station. I would have been there at the exact time the fire broke out had the compelling thought not come to my mind.

REMEMBER TODAY: The Lord guards our going out and coming in, but we must be tuned in to the voice of God. It may save our life today and therein be the salvation of someone's soul tomorrow.

Lilly Gay Stockton
Meadville, MS

Related Scriptures
Isaiah 55:9; Psalm 18:30;
Mark 9:23

October 18
Isaiah 55:8

*For my thoughts are not your thoughts, neither
are your ways my ways, saith the Lord* (Isaiah 55:8).

GROWING IN SMALL WAYS

"Lord, please help me to grow in You and be stronger." I had prayed this prayer many times, but now it was happening. While pastoring our second church, we were invited to go camping with some members. Living away from family made fellowship precious to us. We were packed and ready to go when Angelia, our 4-year-old daughter, came in crying. She had been stung by a wasp. Later we found out she was highly allergic to all types of stings.

After arriving at the campsite, the men went fishing. I noticed Angelia's hand and arm were swelling. After the men returned, we decided to go to the nearest hospital. We were praying the whole time, reminding God of our income and the fact that we did not have insurance. There was no doctor at the first hospital, so we drove to the next one and admitted her for observation. The doctor was concerned that the poison had gotten into her bloodstream. Morning came and we received the good news: no poison.

We wrote a check for Angelia's stay so she could be discharged, even though we did not have the funds. As soon as we arrived home, we found a letter waiting in the mailbox from friends we had not heard from in years. I opened the letter, and a check fell from the envelope. It was for twice the amount of the bill. Yes, God can heal, but that wasn't the lesson to be learned at this time. No matter what the circumstance, God can be trusted!

REMEMBER TODAY: God is interested in our growth and our trust in Him in all circumstances.

Susan LeBuhn
Little Rock, AR

Related Scriptures
Matthew 5:14-16; Luke 10:2;
John 4:35

October 19
Deuteronomy 11:19

*"You shall teach them to your children, speaking of them when
you sit in your house, when you walk by the way, when you
lie down, and when you rise up"* (Deuteronomy 11:19, *NKJV*).

OUR FAMILY—THE HARVEST

A 6-year-old walked into her mother's bedroom one Sunday morning and asked, "Am I saved?" The mother lovingly explained that to be saved, she must ask Jesus to forgive her sins and invite Him into her heart. This burned into the little girl's heart, and she knew she wanted to be saved. So in church that morning she sat on the front pew and patiently waited for the preacher to finish his sermon. When at last the invitation was given, she went to the altar and prayed a simple prayer: "Jesus, if it's nice to be saved, I want to be saved. Please forgive me of my sins and come into my heart."

We never know when the seed might be planted, so we must always be willing and ready to reap the harvest. That morning I was the harvest and God used my mother to be the reaper. Often we overlook the closest souls to us, failing to recognize them as the harvest. It would have been easy for my mother to say, "Go on, we'll talk about it later. I've got to hurry and get ready for church." Had she done so, I might have been lost.

As women of God we must be sensitive to our family's spiritual needs and willing to be used by God in reaching the harvest dearest to us—our loved ones.

REMEMBER TODAY: We must take advantage of every opportunity to reach our loved ones for Christ.

Mary Ruth Stone Cleveland, TN	**Related Scriptures** Philippians 3:8-11; 1 John 3:2; Psalm 42:1-3	**October 20** Philippians 3:10

*That I may know Him and the power of His
resurrection, and the fellowship of His sufferings,
being conformed to His death (Philippians 3:10, NKJV).*

GETTING TO KNOW GOD

Most children grow up knowing their fathers. Most of them have always known their fathers and cannot actually remember when they met. The relationship grew from birth.

It was different for me. I was born a few months after my father was drafted by the U.S. Army to serve in World War II. Until I was 3 years old, I knew him only as a figure in photographs. In those photographs he was always smiling and wearing a uniform. I was aware that these shiny, black and white pictures represented my father, but it was not accurate to say that I knew him. But how I wanted to know him!

My mother, my grandparents and all my extended family told me about the wonderful things that would happen when my daddy came home. We could have our own house and a dog and maybe even a baby. He would love me. We would do this and that, and everything would be wonderful.

I clearly remember the night my father came home—that bittersweet mix of joy and fear as the familiar-looking stranger held me in his arms. We got our house and our dog. We had some wonderful times. But along with the fun of getting to know my father came the discipline that I needed (but did not want) from him. I no longer had my mother's undivided attention. I had to share with him. In getting to know him, I learned obedience and respect along with joy and security.

Knowing and loving God is like that. It is joy and security, but it is also obedience and sacrifice. Anything less would be unbalanced.

REMEMBER TODAY: Seek a well-rounded relationship with God. Seek to know Christ's suffering as well as His security.

Eveylene Holt	Related Scriptures	October 21
Deer Park, TX	1 Corinthians 15:55; John 15:7;	Jeremiah 30:17
	Psalm 118:17	

"'But I will restore you to health and heal your
wounds," declares the Lord'" (Jeremiah 30:17, *NIV*).

BELIEVING GOD'S PROMISES

I awoke from the surgery minus my left breast and 13 lymph nodes. The devastation I felt was like a cloud of blackness enveloping me. I had cancer! I was no longer a whole woman. Would death soon follow? These thoughts plagued me as my church, family, friends and even strangers began to pray for my full recovery.

This dark cloud continued to torment me as I began chemotherapy. During this time my hair fell out, I was nauseated, my energy was drained both physically and emotionally, and the antinausea medication caused hallucinations. I searched the Scriptures daily. One scripture stood out, and I began claiming Jeremiah 30:17 for my healing.

When I finally began to adjust to the chemo, resigning myself to its necessity, I began experiencing severe chest pains. This led to a double bypass on my heart. All through the heart surgery I never doubted that God would heal me. I recovered rapidly from heart surgery but still had several months of chemo ahead. I knew I was healed and didn't need chemo anymore, but my doctor insisted on continuing. For weeks I prayed, asking God for some sign that I was really healed. The sign I asked for was that my doctor, a man determined to do all the correct procedures by the book, would not try to dissuade me from quitting the chemotherapy treatment.

I remained off the chemo until I had fully recovered from heart surgery. However, when I returned for my long-postponed treatment, it was once again postponed due to a low platelet count. I discussed with the doctor my decision to discontinue chemotherapy and, to my surprise, he offered no resistance. I had received the sign I had asked from God. God had kept His promise to make me well again.

God's power is greater than cancer or any human problem. His promises are true.

REMEMBER TODAY: God cannot lie. What He has promised in His Word, He will do.

Gladys Lemons	**Related Scriptures**	**October 22**
Ft. Myers, FL	Isaiah 55:9; Psalms 40:5, 17, 139:17	Jeremiah 29:11

I know the thoughts that I think toward you, saith the Lord, thoughts of peace, and not of evil, to give you an expected end (Jeremiah 29:11).

THINKING OF YOU

When I answered the phone, the voice at the other end said, "Hello, Gladys. This is Nell [Cross]. I was just thinking about you and wanted to chat with you and see how you are."

Nell and I have been friends for most of our lives. We accepted the Lord as young girls, served with our minister husbands and became widows within two weeks of one another. With so much in common, it was easy for us to spend a half-hour on the phone together. We'd speak of joys and pleasures and share some of the recent concerns and needs of our lives. We'd express love and appreciation for the years of shared friendship, say our goodbyes and promise to keep in touch.

While basking in the warm glow of feeling special and loved, I remembered the many times I had received or made one of those "thinking of you" calls. As I breathed a prayer of thanksgiving to God for thoughtful friends and family, my heart exploded with the knowledge of the words of Jeremiah 29:11: "I know the thoughts that I think toward you, saith the Lord, thoughts of peace, and not of evil, to give you an expected end."

The Lord is thinking about me! He tells me in Isaiah 55:9 that His thoughts are higher than mine, and they are more than can be numbered (Psalm 40:5). In Psalm 139:17 I find that His thoughts are precious even when "I am poor and needy; yet the Lord thinketh upon me" (Psalm 40:17).

As I knelt for prayer that evening, I said, "Hello, Lord. This is Gladys. I was just thinking about You. . . ."

REMEMBER TODAY: The Lord is thinking peaceful, precious thoughts about you today.

Laura Griffith	**Related Scriptures**	**October 23**
Salinas, CA	Psalms 23; 37:25; Isaiah 26:3	Psalm 23:1

*The Lord is my shepherd; I
shall not want* (Psalm 23:1).

JESUS—HE'S ALL I NEED

A little girl was asked to repeat the Twenty-third Psalm. She faced the audience, made a little bow, then bravely said in a strong voice, "The Lord is my shepherd; that's all I want!" She bowed and went back to her seat. Mission accomplished!

The source of every good and perfect gift is the Good Shepherd. He is my shepherd. This kind of personal relationship inspires trust and confidence. The psalmist David knew God well. He often communed with God while he watched his sheep. David knew how much the sheep depended on the shepherd for protection, direction, food and water.

David eventually became king of Israel, but he always depended on God for guidance and direction. It is said that David was a man after God's own heart. Even though he failed God, he knew the path of repentance.

The relationship David had with God is reflected in his psalms in the many ways he expressed his closeness to God when he used the names of God. In Psalm 23:1, David portrayed God as Jehovah-raah, "The Lord is my shepherd," and as Jehovah-jireh, the Lord will provide, "I shall not want."

If we sincerely put our faith each day in the Good Shepherd, He will be everything we need. He will be our source—physically, emotionally, financially and spiritually.

REMEMBER TODAY: With the Lord as our shepherd, we can relax and smile, for God has everything under control.

Ina Boling
Little Rock, AR

Related Scriptures
1 Corinthians 15:58; Revelation 14:13

October 24
Hebrews 4:11

*Let us labour therefore to enter
into that rest* (Hebrews 4:11).

WHAT WILL WE REMEMBER?

Last summer I paused during my busy summer rush to reflect upon the summers of my youth.

Into my mind came the memory of wonderful days spent on our farm. Summer on the farm was canning season. There were vegetables to be gathered and prepared for the freezer daily. Then, it seemed an unending task that consumed my precious summer.

And yet as I look back, it's not the work I remember but the fun. Summer brought days of playing in the sprinklers, running barefoot across a freshly cut lawn, chasing butterflies during the day and fireflies at night. It also brought times of family fun and laughter as we labored together.

Those thoughts made me wonder about our days of labor here on earth. When we get to heaven, will we remember the long hard hours of work for the Lord? Or will we only remember the joy of being able to serve Him for a short season?

REMEMBER TODAY: The trials of earth are nothing compared to the triumphs of heaven.

Judy Morgan Fort Mill, SC

Related Scriptures
Mark 14:3-9; Acts 9:36-42;
Matthew 25:31-46

October 25
Mark 14:8

"She has done what she could" (Mark 14:8, *TLB*).

DOING WHAT WE CAN

We all are familiar with the woman who shared the contents of her alabaster box, anointing Jesus' feet. She did what she could. She affectionately showed the Master her love in the greatest possible way, and He memorialized her actions with his tribute in Mark 14:8, 9.

Other godly women also showed their love for their Master. Dorcas, who did not own spikenard or an alabaster box, did what she could as well. She was not privileged to express her love for Him in personal actions, but she ministered to those around her who were in need. Perhaps she knew what Jesus had said in Matthew 25:40: "Inasmuch as ye have done it unto one of the least of these . . . ye have done it unto me." Dorcas sewed garments and "was always doing kind things for others, especially for the poor" (Acts 9:36, *TLB*). Even her name, which in English is *Gazelle*, signifies a lovely animal. She was, indeed, lovely. She did not give to others expecting a return. She gave to those who probably would only smile, hug her and say thank you. Dorcas was restored to life by God's power because of His mercy and her usefulness.

REMEMBER TODAY: Can I do less today than my ability? Will Jesus say of me, "She did what she could"?

Robin Caddell	**Related Scriptures**	**October 26**
Manchester, NH	Psalm 139:1-10; Isaiah 26:3;	Deuteronomy 31:6
	2 Timothy 1:7; 1 Peter 5:7	

Be strong and of a good courage, fear not, nor be afraid of them: for the Lord thy God, he it is that doth go with thee; he will not fail thee, nor forsake thee (Deuteronomy 31:6).

HE CARES FOR YOU

Some days our circumstances cause us to feel isolated from any continuity of life. It's at those times I tend to be so wrapped up in the event that I am not consciously aware of God's omnipresence.

It was late October 1986. My son, Jeremy, and daughter Jaclyn were traveling with me. My husband, Larry, and daughter Jessica were in a Ryder moving truck just ahead of us. It is an undescribable feeling to see the accumulation of all you possess collected in a rectangular box with wheels.

Night had fallen, and road construction had separated the moving van and us by several lengths. Suddenly, I knew I had a flat tire! I tried to pull over but realized there was insufficient road shoulder and also a drop-off. As I watched, the Ryder lights melded with all the others. I felt so alone. "God, where are You?" was my plea. I soon felt that God, as well as the police, had forsaken me! I tried to get the car properly jacked up. One lug nut on the wheel would not budge. As I looked up from my struggles with the tire, a graffiti-covered van stopped. As its passengers approached, a blanket of fear engulfed me. I began to pray. Without any conversation, they returned to the van and left. The sweetest peace replaced the fear, as I realized God had not forsaken me. In my dilemma, He was truly concerned.

Within minutes a man traveling the opposite direction on the access road dodged through the traffic and offered help. During our conversation, I discovered that he had been afraid to stop but felt compelled to do so. He told me he had been raised in the Church of God, and we discovered that we had several mutual friends. Isn't God good?

Deuteronomy 31:6 tells us that He will never forsake us. He cares for us and is concerned about what we are going through, no matter how large or small the crisis.

REMEMBER TODAY: Rejoice whatever the circumstances, for God is in control and He is never too late!

Charlotte Tygart
Yakima, WA

Related Scriptures
Psalms 10:17; 34:15; 86:1-7;
Isaiah 59:1;1 Peter 5:7

October 27
Psalm 88:2

Let my prayer come before thee:
incline thine ear unto my cry (Psalm 88:2).

GOD'S MIRACLE HEARING

Several years ago my mother died of cancer. During her illness I experienced some difficult times. At the same time, I also experienced some beautiful miracles from God.

My husband was youth director in West Virginia, and my mother lived in California. This put many miles between my mother and me. I wanted so much to be with her. One Saturday morning after feeding my children and cleaning the kitchen, I decided to phone her. By this time Mom was having a few good days, but unfortunately more were bad. I got through to her room but learned from the nurse that Mom was in such severe pain that she couldn't talk just then. I hung the phone up, fell on my knees and began sobbing. My words weren't coherent to anyone else, but God has such miraculous hearing that He understood just what I was saying.

I had been sobbing and praying for about five minutes when the phone rang. I really didn't feel like talking to anyone, but I thought there might be an emergency. I picked up the phone and heard my sweet mother's voice on the other end saying, "Hello, my precious daughter, did you want to talk to me?" Did I ever! God had given Mom a healing touch and had responded to the cries of my heart by letting me talk to her that day.

David knew that God heard his cries, because he cried out to Him many times. I had been taught as a child that God hears everything. On this special day God gave me a special reminder that He has time to hear us when we cry out to Him.

You may be crying out loud or just in your spirit, but God has miracle hearing. He not only hears you but responds to your cries.

REMEMBER TODAY: With his miracle hearing, God is attentive to your cries and responds to your needs.

Sherry B. Lee	**Related Scripture**	**October 28**
Cleveland, TN	1 Corinthians 15:10	2 Corinthians 3:5

*Not that we are adequate in ourselves to consider
anything as coming from ourselves, but our
adequacy is from God* (2 Corinthians 3:5, *NASB*).

ADEQUACY

I stood trembling as the spelling bee announcer cleared his throat to pronounce the next word. As representative from the sixth-grade class, I desired to do my best for my class and also for my sense of achievement.

"Adequate," the announcer said. His voice seemed far away. I moistened my lips, closed my eyes and tried to visualize the word.

"Adequate," he pronounced for the last time. The silence was interminable. Was it a-d-i? or a-d-e?

"A-d-i-q-u-a-t-e," I spelled slowly, distinctly.

"Incorrect," the announcer said. "One more try."

Confidence shattered, my body began shaking. I could not collect my thoughts well enough to make a second try. I simply walked offstage and sat down, relieved that the pressure was gone, the whole ordeal over.

Whenever I use or hear the word *adequate*, I still experience an insecure feeling inside. Of course, this word means more to me now and to the mind-set of our present age than I could ever have imagined at the age of 12.

Adequacy is pursued anxiously by all mankind, most of whom act on the belief that it may be personally achieved. Men compete to acquire it, sell their characters to buy it, search everywhere to find it, give unbelievable sums of time and energy to attain it, cheat and steal to keep it. A lack of adequacy motivates many to fear, give up, fail, burn out, escape and resign.

God makes it clear, through the apostle Paul, that we will never possess adequacy in ourselves no matter how much life we live, how many possessions we gain, or how high a position we attain. Adequacy—that secure feeling of knowing who we are, our value and worth as personal beings—can come only from God. *The Living Bible* says it plainly: "Our only power and success comes from God" (2 Corinthians 3:5).

REMEMBER TODAY: I'm learning to feel more secure with the word *adequate*. God not only knows how to spell it, He is the source of adequacy.

Pat Whitehouse
Bloomington, MN

Related Scriptures
Romans 8:28; Psalms 25:5; 28:6, 7

October 29
Galatians 4:4

But when the fullness of the time had come,
God sent forth His Son, born of a woman,
born under the law (Galatians 4:4, NKJV).

IN THE FULLNESS OF TIME

If you are presently experiencing circumstances of life about which you have prayed for years and yet the answer has not come, it is a bewildering place to be. God has answered many of my prayers—some to a greater depth than I could imagine. But at one point I wondered why there was silence in one specific area?

In your concordance look up various instances in the Bible that include these words: "And it came to pass. . . ." Then contemplate the years between the event and the breakthrough. We tend to think answers came quickly, but that was not always the case. "But when the fullness of the time had come, God sent forth His Son, born of a woman, born under the law." Many were looking for the Redeemer throughout their lives. But when He came, they denied Him because He did not match what they anticipated God would send.

Do you have your own idea of how the long-awaited answer to your prayer should come? The answer will come, but don't miss out on it. Ask God to prepare your heart for His answer.

After almost seven years of praying, waiting and agonizing, my prayer was answered. As I reflected on the time I waited, I realized that many pieces of the answer had to be moved into place. Had I moved ahead of God, I might have received a partial answer instead of a complete answer. Neither did the answer come in the way I imagined it would. The circumstances preceding the answer did not "look like God" to me, but they were.

REMEMBER TODAY: If you are in the waiting room for an answer . . . hang on. God is faithful.

319

Naomi R. Donaldson	**Related Scriptures**	**October 30**
Daphne, AL	Psalms 34:7; 91; Hebrews 13:5	Genesis 28:15

"I am with you and will watch over you
wherever you go" (Genesis 28:15, NIV).

SECURITY IN GOD'S CARE

The image is just as clear today as it was when I was a little girl in a starched eyelet dress and patent leather shoes. The vivid image is of a picture a caring teacher had placed on the wall of my Sunday school classroom. I have long since forgotten the teacher but not the scene of a little boy and girl on a bridge stretched above ominously dark waters. And standing just behind them, with arms outstretched to protect them from danger, was the most beautiful angel I could have ever imagined.

Of course the picture was an artist's interpretation of the comforting words penned by the writer of Psalm 91, who wrote that God would give His angels charge over us. But long before I gained that knowledge, countless childhood fears were quieted because of my assurance that I was not alone. I was certain that I too had a guardian angel and was in God's care.

Childish? Perhaps. Foolish? A thousand times no. For in the following years I have come to know that God does indeed watch over me and all His children. His Word declares that not only has He charged His angels with our care, but He will be with us wherever we are. What a comfort to trust those words and know He is with us in every situation!

As a child I felt safe because I saw myself as the little girl in the picture. And just as surely I am secure in God's care today as I claim His promise: " 'I am with you and will watch over you wherever you go.'"

REMEMBER TODAY: There is assurance for every circumstance because there is security in God's care.

Sonjia Lee Hunt
Cleveland, TN

Related Scriptures
1 Corinthians 10:13; 2 Timothy 2:12;
Romans 8:18

October 31
1 Peter 5:10

*And the God of all grace, who called you to his eternal glory in
Christ, after you have suffered a little while, will himself restore
you and make you strong, firm and steadfast* (1 Peter 5:10, *NIV*).

SUFFERING—THE SHORT AND LONG OF IT

God gave David some disciplinary options once, and though none were
pleasant, David chose the one most directly under God's control (2 Samuel
24:13-17). He considered that to be the best because he trusted God to be merciful.

All trials, of course, are not punishment for wrong, but some are meant
specifically to prepare us for further growth. These come into our lives periodi-
cally and should be expected (John 16:33; 1 Peter 4:12). We even are to be joy-
ous in the midst of our trials (James 1:2). The writer of Hebrews says Jesus
learned obedience from His sufferings (5:8). Sufferings are one of God's gifts to
His children (Philippians 1:29). (I must admit that sometimes, if I could, I
would return this particular gift.)

Abraham and Sarah did not know how long their faith would be tested. At
times they gave up on God. About 20 years passed before God moved, but
when Isaac came, he was a gift of life where death had been. He represented
fruitfulness brought out of certain barrenness. He embodied what God can do
when to human eyes all appears dark, hopeless. Though the trial had been
long, its length did not mean God could not or would not act.

Last fall I moved my potted rose into the garage for the winter, intending to
water and care for it. I failed, however, to do so. Eventually, it lost its leaves
and appeared completely dead. When spring came, surprisingly, it put out
new growth and looked rather good for a while. Still I neglected it, and it
"died" again. After a couple of months more, I decided to discard it and get
another rose. There was no trace of life, and it was ugly. Suddenly, and seemingly without cause, my "dead" rose shot out a new stem. On the stem was a
tiny bud. I couldn't believe my eyes.

I'm not one to turn everything that happens to me into a spiritual event.
Maybe I'm too cautious about that. But my most recent trial has been long, and
I have sometimes felt confused and hopeless. I felt like my rose that lost its
leaves, revealing its rough, prickly branches. To me, my resurrected rose is a
sign of what God can and will do in my life.

God gives new life where death has reigned. He gives new hope out of deep
despair. In God's time, trees again produce beautiful green foliage that covers
their scars and produces oxygen for us to breathe. Roses too bloom again when
God sends spring. And He does this without fail *in His time.*

REMEMBER TODAY: If your trials are long and hard to bear, hold on to God.
His time for your "resurrection" will come.

NOTES

Patricia Dempsey
Tampa, FL

Related Scriptures
Psalms 23; 138:7; 143:8; Proverbs 3:23

November 1
Proverbs 3:6

In all thy ways acknowledge him, and
he shall direct thy paths (Proverbs 3:6).

SINGING WHEN I'M SCARED

"God made the moon, the trees and flowers, and He created me."

This simple little line is the lyric to the first song I ever wrote as a 6-year-old child. It came to me as a means of comfort when I was scared of the dark.

We were blessed to have two homes, one in town and one—a rough, oak, barnlike cabin—at Sandy Run Lake. This rustic building that had embraced three generations of Murphys could sleep 20 comfortably. Although we had the luxury of electricity, there was no running water, so we drew from the cistern on the back porch. At the end of the path was "Eleanor's House," the privy, so dubbed by Granddaddy in honor of Eleanor Roosevelt and the WPA projects that built such structures. The 30 steps to the outhouse seemed a great distance to me.

Nights at the lake were a magical mix of chirping crickets, buzzing locusts and incessant "whip-poor-will" calls. The liquid black sky was dotted with starry diamonds that crackled noiselessly, and behind every tree a small girl saw a pirate with his eye patched, a hungry wolf or a huge brown bear.

During the stealthy walk from the back door to Eleanor's, I composed this song to ward off the imaginary captors and the real tremors of fear.

Today my fears have different faces. Pirates, wolves and bears are gone. The principle I learned so long ago for diffusing my fears is still effective, though: I sing in the face of danger, giving praise to God, my Creator; and His peace envelopes me.

REMEMBER TODAY: The smallest sincere cry offered to God will yield comfort and strength.

Irene G. Tunsil
Jacksonville, FL

Related Scriptures
Romans 8:15; Psalms 23:4; 34:4

November 2
2 Timothy 1:7

*For God hath not given us the
spirit of fear* (2 Timothy 1:7).

FROM BLURRED TO CLEAR VISION

One midafternoon while driving down a busy street in my hometown, my vision suddenly became blurred. I could only see circles and colors. Fear gripped me as the traffic surrounded me. I strained to see how to change lanes or pull off the road to safety. All I could distinguish were cars everywhere.

In my distress I started crying and nearly panicked, when a voice spoke to my spirit saying, "God has not given you the spirit of fear!" Immediately, I began to rest on that promise. I cried out to the Lord to restore my sight. By this time the traffic was not as busy, enabling me to pull off the road in the parking lot of a business. I exercised my faith and began to confess to the Lord, "I can see! Lord, I thank You that I can see!" Almost immediately, my vision returned to normal, and I drove back into the flow of traffic with clear vision.

How many times do we panic when Satan attacks us instead of remembering that God is just a prayer away? David said, "I sought the Lord, and he heard me, and delivered me from all my fears" (Psalm 34:4).

REMEMBER TODAY: The secret eyes of God protect us when our eyes are fixed on Him.

Susan C. Kelley
Louisbourg, Nova Scotia

Related Scriptures
1 Thessalonians 5:11, 12;
2 Corinthians 9:5-8

November 3
Philippians 2:4

*Look not every man on his own things, but every
man also on the things of others* (Philippians 2:4).

APPRECIATE ONE ANOTHER

I saw a poster once that did not have any words but portrayed a powerful message. It was a picture of four cows in four adjoining pastures. Each cow had its head over the fence, grazing in the neighbor's paddock.

Sometimes we behave like those cows, wasting time envying and desiring the things of others. I am sure that's not what the apostle Paul had in mind in his letter to the Philippians. Looking at the things of others, we should see them as Christ did, with compassion and love. He always saw the need, even when those around Him were insensitive.

We need to follow His example. We may see a physical need (someone who needs a good meal) or an emotional need (someone who needs a word of praise for a job well done). Imagine not only how good the multitudes that were fed felt but also how gratified the boy who supplied his lunch felt.

Discouragement, depression and a lack of self-worth are common maladies today. We need to give encouragement to one another. We should recognize special talents in others, whether in the arts or apostleship, administration or academics, assistance or athletics. And we should appreciate their use and dedication for the glory of God. Our reward is in heaven, but the perks along the way help to lighten the load.

REMEMBER TODAY: God's solution for the grass-is-greener syndrome is to love and appreciate your neighbor.

Elaine Craig	**Related Scriptures**	**November 4**
Lincoln Center, ME	2 Corinthians 4:16; James 5:11;	Ephesians 4:2
	Matthew 5:9; Philippians 3:13, 14	

With all lowliness and meekness, with longsuffering,
forbearing one another in love (Ephesians 4:2).

THE HEALING OF A HURT SPIRIT

In our earthly Christian walk our emotions are often tender. So it was with me when I was a young Christian. While working in our local church, a close friend whom I admired a great deal became critical of me and said things that hurt me deeply. From that point I became bitter and hard in my spirit. I would not allow myself to become close friends with anyone.

After a time God began speaking to my heart about letting go of the bitterness I was harboring. I had allowed this resentment to grow to the point that it was having negative effects in me. I felt that my salvation experience was at stake.

We need to allow God to renew a right spirit within us and to have patience and long-suffering toward others who hurt us. Not until I was willing to put away the bitterness and forget the thing that was behind could I truly grow and do the work God has had for me to do.

REMEMBER TODAY: Let go of bitterness and let God work through you.

Anita Hughes
Cleveland, TN

Related Scriptures
Isaiah 43:2; Zechariah 13:9;
2 Corinthians 4:17; 1 Peter 4:12-14

November 5
Job 23:10

*When he hath tried me, I shall
come forth as gold* (Job 23:10).

THROUGH THE FIRE

Have you been going through a fiery trial you don't understand? First Peter 4:12-14 tells us to not think it strange or be surprised at such experiences.

The refining process is sometimes very laborious. All of the dross, or imperfections, need to be burned out before pure gold can come forth. Gold symbolizes purity, loyalty, majesty or something of great value.

Job knew the value of gold when he exclaimed, "When he hath tried me, I shall come forth as gold." He had looked all around. Seemingly God was not there.

Do you feel as though you are all alone in your trial? Job settled that question: "But he knoweth the way that I take . . ." (v. 10). God knows right where you are. And though you may feel as if you are going through the fire, you can come forth as pure gold, refined by the Master Refiner.

The purest of gold is soft and pliable and can be easily molded and shined to a brilliant luster. When we are tried as gold, our lives can be molded in His image and the light of His love can shine through.

REMEMBER TODAY: "Our light affliction, which is but for a moment worketh for us a far more exceeding and eternal weight of glory" (2 Corinthians 4:17).

Sandra Miller
Stone Mountain, GA

Related Scriptures
Romans 8:18; 1 Peter 4:12, 13, 16

November 6
2 Timothy 2:12

If we suffer, we shall also
reign with him (2 Timothy 2:12).

SUFFERINGS

"Mom, could you die from a cut on your finger?"

Without thinking, I answered my 9-year-old daughter, "Oh, I suppose so." Seeing the look on her face made me realize I had frightened her with my careless answer. After tending her finger, I asked her if she was afraid to die.

"No," she said, "I am afraid of the suffering before I die." No one is exempt from suffering. It can come at any time. It can come when we think everything is going great. It can come in many forms: an affliction of our body, death of a family member or friend, disappointments, loss of a job, or—maybe one of the most common of all—loneliness. Some suffer greatly just from lack of basic material needs.

Jesus suffered hunger, thirst, ridicule, loneliness, heartbreak and pain. Yet He learned to be obedient to the Father through His suffering. Jesus sought relief from or strength for enduring His suffering in prayer. In Hebrews 5:7 we read, "When he had offered up prayers and supplication with crying and tears. . . ."

I think my 9-year-old was saying she was afraid of the unknown. So am I. But God's Word has many passages that lead us gently through any suffering that comes our way. "If I say, Surely darkness shall cover me; even the night shall be light about me. . . . For thou hast possessed my reins: thou hast covered me in my mother's womb" (Psalm 139:11, 13).

Over the years I have learned that we can be overcome by our sufferings or we can be overcomers made stronger by them.

REMEMBER TODAY: Jesus is the perfect example for us in our suffering.

Evelyn Scogin Robertson	**Related Scriptures:**	**November 7**
Villa Grove, IL	Mark 9:23; Isaiah 30:18	Matthew 19:14

Suffer little children, and forbid them not, to come unto me: for such is the kingdom of heaven (Matthew 19:14).

A SISTER FOR DEANNA

"Please, God, give me a little sister." Each night before I tucked my little girl into bed, she prayed this sincere wish to God. I knew how she felt. I too had never had a sister and always prayed for one.

After Deanna was born, the doctor told us I could never have another child, so we began trying to adopt a child. Years went by, and although we took several children into our home, we never found one we could legally adopt.

Deanna graduated from Lee Academy and agreed to teach in Vacation Bible School that summer. Every evening she talked about the sweet little girl who attended her class. When Bible school ended, the little girl was in my Sunday school class.

One Sunday she came early. Her face was swollen and red from crying. As I counseled with her, she told me her mother was dying with cancer. She would be adopted into another family.

Traveling home from church, I explained her circumstances to the family. My husband said, "We have plenty of room in our home and love in our hearts for a little girl like that." So I went to the courthouse the next day to apply for her. Satan tried in many ways to hinder the adoption, but the Lord helped us to be victorious.

At last Deanna's prayers were answered—she had a sister! What a joy it was to take this child from an ungodly home and lead her in the ways of righteousness, truth and love.

She married a young minister. They have spread the gospel in South Korea, Guam, Germany and the United States.

No wonder Scripture instructs us not to forbid the children to come to the Lord, "for of such is the kingdom of heaven."

REMEMBER TODAY: No matter how long you've been asking, keep asking. Don't give up. God still answers prayer.

Lynn R. Caffrey
Cleveland, TN

Related Scriptures
Galatians 5:14; Philippians 4:8;
James 3:8, 9; 5:9

November 8
Ephesians 4:29

*Do not let any unwholesome talk come out of your mouths, but
only what is helpful for building others up according to their needs,
that it may benefit those who listen* (Ephesians 4:29, *NIV*).

SPEAK LIFE

As a mother of two little girls, I have learned the importance of words. Any small, one-syllable utterance from my 1-year-old will elicit an appropriate action or response from me. On the other hand, my 3-year-old wants a long, detailed explanation for every word I speak. How readily we communicate our thoughts through words.

How powerful our words are: they have the power to build up or tear down. In Ephesians 4:29 the apostle Paul clearly articulated that our speech is to be wholesome and should be used exclusively for the building up of those who are listening. Too often we forget that our words speak life or death.

Scripture also tells us that "out of the abundance of the heart the mouth speaketh" (Matthew 12:34). What are we thinking about, and subsequently speaking about? We need to examine our hearts daily.

Paul reminds us, "Finally . . . brother whatever is pure, whatever is lovely, whatever is admirable—if anything is excellent or praiseworthy—think about such things" (Philippians 4:8, *NIV*). Let us seize opportunities to build each other up in Christ.

REMEMBER TODAY: Think on good things and speak life to those who are listening.

Shana Garner
Cleveland, TN

Related Scriptures
Proverbs 11:27; Galatians 6:10;
Colossians 3:23-25

November 9
Galatians 6:9

*And let us not grow weary while doing good, for in due season
we shall reap if we do not lose heart* (Galatians 6:9, NKJV).

WEARY IN DOING GOOD

Living in a dorm suite with three other girls was fun. Sometimes. I love people and dislike confusion and trouble. It was my nature to make sure everyone was happy, even at my own expense. But some days were harder than others.

"I'm getting sick and tired of always being the nice guy. It never pays to do good. Everyone just takes advantage of you," I said as I stormed out of my dorm room.

When I returned, my roommate had marked Galatians 6:9 in my Bible and left me a note that read, "They may not tell you thanks for being so nice or for doing the right thing, but believe me, they would not like you if you weren't so sweet. And besides, you are doing what God would want you to do."

That verse and note really spoke to me that day. I was trying to do good because it was the right thing, not for selfish motives. I knew that, but I needed to be reminded.

There are times when we do all the right things. We are helpful and considerate of others. Our lives are a testimony of good works. But if we are waiting for compliments or accolades from our friends, it may appear that our good works are in vain.

God's Word in Colossians 3:23, 24 tells us that our works should be done "heartily, as to the Lord . . . knowing that of the Lord ye shall receive the reward of the inheritance." And Galatians 6:7 says we will reap what we sow. We will receive a harvest of blessing for doing what is right.

It is wonderful to realize that God is keeping a record. As long as we obey God's Word, we have the promise of our inheritance. In His perfect timing, He will reward us.

REMEMBER TODAY: God will reward us for doing good.

Kathy Sanders **Related Scriptures** November 10
Lexington, KY 2 Corinthians 5:17; Jeremiah 29:11; Isaiah 40:31
1 Corinthians 10:13

. . . They shall mount up with wings as eagles (Isaiah 40:31).

STRENGTH IN MY WINGS

I've always been fascinated by comparing my spiritual life to the metamorphosis process of the butterfly emerging from its cocoon. I became even more excited watching a documentary film on *Raising Showcase Butterflies* and comparing yet another phase to my spiritual walk.

The transformed butterfly begins pumping its wings, causing thick secretion to flow from its body into the tiny veins in the wings. The wings, strengthened by this secretion, begin to expand and crack the cocoon so the butterfly can emerge. Without this strengthening process, the butterfly could not fly.

The film showed how man helps to make showcase butterflies' wings supernaturally strong. When a butterfly begins pumping its wings to break the cocoon so it can emerge, the cocoon is sprayed with a type of starch which keeps the cocoon from breaking. The butterfly pumps harder and faster, manufacturing a thicker secretion. When the butterfly has almost given up, man takes a razor and splits the cocoon about one-fourth of an inch. The butterfly, feeling the separating of the cocoon, begins his pumping activity again. While closely observing, once again the man sprays the cocoon. When the butterfly exhausts himself again, the cocoon is cut out and the butterfly resumes the pumping process. After several exchanges of pumping, spraying, pumping, cutting and pumping again, the most gorgeous butterfly emerges with such strength in its wings it can fly above all its surroundings.

Is this what You do to me, God, in the midst of a trial? I have almost given up, then You give me a ray of hope. I receive new energy, yet You still want me stronger. The test is still there, but I see another ray of light. New strength . . . more testing . . . renewed faith . . . more testing. Then at last I emerge, rising above my circumstances with wings having the strength of an eagle.

REMEMBER TODAY: God's will for you is that you become stronger in Him.

Katherine L. Cantrell
Cleveland, TN

Related Scriptures
Ephesians 2:14-18; 6:12; John 14:27

November 11
Psalm 29:11

The Lord will give strength to His people; the Lord
will bless His people with peace (Psalm 29:11, NKJV).

THE BATTLE FOR PEACE

During the Persian Gulf War, millions watched the news daily with the hopeful expectation that there would be a declaration of peace. The men and women of the allied forces traveled to foreign soil to fight for peace. This seems such a paradox. But let us compare it with the Christian walk.

As it appeared, the only way to bring about a solution to the gulf crisis was through the events of war. The peace sought cost everyone a great deal. As Spirit-filled Christians we battle not against flesh and blood but "against principalities, against powers, against the rulers of the darkness of this world, against spiritual wickedness in high places" (Ephesians 6:12). Just as a soldier fights to defend the freedom of self and others, so the Christian must engage in spiritual battle to defend the faith.

By winning the battle against Satan, Jesus Christ made the way for us to find peace. He is our peace. Now we, as God's children, have a battle to fight every day in our prayer closets as warriors for the Lord.

In your heart, is there turmoil, confusion, war? Do you long for peace? Only Jesus can calm the storm in your life. Only He can bring everlasting peace.

While the nations of this world continue their search for peace, let us accept the peace of Christ, who said, " 'Peace I leave with you, My peace I give to you; not as the world gives do I give to you. Let not your heart be troubled, neither let it be afraid'" (John 14:27, *NKJV*).

Jesus went through an unpeaceful ordeal to become our peace. We can trust Him to keep us through any turmoil, strife or war that is raging around us.

REMEMBER TODAY: Let us trust in Jesus to give us His everlasting peace.

Wendy Obenauer	**Related Scriptures**	**November 12**
Billings, MT	Proverbs 13:12; John 15:11; Jeremiah 29:11	Hebrews 12:2

Looking unto Jesus the author and finisher of our faith; who for the joy that was set before him endured the cross, despising the shame, and is set down at the right hand of the throne of God (Hebrews 12:2).

THE JOY OF THE LORD IS MY STRENGTH

"When are you guys going to start having kids?" they asked me.

How many times would I have to swallow the lump in my throat and answer that question? Thinking back over the seven years of waiting and waiting again for our dreams of having a little one to come true is painful. I remember the miscarriages and the emotional pain associated with them. It was a crucifying experience, but the joy of the Lord was sufficient to see me through. There is a calm delight in knowing God continued to care for me and had a plan for our lives.

Jesus agonized as He faced Calvary, but He endured that we might have Christ within, the hope of glory (see Colossians 1:27), and that we might have fullness of joy (see John 15:11). Proverbs 13:12 tells us, "Hope deferred maketh the heart sick: but when the desire cometh, it is a tree of life."

Though Jim and I experienced a period of waiting and endurance before our first child was born, we found strength and encouragement in the same joy Jesus experienced as He faced Calvary. He knew there was something better coming, and so did we. So we praise God together, knowing that even when we experience our own kind of sorrow and suffering, God has a plan for us.

"For I know the thoughts that I think toward you, saith the Lord, thoughts of peace, and not of evil, to give you an expected end" (Jeremiah 29:11).

REMEMBER TODAY: In times of sorrow and suffering, rest in the calm delight of knowing God has a perfect plan for your life.

Carolyn Wiggins
Rocky Mount, NC

Related Scripture
1 Corinthians 13:13

November 13
Romans 8:28

And we know that all things work together for good to them that love God, to them who are the called according to his purpose (Romans 8:28).

LIQUID LOVE

"Nana, you're the best nana in the whole wide world!" Those words pierced my heart as I stared into the eyes of my beautiful granddaughter. My mind instantly raced back to the delivery room as I watched my 17-year-old, unwed daughter give birth to this 6-pound baby girl.

"Mom, this is my daughter. Will you hold her?" I stood there, empty of all feelings. For nine months I had supported her in every way through thoughts of suicide, abortion, loneliness and guilt. I had managed to hide my true feelings of hurt and disappointment, but our "perfect family" had been destroyed. Hostility from peers was endured. Feelings of hurt and embarrassment haunted my younger daughter as she watched her dad minister from the pulpit—broken, yet ministering with love. Often in self-pity I had prayed to die, trying to escape where I now stood. Just minutes before, I was beating the walls in the waiting room, screaming, "Why, God?" But now the words echoed, "Mom, this is my baby. Please hold her."

"Sure I will, honey," I quickly replied. As I reached out to take this small bundle, I prayed, "God, please give me a love for this child." Simultaneously, the warmth of the baby's body touched my hands and I felt the warm sensation of God's love, like liquid, pour on my head and flow through my body. She was so very beautiful. She was my granddaughter.

At that moment God taught me forgiveness and filled me with His greatest gift—love. He had turned an ugly situation into a beautiful blessing. Money could never buy the greatest of all compliments: "Nana, you're the best nana in the whole wide world!"

REMEMBER TODAY: God's love is a healing balm when we allow it to flow. His grace is sufficient, regardless of the circumstance.

Enetha McClung
Cleveland, TN

Related Scriptures
Proverbs 16:3; 3:5, 6; 2 Corinthians 3:18

November 14
Psalm 37:5

Commit your way to the Lord; trust in
him, and he will act (Psalm 37:5, RSV).

A THING OF BEAUTY

Standing on a city street in Turkey one day, I watched the making of a beautiful carpet. The cloth was placed on a large vertical frame, with the weavers on one side and the master weaver on the other. The master weaver knew the pattern he wanted and directed the others in achieving it. He indicated a place on the cloth for one of the weavers to push the needle and thread through. This process continued until the carpet was finished. None of the weavers could see the design being made. They had to trust the master weaver to make everything come out all right. The pattern on their side did not make sense. In fact, many times it appeared quite ugly.

Later I made these observations about the carpets I saw that day. Some were almost finished, others just begun. Some were rough, without design, while others, almost completed, were beautiful. How like those carpets we are! We are in the hands of our Master Weaver, and He cares for and directs the lives of each of us individually! No carpet was without value; indeed, each would become a prized possession cherished by the maker and desired by the onlooker.

If you feel rough, unlovely or incomplete, remember the same principle applies to our lives. God has a plan for each of us. We must commit ourselves to Him and, by faith, trust that He knows the best method to make our lives the beautiful design that will reflect His image and likeness, making us a thing of beauty in a world of ugliness.

REMEMBER TODAY: God sees us as someone of worth; we have great value to Him.

Sharon L. Landreth
Hamilton, OH

Related Scriptures
Psalm 29:11; John 16:33; Ephesians 2:14;
Colossians 3:15; 2 Thessalonians 3:16

November 15
John 14:27

*Peace I leave with you, my peace I give unto you:
not as the world giveth, give I unto you. Let not your
heart be troubled, neither let it be afraid* (John 14:27).

THE LIGHT OF PEACE

Peace. We sing about it, talk about it, preach about it, pray for it. But do we really know peace in troubled times? Can we find peace in our darkest hour?

My darkest hour was on a November day as I sat with my family in a hospital room. The doctor entered the room and informed my father that he had a brain tumor that could not be treated entirely with surgery. I remember thinking of all the times I'd said I would fall apart if anything ever happened to one of my parents. Could I face one of my worst fears and be victorious?

Luke 1:78, 79 says, "Whereby the dayspring from on high hath visited us, to give light to them that sit in darkness and in the shadow of death, to guide our feet into the way of peace." As I sat in my own personal darkness and shadow of death, I felt the Spirit of God rise up in me. Suddenly I knew in my spirit that God had everything under control, and He would take care of my father and my family. I found true peace.

"Acquaint now thyself with him, and be at peace: thereby good shall come unto thee" (Job 22:21). True peace is achieved by truly knowing God. If we know His love and power in our lives, nothing we face in this life can take away the gift of God's peace.

By walking in peace and faith, good came to my family. When Dad had the tests repeated in February, there was no tumor. I'm thankful for the miracle of healing God performed in my father. I am also thankful for the gift of God which allowed me to walk through the darkness with the light of peace in my heart.

REMEMBER TODAY: "Thou wilt keep him in perfect peace, whose mind is stayed on thee: because he trusteth in thee" (Isaiah 26:3).

Geraldine Ballard **Related Scripture** November 16
Columbus, IN Philippians 4:13 Philippians 2:13

*For it is God which worketh in you both to will
and to do of his good pleasure* (Philippians 2:13).

SAYING "I CAN'T"

As a young Christian I was taught, "Never say 'can't.' " This is good advice for developing self-confidence; however, there were times I discovered self-confidence was insufficient.

It was difficult to say, "I can't." I was going against the grain of this well-established lesson, but I found myself crying loudly and clearly, "I can't!" I needed more than what I had! Self-resources could not carry me through!

Have you ever come to a crossroad such as this in your life? Most people have. You too can say "I can't" and learn a greater lesson revealed in Philippians 2:13. The apostle Paul said, "For it is God which worketh in you both to will and to do his good pleasure." The greater lesson is that you can say "I can't" and feel good about it. It's all right. It's a new discovery of truth. We are to be totally dependent, not upon resources of self, but upon the efficiency of what God is in us. He is the source that is all-sufficient. He is working in us, by His Spirit, to fulfill His pleasure and to help us do all that is within His will.

REMEMBER TODAY: Paul said in Philippians 4:13, "I can do all things through Christ which strengtheneth me." I can't . . . you can't . . . but God can!

Linda M. Holdman
Minot, ND

Related Scriptures
Psalm 139:13-18; Matthew 6:25-34;
Romans 8:28

November 17
Jeremiah 29:11

For I know the plans I have for you, says the Lord. They are plans for good and not for evil, to give you a future and a hope (Jeremiah 29:11, *TLB*).

THE PLANS

"If you had come one hour later, it would have been too late," the doctor informed my mother as he completed his examination. "We'll have to keep her here for a few days." He was talking about me. I was 2 years old and sick with double pneumonia.

My mother has retold this story many times throughout the years, always ending the account by saying that she would never forget how she felt the Lord had a plan for my life when she looked into my infant eyes. She has repeatedly encouraged me with the words "He spared your life for a purpose. You are special to Him."

One reason she clings to this opinion is the fact that my uncle came to our farm that specific night in the middle of a storm, without having been contacted. He came bursting into our home, not taking time to remove his coat, and said, "Sis, what's wrong? I felt I just had to come." My mother covered me carefully, assured my sisters and brothers she would be back soon, and told my uncle that we must get to the hospital. If he had come one hour later, it would have been too late. But God had a plan for "a future and a hope." He was in control. He knew my mother could not drive, so He sent a driver. He chose not to heal but to provide.

Now that I am a mother of three sons, I think I know somewhat how Mother must have agonized with feelings of helplessness. But her help came from the Lord. Thank God for her strong faith and belief in God's power and plans!

From childhood I have experienced God's marvelous works in my life, beginning with salvation at age 8 and receiving the baptism of the Holy Spirit at age 13. Life has brought unique experiences—sometimes opportunities came disguised as obstacles—some hopeful, some hurtful, but all designed by the Master Planner.

God has given me a full life, "a future and a hope." He has an individual life plan for each of His children. We matter to Him.

The psalmist says in 139:17, 18, "How precious it is, Lord, to realize that you are thinking about me constantly! I can't even count how many times a day your thoughts turn towards me" (*TLB*).

REMEMBER TODAY: God has a plan for our lives—a perfect plan that will give us perfect peace.

Patty Stallings | Related Scriptures | November 18
Rapid City, SD | John 13:34, 35; 15:9-17; 1 John 4:7-11; | John 15:12
 | 1 Corinthians 13; Galatians 2:20; |
 | Colossians 3:12-14 |

"Love each other as I have loved you" (John 15:12, *NIV*).

OPEN-ARMED LOVE

We often say Christ loves us so much that He died for us. Think for a moment how Jesus was positioned when He made that statement of love. It is significant that His arms were outstretched. If you can, read the rest of this page with your arms literally outstretched in the manner Christ stretched out His arms on the cross.

The position physically exposes your most vulnerable organs. You have little defense against oncoming blows. You have opened yourself to be wounded by those who choose to do so.

If we love others as Christ loves us, then we must stretch our arms out spiritually, just as Christ did physically. Yes, you do make yourself open and vulnerable. Others may wound you. When this happens, you can choose to crawl into a corner, you can strike back in self-defense, or you may allow God to heal the wound so you can stretch out your arms again and love others as Jesus loves you.

Jesus said the strongest evidence we can offer to prove we belong to Him is loving people in the manner that He loves us (John 13:34, 35). When we have crucified ourselves, then Christ's love can flow through our outstretched arms into the lives of others.

❦

REMEMBER TODAY: Follow Christ's example of love, and others will follow your love to find Christ.

Elizabeth S. Sikes
Alma, GA

Related Scriptures
1 John 1:9; Lamentations 3:22, 23;
1 Corinthians 1:9

November 19
Deuteronomy 7:9

> *Know therefore that the Lord thy God, he is God, the faithful God, which keepeth covenant and mercy with them that love him and keep his commandments* (Deuteronomy 7:9).

GOD IS FAITHFUL

The quietness of the emergency room was broken by the sound of arriving ambulances. A car accident had sent five young people to the hospital. As our team worked with the most seriously injured young man, he opened fearful eyes and asked me to help him find the Lord as his Savior. I quickly prayed the sinner's prayer with him. A smile crossed his face as God's amazing grace flowed into his fragile life. He asked me to share with his mother what had happened and to thank her for not giving up on him.

As she was told of his death, the mother's heart broke. I told her how God's love had been wrought in the life of her dying son. In great victory, she worshiped God—the faithful God.

God is faithful to His people and faithful to fulfill all His promises. He did not save us to forsake us during difficult circumstances. When the game of life is "on the line," He is entirely faithful. His commitment to us is deep. On the basis of His faithfulness, we can call to Him for help, knowing He is always with us. How marvelous is His love to us!

Do you ever doubt God's faithfulness? Does your inconsistency change His faithful commitment to you? Of course it doesn't!

We can relax, knowing His loving faithfulness will see us through every situation.

REMEMBER TODAY: Regardless of the valley, God—who is ever faithful—never leaves you alone. He is with you even now! Call upon Him. He is present.

Joy Hostetler	**Related Scriptures**	**November 20**
Parsons, WV	Ezekiel 22:30; Colossians 3:9;	Isaiah 59:15, 16
	1 Timothy 2:1-8	

*Then the Lord saw it, and it displeased Him that there was no justice.
He saw that there was no man, and wondered that there was no
intercessor; therefore His own arm brought salvation for Him; and
His own righteousness, it sustained Him* (Isaiah 59:15, 16, *NKJV*).

PLEASE PRAY FOR ME

Betty had moved to our town because her husband had been incarcerated in a local institution and she wanted to live close enough to visit him.

I had seen her in the store where I worked, and a friend had even brought her to our church a few times. There was nothing unusual about her, just a single parent trying to keep her family together. She had accepted the Lord and was experiencing the ups and downs of her new faith.

I remember the day she walked into the store and came directly to my station. She struck up a conversation, which came around to her telling me she was having a battle with a habit.

"I'm really trying to quit smoking, but it's so hard. Please pray for me."

"I will," I assured her.

I didn't see her again for two or three weeks. Then one day she came into the store again. She told me she was still fighting her habit. Then she looked directly into my eyes and asked, "Have you been praying for me?"

I was tempted to utter a quick, silent prayer and tell her I had prayed for her. I chose one of the hardest things I've ever had to do. I admitted I had not sincerely prayed for her. Right then and there, I vowed to work on my memory and not take prayer requests lightly.

How many times have we casually promised to pray for someone and then forgotten the promise? When people ask us for prayer, they have confidence that we will intercede on their behalf.

Someone has said that honest confession is good for the soul; but in my case, confrontation was better.

REMEMBER TODAY: We have an awesome responsibility when someone asks for prayer. We become a "gap filler" between God and man.

Mary Hocker	**Related Scripture**	**November 21**
Camden, OH	Hebrews 4:14, 15	Hebrews 4:16

Let us therefore come boldly unto the throne of grace, that we may obtain mercy, and find grace to help in time of need (Hebrews 4:16).

ON SPEAKING TERMS

The sidewalk connecting the back door of the Sunday school annex to the parsonage was the way my 2-year-old son and I went back and forth to church. On a particular Sunday the sun was shining, birds were singing, and my son and I walked slowly to church. With his hand in mine, I heard him say, "Hi, Jesus!" I looked at him and followed his gaze heavenward as he raised his chubby little hand in salute. Then just as quickly he dropped his hand, looked at me and smiled.

He didn't say the words loudly as if Jesus were far away; neither did he whisper them as if he were fearful or ashamed. He said it very naturally, as though it was his usual way to greet Jesus, the Son of God. He said the words as though he knew perfectly well that Jesus was observing us as we walked home from church, enjoying His beautiful creation. In those two words, "Hi, Jesus," I could sense my son's assurance that there truly is a Savior who is Lord of his life. This Lord is a personal, approachable friend.

Scripture tells us, "We have not an high priest which cannot be touched. . . . Let us therefore come boldly unto the throne of grace . . ." (Hebrews 4:15, 16). "Through him [Jesus] we both have access by one Spirit unto the Father" (Ephesians 2:18).

Tears filled my eyes that day as I remembered days when I had not communicated with my Lord. I also recalled Christ's words, "Except ye be converted, and become as little children, ye shall not enter into the kingdom of heaven" (Matthew 18:3). I breathed a prayer right then, determining to stay on "speaking terms" with my Lord regularly, whether for an hour or two short words. You see, His Word admonishes us, "Be not children in understanding: howbeit in malice be ye children, but in understanding be men" (1 Corinthians 14:20).

REMEMBER TODAY: Stay on speaking terms with God the Father. He is personal and approachable.

Patricia A. Allen   **Related Scriptures**   November 22
Warner Robins, GA   Matthew 10:8, 42; 25:34-45;   Luke 6:38
                       Deuteronomy 15: 14, 15

"Give, and it will be given to you. A good measure, pressed down, shaken together and running over, will be poured into your lap. For with the measure you use, it will be measured to you" (Luke 6:38, NIV).

INTERRUPTED AGAIN?

No one likes to be viewed as self-centered. But let's face it, each of us has a strong tendency to live for self. If you don't think so, just look back at the times when unexpected company interrupted your plans. Suppose you are invited to visit the sick or Sunday absentees—does your whole countenance change?

At times I don't want anyone intruding upon my private time with my family. (The telephone is a story in itself.) Self-centered? Not always. But many times a bad attitude erupts when plans are interrupted.

Christ instructs us to show His love. As we show love to others, we are also loving Christ. In turn, the more love we show, the more we receive.

The next time your husband comes home with a visitor or changes the family plans, check your attitude and pray before turning down a wonderful opportunity to be Christlike. "Lord, here I am again. Teach me how not to just receive but to give from the heart."

REMEMBER TODAY: "Inasmuch as ye did it not to one of the least of these, ye did it not to me" (Matthew 25:45).

Rachel Quinley	**Related Scriptures**	**November 23**
Loxley, AL	Deuteronomy 6:6-9; John 3:16	Job 19:23

Oh that my words were now written! (Job 19:23).

ENCOURAGING WORDS

Can you think of someone you have tried to reach for the Lord and just could not? No song, no message—nothing seemed to touch the heart of the person.

Is there anything else to do when spoken words fail? Try one more thing—write a letter.

There is no way to evaluate the value of one letter. When my son was a young teenager he became burdened for a young man who had drifted from God and the church. Ernie decided to write him a letter, telling him he was praying for him. It was a simple but powerful letter.

A few nights later the young man went to church and gave his heart to God. He testified, "I could not get away from Ernie's letter."

When spoken words fail, try a letter. You may be surprised at the number of people whose hearts can be touched with a piece of paper and a pen.

Try a letter of appreciation and encouragement for those who never miss a Sunday at your church. Write a letter to a parent who has had problems with a teenage son or daughter. A short note of appreciation may give your pastor the lift he has been needing.

Stop reading and start writing! The hardest task is getting started. Waiting until you have a box of beautiful stationery or until you get a new typewriter ribbon or until your work load slows down is in reality procrastination—and procrastination is a thief of time.

Don't put it off another day. A letter will mean a lot to someone. And the satisfaction of encouraging someone through a few written words will mean even more to you.

REMEMBER TODAY: The greatest letter ever printed was written by Jesus Christ. Read John 3:16—it's a letter just for you.

Nancy A. Neal   **Related Scriptures**   November 24
Cleveland, TN   1 Thessalonians 5:18;   Psalm 92:1
Psalms 40:5; 50:14; 105:1, 5

It is a good thing to give
thanks unto the Lord (Psalm 92:1).

THE LITTLE THINGS

Outpatient surgery for some reconstruction on my left foot seemed like no big deal initially. Mother was available—fixing meals, getting pain pills in the middle of the night, answering the phone, straightening household clutter. But after five days, she had to go home . . . some 300 miles away. In her place, reality moved in.

Every little detail had to be carefully planned. Even brushing my teeth proved to be an ordeal. My walking cast, fashioned after some giant robot, made me "mobile." But after I lugged it around all day, my spine was completely out of alignment, I was exhausted, and preparing a meal was simply out of the question.

Granted, I could take the cast off during the evenings, but then I had to resort to crutches to get around. My size 4 1/2 with the wire protruding from the side was not allowed to touch the floor. Crutches simply aren't conducive to making quick trips to the fridge for a snack, scurrying to catch the phone or even checking the mail for hospital bills.

In frustration I began to regret the decision to have surgery. When I fell and had no one to help me up, I threw big pity parties. I longed for the days when it didn't require an Act of Congress to walk 30 feet to take out the garbage.

I was made keenly aware of just how much I take even my little feet for granted. In the final analysis, I determined that in our absorption with our own peculiar set of circumstances, we quite regularly fail to be thankful for the little things.

*Adapted from "The Little Things," *Church of God Evangel*, January 1989.

REMEMBER TODAY: Indeed, we should give thanks for those aspects of our lives that sometimes we see as annoyances—the ringing telephone, grocery shopping, bill paying, vacuuming—especially if we still have the ability to accomplish these tasks.

Brenda W. Crisp
Anderson, SC

Related Scriptures
Psalm 23; Isaiah 45:3; 60:1, 2;
Acts 27:22-25

November 25
Psalm 23:4

*Yea, though I walk through the valley of the shadow
of death, I will fear no evil: for thou art with me;
thy rod and thy staff they comfort me* (Psalm 23:4).

BUGBEAR, BE GONE

Debbie, my daughter, and I were alone in the room long after the anonymous voice had authoritatively announced for the last time: "Visiting hours are over in the hospital. All visitors please leave immediately."

Debbie was so fearful; I just couldn't leave her alone. She was scheduled for surgery early the next morning, and the doctors had informed us they would have to remove most of the left lung in order to excise a massive tumor. She looked out the window into the dark night and tearfully rehearsed all the same questions over again: "Why me?" "Am I going to die?" "How bad will the scar be?" "Why hasn't God healed me?"

I felt so helpless in my efforts to comfort her. Then the Holy Spirit seemed to give me a spiritual *deja vu*. Suddenly my memory flashed back 20 years. Debbie and I were in the bedroom of a small parsonage in rural North Carolina. Momentarily startled, my little 4-year-old had frantically clasped the drapes together to shut out the darkness. She cried, "Bugbears, Mommy, bugbears! Make 'em go away." I tried to explain to her that God was outside walking in the darkness, as well as being right there in the bedroom with us. I told her the ones who really needed to be afraid were the bugbears. To my surprise, her courage must have surged. She pressed her face to the drapes and yelled in her biggest voice, "Bugbear, be gone. Be gone, Bugbear."

As we shared this together, I reminded Debbie that the surgery she was facing was one of the real "bugbears" in life. Although the diagnosis was dark, she could count on God's presence. She was not alone. She could confidently face the darkness with childlike faith and declare, "Bugbear, be gone. Be gone, Bugbear." Afterward both of us had a deep, settled peace that transcended the dark circumstances.

Today Debbie is in great health and enjoys full life in Christ.

REMEMBER TODAY: Even when it is too dark to see Him, God is there and we need not fear.

Marion M. Spellman
Somerset, PA

Related Scriptures
Psalm 94:19; Philippians 4:8

November 26
Philippians 4:6

*Be anxious for nothing, but in everything by prayer
and supplication with thanksgiving let your requests
be made known to God* (Philippians 4:6, *NASB*).

GIVE THANKS

Have you ever watched an episode of *Little House on the Prairie* and found yourself longing for a simpler time?

Society has changed direction to such an extent that we seldom have time for such carefree activities as taking a stroll, baking pies, or even sitting down together as a family to enjoy one another's company and discuss the events of the day. The extended family is nearly alienated simply because of distance and lack of time to visit.

Progress, while it has made things easier for us in terms of chores and daily routines, has complicated our lifestyles so much that we can scarcely pick up a magazine without seeing an article on how to reduce stress. In our quest for success and in keeping up with demands, we find ourselves bogged down with pressures. We become overwhelmed with life in general.

As housewives who often must also work outside the home, a daily routine demands a superhuman to organize schedules, baby-sitters, piano lessons, after-school activities, sports and all the events our children are involved in. This doesn't include the never-ending housework that still must be done.

The Lord made provision for us by encouraging us in Philippians 4:6 to make our requests known to Him. Do not fret or be anxious, but in *everything* by prayer and supplication *with thanksgiving*, give it to Him.

I wonder if in our hectic schedules we sometimes forget to give thanks to Him for all He has done for us, for the privilege of even seeing another day.

REMEMBER TODAY: Be anxious for nothing, but give thanks for all things.

Roxanne Pasanen
Medway, ME

Related Scriptures
Matthew 19:14; Mark 10:14

Suffer little children to come unto me,
and forbid them not . . . (Luke 18:16).

GOD BLESS THE CHILDREN

This verse was going through my mind one November day as I walked up my steps over a new-fallen snow. I had just come from the store where I had picked up two new bed frames. I was expecting not one but two children and needed more bed space.

As I opened the door and stepped inside, I saw little islands of snowy foot-prints on my living room rug. Then I saw a set of large, frightened eyes. My new ones had arrived. They were abused, skinny, very frightened and trauma-tized. These were not my first foster children, nor would they be my last. But because of the severity of their trauma, having witnessed multiple murders to primary care givers just weeks previously, they were the two I spent the most time praying for, nurturing and training.

Two and a half years later, the little girl recovered enough to return home to her mom. But it was 10 and a half years before the little boy could process everything he had suffered. He finally did forgive his mother and was able to return home as a young man who had learned some valuable lessons.

Could Jesus have had such children in mind when He said those beautiful words, "Allow the little children to come to Me" (*Amp.*)? I think these two little ones would have fit very well on the lap of the Master.

REMEMBER TODAY: Let us be watchful of ourselves that we do not over-look all the children who need someone to lead them to Jesus.

Andrea C. Reid   **Related Scripture**   **November 28**
Simpsonville, MD   Isaiah 46:4   Isaiah 40:11

He shall feed his flock like a shepherd: he shall gather the lambs with his arm, and carry them in his bosom, and shall gently lead those that are with young (Isaiah 40:11).

HE WILL CARRY YOU

"If you carry me now, when I get big I will carry you!"

The day was wonderful! Bill and I had both sets of parents for the whole weekend. Our time together was busy with train rides and sight-seeing. Our sons, Alex and Warren, were with us. They were having the time of their lives. Our youngest son, Warren, grew tired from the day's activities. As we were walking along, he looked up at his granddad and said, "Granddad, if you will carry me now, when I get big I'll carry you!"

Many times since that day I have remembered the promise of a little boy. As he spoke, you could see the love and care he had for his beloved grandparents.

More than once in working for the Lord, I have become weary. When I do not think I can go on, I look to the Lord and think of Isaiah 40:11.

If you grow weary, just remember: He wants to carry you until you are strong again. Do not be afraid; let God gather you to His bosom.

REMEMBER TODAY: The Shepherd will carry you gently in His arms today!

Clarice Weaver
Pulaski, VA

Related Scriptures
Matthew 21:22; 6:6; Psalm 21:2

November 29
John 14:13, 14

And whatsoever ye shall ask in my name, that will I do,
that the Father may be glorified in the Son. If ye shall
ask any thing in my name, I will do it (John 14:13, 14).

PRACTICE WHAT YOU PREACH

After spending the Thanksgiving holidays in 1988 with my family in Clearwater, Florida, we flew back into Nassau. We proceeded through customs and immigration and made our way to the parking lot to drive home, which was about 45 minutes from the airport. It was nearing 1 a.m.; we were tired and longing to be home. Hurriedly we threw the luggage in the car and buckled up, but to our dismay, the car would not start. After trying several times, my husband threw his hands on the steering wheel and said, "Well, what do we do now?"

From the backseat our teenage daughter said, "Practice what you preach."

"OK," my husband said, "let's pray." And we did. Trying the starter again, nothing happened. So in unison we prayed aloud, "In the name of Jesus, let this car crank." We began praising God for letting it start. On the third try, it cranked immediately. Then we really praised God.

My daughter will never forget the day we practiced what we were preaching as instructed in John 14:13, 14. We asked in Jesus' name and He heard our prayer.

When you've prayed, then you must believe God for the right answer for you. He may say no, or He may say yes. We must accept His answer, regardless of the nature.

People are watching you every day. They are peeking around doors, listening through cracks in the wall, hiding behind bushes—watching to see if you practice what you preach.

REMEMBER TODAY: If we say God will do it, let's put it into action and let the world see it.

Phyllis M. Sustar
Cleveland, TN

Related Scriptures
Psalm 56:11; 2 Timothy 1:12;
Mark 4:39, 40

November 30
Psalm 56:3

What time I am afraid, I will trust in thee (Psalm 56:3).

BE NOT AFRAID

A couple of years ago my daughter, Sonya, and I were flying home from Pennsylvania after the Thanksgiving holiday. Our plane was already an hour late leaving Pittsburgh. The plane was full, and the stewardess was asking for volunteers to give up their seats in return for a free round-trip ticket. I considered suggesting to my daughter that we volunteer our seats, but I knew I needed to be at work on Monday morning and she had a full day of college classes.

Finally we were on our way, and I breathed a long sigh and settled down in my seat for what I thought would be a usual trip home. However, about 30 miles outside of Nashville, the plane began to go through rough turbulence. The further west we flew, the worse our situation became. The captain announced we were in a violent storm and would have to continue through it for our descent into Nashville. Tornadoes had been sighted in the storms coming from the west. As the plane continued to shake and sway, it seemed we were destined to crash.

My daughter reached over and clasped my hand. We began to pray and ask God to bring us safely through the storm. Words cannot describe the devastating feelings we experienced, but we trusted God. Finally, the wheels touched down on the runway, and we knew we had arrived safely.

Afterward, while sitting in the hotel room before our flight home the next day, the words of the song "Till the Storm Passes By" flowed through my mind. I knew God had brought us safely through the storm.

REMEMBER TODAY: How wonderful to know that even through our fears, we can depend on Him to be with us! He will give us calmness when everything around us is turbulent.

Shirley Moss	**Related Scriptures**	**December 1**
St. Joseph, MO	James 4:15; Psalm 39:1-7;	James 4:14
	Ecclesiastes 6	

What is your life? It is even a vapour, that appeareth
for a little time, and then vanisheth away (James 4:14).

THE GREATEST GIFT

"It doesn't matter what I get for Christmas this year; really, I can't think of anything," I said as my voice dissipated into the air. The department store was less than exciting on that December day. Oh, yes, all the decorations were gaily strewn throughout the store, but somehow they didn't draw my attention as they had in years before. The memory of the cancer surgery I'd had less than a month before seemed to hover over me continually.

I found myself standing in the main aisle between the Children's Department and the Junior Department. My 11-year-old daughter was growing quickly and probably could use a junior size, but I steered my husband, my 3-year-old son and my daughter toward the Children's Department, hoping to keep her from the junior sizes— at least for one more year.

Suddenly, without remembering the real reason we were in the store, my husband said to me, "While you're here, give me some ideas for your Christmas gift." Somewhat ignoring his words, I began to search for a coat. It didn't take long to find it. I needed to get to the car. My strength wasn't lasting today.

Again, my husband requested an idea for my Christmas gift. I turned, looked into his loving eyes, and with quivering lips I said, "I don't want anything from the store this year—I only want to live." Perhaps it was just one of those postsurgical-syndrome days, but amid all of the beautiful clothes, furniture, household items and Christmas music, one realization remained. Many times cancer takes a person's life. Even a mother of two and companion of a minister was subject to its devastation. So nothing but life really mattered—just life.

The writer James posed a question: "What is your life?" (4:14). Swiftly he gave us the answer: "It is like a puff of smoke visible for a little while and then dissolving into the air" (*Ph.*). He reminded us of one thing—that which we love often comes speedily to an end.

While reflecting on the past 22 postcancer years, my words are the same as they were on that December shopping day: "I just want to live."

REMEMBER TODAY: Through Christ we have life in this present world and also is the world to come.

Teresa Conlon
Curran, Ontario

Related Scriptures
Mark 9:50; Luke 17:32;
2 Corinthians 2:14

December 2
Matthew 5:13

Ye are the salt of the earth: but if the salt have lost his savour,
wherewith shall it be salted? it is thenceforth good for nothing,
but to be cast out, and to be trodden under foot of men (Matthew 5:13).

SALT—OUR LEGACY

Why was Lot's wife turned into a pillar of salt? Wouldn't a stone block be a more enduring memorial of her rebellion for future generations? Perhaps the Lord chose a pillar of salt to ask the question "How salty is your salt?" The Bible teaches that Christians are to be as salt. This illustrates many truths that pertain to a believer's influence on others. We should, like salt, provide healing, add flavor, act as a preservative and create thirst. Salt represents the holiness of Christ in the Old Testament, for no sacrifice was to be offered without it (Leviticus 2:13).

So what has all this to do with Lot's wife? Everything. Her longing for life in Sodom, which God had judged as vile, left an enduring legacy for the nation of Israel through her two daughters.

Their mother had lost her salt. She did not have the ability to make her children thirsty for righteousness, to preserve them from corrupting influences and to heal their hurts through a God-fearing love. Her influence failed to show the truth of the scripture "Taste and see that the Lord is good" (Psalm 34:8). She had lost her savor.

This mother became a pillar of salt to be eroded by the elements, dissolved into the earth and ultimately trodden under by the feet of men—a chilling fulfillment of Matthew 5:13. Salt can lose flavor but not potency. A tasteless salt can still corrupt and corrode.

Lot's daughters were the legacy of a saltless and flavorless mother. Could it be that her corrupt legacy continued when her daughters mothered Israel's enemies?

Is your mothering flavorful and salty? We will be accountable as mothers for what we have communicated and for the legacy we pass down to the next generation. Is your influence salty, or is it in danger of becoming "good for nothing" by losing the savor of Christ? Any legacy "worth its salt" will bear the imprint of Jesus etched into our lives and the lives of those who follow us.

REMEMBER TODAY: Our lives are written into the lives of others.

Nancy M. O'Bannon
Cleveland, TN

Related Scriptures
Psalm 103:1-18; Romans 8:37-39;
1 John 4:7-10

December 3
John 11:36

*Then said the Jews, Behold
how he loved him!* (John 11:36).

GOD LOVES YOU!

A number of years ago I received news from the doctors that I had kidney failure. In 1969 dialysis and kidney transplants were so new I received no assurance either would work. I needed to be prepared for death.

An uncle who was a minister, known as one who could really "touch God" in prayer, came to visit me in the hospital. In times past he had shared with me miracles of healing in his own life and ministry. I expected him to read a passage of Scripture about healing. Instead he read from John 11, which tells how Christ raised Lazarus from the dead. Rather than stressing the miracle, he focused on Christ's arrival at the grave site with Mary and Martha, at which time He wept.

"Then said the Jews," he read, "Behold how he loved him!"

Then he said, "No matter how much you love your husband and children, remember that God loves them more."

My children were 10, 6 and 4. When faced with the possibility of my death, my main concern was for them. What would happen to my children? But as my uncle had pointed out, however great my love for them was, God's love was greater. His love is infinite. What comfort!

For years I have held the assurance that God loves me—now, in this life, not just for eternity. God loves my family—now, in this life, not just for eternity. God has answered my prayer by allowing me to live not only to see my children grow into adults but also to see my three wonderful little granddaughters.

God doesn't always answer prayer in the same way He answered mine. We can be assured, however, of God's love—now and always. Throughout Scripture, God reminds us over and over of His love. In Psalms, the *New International Version* tells us of God's unfailing love at least 24 times. If you are feeling depressed and unloved, search out the Scriptures that remind you of His love.

REMEMBER TODAY: God loves you now as well as for eternity; His love is unfailing.

Karleen McCarn
Macon, GA

Related Scriptures
1 Corinthians 4:5; 2 Corinthians 4:6;
1 Peter 2:9; 1 John 2:8

December 4
Psalm 112:4

Unto the upright there ariseth
light in the darkness (Psalm 112:4).

DARKNESS

My Christmas cactus had plenty of foliage, but it had never bloomed. I read an article saying that to force blooms I should put it in a cool, dark place for 12 hours a day. So I began my daily ritual.

Each evening when I began to prepare the family meal, I would take the plant to the linen closet. I put it on a shelf and made sure I blocked out the heat and light. Each morning when the children left for school, I would take the plant from the closet and put it back with my other plants in the kitchen window.

We had been going through traumatic times. Church members whom we loved dearly had become bitter enemies. The area economy had taken a nosedive, thus affecting the church's finances and attendance. We had spent hours in prayer seeking God's will, guidance and direction for our lives as well as for the church.

One morning when I took the plant from the closet, I was praying, "God, have You forsaken us? Do You know where we are? Do You know that we hurt? Do You care?" As I placed the plant beside the others, God spoke, "I have let you experience darkness, coldness and isolation so that you will bloom for Me."

REMEMBER TODAY: No matter how dark or stormy the night may have been, morning has never failed to come.

Norma Johnson
Vienna, WV

Related Scriptures
Psalm 91; Proverbs 3:5, 6;
Romans 1:17

*For we walk by faith, not
by sight* (2 Corinthians 5:7).

BLIND FAITH

After pastoring for many years, my father retired but remained active in the ministry. He traveled by bus to various states preaching revivals. My family and I worried about him and expressed our concern every time we saw him board a bus to travel hundreds of miles. After one of Dad's trips, he related a story to me that I have never forgotten.

While traveling to Florida for a meeting, he met a blind man. During the trip they engaged in conversation. When the bus pulled into the busy terminal in Atlanta, everyone quickly exited, leaving the blind man on the bus. My father turned and asked the man, "Sir, may I help you find your connecting bus?" Gratefully the blind man said yes. Then my father asked him, "Aren't you afraid to travel alone, afraid you'll get on the wrong bus?" Without hesitation, the blind man said, "No! God always has someone there to see about me—like you!"

So many times in life we travel a path that is strange and unknown to us. We wonder what we will face around the next bend. But God takes care of His own! No matter where life's path may lead, His hand is guiding us. If necessary, He will dispatch a host of angels to come to our rescue. Don't be concerned about tomorrow. When we get there, God will provide someone there to help us on our way!

REMEMBER TODAY: It isn't really faith until faith is all you have. But when faith is all you have, it's all you need!

Annette Ballard	Related Scriptures	December 6
Terre Haute, IN	Isaiah 40:31; 58:11; 2 Timothy 2:15	Psalm 84:6

Who passing through the valley of Baca make it a well; the rain also filleth the pools (Psalm 84:6).

THE VALLEY OF BACA

"Tears Are a Language God Understands" is the title of a once-popular Christian song, and for us ladies, it's a good thing He does understand! Tears become an expression or an outlet for us. We cry when we're happy, when we're sad, when we're tired, when we're mad, when we're hurt or frustrated, or just for no good reason at all! Crying can be perceived by others as a weakness, but God created us with these emotions, and our tears can serve a purpose.

Have you ever come to a place in your life when tears were just beneath the surface? Maybe you didn't even know why. The Scriptures call this "weeping place" the Valley of Baca. It's not actually a physical location but rather a description of an emotional plateau in our lives. The verse indicates that it is a place we will pass through and make it a well. To make a well it is necessary to dig. The verb *dig* denotes an effort on our part to rightly divide the Word of truth. We're encouraged to use the Valley of Baca in our lives as an opportunity to draw us into the presence of our Father, planting ourselves at His feet and waiting on Him.

This precious time with the Lord will become a spring of life to us. He understands, and He will transfer these streams of tears into pools of blessing.

REMEMBER TODAY: The Valley of Baca can be a very special place when we allow our tears to become a vehicle that guides us into our Father's presence.

Jimmi N. Campbell
Aiea, HI

Related Scriptures
Acts 2:39; Hebrews 6:12;
2 Peter 1:4

December 7
1 Kings 8:56

*There hath not failed one word of
all his good promise* (1 Kings 8:56).

PRECIOUS PROMISES

The view from the lanai of our home, high on a hillside overlooking Pearl Harbor Bay, is always beautiful and serene. Often the sun shines brightly in the valley while a few miles away there is a gentle rain falling. Even before I search the skies, I know there will be a lovely rainbow gracefully arching the island.

The colors are luminous. The most talented artist could never capture the radiant beauty I see. As I whisper a prayer of thanksgiving, I am reminded that this rainbow is symbolic of a promise I have inherited as His child. How many promises has He given to us? How many times have I claimed those promises?

When our children were small and became ill during the dark hours of night, I claimed those promises for cooling their fevered brows.

Years later when my child was on drugs and alcohol and hope was almost gone, I claimed these promise: "There hath not failed one word of all his good promises."

REMEMBER TODAY: God is faithful and His promises are an everlasting inheritance to the believer.

Erlene J. Burton
Kalamazoo, MI

Related Scripture
1 Corinthians 12:12-27

December 8
1 Corinthians 12:27

*You are the body of Christ, and each one
of you is a part of it* (1 Corinthians 12:27, *NIV*).

I BELONG TO YOU AND YOU BELONG TO ME

Isolated, lonely and having low self-esteem describes the condition of many individuals these days. Busy schedules leave little time for meeting social needs. This can result in shallow relationships, casual friendships with no real commitments.

As a part of the body of Christ, we need to understand that one part really cannot function without the others. For me to do my job, I need to work with the body. A child's song says it well: "For my work is your work and our work is the Lord's work. If we all pull together, how happy we'll be." Many times the key is found when we recognize our place in the body. Knowing that we belong together as a unit gives us a sense of kinship with other believers.

Refuse to be isolated. Become involved. This may require you to take the initiative. Loneliness can cripple your effectiveness. God made us to be social beings. We need one another.

REMEMBER TODAY: I belong to you, and you belong to me. We are all part of the body of Christ.

Louise Daniels
Rogers, AR

Related Scriptures
Isaiah 40:29-31; 2 Corinthians 4:16-18

December 9
2 Corinthians 12:9

And he said unto me, My grace is sufficient for thee: for my strength is made perfect in weakness (2 Corinthians 12:9).

GRACE SUFFICIENT

I went to work as usual, but before the day was over I began experiencing pain in my lower left side. This continued for a week, with the pain becoming worse each day. What began as a trip to the doctor for an examination to determine the cause of this pain started endless series of visits to the doctor and four hospital stays. I was admitted to the Mayo Clinic for two weeks of testing—but still no diagnosis.

I discovered that when I sat for long periods of time, the pain became unbearable. Therefore, I was transferred to a job where I could stand and work. This brought some relief, but the pain continued.

To this day I still have the pain, and there seems to be no medical reason for it. But through my suffering, God has spoken peace to me through His presence and His Word. I have become a much stronger Christian, and my husband has accepted Christ as his personal Savior. God has surely given strength in my weakness.

REMEMBER TODAY: No matter what we have to endure, God's grace is sufficient.

Kathy Countryman
Big Timber, MT

Related Scriptures
John 12:1-8; 2 Corinthians 2:14-16

December 10
John 12:3

And the house was filled with the
fragrance of the oil (John 12:3, *NKJV*).

THE FRAGRANCE OF JESUS

At Christmastime I spent a day in the mall, buying gifts, window-shopping, and absorbing all the sights and sounds of the season—even the scents of Christmas mingling in the air. I smelled pizza cooking, cookies baking, and the fresh aroma of evergreens standing tall and elegant. Every few steps the fragrances changed. I remember walking by the perfume aisle with sweet, heavy, spicy scents hanging in the air. Then I passed by the chocolate shops—mmm!

Later that evening I was meditating on Mary and how she brought precious ointment in the alabaster box to Jesus. In those days ointment was a sweet-perfumed mixture of aloes, spices and oil. When she broke the box, she poured it out in ministry to the Lord. That was her only motive and desire— ministering to Him. John's account says, "The house was filled with the fragrance of the oil."

I thought to myself, *What kind of fragrance am I leaving?* When I leave a room, do people remember the sweetness of the Lord's life flowing through me? When I leave a friend, does the sweet Rose of Sharon linger in her mind and touch her spirit? What fragrance are we leaving to those around us?

REMEMBER TODAY: When we have been in His presence, we will leave behind His fragrance.

Brenda Short	**Related Scriptures**	**December 11**
Chattanooga, TN	John 3:16; 2 Corinthians 5:21	Proverbs 14:26

In the fear of the Lord is strong confidence: and his children shall have a place of refuge (Proverbs 14:26).

CONFIDENCE FOR TODAY

"I want to be more confident" is a statement I hear often as I travel across the states teaching. The word *confidence* means "a feeling of assurance, trust in a person or thing." God wants us to be confident women. He doesn't want us to be intimidated. In order to have self-confidence we must realize our worth to God. "For God so loved the world, that he gave his only begotten Son, that whosoever believeth in him should not perish, but have everlasting life" (John 3:16).

How much are you worth? You are worth the very life of Jesus Christ. If you had been the only woman on earth, God would still have sent Jesus to die for you. You are somebody because of Jesus. "For he hath made him to be sin for us, who knew no sin; that we might be made the righteousness of God in him" (2 Corinthians 5:21).

The word *righteous* means "standing morally right, meeting the standards of what is right and just." You are righteous in the sight of God. Your works do not make you righteous; it is, rather, the sacrifice of Jesus Christ.

God has given each of us gifts and abilities. We are to be bold women of God who know that confidence comes from Him. As He opens doors of opportunity, we must walk through them with confidence, knowing that if He calls us, He will also equip us.

We belong to the Most High God. He is our refuge, our strength and our strong confidence for each day.

REMEMBER TODAY: Don't trust in your abilities. Trust His ability within you.

Dorothy J. Driggers Honea Path, SC	**Related Scriptures** Matthew 5:44, 45; Luke 6:22-38	**December 12** Matthew 5:46

*"For if you love those who love you, what
reward have you?"* (Matthew 5:46, *NKJV*).

LOVE A BEAR!

Love is a complicated feeling that motivates our thoughts and actions. Love is a vital part of our lives. It isn't difficult to love someone who is nice to us. But what about those who aren't?

A few days ago my husband brought me a card with a large bear on the outside with a tag attached: "Please Look After This Bear." Inside was a verse thanking me for loving a bear. This made me stop and think.

Have you ever accused someone of acting like a bear—clumsy or grouchy? That person still needs someone to "look after" him and show him love, God's love. When we meet people who are grumpy, sharp-tongued or short-tempered, our first impulse is to treat them in the same manner. But we should allow the Spirit to check our response. This "bear" may just need a hug, a kind word or a smile. Perhaps the individual is having a bad day or carrying a heavy burden. Perhaps he doesn't know Jesus as Savior and friend. Showing love and concern for that person will give us a feeling of peace and satisfaction because we know we are pleasing God.

There have been times I have felt and acted like a bear, but not once did God stop loving me. Not once did He fail to reach down and touch my wounded spirit. He always let me know He loved me. How comforting it is to know that in spite of our imperfections we are still loved!

REMEMBER TODAY: Let God's love reach out through us to touch the unlovable.

Dorlene Harris
Tifton, GA

Related Scriptures
Psalm 55:22; 1 Peter 5:7

December 13
Matthew 11:28-30

Come unto me, all ye that labour and are heavy laden,
and I will give you rest. Take my yoke upon you, and
learn of me; for I am meek and lowly in heart: and ye
shall find rest unto your souls. For my yoke is easy,
and my burden is light (Matthew 11:28-30).

HIS YOKE FITS PERFECTLY

"Father, I am so tired and overworked," I prayed anxiously.

He said, "Come unto me . . . and I will give you rest."

"But God, this burden is unlike any I have carried before; I don't know how to handle it," I cried impatiently and tearfully.

He gently instructed me with these words: "Take my yoke upon you, and learn of me . . . and ye shall find rest unto your souls."

So often I had read these words of Jesus' as a comfort during stressful times, but a simple truth came to life one day when I was made to realize the relevance of the yoke of Jesus.

During His life on earth, Jesus worked as a carpenter alongside Joseph, His earthly father. One of the responsibilities of the carpenter in those days was to manufacture yokes for the neck of oxen to help carry loads or pull a plow. When a yoke was needed for a specific task, it was carefully made by hand to withstand the pressure of the burden it was to pull or carry.

As the Son of Man on earth, Jesus was skilled in His trade. He knew how to make the wooden yoke to bear physical burdens. How thrilling, however, to know that as the Son of God, He also knows how to make the spiritual yoke to bear the load we must carry. *The Living Bible* translates the words of Jesus, "Wear my yoke—for it fits perfectly—and let me teach you."

Too often we endeavor to use the yokes of self-reliance or man's philosophy in devising ways to handle trials, heartaches or stress, when all the time Jesus has the yoke that will make our burden light and give us rest.

REMEMBER TODAY: Trust Jesus today to provide the yoke to bear the burden you carry.

Wanda Griffith
Cleveland, TN

Related Scriptures
1 Timothy 6:11; 2 Timothy 2:24; James 1:4

December 14
Ecclesiastes 7:8

And the patient in spirit is better than the proud in spirit (Ecclesiastes 7:8).

PATIENCE 101

The holiday season was in full swing with the usual baking, parties, shopping and counting down the last few days until Christmas. Instead of spending the holidays in Cleveland, my husband, Bob, and I were flying to Mather Air Force Base in California to spend Christmas with our son, Rob, and his wife. I still had many items on my "to do" list to complete before we left. How would I ever finish?

One of my early presents was a gift certificate for a manicure. This held high priority on my list because I thought I deserved to be pampered after working so hard preparing for this trip. My appointment was for 10 a.m. I was assured it would only take an hour. That would give me two hours to check by the office, pack the car, make arrangements for the dog and get to the airport on time.

When I arrived at the beauty shop, the receptionist asked me to have a seat because Becky, the girl doing my nails, was running a little late. *Running late*, I thought. *How dare she be late! Doesn't she know I have to be out of here in an hour?* The clock on the wall read 10:10. Now my blood pressure was beginning to rise.

This is inexcusable, I thought. *My time is too valuable for me to be sitting here waiting for someone to do my nails.* But the clock clicked on over to 10:20. *Well, this is the limit! I will just tell them to cancel my appointment and reschedule after Christmas.*

Just as I made my decision, Becky walked in. I could tell her day was not going any smoother than mine. As we sat down, she said, "I'm sorry I'm late. Please be patient with me today. I lost my father last week, and I'm not doing well today."

My heart melted. At the same time I felt like a big jerk. My busy schedule and problems were so insignificant in comparison to Becky's. How could I have been so impatient and self-centered?

The painful memory of returning to work after my own father's death remains fresh. I remember wanting to shout, "Stop the world! My heart is breaking! Doesn't anyone care?" I needed more than patience—I needed understanding. And Becky did too.

Yes, I really did care about Becky, even though we were strangers. After noticing a small pen on her jacket which read, "Jesus is the reason for the season," I began talking about the Lord, church and the child she was carrying. The hour passed quickly. My blood pressure returned to normal, my nails looked great, but most of all, I had passed a course in Patience 101.

REMEMBER TODAY: "Let it [patience] grow . . . when your patience is finally in full bloom, you will be ready for anything" (James 1:4, *TLB*).

Freeda May
Cleveland, TN

Related Scriptures
Exodus 14:19; 23:20; Psalm 34:7

December 15
Psalm 34:15

The eyes of the Lord are upon the righteous, and
his ears are open unto their cry (Psalm 34:15).

O LORD, HELP ME!

We had been to Arkansas to visit our families during Christmas and were on our way back to Georgia. Our son, his wife and two daughters were with us. After spending the night in Memphis, Tennessee, we arose early the next morning to return home. We discovered that a severe ice storm had occurred during the night and the roads were very dangerous.

My husband was driving carefully, about 15 miles per hour, when a car started to pass us. As he did, he began to slide and almost hit us. Larry stepped on his brakes to avoid hitting him, and we began sliding. We slid around and headed toward a deep ditch. Both front wheels were almost over the embankment. We were all praying when Larry said, "O Lord, help us." Immediately we stopped. Had not the hand of the Lord protected us, we would have fallen into the ditch. The car that passed us landed in the ditch, but we were stopped right on the brink of a deep embankment. A good samaritan came by with a truck and pulled us back onto the road, and we continued slowly on our way.

When these kinds of situations arise and Satan attacks us in forceful ways, we cry, "O Lord, help me!" The Lord touches us and says, "Back off, Satan. Take your hands off My child." It's wonderful to know that we have a heavenly Father who loves and cares for us.

REMEMBER TODAY: God is always mindful of His children. He wants us to trust Him.

Melody A. Skoog
Lakeville, MN

Related Scripture
Luke 6:47-49

December 16
Hebrews 12:28

*Therefore, since we are receiving a kingdom which cannot be
shaken, let us have grace, by which we may serve God acceptably
with reverence and godly fear* (Hebrews 12:28, NKJV).

UNSHAKABLE KINGDOM

The church nursery is a wonderful place to learn some precious spiritual truths. One particularly cold Sunday morning my husband and I were busy caring for the little lambs left in our charge when Jenny summoned my attention. A bright 3-year-old, she was building a structure of blocks on top of a small table. As I complimented her grand creation, Jeffrey, an energetic 2-year-old, ran over and aggressively shook the table, bringing every block tumbling to the floor. None of Jenny's labor of love remained, which brought a flood of tears.

As I comforted Jenny, the Holy Spirit reminded me that only earthly things can be shaken. Oh, how wonderful it is to know that the kingdom of God cannot be shaken! Too often I forget this truth. How easy it is to become attached to earthly things that do not last. Even good things, in the end, will not remain. I have observed times when things in my life, the lives of my friends and loved ones, and even those in the church have been shaken. When I become overwhelmed and lose sight of who is on the throne, my Comforter whispers, "What is of God will remain," and His peace floods my soul. What is built on Christ, the solid Rock, will stand. Are we busy building what will remain?

REMEMBER TODAY: The kingdom of God cannot be shaken.

Linda Lippolt   Related Scriptures   December 17
Amityville, NY   1 Peter 2:6; Psalm 46:1   Luke 7:19

John sent them to the Lord, saying, "Are You the Expected
One, or do we look for someone else?" (Luke 7:19, NASB).

FACING DOUBTS

How strange it is that John the Baptist would ask this question. For it was he who identified Christ as the "Lamb of God" at the Jordan River; it was he who beheld the Spirit of God descending upon the Lord and heard the voice of the Father from heaven proclaiming Christ's identity. Even much earlier, when an unborn child, he recognized the Lord, for he leaped with joy in his mother's womb upon her encounter with Mary, who was carrying the unborn Christ.

John knew the Lord. He knew his own calling as well: "I am not the Christ . . . . but I have been sent before Him . . . one mightier than I . . . . He must increase, but I must decrease" (John 3:28, *Amp.*; Mark 1:7; John 3:30). Why then would he ask such a question, "Are You the Expected One?"

Perhaps his persecution and imprisonment had begun to bring about discouragement and doubt. Any number of reasons could be offered. But did this mar his testimony, his credibility? No. Even after this confession of doubt, the Lord gave John the highest appraisal: "'Truly, I say to you, among those born of women there has not arisen anyone greater than John the Baptist'" (Matthew 11:11, *NASB*). Christ did not rebuke him or cast him aside for his momentary uncertainty.

We as servants of the Lord, however faithful, will also be faced with doubts from time to time. We may doubt God's love, His presence during a trial or even our own faith. But this does not change our Lord, nor does it mean we have utterly failed. God wants us to have faith in Him, but He is present to comfort and assure us when we become doubtful or discouraged.

REMEMBER TODAY: If you are facing doubt or discouragement, turn to the Lord for help. Those who trust in the Lord will never be disappointed.

Sue Perritte
Jacksonville, FL

Related Scriptures
Psalms 120:1; 37:7; 56:3;
Hebrews 13:6; 1 Peter 5:7

December 18
Hebrews 13:5

*"Never will I leave you; never will
I forsake you"* (Hebrews 13:5, *NIV*).

STANDING ON HIS PROMISES

How easy it is to have faith and praise the Lord when things are going well! How about when things are not going so well? Yes, we can have peace in Jesus when family members disappoint us and friends betray us. When our world is falling apart, we can be assured of God's love. The writer of Psalm 120:1 said, "In my trouble I pled with God to help me and he did!" (*TLB*).

My husband and I experienced a horrible rejection by some people in our congregation who we had thought were our friends. As a minister's daughter, I had been in the church all my life; however, I had never felt the hurt, disappointment and rejection I was feeling at this particular time. I found myself pleading the blood, fasting and staying in an attitude of prayer all day and into the night. I had come to the place that I thought I would never be able to minister to anyone again. I could not feel God, although I was doing everything I knew to do. I constantly claimed His promises through Scripture.

How exciting when we learn to cast all our cares on Him! He will never leave us and never forsake us. Jesus always goes before us and prepares the way.

This conviction came alive to me when we were relocating and assuming a new pastorate—carrying all the hurt, bruises, disappointments and discouragement. Although I had thought, *I can never love, minister or be a part of any congregation again*, the Lord honored our prayers and our faithfulness to Him. And yes, He went ahead of us and made a way.

In a short time the Lord did a wonderful inner healing, and we are enjoying ministry more than ever. We found a congregation that needed love as much as we did. I have never seen more loving people. God has blessed, and we are growing in every way.

Yes, many times I have had to stand on His promises when I didn't feel like it. But joy comes in the morning if we hold on to His promises.

REMEMBER TODAY: Our trials and disappointments don't last forever. Joy comes in the morning when we stand on His promises.

Delta Schrade	**Related Scriptures**	**December 19**
Arvada, CO	Romans 4:20; 12:3-6; 2 Corinthians 10:15;	Romans 10:17
	2 Thessalonians 1:3-5; James 1:22-25	James 1:22

Faith comes from hearing the message, and the message is heard through the word of Christ. . . . Do not merely listen to the word. . . . Do what it says (Romans 10:17; James 1:22, *NIV*).

THE FAITH WORKOUT

My muscles had not been routinely exercised in over a year. So why was I surprised that I couldn't make it through half of one side of my aerobics tape. Earlier I had enough energy to complete the entire tape. But how could I expect to achieve immediately what had previously taken months of hard work?

Faith is like a muscle; it too must be exercised. When beginning a workout program, one starts slowly with a set of weights he or she can lift. No one goes immediately to the bench and presses 300 pounds. Often, however, in our spiritual workouts we neglect the feeding of the spirit-man, and when a big bad problem lands, we walk over to it and with our untoned muscle of faith command it to be gone.

As Christian women we need to begin a conscious faith workout program, so our faith will be a strong muscle when we must lift heavier trials. To begin, practice exercising the faith you know already exists within you. For example, practice saying, "I know I'm saved. There is not a demon, a doctrine or a device that can trick me into believing my salvation isn't settled." The spirit-man is full of the Word of God ("Thy word have I hid in mine heart, that I might not sin against thee" [Psalm 119:11]), which is another part of the spiritual workout. Then one can refer to Jude 24, which tells me He is able to keep me from falling and to present me before His glorious presence without fault.

Another faith muscle I can build is in the area of healing. James 5:15 says, "The prayer offered in faith will make the sick person well" (*NIV*). Luke 6:38 can be the next weight which can tone the way I pray about finances.

With each weight added, the muscle of faith grows stronger and stronger. Without faith it is impossible to please God, so with faith I am pleasing my Lord.

REMEMBER TODAY: A conscious effort in a faith workout program will build strong faith muscles, which will result in answered prayer.

Wanda R. Baker
Oklahoma City, OK

Related Scriptures
Matthew 7:2-5; Romans 14:13

December 20
Matthew 7:1

Judge not, that ye be not judged (Matthew 7:1).

A LESSON IN JUDGING

My 7-year-old grandson, Andrew, got a bicycle for Christmas, but now he needed a helmet and shin guards. We discussed the matter, and then we made a deal. He had a quarter bank, so I suggested that he save quarters. I promised to save all the quarters I received if he would promise not to spend any of them until he had enough for the helmet and shin guards. When he left for home, he already had $3.07 in his bank.

In a few weeks I was on my way to Andrew's house with a purse full of quarters. While waiting for just the right moment to count out the quarters, I helped my daughter put away laundry. I opened a drawer and there it was—the quarter bank—empty! I shut the drawer and said to myself, *Just as I thought! He's spent it all on candy or junk.*

That evening I decided it was time for Grandmother to teach Andrew a lesson. I began by asking, "Andrew, how many quarters do you have now?"

He shifted a little, and I waited. He took a deep breath. "Well, you see, Grandmother, my brother is having to stay after school to improve his writing. I saw this book in the school bookstore that would help him, so I bought it for him to use in practicing his cursive writing. It cost $2.50, and now I only have 57 cents."

Andrew's lesson was over. Grandmother's lesson was beginning.

How often we leap to wrong conclusions. It's easy to give in to the fault of always judging others. This is misjudging, and it hurts the one who misjudges as much as the person who is misjudged.

"Stop judging by mere appearances, and make a right judgment" (John 7:24, *NIV*).

REMEMBER TODAY: In the same way you judge others, you will be judged.

Debbie Lanier
Winston-Salem, NC

Related Scriptures
Exodus 15:2; Psalm 73:26;
Isaiah 41:10

December 21
Isaiah 40:31

*Those who wait for the Lord will gain
new strength* (Isaiah 40:31, *NASB*).

DECEMBER MOURNING

It was so cold. The frigid weather, however, could not compete with the bitter cold inside me. December 21, 1989, would be forever frozen in my memory. As I lay in the emergency room, I looked at my little boy and girl who were born prematurely and realized they would also die prematurely. In the hours that followed, I dealt with endless questions. The hospital's standard questionnaire asked, "What is your favorite color?" The funeral director wondered, "Do you want your twins buried in the same casket?"

I questioned, "Why a casket? Why not in my arms?" Questions. Questions. Endless questions.

As holiday lights flickered, the world celebrated the birth of the Christ child. There would be no Christmas for me this year. Dear friends tried to assure me that the heavy grief would become easier to bear. What I learned, however, is that a 500-pound stone will always weigh 500 pounds. Time does not lessen its weight. God's grace, however, provides new strength to carry a heavy heart. I had never known such strength before . . . but I had never needed it before.

Today I am a stronger person. I hold my newborn daughter, Kaylyn, with stronger arms. As she grows, I will share with her the strong faith I found during a cold December mourning.

REMEMBER TODAY: When it seems you're praying against a wall, God is on *your* side of the wall!

Judy L. Poteet
Cleveland, TN

Related Scriptures
Psalm 37:4; Matthew 6:25; 7:7, 8;
John 15:7

December 22
Matthew 21:22

And all things, whatsoever ye shall ask in prayer,
believing, ye shall receive (Matthew 21:22).

TRYING TO FIT THE WRONG PIECE

Several years ago we started a tradition in our home at the beginning of each new year. My family and I shop for the most complicated puzzle we can find.

Spreading the puzzle pieces on the dining room table, we begin working the puzzle with great excitement and enthusiasm. As the days turn into weeks, enthusiasm begins to fade. In our eagerness to see the puzzle completed, we pick up a piece that looks as if it may fit. It has the right shape, the right color, but regardless of how we turn, push or pry the piece, it just will not fit.

Many times the pieces of my life have seemed as scattered as the puzzle pieces spread on the table. Nothing seemed to fit right in my life. I realize that much of this came as a result of my impatience. Many times I prayed for an answer to a specific need in my topsy-turvy world. As the days passed and the answer I expected did not come, I substituted my solution for God's answer. Regardless of how I reasoned, rationalized or justified the decision, my solution fit the situation no better than the wrong piece we often tried to squeeze into the almost-completed puzzle.

For a short time I forgot how easily God's answer to my every problem makes my life complete and peaceful. Not until God's grace touched my life once again did the pieces of my life fit back together and I remembered that God's answer always comes just in time.

REMEMBER TODAY: Nothing will "fit" in your life if God is not Lord of all and the center of everything you undertake.

Edith Bean
Brownfield, TX

Related Scriptures
2 Chronicles 16:9; Psalm 90:8;
Isaiah 1:18; Romans 4:7, 8

December 23
Matthew 10:26

*For there is nothing covered, that shall not be revealed;
and hid, that shall not be known* (Matthew 10:26).

OUR SINS ARE COVERED

Visiting relatives on a farm in New Mexico was fun. But as night fell, I realized I had a sore throat. Our host gave me a Mercurochrome tablet to dissolve in my mouth. I did not like the taste and looked for an inconspicuous place to dispose of it. I found a large container where they saved table scraps and extra milk to give to their pigs. This looked like a suitable place to me. The next morning everyone in the house knew my secret. The entire contents of the container had turned a crimson red.

So many times we hide our sins from the world, but God sees and knows everything about us. If we will ask Him, He will forgive our sins, though they are as red as scarlet, and wash us in Jesus' blood so that we may be white as snow. He casts our sins in the sea of forgetfulness and remembers them against us no more.

If your life has hidden sins that no one knows about except you and God, He stands ready to forgive, cleanse and make you whole.

REMEMBER TODAY: "All have sinned, and come short of the glory of God" (Romans 3:23). We do not have to be burdened with a weight of guilt, because Jesus experienced Calvary in our place so that we might be cleansed and forgiven.

Katherine Lankford
Bramalea, Ontario

Related Scriptures
Galatians 4:5-7; Ephesians 1:7;
Colossians 1:14; Revelation 5:9; 14:3, 4

December 24
Galatians 4:5

> *. . . to redeem those who were under the law, that we might receive the adoption as sons [daughters]* (Galatians 4:5, *NKJV*).

LITTLE WATCH TWICE OWNED

It was Christmas Eve and I was so excited. My mind was on my boyfriend who would be here any minute. He came in smiling and took from his pocket a beautiful 21-jewel Elgin watch. Then he asked me to be his wife.

Years later I was in a jewelry shop and found another beautiful watch. I wanted it so bad, although I knew we couldn't afford it. We were pioneering a new church, and finances were limited. I asked my husband to buy the watch for me. He agreed, only if I would trade the old watch in as a down payment.

Reluctantly, I took off my cherished watch and made a deposit on the new one. When I returned home and realized what I had done, I began to cry. So my husband went back to the jewelry store and redeemed my precious watch.

Many years ago I was sold to Satan by Adam and was under bondage and slavery to sin. But I thank God that I cried to Jesus. He paid my debt and set me free. "If the Son therefore shall make you free, ye shall be free indeed" (John 8:36). Thank God, I am redeemed by the blood of the Lamb.

The songwriter penned, "Sweet is the song I am singing today; I'm redeemed! I'm redeemed! Trouble and sorrow have vanished away; I have been redeemed! I'm redeemed by love divine, Glory, glory, Christ is mine, All to Him I now resign, I have been redeemed!" (S.A. Ganus and James Rowe).

REMEMBER TODAY: If you are in bondage, Christ has paid the price for you also. Ask and you shall receive.

Miranda Stuthridge
Fremont, CA

Related Scriptures
Psalm 91; 50:15; Zechariah 13:9

December 25
Psalm 91:11, 12

For He shall give His angels charge over you, to keep you in all your ways. They shall bear you up in their hands, lest you dash your foot against a stone (Psalm 91:11, 12, *NKJV*).

HE SENDS HIS ANGELS . . . ?

"This beautiful new car is going to be our tomb!" These words gripped my heart with terror as we sat encased in snow with no hope of rescue.

The Christmas morning service in 1984 had concluded, and we were on our way from Kentucky to Pennsylvania to visit our daughter. Many miles and hours later we entered the Allegheny Mountains during a blizzard. My husband's pride and joy of the moment was his white Cutlass Ciera with a diesel engine. As we crested the mountain pass, the diesel oil thickened, causing the engine to stall. The temperature was 40 degrees below freezing.

After doing all the things we knew to do, my husband got back into the car. Fifteen minutes had passed and already our white car was buried in the snow! We tried flagging passing vehicles, but no one responded! Reaching into my purse, I pulled out my Bible and turned to Psalm 91. In desperation I reminded God—rather loudly—about His promise to give His angels charge over us. We prayed—urgently!

Several long minutes later a tow truck arrived and hooked up our car. As we headed back to town, I asked the driver if he spent nights such as this cruising the pass, searching for stranded motorists.

He replied, "Oh, no ma'am. You were called in. We received a phone call telling us that two people in a white Cutlass Ciera were stranded at the crest of the mountain." No one except God could possibly have known that there were only two people in that car. Furthermore, they could not have possibly known what kind of car we were driving!

Yes, He sends His angels!

REMEMBER TODAY: Call on Him in your time of trouble; He will send His angels to take charge over you!

Dorothy Black
Cleveland, TN

Related Scriptures
Genesis 1:27; 2:21, 22;
1 Corinthians 11:11, 12

December 26
Genesis 5:2

*Male and female created he them; and blessed them, and called
their name Adam, in the day when they were created* (Genesis 5:2).

ADVANTAGES OF WOMANHOOD

Over the last 20 years or so, we have heard much from voices in the feminist movement about the disadvantages of being a woman in a male-dominated world. Without question, women face very real inequalities and disadvantages, even in the modern world. Nevertheless, there are advantages in being a woman.

God created both man and woman in His own image. They were different in important ways, but they were created equal; and the woman, no less than the man, was created to reflect characteristics of the Creator. But now, after thousands of years of human history, it seems that women have certain advantages over men. Some say these advantages arise from the innate feminine nature of women; others speculate they are the product of cultural conditioning. However these advantages have come, we should not overlook them.

To begin with, women seem to have a spiritual advantage. Historically, more women than men have been receptive to the gospel and concerned about the spiritual welfare of their families. Jesus taught that to enter the kingdom of God, we must become like little children. Women, because of their association with children through childbearing, child training and child caring, seem to find it easier than men to have the childlike attitude needed to enter the Kingdom.

Despite all the rapid changes in male-female relationships over the past three decades, women are still less violent, less aggressive and less competitive than men. Finally, this translates into a moral and ethical advantage for women.

But are these advantages of womanhood really feminine characteristics? No, I would rather think they are reflections of the image of God. And does this mean that men should be more like women? No, it means that both women and men should strive to be more like God.

REMEMBER TODAY: The crowning advantage of womanhood is the privilege of living a Christlike life.

Evaline Echols	Related Scriptures	December 27
Cleveland, TN	Psalm 37:7; Isaiah 40:31	Psalm 37:4

Delight thyself also in the Lord; and he shall
give thee the desires of thine heart (Psalm 37:4).

WINGS OF DELIGHT

Have you ever watched an eagle as it soars high into the sky, delighting in the high winds that would drive other creatures to destruction?

On wings of delight we can learn to soar above the billows of disappointment, sorrow and suffering—even heartbreak. We can learn to rise, as the eagle, above things and circumstances. As we wait on the Lord, we discover that our strength has been renewed and our breadth of view is enlarged.

A few years ago I learned an important lesson about the art of waiting. While en route to Israel with the President's Council from Lee College, we were forced to wait at the London airport for three hours, which caused us to arrive in Israel three hours later than we had planned. Did we enjoy waiting? No. Was it for our good? Yes.

During those hours of waiting, I watched intensely as the mechanics at Heathrow Airport worked feverishly to determine what was causing the technical difficulties. However, when the problem was discovered, our waiting would have been in vain had the mechanics not been allowed to correct the problem. This wait involved action. I must admit I was perfectly willing to trust the captain's orders to wait before we continued our flight to Israel. Even though my knowledge of flying was limited, and it would not have been possible for me to understand the reason for this period of waiting, it was necessary for me to trust his judgment that at this particular time it was more advantageous for me to wait than it was for me to fly.

When we "delight ourselves in the Lord," praying that He will give us the desires of our heart, we may be forced to wait for His perfect timing. During these enforced times of waiting (or aloneness), perhaps our Captain is checking for "technical difficulties." These times of waiting on God are necessary not only to discover weaknesses and frailties but to learn to commit them to Him, the Master Captain, and to allow Him to fill the void or vacuum.

REMEMBER TODAY: With eagle's wings we can soar on wings of delight, no matter which way the wind blows.

Margaret Hughes	**Related Scriptures**	**December 28**
Magnolia, OH	Psalm 37:1-5; Galatians 5:22, 23	Philippians 4:13

I can do all things through Christ which
strengtheneth me (Philippians 4:13).

HEY! LOOK AT THE FAT LADY!

These painful words still echo loudly and clearly in my ears. I will never forget the feelings I experienced when I realized the group of young people yelling these words from a passing school bus were talking about me. It was hard to remove those taunting words from my mind. I realized I was overweight, but I guess I didn't want anyone else to notice!

That day I began to realize that I needed to depend on God to help me with the difficult task of losing weight. I knew that Proverbs 3:5, 6 said, "Trust in the Lord with all thine heart; and lean not unto thine own understanding. In all thy ways acknowledge him, and he shall direct thy paths." In my case I had learned to "trust in a bologna sandwich when troubles and trials come your way, resort to food, for therein lies the comfort you seek." It was a terrible feeling to realize I was hooked on food the way some people are hooked on soap operas, cigarettes and alcohol. I was out of control!

Since that experience I have had several children remark about the "fat lady." I almost became paranoid every time I saw someone talking. I was sure I was the subject of their conversation and that I was being ridiculed.

Today I am happy to tell you I have discovered the secret of getting rid of the "fat lady." I resolved to lose 100 pounds and make the temple, in which the Holy Spirit lives, an acceptable one. God's Word instructs me in Psalm 37:1-5 to fret not, to trust, to delight and to commit myself to Him. If I follow those instructions, I will have the desires of my heart. I believe I will reach my goal of losing 100 pounds. I have already lost 45 of those 100 pounds. I don't have to hide in shame anymore, because I realize that the fruit of the Spirit dwells in me and self-control is mine! It is His desire that I accomplish all things through Him.

REMEMBER TODAY: You are the handiwork of God, His creation. Give Him what you have and He will make it better!

Debbie Irwin
Pell City, AL

Related Scriptures
Matthew 18:3-5; 19:14;
Psalm 127:3-5

December 29
Mark 10:15

"Whoever does not receive the kingdom of God as a little child will by no means enter it" (Mark 10:15, *NKJV*).

THROUGH THE EYES OF A CHILD

We had just moved into our new home! As a pastor's wife for many years, I had dreamed of owning my own home and choosing my own furniture. My dream had finally come true! But now, through circumstances beyond my control, it looked as if we might have to sell. I was devastated!

As I tucked my 6-year-old daughter in bed that Monday night, my routine was the same as every night. Hurriedly I said, "Say your prayers and give me a good-night kiss." But instead of praying, Rachael stared thoughtfully into space and said, "Mother, I remember when there was nothing but woods where our house is now." I hurried her, "That's right. Say your prayers." But Rachael continued, "And then we put a few pieces of wood together, didn't we, Mom?" Beginning to listen more intently, I agreed. "And then we added a few more pieces of wood. You know, Mother, a house is really just a few pieces of wood put together. That's all."

I was speechless! It was as if God himself were speaking directly to my heart. In those few seconds I really understood that a house is just a house, but a home is a place—any place—where there is love, understanding and peace of mind.

God allowed me to keep my home, but I have a totally different attitude. My first obligation is being submitted to God and His will, not mine. "'But seek first the kingdom of God and His righteousness, and all these things shall be added to you'" (Matthew 6:33, *NKJV*).

REMEMBER TODAY: Material things will pass away, but the things most precious are eternal.

Martha S. Wong	Related Scriptures	December 30
Cleveland, TN	Mark 12:30, 31, 41-44;	Mark 12:41, 42
	Luke 6:38; 21:1-4	

And Jesus sat over against the treasury, and beheld how the people
cast money into the treasury. . . . And there came a certain poor
widow, and she threw in two mites (Mark 12:41, 42).

THE WIDOW WHO OUTGAVE THEM ALL

Two mites (the word means "flake" in the original Greek) equaled a farthing, which was only half a penny. This widow was obviously poor and perhaps suffered deprivation, as many widows still do.

Let us identify with her situation. She may have been younger with several children to clothe and feed, or she may have been older with few earthly goods.

As she headed toward the Temple treasury to give her meager offering, she may have been oblivious to those who were giving great sums of money at the treasury box, or she may have trembled with self-consciousness as a poor and needy woman among wealthy men.

Apparently she had no male relative who was old enough, living near enough or willing enough to perform this act of worship for her. If she was going to give to God at all, she would have to go alone—aware that she and her gift, and the immensity of her sacrifice, might be despised or ignored.

"And Jesus . . . beheld how the people cast money into the treasury." She did not know the Savior of the world was watching, observing her every move. The moment she dropped her meager gift into the treasury, He appreciated the significance of her amazing act of worship. This one act would be recorded for all eternity. Jesus "beheld" her courage, determination, sacrifice and humble spirit. He observed her absolute, complete devotion to God and her willing heart to give all she had.

Not once did our Lord suggest that she should not have given her last mite! Her giving revealed tremendous trust and abandonment to the loving care of God. She would receive many blessings money could never buy. Indeed, she gave all she had to God as He would give all He had for us.

REMEMBER TODAY: "This poor widow hath cast more in, than all they which have cast into the treasury: for . . . she of her want [poverty] did cast in all that she had, even all her living" (Mark 12:43, 44).

Deborah Schierbaum Claudio
Antioch, TN

Related Scripture
Ruth 3:11

December 31
Philippians 1:9, 10

And this is my prayer: that your love may abound more and more in knowledge and depth of insight, so that you may be able to discern what is best and may be pure and blameless until the day of Christ (Philippians 1:9, 10, NIV).

PORCELAIN WOMAN

They come to you in the still moments—occasional glimpses of the woman you had envisioned yourself to be by now. Dreams of someone whose appearance exudes youth and elegance. A glimmer of hope reappears every time you see her, believing there is still within you the chance to become the woman of your dreams.

Chances are you're fooling yourself. Is that blatant discouragement? Definitely not! It is outright celebration. More than likely, to become the woman of your dreams would mean finding a neat, cozy box somewhere and staying there until you matured. There could be no running to the grocery store at 11:30 in the evening to get hose for the next day. No laboring over the checkbook to find a way to pay those tithes you should have paid at the first of the month. No crying on your pillowcase over the call you had anticipated but never received. No waiting for that ideal job that was eventually offered to someone else.

Considering this, it is safe to say the woman of every woman's dreams is not so wonderful after all. For in her lifetime she has taken few chances, invested very little of herself in others, and run in smaller circles than those you see around your eyes some mornings.

The very sweeps of the chisel that you thought were hindrances were actually the mighty acts of life that have given you true character and a deep sense of purpose.

The image you are beginning to resemble may not be that of the perfect woman you had hoped to become. Instead, your hands may hint at hard work and great sacrifice. Your feet may have rough edges and many miles on them. Your heart may be dotted with more tears than trophies. The image you resemble may be less that of a porcelain woman and more of a prophetic man—Jesus Christ.

REMEMBER TODAY: Celebrate the freedom of being you, a unique daughter of God whose life is a simple, yet radiant, resemblance of His eternal image.

NOTES